# BEACON
## BIBLE COMMENTARY

# BEACON
## BIBLE COMMENTARY

*In Ten Volumes*

## Volume V
### *The Minor Prophets*

HOSEA, JOEL, AMOS
  *Oscar F. Reed, M.Th., Ph.D.*

OBADIAH, JONAH, MICAH
  *Armor D. Peisker, M.A.*

NAHUM, HABAKKUK, ZEPHANIAH, HAGGAI
  *H. Ray Dunning, B.D., M.A.*

ZECHARIAH, MALACHI
  *William M. Greathouse, M.A., D.D.*

BEACON HILL PRESS OF KANSAS CITY
Kansas City, Missouri

# BEACON BIBLE COMMENTARY

## *In Ten Volumes*

# BEACON BIBLE COMMENTARY

## In Ten Volumes

I. Genesis, Exodus, Leviticus, Numbers, Deuteronomy

II. Joshua, Judges, Ruth, I and II Samuel, I and II Kings, I and II Chronicles, Ezra, Nehemiah, Esther

III. Job, Psalms, Proverbs, Ecclesiastes, Song of Solomon

IV. Isaiah, Jeremiah, Lamentations, Ezekiel, Daniel

V. Hosea, Joel, Amos, Obadiah, Jonah, Micah, Nahum, Habakkuk, Zephaniah, Haggai, Zechariah, Malachi

VI. Matthew, Mark, Luke

VII. John, Acts

VIII. Romans, I and II Corinthians

IX. Galatians, Ephesians, Philippians, Colossians, I and II Thessalonians, I and II Timothy, Titus, Philemon

X. Hebrews, James, I and II Peter, I, II, and III John, Jude, Revelation

# Preface

"All scripture is given by inspiration of God, and is profitable for doctrine, for reproof, for correction, for instruction in righteousness: that the man of God may be perfect, throughly furnished unto all good works" (II Tim. 3:16-17).

We believe in the plenary inspiration of the Bible. God speaks to men through His Word. He hath spoken unto us by His Son. But without the inscripted Word how would we know the Word which was made flesh? He does speak to us by His Spirit, but the Spirit uses the written Word as the vehicle of His revelation, for He is the true Author of the Holy Scriptures. What the Spirit reveals is in agreement with the Word.

The Christian faith derives from the Bible. It is the Foundation for faith, for salvation, and sanctification. It is the Guide for Christian character and conduct. "Thy word is a lamp unto my feet, and a light unto my path" (Ps. 119:105).

The revelation of God and His will for men is adequate and complete in the Bible. The great task of the Church, therefore, is to communicate the knowledge of the Word, to enlighten the eyes of the understanding, and to awaken and to illuminate the conscience that men may learn "to live soberly, righteously, and godly, in this present world." This leads to the possession of that "inheritance [that is] incorruptible, and undefiled, and that fadeth not away, reserved in heaven."

When we consider the translation and interpretation of the Bible, we admit we are guided by men who are not inspired. Human limitation, as well as the plain fact that no scripture is of private or single interpretation, allows variation in the exegesis and exposition of the Bible.

*Beacon Bible Commentary* is offered in ten volumes with becoming modesty. It does not supplant others. Neither does it purport to be exhaustive or final. The task is colossal. Assignments have been made to thirty-nine of the ablest writers available. They are trained men with serious purpose, deep dedication, and supreme devotion. The sponsors and publishers, as well as the contributors, earnestly pray that this new offering among Bible commentaries will be helpful to preachers, teachers, and laymen in discovering the deeper meaning of God's Word and in unfolding its message to all who hear them.

—G. B. WILLIAMSON

# Acknowledgments

Permission to quote from copyrighted material is gratefully acknowledged as follows:

Abingdon Press: Albert C. Knudson, *Beacon Lights of Prophecy.*

Doubleday and Company: George L. Robinson, *The Twelve Minor Prophets.*

Macmillan Company: Martin Buber, *The Prophetic Faith.*

Thomas Nelson and Sons: Stuart E. Rosenberg, *More Loves than One: The Bible Confronts Psychiatry.*

Scripture quotations have been made from the following copyrighted sources:

*The Amplified Old Testament.* Copyright 1964, Zondervan Publishing House.

*The Berkeley Version in Modern English.* Copyright 1958, 1959, Zondervan Publishing House.

*The Bible: A New Translation,* James Moffatt. Copyright 1950, 1952, 1953, 1954 by James A. R. Moffatt. Used by permission of Harper and Row.

*The Bible: An American Translation,* J. M. Powis Smith, Edgar J. Goodspeed. Copyright 1923, 1927, 1948 by The University of Chicago Press.

*Four Prophets: A Modern Translation from the Hebrew,* John B. Phillips. Copyright 1963, The Macmillan Company.

*Living Prophecies: The Minor Prophets Paraphrased,* Kenneth N. Taylor. Copyright 1965, Tyndale House, Publishers, Wheaton, Illinois.

*Revised Standard Version of the Holy Bible.* Copyright 1946 and 1952 by the Division of Christian Education of the National Council of Churches.

## Quotations and References

Boldface type in the exposition indicates a quotation from the King James Version of the passage under discussion. Readings from other versions are put in quotation marks and the version is indicated.

In scripture references a letter (*a, b,* etc.) indicates a clause within a verse. When no book is named, the book under discussion is understood.

Bibliographical data on a work cited by a writer may be found by consulting the first reference to the work by that writer, or by turning to the bibliography.

The bibliographies are not intended to be exhaustive but are included to provide complete publication data for volumes cited in the text.

References to authors in the text, or inclusion of their books in the bibliography, does not constitute an endorsement of their views. All reading in the field of biblical interpretation should be discriminating and thoughtful.

# How to Use "Beacon Bible Commentary"

The Bible is a Book to be read, to be understood, to be obeyed, and to be shared with others. *Beacon Bible Commentary* is planned to help at the points of understanding and sharing.

For the most part, the Bible is its own best interpreter. He who reads it with an open mind and receptive spirit will again and again become aware that through its pages God is speaking *to him.* A commentary serves as a valuable resource when the meaning of a passage is not clear even to the thoughtful reader. Also after one has seen his own meaning in a passage from the Bible, it is rewarding to discover what truth others have found in the same place. Sometimes, too, this will correct possible misconceptions the reader may have formed.

*Beacon Bible Commentary* has been written to be used with your Bible in hand. Most major commentaries print the text of the Bible at the top of the commentary page. The editors decided against this practice, believing that the average user comes to his commentary from his Bible and hence has in mind the passage in which he is interested. He also has his Bible at his elbow for any necessary reference to the text. To have printed the full text of the Bible in a work of this size would have occupied approximately one-third of the space available. The planners decided to give this space to additional resources for the reader. At the same time, writers have woven into their comments sufficient quotations from the passages under discussion that the reader maintains easy and constant thought contact with the words of the Bible. These quoted words are printed in boldface type for quick identification.

## ILLUMINATION FROM RELATED PASSAGES

The Bible is its own best interpreter when a given chapter or a longer section is read to find out what it says. This book is also its own best interpreter when the reader knows what the Bible says in other places about the subject under consideration. The writers and editors of *Beacon Bible Commentary* have constantly striven to give maximum help at this point. Related and carefully chosen cross-references have been included in order that the reader may thus find the Bible interpreted and illustated by the Bible itself.

## Paragraph Treatment

The truth of the Bible is best understood when we grasp the thought of the writer in its sequence and connections. The verse divisions with which we are familiar came into the Bible late (the sixteenth century for the New Testament and the seventeenth century for the Old). They were done hurriedly and sometimes missed the thought pattern of the inspired writers. The same is true of the chapter divisions. Most translations today arrange the words of the sacred writers under our more familiar paragraph structure.

It is under this paragraph arrangement that our commentary writers have approached their task. They have tried always to answer the question, What was the inspired writer saying in this passage? Verse numbers have been retained for easy identification but basic meanings have been outlined and interpreted in the larger and more complete thought forms.

## Introductions to Bible Books

The Bible is an open Book to him who reads it thoughtfully. But it opens wider when we gain increased understanding of its human origins. Who wrote this book? Where was it written? When did the writer live? What were the circumstances that caused him to write? Answers to these questions always throw added light on the words of the Scripture.

These answers are given in the Introductions. There also you will find an outline of each book. The Introduction has been written to give an overview of the whole book; to provide you with a dependable road map before you start your trip—and to give you a place of reference when you are uncertain as to which way to turn. Don't ignore the flagman when he waves his warning sign, "See Introduction." At the close of the commentary on each book you will find a bibliography for further study.

## Maps and Charts

The Bible was written about people who lived in lands that are foreign and strange to most English-speaking readers. Often better understanding of the Bible depends on better knowledge of Bible geography. When the flagman waves his other sign, "See map," you should turn to the map for a clearer understanding of the locations, distances, and related timing of the experiences of the men with whom God was dealing.

This knowledge of Bible geography will help you to be a better Bible preacher and teacher. Even in the more formal presentation of the sermon it helps the congregation to know that the flight into Egypt was "a journey on foot, some 200 miles to the southwest." In the less formal and smaller groups such as Sunday school classes and prayer meeting Bible study, a large classroom map enables the group to see the locations as well as to hear them mentioned. When you have seen these places on your commentary maps, you are better prepared to share the information with those whom you lead in Bible study.

Charts which list Bible facts in tabular form often make clear historical relationships in the same way that maps help with understanding geography. To see listed in order the kings of Judah or the Resurrection appearances of Jesus often gives clearer understanding of a particular item in the series. These charts are a part of the resources offered in this set.

*Beacon Bible Commentary* has been written for the newcomer to Bible study and also for those long familiar with the written Word. The writers and editors have probed each chapter, each verse, every clause, phrase, and word in the familiar King James Version. We have probed with the question, What do these words mean? If the answer is not self-evident we have charged ourselves to give the best explanation known to us. How well we have succeeded the reader must judge, but we invite you to explore the explanation of these words or passages that may puzzle you when you are reading God's written Word.

### Exegesis and Exposition

Bible commentators often use these words to describe two ways of making clear the meaning of a passage in the Scriptures. *Exegesis* is a study of the original Greek or Hebrew words to understand what meanings those words had when they were used by men and women in Bible times. To know the meaning of the separate words, as well as their grammatical relationship to each other, is one way to understand more clearly what the inspired writer meant to say. You will often find this kind of enriching help in the commentary. But word studies alone do not always give true meaning.

*Exposition* is a commentator's effort to point out the meaning of a passage as it is affected by any one of several facts known to the writer but perhaps not familiar to the reader. These facts may be (1) the context (the surrounding verses or chapters), (2) the historical background, (3) the related teachings from other parts of the Bible, (4) the significance of these messages from God as they relate to universal facts of human life, (5) the relevance of these truths to unique contemporary human situations. The commentator thus seeks to explain the full meaning of a Bible passage in the light of his own best understanding of God, man, and the world in which we live.

Some commentaries separate the exegesis from this broader basis of explanation. In *Beacon Bible Commentary* writers have combined the exegesis and exposition. Accurate word studies are indispensable to a correct understanding of the Bible. But such careful studies are today so thoroughly reflected in a number of modern English translations that they are often not necessary except to enhance the understanding of the theological meaning of a passage. The writers and editors seek to reflect a true and accurate exegesis at every point, but specific exegetical discussions are introduced chiefly to throw added light on the meaning of a passage, rather than to engage in scholarly discussion.

The Bible is a practical Book. We believe that God inspired holy men of old to declare these truths in order that the readers might better understand and do the will of God. *Beacon Bible Commentary* has been undertaken only for the purpose of helping men to find more effectively God's will for them as revealed in the Scripture—to find that will and to act upon that knowledge.

## HELPS FOR BIBLE PREACHING AND TEACHING

We have said that the Bible is a Book to be shared. Christian preachers and teachers since the first century have sought to convey the gospel message by reading and explaining selected passages of Scripture. *Beacon Bible Commentary* seeks to encourage this kind of expository preaching and teaching. The set contains more than a thousand brief expository outlines that have been used by outstanding Bible teachers and preachers. Both writers and editors have assisted in contributing or selecting these homiletical suggestions. It is hoped that the outlines will suggest ways in which the reader will want to try to open the Word of God to his class or congregation. Some of these analyses of preachable passages have been contributed by our contemporaries. When the outlines have appeared in print, authors and references are given in order that the reader may go to the original source for further help.

In the Bible we find truth of the highest order. Here is given to us, by divine inspiration, the will of God for our lives. Here we have sure guidance in all things necessary to our relationships to God and under Him to our fellowman. Because these eternal truths come to us in human language and through human minds, they need to be put into fresh words as languages change and as thought patterns are modified. In *Beacon Bible Commentary* we have sought to help make the Bible a more effective Lamp to the paths of men who journey in the twentieth century.

A. F. HARPER

# Table of Contents

## VOLUME V

# Abbreviations and Explanations

## The Books of the Bible

| | | | |
|---|---|---|---|
| Gen. | Job | Jonah | I or II Cor. |
| Exod. | Ps. | Mic. | Gal. |
| Lev. | Prov. | Nah. | Eph. |
| Num. | Eccles. | Hab. | Phil. |
| Deut. | Song of Sol. | Zeph. | Col. |
| Josh. | Isa. | Hag. | I or II Thess. |
| Judg. | Jer. | Zech. | I or II Tim. |
| Ruth | Lam. | Mal. | Titus |
| I or II Sam. | Ezek. | Matt. | Philem. |
| I or II Kings | Dan. | Mark | Heb. |
| I or II Chron. | Hos. | Luke | Jas. |
| Ezra | Joel | John | I or II Pet. |
| Neh. | Amos | Acts | I, II, or III John |
| Esther | Obad. | Rom. | Jude |
| | | | Rev. |

| | |
|---|---|
| Vulg. | The Vulgate |
| LXX | The Septuagint |
| ASV | American Standard Revised Version |
| RSV | Revised Standard Version |
| Amp. OT | Amplified Old Testament |
| NASB | New American Standard Bible |
| NEB | New English Bible |
| Living Prophecies | Kenneth N. Taylor, *Living Prophecies* |
| Berk. | The Berkeley Version |
| Phillips | John B. Phillips, *Four Prophets* |
| IB | Interpreter's Bible |
| IDB | The Interpreter's Dictionary of the Bible |
| ISBE | International Standard Bible Encyclopedia |
| NBC | The New Bible Commentary |
| NBD | The New Bible Dictionary |
| BBC | Beacon Bible Commentary |
| HDB | Hastings' Dictionary of the Bible |

| | | | |
|---|---|---|---|
| c. | chapter | OT | Old Testament |
| cc. | chapters | NT | New Testament |
| v. | verse | Heb. | Hebrew |
| vv. | verses | Gk. | Greek |

*The Book of*

# HOSEA

Oscar F. Reed

# Introduction

Amos is viewed as the leader of those who would free religion from its unnatural relationship with tyranny, selfishness, ceremonialism, and superstition. In contrast, Hosea is to be viewed as the earliest prophet who interpreted the nature of Jehovah in terms of love. As George Adam Smith has observed, "There is no truth uttered by later prophets about the divine grace, which we do not find in germ in him . . . He is the first prophet of grace, Israel's first evangelist."[1]

The burden of the prophecy is a dynamic and earnest witness against the Northern Kingdom because of its apostasy from the covenant. The nation's corruption, at the levels of both public and private interests, was well known.

Thus the purpose of Hosea was to convince his countrymen of the need of repentance, the reestablishment of the covenant relation, and dependence upon a patient, compassionate, and forgiving God. "Both threat and promise are presented from the standpoint of Yahweh's (Jehovah's) love to Israel as his own dear children and as his covenant wife."[2]

Though his doctrine of divine love was not absolutely new, yet it was expressed with clarity and finality. While his prophecy is not listed among the major prophets because of the brevity of his utterance, yet it must be listed as among the most important in insight. Hosea was more a poet than a theologian—the St. John of the Old Testament.[3]

[1]Quoted in Albert C. Knudson, *The Beacon Lights of Prophecy* (New York: The Methodist Book Concern, 1914), p. 93.

[2]Gleason L. Archer, Jr., *A Survey of Old Testament Introduction* (Chicago: Moody Press, 1964), p. 93. While Amos identified the nation's sinfulness in terms of nonconformity to divine righteousness, Hosea spoke of sin as the breaking of a covenant. The Hebrew word *chesed* is usually translated "covenant love." *Chesed* speaks of a contractual relationship "where both parties are bound together by obligations which must be honored with steadfast zeal and patience. Into such a relationship of *chesed* Yahweh entered with His people at Sinai; the people's sin therefore lay in their failure to honor their obligations. See "Hosea," IB, pp. 556-57. Cf. N. H. Snaith, *The Distinctive Ideas of the Old Testament*, II (Philadelphia: Westminster Press, 1946), 122-23.

[3]George L. Robinson, *The Twelve Minor Prophets* (New York: George H. Doran and Co., 1926), p. 16.

## A. Authorship and Date

The name "Hosea," like "Joshua" and "Jesus," springs from the Hebrew root meaning "salvation." It is identical to the name of the last king of Israel, though for purposes of distinction the English Bible usually eliminates the second *h* from the prophet's name.

Commonly acknowledged to have been a native of the Northern Kingdom, Hosea knew the entire life of Ephraim intimately. He writes as an eyewitness. Little detail is given of his life outside of his marriage to Gomer and the name of his father. It is conjectured that he was a priest, though there is nothing to indicate absolutely that this was true. He had a high conception of the duty of the priesthood and makes numerous references to the priests (4:6-9; 5:1; 6:9), to the *Torah* or law of God (4:6; 8:12), to unclean things (9:3), to abominations, and to persecution of the "house of God."[4] He was acquainted with the written law and had firsthand knowledge of Israel. Of his actual ministry we know little save that he was perhaps persecuted for his prophetic work (9:7-8).

Hosea gives us the date of his prophecy in the superscription of his book: "The word of the Lord that came unto Hosea, the son of Beeri, in the days of Uzziah, Jotham, Ahaz, and Hezekiah, kings of Judah, and in the days of Jeroboam the son of Joash, king of Israel" (1:1).

There is considerable difference of judgment as to the duration of Hosea's ministry. The fragmentary character of the prophecies suggests that not all of them were delivered at the same period in his life. Archer concludes that a part of the writing must be dated before the death of Jeroboam II (753 B.C), "since chapter I interprets the symbolic meaning of Jezreel to signify that the dynasty of Jehu is to be violently ended."[5] When Shallum murdered Zechariah, the son of Jeroboam, the prophecy was fulfilled. On the other hand, chapter 5 seems to be directed toward King Menahem (752-742). Since chapter 7 deals with the "double-diplomacy" of pitting Assyria against Egypt (not known before the reign of Hoshea, 732-723 B.C.), it must have followed chapter 5 by ten to twenty years. Evidently the book represents selections from sermons delivered over a period of time. Archer concludes that Hosea's ministry spanned a period

---

[4] A. B. Davidson, "Hosea," *Dictionary of the Bible*, ed. James Hastings, et al., II (New York: Charles Scribner & Sons, 1909), 420.

[5] *Op. cit.*, p. 310.

of at least twenty-five years—the final compilation finished and published by 725 B.C., some thirty years after the prophet's ministry had begun.[6]

On the other hand, Carl Keil, the German scholar, believes Hosea to have held his prophetic office between sixty and sixty-five years. (The discrepancy is between the duration of the "office" as over against the actual time of the prophetic utterances.) That reckoning is twenty-seven to thirty years under Uzziah, thirty-one years under Jotham and Ahaz, and one to three years under Hezekiah.[7] We are justified in assuming that while Hosea's ministry spanned the time that is indicated in 1:1, the internal evidences of the book point up the widely divergent times of the actual utterances—a time span which may have been considerably shorter than the superscription would seem to indicate.

While the actual length of Hosea's ministry may remain in doubt, we know that Amos was contemporary to Hosea in the earlier part of his ministry and Isaiah, Micah, and Obadiah during the later part.

## B. BACKGROUND

If we are to understand the writings of Hosea in relation to the concept of divine love, the central teaching of the book, it is necessary that we view briefly the circumstances under which he exercised his ministry. As with others, we cannot understand the man or his message apart from his own peculiar environment. A prophet is both influenced by and influences the culture in which he lives.

The reign of Jeroboam II in Israel was an era of peace, prosperity, and luxury. However, anarchy, feud, and broken covenant followed his death. Knudson. in summarizing the situation, writes:

> Jeroboam . . . was succeeded by his son Zechariah who after a brief reign of six months was assassinated by Shallum. Shallum ascended the throne and after ruling for a month was himself put to death by Menahem. Menahem ruled for two or three years, and was then followed by his son, Pekahiah, who after a reign of two years was assassinated by Pekah. Pekah ruled for a year or two, and then was slain by Hoshea, who ascended the throne as the Assyrian vassal and was the last of the kings of Israel. There

[6]*Ibid.*

[7]C. F. Keil and F. Delitzsch, "Hosea," *Biblical Commentary on the Old Testament,* The Twelve Minor Prophets, I (Grand Rapids: Wm. B. Eerdmans Co., 1954), 15.

was thus within eight or nine years, from B.C. 740 to about 732, no less than seven different kings of Israel, and of these, four were assassinated by their successors.

The period then following the death of Jeroboam II was one of anarchy. The kingdom was on the road to ruin. This state of affairs is clearly reflected in the last eleven chapters of the book of Hosea.[8]

Following Jeroboam's death, Israel was weak politically. It was undermined by plots, deceit, and intrigue. The nation was ripe for conquest. Yates adds to the picture by observing that "silly princes who led the people to trust in Egypt hastened the end. Egypt promised much but was never able to carry out any of her promises. She was utterly without an ally."[9] The outcome was inevitable and came in its first wave in 733 B.C. when Tiglath-pileser captured Damascus, ravaged Israel's territory, and carried large numbers of her leaders into exile. Sargon finally captured the capital city of Samaria in 722-721 B.C. Of this grave disaster Hosea had no illusions. The punishment of Israel's sins was imminent, but was still in the future.

The political disintegration in Israel at the time of Hosea was perhaps an indication of a more serious social malady. It was a time of crime, corruption, and immorality. The degradation of the priesthood, the impotence of rulers, the folly of sin and injustice all contributed to the decline and fall of the Northern Kingdom. There was laxness in personal behavior. Property was worthless. The dignity of the individual was sacrificed to personal anarchy, and uncertainty gripped the nation.

The widespread presence of the fertility cults had its effect in breaking down family life. The home was no longer sacred and marriage vows meant little. The orgies connected with the fertility cults turned many Israelites into drunkards, and there was suspicion that many of the women had become sacred prostitutes.

On every hand there was class hatred. The rich became richer and the poor only poorer. There was oppression of the poor by the rich and even enslavement.[10] The condition was ripe for Hosea to fulfill the traditional role of the prophet as the champion of the poor and the pleader for social reform.

[8]*Op. cit.*, pp. 92-93.
[9]Kyle M. Yates, *Preaching from the Prophets* (Nashville: Broadman Press, 1942), p. 55.
[10]*Ibid.*, pp. 55-86.

22

It is apparent that the prophet quickly traced the political and social degradation to its root: religious and moral failures—sin. Idolatry was the source of Israel's disease. Hosea labels it "whoredom." Eiselen writes of the situation: "Israel, the spouse of Jehovah, had proved faithless to the husband. The evidences of her unfaithfulness were seen in the sphere of religion, of ethics and of politics, and the sins provoking the anger of Jehovah and of his prophet center around these three heads."[11] There was only a nominal regard for Jehovah (8:2). The people abandoned themselves to superstition and licentiousness.

The priesthood failed in its duty to God and people. It rejoiced in the sins of the people because they augmented its revenues. The priests became bandits (6:9). The nation herself became "prostitute." The state of Israel was one of religious apostasy resulting in moral, social, and political degradation.

### C. The Theology of Hosea

Hosea centers his attention on the relation of God to Israel. While Amos is concerned with divine sovereignty and Jehovah's concern for other nations, Hosea's approach is an exclusive concern with Israel's covenant relation to God. "The nation has forsaken its husband Yahweh, and has played the harlot by setting its trust upon the Baals . . . Sin is not defined in any legalistic way . . . for him the essence of sin for Israel is to rely upon anyone or anything other than God for the guiding and sustaining of life."[12] For this reason, the prophet severely censures every form of idolatry.

Hosea's whole interpretation of Israel's history centers around the ideas of divine love and the knowledge of God. Behind the two figures of fatherhood and marriage are two Hebrew words, both of which Hosea uses, *'ahab* and *chesed*. The first is normally taken to be the Hebrew equivalent of the English word *love*, being used of both human and divine love, both pure and impure. The second (*chesed*) is the word usually rendered "lovingkindness" in the KJV and always rendered "steadfast love" in the RSV. The NASB translates it "covenant love." When used of God it is the Hebrew equivalent of "faithfulness" and when used of man develops into the sense of "piety." The word *'ahab* is usually taken to be the narrower of the two, while

[11]Frederick Carl Eiselen, *Prophecy and the Prophets* (New York: The Methodist Book Concern, 1909), p. 54.

[12]J. D. Smart, "Hosea," *The Interpreter's Dictionary of the Bible* (New York: Abingdon Press, 1962), p. 652.

*chesed* is the more noble. However, there are times when *'ahab* has its elements of great nobility. *'Ahab* is used to denote the "election love" of God and forms the basis of the covenant. It indicates His redemptive action in history and choice of Israel as His people.

There were, however, two questions the law could not answer about itself. The first concerned the reason for its own establishment. The only answer was found in God's love (*'ahab*). God's "election love" for Israel was the very basis and the only cause of the existence of the covenant between God and Israel. Indeed if it were not for God's "election love" there would never have been any covenant and therefore no Israel. Also, according to the covenant, it was Israel's continued obedience to God which made its existence possible.

But what if Israel was disobedient? The law could give no answer! Only God's faithful love could offer a solution. This provides us with the second synthesis between law and love in Hosea. It is most graphically illustrated by Hosea's relationship to his adulterous wife. God's love finds its peak of expression in 11:8 when Jehovah cries, "How can I give you up, O Ephraim! How can I hand you over, O Israel!" (RSV) Hosea consistently uses the word *chesed* (love) to denote Jehovah's attitude toward the covenant. *'Ahab* is the cause of the covenant and *chesed* is the means of its continuance. Thus *chesed* should be the attitude expressed toward the covenant on the part of both God and Israel.[13]

In the progress of the idea of love in Hosea there are three important points to be noted. First, love is the basis of the covenant. Second, love is the answer to the broken covenant and the continued existence of Israel. Third, "steadfastness" or "faithfulness" is the central element in love. The basis of the covenant, then, is love, not law. But God's holiness still demands that the law, the content of His love and covenant, be kept and that the transgressor be excluded from His fellowship.

Even as there is a love (*chesed*) of God to Israel, there must be a *chesed* to God from Israel. It is a reciprocal relation. God initiates that love and Israel gratefully responds. This is the

[13]Snaith, *op. cit.*, p. 119. See also Gerhard Kittel, *et al., Bible Key Words,* trans. & ed. J. R. Coates (New York: Harper and Bros., 1951), pp. 18-19; Gustave F. Oehler, *Theology of the Old Testament* (Grand Rapids: Zondervan, n.d.), p. 178; Otto J. Baab, *The Theology of the Old Testament* (New York: Abingdon-Cokesbury Press, 1949), p. 18; Anders Nygren, *Agape and Eros,* trans. Phillip S. Watson (Philadelphia: The Westminster Press, 1953), pp. 75-76.

sense in which love (*'ahab*) is used of an inferior toward a superior, the sense of humble, dutiful love. Man's love for God in the Old Testament is based on God's love for man.

While the relation is not worked out in a systematized form, it is nevertheless there. If Israel needed to be grateful to God for her election, much more did she need to be grateful for God's steadfast love and faithfulness after she had broken the covenant.

Thus we see that the background of the covenant between Jehovah and Israel is gracious, not legal. One might say that the law, as an expression of God's holiness, furnished the content of His love (*chesed*) and therefore of His covenant with His people.

The problem of God's *chesed* and the broken covenant resolves itself into a tension between His holiness and love. What then is the balance between mercy and justice? The Book of Hosea is an excellent example of this tension between the message of God's doom and His mercy. Jehovah was steadfastly faithful to His part of the covenant, and it is this element of God's love which is ultimately to bring about the resolution of the tension between His love and His holiness. God would himself bring about that repentance which He required (12:6) and furnish the atonement which His holiness and justice demanded (Isaiah 53). It is thus the idea of love (*chesed*) in the covenant relationship, however broken, which develops into the idea of grace in the New Testament. It is also this element that furnishes the background for the new covenant prophecy in Jeremiah and the foundation of the Messianic hope.

The second element in Hosea is the knowledge of God. It arises out of the "communion" that results from "covenant love." Such communion in Hebrew thought becomes the method of knowing God. Vriezen comments: "This knowledge of God is essentially a communion with God, and it is also religious faith. It is something altogether different from intellectual knowledge: it is a knowledge of the heart and demands man's love (Deut. vi); its vital demand is walking humbly in the ways of the Lord (Micah 6:6); it is the recognition of God as God, total surrender to God as the Lord."[14]

With this in mind one can understand why Hosea's cry that there was no "knowledge" of God in Israel was so serious. It indicates that there was no faithfulness to God, no love to God,

[14]M. C. Vriezen, *An Outline of Old Testament Theology* (Boston: Charles T. Bradford Co., n.d.), p. 126.

and no communion with Him. It is not an intellectual knowledge but a spiritual relationship that Hosea is referring to. Vriezen indicates this when he writes that in the Old Testament "the knowledge of God does not imply a theory about the nature of God, it is not ontological, but existential: it is a life in the true relationship to God."[15]

The above discussion indicates two things about "knowledge" in the Old Testament. First, it is spiritual and relational rather than intellectual. Second, it has ethical implications. Snaith illustrates this second point when in writing on Hos. 4:2, he says that "Israel's true *chesed* (love) to Jehovah involves . . . primarily knowledge of God, and issuing from that, loyalty in true and proper worship, together with the proper behaviour in respect to the humanitarian virtues."[16] The fact that knowledge is essentially communion and that this is based upon the covenant relationship with Jehovah necessarily involves ethical implications. For if love is the basic element in the covenant, it cannot be separated from law which furnishes its content. The knowledge of God then provides the transition between religion and ethics; thus, the justification of the prophetic cry for social righteousness and the insistence that true religion is much more than ritual observance.

It is evident, then, that the "ethics" of Israel was deeply personal and based upon the covenant conception of *chesed* (love) which is so deeply reflected in the writings of Hosea. Since its main thrust is in relations between persons and its aim is union or knowledge in the fullest sense of the Hebrew word, *chesed* is the means of overcoming alienation and estrangement. This is because the Hebrew mind viewed man, in himself, as incomplete, as something less than man when he stands outside the covenant relationship. He becomes truly himself only in discovering his relationship to God and man.

The reconciliation is through the love of Jehovah for man and through man's humble response in love. It is through love, then, that man realizes the true essence of his being. Rosenberg writes:

> Love is the rational demand for wholeness, human integrity, and correlation; it is the quest for a union of our own half-worlds with what fulfills us as persons. . . . To love, then, is to be reunited with what we feel separated from; it is rational enterprise, emerging from our will to see justice done to ourselves through our rela-

[15]*Ibid.*, p. 129.
[16]*Op. cit.*, p. 155.

tionship to others. The "commandment to love" is thus not an impossible imperative demanding an unnatural emotional response but rather an expression of the fundamental, irreplaceable human need for personal integrity. "Know thy neighbor as thyself" is what the Old Testament means when it commands that we love him. Know him as one related and connected to you—as an expression of yourself which helps restore your own fulness as a complete person.[17]

Thus, Hosea with his theology of love prepares the background for the New Testament idea that life is realized only in relationship to God, and the fullest life is realized in *koinonia* (love fellowship). The summit is reached in the writings of John and especially in I John 4:16-17: "God is love, and he who abides in love abides in God, and God abides in him. In this is love perfected with us" (RSV).

In Hosea's day, Israel seemed unable to repent and God's holiness could not abide with sin. Yet God's steadfast love would somehow find a way to bring His people back to Him. Although God pronounced certain doom on the sinful, He promised He would never let Israel go. Israel must meet judgment, but God in His love (*chesed*) could not destroy her. This creative tension reaches its fullest expression in Hos. 11:8-9, where after predicting the Assyrian exile Jehovah cries:

> *How can I give you up, O Ephraim!*
> *How can I hand you over, O Israel!*
> *How can I make you like Admah!*
> *How can I treat you like Zeboiim!*
> *My heart recoils within me,*
> *my compassion grows warm and tender.*
> *I will not execute my fierce anger,*
> *I will not again destroy Ephraim;*
> *for I am God and not man,*
> *the Holy One in your midst,*
> *and I will not come to destroy* (RSV).

[17]Stuart E. Rosenberg, *More Loves than One: The Bible Confronts Psychiatry* (New York: Thomas Nelson and Sons, 1963), p. 34.

# *Outline*

(NOTE: The author is indebted to his student, Mr. Otho Adkins, for his research in Hosea and Joel while a student at Pasadena College, 1963-64.)

  I.  Experience and Insight, 1:1—3:5

    A.  Hosea's Personal Life, 1:1—2:1
    B.  Personal Tragedy and Redemptive Love, 2:2-23
    C.  Hosea's Dealing with Gomer, 3:1-5

 II.  The Sin of Israel, 4:1—13:16

    A.  Israel's Infidelity and Its Cause, 4:1—6:3
    B.  Israel's Infidelity and Its Punishment, 6:4—10:15
    C.  The Love of Jehovah, 11:1—13:16

III.  Repentance and Renewal, 14:1-9

    A.  Final Appeal to Repentance, 14:1-3
    B.  Promise of Ultimate Blessing, 14:4-8
    C.  Epilogue, 14:9

# Section I  *Experience and Insight*

## A. Hosea's Personal Life, 1:1—2:1

God uses the experiences of His people to reveal himself progressively in the Old Testament, looking forward to the fullest expression of himself in His Son, Jesus Christ. Such was the case with Hosea, through whom we begin to catch an insight into God's love for man.

### 1. *Superscription* (1:1)

The prophecy begins with a most meaningful phrase, **The word of the Lord that came unto Hosea** (1). These words may be translated, "The beginning of that which Jehovah spake by Hosea." God was not only speaking to Hosea, but through the prophet He was speaking to others.

The conviction that **the word of the Lord** comes to a prophet (cf. Jer. 1:2; Joel 1:1; Mic. 1:1; Zeph. 1:1; Hag. 1:1; Zech. 1:1) is fundamental to Hebrew prophecy. The prophet's inspiration is not of himself, but of God, who is willing to reveal himself and His will through the prophet to His people.[1]

Hosea was **the son of Beeri.** We know nothing of his father, but the name itself means "my well," or "the well of Jehovah." The fact that Hosea was so familiar with holy things might well indicate that his father was a priest.

The time of the prophecy is indicated as taking place during the reigns **of Uzziah, Jotham, Ahaz, and Hezekiah, kings of Judah, and in the days of Jeroboam the son of Joash, king of Israel.** (See Introduction for explanation of the duration of Hosea's ministry.)

### 2. *Hosea's Marriage* (1:2-3)

**And the Lord said to Hosea, Go, take unto thee a wife of whoredoms** (2). Authorities disagree as to whether this passage introduces an extended parable or whether it is to be taken literally. "Would Jehovah have commanded a holy man to do

[1]*The Oxford Annotated Bible,* RSV (New York: Oxford Univ. Press, 1962), p. 1088 (notes).

that which was expressly forbidden to the priests and frowned upon for Israel as a whole?"[2] Augustine forbade a literal interpretation on the hermeneutic principle that a literal interpretation that was incongruous and morally improper was to be held inferior to the figurative sense. The experience was obviously not a vision. Many, including Keil, regard it as "an inward and spiritual intuition in which the word of God was addressed to the prophet."[3] That is, it was a parabolical representation.

Perhaps the most serious objection to an allegorical interpretation is the straightforward narrative given by Hosea. There is no indication that it was to be understood in any other way. Gomer's father, **Diblaim** (3), is named, though nothing further is known about him. A stronger hermeneutical principle than the one cited by Augustine is that, unless otherwise indicated, the Scripture is to be taken in its plain and obvious sense.

The author believes the best solution is in the conjecture that Gomer at the time of her marriage was not a woman of loose morals. Archer concludes his discussion by saying: "If Hosea delivered his message in later years, he may well have looked back upon his own domestic tragedy and seen in it the guiding hand of God. Hence the Lord's encouragement to marry her in the first place, though her future infidelity was foreknown to God, would have been tantamount to a command: Go marry an adulterous woman, even though the command did not come to the prophet in precisely those words."[4] God thus used Hosea's tragic personal experience to reveal the sin of His chosen people and the character of His will to woo them back to himself.

### 3. The Children (1: 4-9)

Gomer was probably one of the common people, as indicated by the fact that the name of God (*El* or *Jah*) was not included in her name, as was true of most of the upper class.

The first child of Hosea and Gomer was **Jezreel** (4). The Lord commanded Hosea to give the child this name, which meant "God sows" or "God scatters." Thus, symbolically, the reference was an act of judgment which was to come in the destruction of Israel.

[2]Archer, *op. cit.*, p. 310.
[3]*Op. cit.*, p. 27.
[4]*Op. cit.*, p. 311.

**The blood of Jezreel** refers to the city of Ahab and Jezebel. It was in this city that the massacre of the house of Ahab took place (II Kings 9:21-37). Because **Jehu** acted with cruelty, judgment was to visit his own house. Hosea's prophecy spoke the beginning of the end for Israel, although it must have been uttered forty to sixty years before the fall of Samaria (see Chart *A*).

**The bow of Israel** (5) which was to be broken **in the valley of Jezreel** is representative of the power of Israel. Nothing more defenseless could be imagined than an Israelite warrior with a broken bow. **The valley of Jezreel,** which was later to be known as the "valley of Esdraelon," has been the battleground of the Near East from Deborah to Allenby. "Where Jehu had sinned, there in his posterity should sin be punished."[5]

In naming his son **Jezreel,** the prophet symbolized both the bloodshed at Jezreel when Jehu ascended the throne and also the anticipated judgment of God upon the dynasty of Jehu for the massacre.

The second child was a daughter, concerning whom God commanded Hosea, **Call her name Lo-ruhamah** (6). The name in the Hebrew means "unfavored" or "she that is unpitied." It indicates that the child was illegitimate, born without a father's love. Symbolically, the daughter was named to show that the Lord would not long continue to show compassion towards a nation that was rebellious against Him. God's mercy towards Israel was exhausted. He would save no longer. There is a finality in the closing words, **but I will utterly take them away.** Once Israel was taken captive, there would be no return as was experienced by the Southern Kingdom in the restoration. Israel is to learn that the covenant is dissolved—that Jehovah is no longer her God, that He considers her an idolatrous nation.

In contrast, God declared, **But I will have mercy upon the house of Judah, and will save them by the Lord their God** (7). Observe that the pronoun I is replaced by the proper noun, **the Lord their God.** Though **Judah** was not exempt from the curse of exile, she was saved from final apostasy through the favor of God. While Hosea does not ignore the religious and moral state of **Judah,** he promises deliverance.

[5]John W. Horine, "The Book of Hosea," *Old Testament Commentary,* eds. Herbert C. Alleman and Elmer E. Flack (Philadelphia: Muhlenberg Press, 1948), p. 795.

The prophecy concludes by showing that Judah will not be saved by force of arms, but **by the Lord their God.** Israel had relied upon earthly resources (10:13), but only those who finally relied upon the Lord and worshipped Him could envision deliverance with confidence.

The threat to Israel refers to the punishment immediately in the future (2:1-3) when judgment was to consummate the history of the ten tribes. Nevertheless, as Keil points out, "it has also a meaning which applies to all times, namely, that whoever forsakes the living God, will fall into destruction, and cannot reckon upon the mercy of God in the time of need."[6]

The third child delivered by Gomer, a son, was named **Lo-ammi: for ye are not my people, and I will not be your God** (9). The cycle is complete. The third child is also illegitimate and Hosea acknowledges that Gomer has played the adulteress. The name suggests the uninterrupted succession of tragedies to be visited upon Israel. **Not my people**—thus should Israel be designated. The covenant is completely dissolved. In the last clause, the words pass with great emphasis into the second person, "I will not be to you" or "I will no longer belong to you" (cf. Exod. 19:5; Ps. 118:6; Ezek. 16:8). The fulfillment of the prophecy is found in the tragic story of II Kings 17:18.

### 4. *Restoration and Renewal* (1:10—2:1)

Rather abruptly Hosea turns from tragedy to promise. In the midst of judgment, the Lord remembered mercy. This appendix to c. 1 is the saving announcement of the final restoration to those who return to the Lord. The number of the posterity of Israel is to be **as the sand of the sea, which cannot be measured nor numbered** (10). The final punishment predicted must be modified by the eternal "nevertheless" of the promises to Abraham in Gen. 22:17 and 32:12. Hosea could not erase the possibility of salvation which had been originally promised by God. As *The Biblical Illustrator* has suggested, "When God threatens most dreadfully, yet he promises most graciously."[7]

The promise is graphically expressed in that men called Lo-ammi **(not my people)** shall be called **the sons of the living**

[6]*Op. cit.,* p. 45.

[7]Joseph S. Exell, editor, "Hosea," *The Biblical Illustrator; The Minor Prophets,* I (New York: Fleming H. Revell Co., n.d.), 9.

**God** (10). This change is to take place in the land of the Exile, for both Israel and Judah (11). Here Jehovah is called *El chai*, **the living God,** in opposition to the idols which Israel had created or borrowed from her neighbors. This seems to be the first prediction of divine adoption of the Gentiles to which Paul refers in Rom. 9: 24-26.

The magnificent Messianic promise of **the living God** speaks of the healing of the breach between Israel and Judah: **Then shall the children of Judah and the children of Israel be gathered together** (11). There is more here than in the return from captivity alone. Rather, v. 11 speaks of **the day of Jezreel,** when under **one head,** the King Messiah, they shall go unto their own land. Thus, if the initial fulfillment of the prophecy was the return of Judah from Babylon joined by many Israelites, the final fulfillment may be the "restoration of the Jews, converted and believing in the Messiah under Divine guidance to their own land."[8]

Although the names of the prophet's children were omens of impending tragedy, the picture is suddenly reversed. The curse is now a blessing. **The day of Jezreel** is not a "scattering," but a "bringing together" in the final spiritual consummation. **Not my people** becomes "my people" and "she that is unpitied" becomes pitied or loved with compassion (2:1). "Great, then, shall be the day so signalized by Divine goodness, so glorious in Divine grace, and so conspicuous for the wondrous works of the covenant-keeping God."[9]

To confirm this joyful event, the Messianic promise closes with a summons in 2:1. "Speak to your brothers and call them now, My people, and call your sisters Beloved" (Phillips). Since divine mercy is now extended, the spiritually related are urged to accost one another joyfully with the "new name" given to them by the Lord himself.

A suggestive exposition of c. 1 might include: (1) God's revelation in the face of human experience, 1*a*, 2*a*; (2) Man's obedience in the face of obvious questions, 3*a*, 4*a*, 6*b*, 9*a*; (3) God's promise in the face of insurmountable obstacles, 10.

---

[8]J. J. Given, "The Book of Hosea" (Exposition and Homiletics). *The Pulpit Commentary*, ed. H. D. M. Spence and Joseph S. Exell (New York: Funk and Wagnalls Co., n.d.), p. 9.

[9]*Ibid.*

## B. Personal Tragedy and Redemptive Love, 2:2-23

In c. 2 the narrative is retold in poetic style (cf. Moffatt, RSV), though the characters change in the drama. Jehovah himself appears as the injured Husband indicting Israel as His adulterous wife. God seems to be the One speaking, while the few faithful Israelites are the ones addressed.

### 1. *Israel's Shame* (2:2-13)

**Plead with your mother, plead: for she is not my wife, neither am I her husband** (2). God is calling to the faithful remnant (I Kings 19:18) to lead His cause against the idolatry and iniquity of the land. It is an urgent and emotion-packed call to conversion. Thus the "significant pair gives place to the thing signified: Israel itself appears to be the adulterous woman."[10]

The import of the address to the children rather than to the wife seems significant. Though Jehovah addresses the idolatrous nation, yet He recognizes that individual persons were not equally involved and guilty of transgression. The observation points out the teaching of the prophets so prevalent during and following the Exile: While Israel was sanctified as the chosen nation, yet each individual was responsible for his own spiritual integrity. The Lord has had not only the seven thousand during the time of Elijah (I Kings 19:18), but in every generation there have been those who were faithful to the covenant even in the midst of a sinful nation.

**The children** (4), or the faithful among the children, had urgent cause to **plead** (reason, 2), for God had dissolved the covenant. **She is not my wife, neither am I her husband.** The Lord, as Husband, severed His marriage relationship with Israel, because of her adulterous addiction to gross idolatry.

Pusey has an intriguing exposition of the passage in analogy when he observes that: (1) The prophets always close the threats of coming judgments with the dawn of after-hopes; (2) The mother is the Church or nation; (3) The children are its members; (4) The children are to plead with their "mother" rather than to accuse God; (5) God's final plea was more gracious than legal.[11]

[10]Keil, *op. cit.*, p. 51.

[11]E. B. Pusey, *The Minor Prophets* (New York: Funk and Wagnalls, 1886), p. 28.

The shameless way in which Israel practiced idolatry is represented in v. 2: **Let her therefore put away her whoredoms out of her sight, and her adulteries from between her breasts.** The conduct is spoken of as **whoredoms,** but for the wife it is adultery. The **whoredoms** (idolatry) of Israel were brazen and open. The Scripture is candid, with Oriental frankness. Schmoller writes of v. 2: "Israel is like a public barefaced whore, who displays her profession in her face and (bared) breasts."[12]

The call to repentance is impressively emphasized by reference to the punishment: **Lest I strip her naked, and set her as in the day that she was born, and make her as a wilderness, and set her like a dry land, and slay her with thirst** (3). In Ezek. 16:4-14 the nation is represented as a filthy, naked child whom the Lord took and covered with clothes and costly ornaments and with whom He made His covenant. In like manner, Hosea alludes to that covenant love through which the Lord adorned His wife (Israel) during marriage. Because of her adulteries, He will leave her **naked,** i.e., poor and bare. **The day that she was born** is symbolic of the birth of the nation in the time of its helplessness in Egypt. **Wilderness** does not refer to the land, but to Israel itself, which was as barren as the desert, without the resources of minimal maintenance. The **dry land** indicates the state of spiritual "dehydration" which would come because of their separation from the Source of "living waters," the Lord himself.

**And I will not have mercy upon her children; for they be the children of whoredoms** (4). This is admittedly a difficult verse if the meaning is taken out of context and treated in isolation. The sentence, though independent in form, is dependent upon **lest** (3; *pen*) for its meaning. Thus, "Plead, lest I will not have mercy upon her children." The children are one with the mother.[13] They are designated the "sons of whoredom," not alone as members of the nation, but because their inheritance has elicited the same conduct. They too are personally defiled. They have endorsed the sin of their mother. They approve of idolatry in the shrine and palace. Keil remarks: "The fact that the children are especially mentioned after and along with the mother,

---

[12]Otto Schmoller, "Hosea," *Commentary on the Holy Scriptures,* ed. J. P. Lange, XIV (Grand Rapids: Zondervan Publishing House, n.d.), 35.

[13]This particular interpretation seems to be contradictory to the former one in which the children are spoken of as the "faithful few." The change of figure is not foreign to Hosea.

when in reality mother and children are one, serves to give greater keenness to the threat, and guards against that carnal security in which individuals imagine that, inasmuch as they are freed from the sin and guilt of the nation as a whole, they will also be exempted from the threatened punishment."[14]

The charge of idolatry is reiterated: **For their mother hath played the harlot** (5). This sentence is introduced to confirm the last clause of v. 4.[15] The emphasis is given again to confirm the thought that **the children of whoredoms** will find no mercy.

**Hath done shamefully** (5) is literally "hath practiced shame" or "hath done shameful things." The nature of that shameful conduct is now made articulate. **For she said, I will go after my lovers, that give me my bread and my water, my wool and my flax, mine oil and my drink.** These **lovers** are the many Baals to which the infatuated people ran and to which they attributed those material benefits which were in reality given by Jehovah. Reynolds observes that the modern counterpart of this sin of Israel is the speaking of fortune, nature, destiny, or law as the giver of good things, "as though it were superstitious or heretical to speak of God as the giver."[16]

The delusion that the **lovers** (idols) gave food, clothing, and the delicacies of life was borrowed from the Assyrians and Egyptians, with whose idols Israel committed spiritual fornication. The Israelites looked at the wealth of their neighbors and attributed it to their neighbors' gods. The fact that the majority accepted the spiritual perversion indicates the extent of their alienation from God and His will. "For as long as a man continues in undisturbed vital fellowship with God 'he sees with the eye of faith the hand in the clouds,' from which he receives all by which he is guided, and on which everything, even that which has apparently the most independence and strength, entirely depends" (Hengstenberg).[17]

The commitment to idolatry that is suggested in **I will go** (5), notwithstanding all that Jehovah had done for her, indicates the extent of Israel's apostasy. Her mistake, carnally influenced, was to identify the resources of life with lifeless idols rather than

---

[14]*Op. cit.,* p. 53.

[15]*Ibid.*

[16]H. R. Reynolds, "Hosea," *Old Testament Commentary,* ed. Charles J. Ellicott, V (London: Cassell and Co., 1897), 415.

[17]Keil, *op. cit.,* p. 54.

with the living God. "I will pursue those alliances and depend
upon them," said Israel. But Jehovah replied, "Because of thy
persistence **I will hedge up thy way with thorns, and make a
wall, that she shall not find her paths (6)**. The figures of the
hedge of thorns and the wall indicate God's purpose to cut off
Israel from her idolatries even though she be in the midst of an
idolatrous nation in exile. Phillips expresses it, "Therefore will
I block all her paths with thorns, I will wall her in so that she
cannot find her way out." Jehovah concluded that the most
extreme treatment was the only means of turning His people
back to himself, who both "smites and heals" (6:1).

The conviction of 6 is confirmed and reiterated in 7 in a
form of parallelism that is quite common to Hebrew poetic
structure. **And she shall follow after her lovers, but she shall
not overtake them; and she shall seek them, but shall not find
them: then shall she say, I will go and return to my first husband; for then was it better with me than now (7)**. The lovers
appear to represent the idolatrous nations from which Israel
sought support and their idols which were involved in the immoral fertility rites of the Canaanite religion. If so, Israel is to
be disappointed, for they will do her no service. **She shall seek
them, but shall not find them.** The satisfaction which Israel
expected will escape her. The gods that she counted on can do
nothing for her. Matthew Henry notes: "(1) that those who are
most resolute in their sinful judgments are commonly most
crossed in them" (Prov. 22:5), and, "(2) God walks contrary to
those that walk contrary to him (Ps. 18:26; Lev. 26:23, 24; Lam.
3:7-9)."[18]

These difficulties (hedges and walls) that God has raised
shall inevitably stimulate thoughts of turning back. "And then
shall she say, Let me go back to my first husband. It was better
for me than now" (Phillips). Israel was to increase her affection for her idols, then suddenly to realize that the idols gave
her no help. In them she anticipated deliverance, but found only
calamity in her eager pursuit. **Follow after** (Heb., *riddeph, piel*)
indicates an intensive search—"to pursue eagerly."

In v. 7, there is a just acknowledgment, **for then was it
better with me than now**, and a good purpose, **I will go.** There
was no question on the part of Israel that God would receive her

[18]Matthew Henry, *Exposition of the Old and New Testament* (New
York: Fleming H. Revell, n.d.), VI, 764.

again into covenant relationship if she came with humility and repentance.

The thought concerning the futility of idolatry is expanded in v. 8: **For she did not know that I gave her corn, and wine, and oil, and multiplied her silver and gold, which they prepared for Baal.** The irony was in giving the very foundation of the nation's wealth (corn, oil, and wine exchanged into gold and silver) to the Baals. The people used their wealth not alone in the creation of the idol, but also in the maintenance of Baal worship. The sin of ignoring the Author of Israel's blessings was compounded by squandering the very resources given by God. **Baal** does not mean a particular Baal, but is a general expression for all idols. (Cf. I Kings 14:9, "other gods.")

Because of Israel's perfidy, Hosea represents Jehovah as taking away the very resources He had given. **Therefore will I return, and take away[19] my corn in the time thereof, and my wine in the season thereof, and will recover[20] my wool and my flax given to cover her nakedness (9).**

God justifies His punishments by the abuses He has experienced (6-8) and warns Israel of the deprivation of the blessings He has given. The food was to be snatched from their mouths and the cup from their lips. The **wool** and the **flax**, the source of raiment, would also be taken away, leaving Israel in **nakedness,** i.e., abject poverty. Whether the tragedy was to be in the form of invasion or from natural causes is not stated, but in any case it was to be sudden. The judgment would come as an unexpected calamity **in the time thereof.**

Hosea lists in vv. 10-13 the punishments which were to be visited upon Israel because of her idolatries. In 10 there is the shame of exposure **in the sight of her lovers,** and their inability to save her. "And no man shall rescue her from my hand" (Phillips). **Lewdness** (Heb., *navluth*) means "slackness," "laxness," or "withered state." Neither her idols nor the Assyrians or Egyptians deliver her. No one is able to save Israel from the wrath of Jehovah, the "husband" sinned against.

Israel's **mirth** is **to cease** along with **her feast days** and **sabbaths** (11). The Hebrew festivals were occasions when families joined in pilgrimage to the sacred shrines. But they were more than religious occasions; they were times of pleasure and merri-

---

[19]"Snatch away."

[20]A Hebraism for "take away."

ment as well.[21] Israel was also to lose the produce of her land
and face starvation. The land would be desolate as **a forest** (12)
and overrun with wild **beasts,** implying depopulation and exile.
Thus Israel was to be forcibly separated from the objects of
which she had said, **These are my rewards that my lovers have
given me.**

**The days of Baalim** (13)[22] were the sacred days which Israel
was commanded to keep sanctified before Jehovah, but which
she had turned into celebrations for the idols. There does not
seem to be any ground for believing that there were special festival occasions peculiar to the Baal worship. The second clause,
**she decked herself with her earrings and her jewels,** deals with
the coquetry of a woman by which she excited the admiration of
**her lovers** (cf. Jer. 4:30; Ezek. 23:40). Phillips expresses the
meaning of 13 graphically: "And I will see that she pays for the
feast-days of the Baals, when she burned incense in their honour,
and decked herself with that ring of hers and all that jewelry,
and pursued her lovers and forgot me, says the Lord." But there
is a pathetic note even in the judgment of God. One senses the
"nevertheless" of compassion. Israel's sin was in forgetting God,
the true Source of her salvation.

### 2. *God's Redemptive Love* (2:14-23).

Some of the prophets look upon the wilderness period as a
time of happy union between Israel and her Lover, Jehovah.
Even though God is now ready to allow judgment its turn, He
is not ready to let Israel go. Here is true love! **Therefore, behold,
I will allure her** (14, go and woo her) . . . **and speak comfortably
unto her** (speak to her heart). God will make love to Israel
again **and bring her into the wilderness** of a second honey-
moon.[23] Thus, from the language of severity comes a new note
of strange tenderness.

---

[21]George A. F. Knight, *Hosea* (London: SCM Press, Ltd., 1960), pp. 55 ff.
Passover, Pentecost, and Tabernacles were the three annual festivals. The
festival of the "new moon" was celebrated at the first of each month. The
Sabbath, from sundown on Friday to sundown on Saturday, was the one
day in seven dedicated to Jehovah.

[22]**Baalim** is Baal in the plural, or baals. While there are various forms,
including Baal-peor, Baal-berith, Baal-zebub, etc., the name Baal came to
designate any idol or false god.

[23]Knight, *op. cit.,* p. 56.

**And I will give her her vineyards from thence** (15). The vineyards rightfully belonged to the faithful wife, Israel. They had been taken away (12), but they were to be returned. **The valley of Achor** is situated to the north of Gilgal and Jericho (Josh. 7:26; see map 2). The vineyards and fertile valleys were the first installments of God's promise of restoration. **The valley of Achor** thus will become a **door of hope.** Two ideas are here placed in conjunction with each other: troubling and hope. When entering the Promised Land, Israel sinned at Achor (cf. Josh. 7:20-26; Isa. 65:10). The place of troubling was now to be the occasion for **hope.**

Morgan observes that "it is this connection between troubling and hope which reveals God. It is the relation between Law and Grace. Law creates troubling as the result of sin. Grace creates hope through the troubling."[24]

**And in that day will I make a covenant for them** (18). We now have a definite eschatological flavor. Hosea evidently was familiar with Genesis 3 and God's curse upon the serpent and the ground. He was also aware that the judgment of God still rested upon His creation (cf. Rom. 8:19-21).

**In that day** God's covenant with the beasts will impose an obligation to hurt man no more. The three classes of animal life dangerous to men are listed (cf. Gen. 9:2): **beasts of the field** (18) as distinguished from domestic animals; **fowls of heaven** (birds of prey); and **creeping things** (Heb., *remes*) **of the ground.** (*Remes* does not mean reptiles, but small animals that move rapidly.)

In addition, Jehovah will destroy the dangers of war—both the instruments of war, **the bow and the sword,** and war itself, **the battle.** The promise is also given in Lev. 26:3-8 and expanded in Ezek. 34:25-28. (Cf. Isa. 2:4; 35:9; and Zech. 9:10.)

Hosea is the first of the prophets to envision the outcome of God's plan as a marriage with Israel. He here looks forward to that day of glorious consummation. **And I will betroth thee unto me for ever; yea, I will betroth thee unto me in righteousness, and in judgment, and in lovingkindness, and in mercies. I will even betroth thee unto me in faithfulness; and thou shalt know the Lord** (19-20). The Hebrew word **in** represents the

---

[24]G. Campbell Morgan, *Hosea* (London: Marshall, Morgan and Scott, Ltd., 1948), p. 15.

idea of bringing a dowry. In this marriage, the bride brings nothing. Jehovah is the Source of all. He is the One who offers **righteousness** and **judgment** (justice), both of which are noble elements of a true marriage. Jehovah also offers to Israel His **lovingkindness** and **mercies.** The term **lovingkindness** is a lovely English word coined by Miles Coverdale in his Bible translation. While it does not cover the full meaning of *love* (*chesed;* see Introduction), in the present context, it certainly means "gratitude," "loyalty," or humble dependence on Israel's part. On God's part *chesed* implies loyalty, which is suggested by His **mercies, lovingkindness,** and above all by His **faithfulness** (20).

Out of the proposed union, which shall be **for ever,** Israel shall come to **know the Lord** (20; see Introduction). This knowledge is not merely cognitive. It is a personal, living relationship— a communion of Jehovah with His people (as husband with wife). Martin Buber observes, "This last word 'knowing' is in the book of Hosea the proper concept of reciprocity in the relationship between God and the people. To know here does not signify the perception of an object by a subject, but the ultimate contact of the two partners of a two-sided occurrence."[25]

The last three verses of c. 2 deal with the consummation of the marriage between Jehovah and Israel. All depends upon God. In that day of betrothal, God will answer **the heavens** (21) with His blessings. "The heavens will answer the asking earth; the earth receiving the rain will answer the field, vine and olive asking for moisture; and all these shall answer Jezreel ('God sows') asking for their products as the means of subsistence and life."[26]

Even though the heavens have been as "brass" and the earth as "dust," now the heavens shall bring forth and the earth respond. God once threatened to take away corn and oil (v. 8), but now He will give them freely. Hence Israel is now the people whom "God sows" and not the people whom He scatters, as in 1:4. The parallel is continued in v. 23. The sowing continues, and Lo-ammi ("not my people") now becomes **my people,** whom God will bless, protect, and provide for. In response, the people will answer in the renewed covenant relationship, **Thou art my God.**

[25]*The Prophetic Faith* (New York: The Macmillan Co., 1949), p. 115.
[26]Horine, *op. cit.,* p. 797.

The divorce is now reversed. The people are again to realize covenant love (*chesed*) and to enjoy the communion originally anticipated by Jehovah in Egypt. The initiative in this saving and redemptive work is wholly with God—but the response must be of man in willing obedience to the divine call. "God may draw man to himself by the cords of love but these cords will in the end be broken if man does not respond to their pull and approach God."[27]

Chapter 2 becomes a satisfying symbolism of the covenant relation that man has with God. Observe: (1) The nature of the covenant—a marriage relationship, 19*a*; (2) The duration of the covenant—forever, 19*b*; (3) The manner of the covenant—in righteousness and judgment, 19*c*; (4) The end of the covenant— knowledge and communion, 20.

In c. 3, Hosea turns to his experience of personal domestic tragedy. Gomer had left her husband for her lovers. This short autobiographical insight becomes the key to Hosea's understanding of Jehovah's compassion. He was shown through his own action how God would carry out His promise. If there is a disposition within the heart and soul of the prophet to love a woman not worthy of his love, then there is a disposition in the Maker of the prophet to love a nation that is not worthy of His love.

## C. Hosea's Dealing with Gomer, 3:1-5

### 1. *The Prophet's Experience* (3:1-3)

**Then said the Lord unto me, Go yet, love a woman beloved of her friend, yet an adulteress, according to the love of the Lord toward the children of Israel, who look to other gods . . . So I bought her to me (1-2).**

It is not to be suggested that Hosea was seeking out a second wife. But in realizing God's suffering love, he was to go and seek Gomer, who was now an adulteress **beloved of her friend** (a paramour). **Flagons of wine** (1) is rather raisin cakes, offerings to the Baals at their vintage festivals (cf. Jer. 7:18).

There is a paradox in v. 1 in the fact that Israel was beloved of Jehovah, **yet an adulteress** (1). His love was wasted, yet

[27]John Mauchline, "Hosea" (Exegesis), *The Interpreter's Bible,* ed. George A. Buttrick, *et al.* (New York: Abingdon Press, 1956), VI, 593.

not lost. It was His wasted love that made reconciliation possible.

From whom did Hosea buy Gomer? Did he purchase her from a brothel, or from the man with whom she was living, or from the master of the slave-mart, overseer of those prostitutes[28] who participated in the cult of Baal?[29] The last seems the most probable answer.

While the Bible does not explicitly state, it is known that Hosea purchased Gomer for the price of a slave. A homer and a half of barley (twelve bushels) was worth about fifteen pieces of silver. Thus the value of the barley plus the **fifteen pieces of silver** made up the price of a slave, i.e., thirty pieces of silver.

**Thou shalt abide for me many days; thou shalt not play the harlot, and thou shalt not be for another man: so will I also be for thee** (3). Gomer was physically and spiritually unclean when taken home by her husband. Thus she was for a time deprived of full conjugal fellowship and excluded from intercourse. **Shalt abide** is the equivalent of remaining quiet: a discipline imposed out of Hosea's affection for her to prepare her for himself. The expression **so will I also be for thee** can only mean that she would be fully restored to her place in the home.

### 2. *God's Message to Israel* (3:4-5)

The parallel between Jehovah and Israel is found in vv. 4-5. **For the children of Israel shall abide many days without . . . afterward shall the children of Israel return** (4). The objects which are withheld from Israel are in three pairs: **king** and **prince, sacrifice** and **image** (monument), and **ephod** and **tera-**

---

[28]The Baal cult: Ashtoreth was worshipped under various names in the Near East as the goddess of fertility. She was the consort of El (generic for "god") and/or Baal. She was both sensual and savage with an exaggerated emphasis upon her sex. She was also known as Astarte, the cow-deity, with shrines (asherahs) on the hilltops (I Kings 14:23; Hos. 3:4). The temptation to the ordinary man was great, for the renewal of life as represented in the conduct of the prostitutes of the pagan temples was closely related to renewed fertility of the earth in the early spring. "The inducing of life within the womb of the female 'holy-one' was supposed to indicate the new life in the Spring" (Knight, *op. cit.*, p. 19). While contact with the temple prostitute was forbidden in Deut. 23:17-18, it was still quite common in Jeremiah's day, a century after Hosea (II Kings 23:6-7).

[29]Knight, *op. cit.*, p. 62.

phim (media in searching the future).[30] These are elements of civil government, religious worship, and prophecy.

Hosea's great analogy is pressed again in vv. 3 and 4. To be without king or priest was to be without the representative of God to the people (the priesthood always represented delegated authority under the "divine right" of kings). "To be without a king, then, was to be out of touch with one's God, as a woman shut up alone in a room could have no physical contact with her husband."[31]

The **sacrifice** was a "means of grace." In Hosea's day the **image** was still accepted (though see Deut. 16:22) Evidently the teraphim, too, were accepted though forbidden in Josiah's reformation a generation later (II Kings 23:24).

In the last words of c. 3, the Lord is represented as expecting the humble return of Israel after judgment and punishment. He is sure that the "troubling" will lead them back in contrition from idols to the living God (2:15).

The prediction of v. 4 was fulfilled when Israel was carried away by the Assyrians into captivity (722-21 B.C.). In v. 5, Hosea predicts that afterward **shall the children of Israel return, and seek the Lord their God, and David their king; and shall fear the Lord and his goodness in the latter days.**

This section, like c. 1, closes with a Messianic promise which is added to the autobiographical theme (Hosea does not mention his family again after chapter 3). Keil interprets the passage as to suggest that the return of Israel to the Lord cannot take place without the return to **David their king** or reunion with Judah, since David is the only true king of Israel. The Messiah, then, is to be as David to the "Israel of God." The return was not to take place till **the latter days** (*acharith hayyamim,* the end of days), the closing future of the kingdom of God, commencing with the coming of the Messiah (cf. Gen. 49:1, 10; Isa. 2:2).[32]

Hosea foresees that Israel **shall fear the Lord** (*pachadel Yahweh;* i.e., shake or tremble before the Lord). The people

[30]**Ephod** was a priestly garment (I Sam. 2:18; 22:18; II Sam. 6:14). In Exod. 28:28-29; 35:27 it is described as a costly shoulder garment of gold, blue, purple, and scarlet to which was attached the oracle pouch containing *Urim* and *Thummim* (with which the Israelites ascertained the will of God). See IDB, p. 118; Hastings, DB, p. 955. **Teraphim** were household deities employed for divination.

[31]Knight, *op. cit.,* p. 63.

[32]Keil, *op. cit.,* p. 72.

would turn and come with trembling at the holiness of God in the awareness of their own sinfulness. Thus affliction was to drive them to the Lord, and with penitence they were to wait for **His goodness.**

Chapter 3 is most expressive of the awe-inspiring love of God. An exposition might treat the theme as the following: (1) The extent of God's love, 1; (2) The discipline of God's love, 3; (3) The results of God's love, 5. Or: (1) Love profaned, 1; (2) Love extended, 3; (3) Love accepted, 4; (4) Love fulfilled, 5.

# Section II  The Sin of Israel

Hosea 4:1—13:16

## A. ISRAEL'S INFIDELITY AND ITS CAUSE, 4:1—6:3

Hosea leaves the interpretation of his personal tragedy in c. 3 to deal with its implications for Israel in the balance of the prophecy. His insights revealed a God who loved Israel deeply and strongly, yet he saw the fatal nature of his country's corruption. He therefore employed the most urgent persuasions to Israel to turn and be saved, while at the same time he announced her inescapable doom.

### 1. *The Lord's Controversy* (4:1-19)

As in 2:2, the Israelites are called into a controversy with the Lord (cf. Isa. 3:13; Jer. 2:9; 25:31). **Hear the word of the Lord, ye children of Israel: for the Lord hath a controversy with the inhabitants of the land, because there is no truth, nor mercy, nor knowledge of God in the land (1).**

Three key words analyze the nature of the condemnation of Israel. **There is no truth** (*emeth*). The RSV renders it "faithfulness," since it is not only knowing what is right, but committing oneself to the right. "Faithfulness" is frequently associated with **mercy** (*chesed*), which in various contexts has been translated love, loving-kindness, or covenant love. Both are related to knowledge, since they are the fruit of the **knowledge of God** (cf. Isa. 9:9; Jer. 22:16). Again, the **knowledge of God** rests upon communion rather than an intellectual cognition. It is through **truth** and **mercy** that the **knowledge of God** is made possible. The absence of such knowledge in the land also indicated an ignorance and disregard of the law. These three great words go to the heart of Hosea's burden. Faithfulness, love, and knowledge are at the center both of the analysis of Israel's plight and of the ideal of fellowship desired by God (cf. 2:19-20; 4:6; 5:4-7; 6:3, 6; 10:12; 11:3-4, 12b; 12:6).[1]

---

[1]See Introduction for a fuller explanation of faithfulness, love, and knowledge.

46

Israel's decadent religious and social environment is shown in God's charges against **swearing, and lying** (2). (*Alah*, to swear, in combination with *kichesh*, speaks of false swearing.) Added to that was **killing, and stealing, and committing adultery. They break out,** i.e., they break all bounds in sin. **Blood** (*damin*) indicates blood shed with violence, a capital crime.[2] **Blood toucheth blood** means that one murder led to reprisal until it became as a contagious disease in Israel. Sin breeds sin. Five of the Ten Commandments were broken in Israel's depravity, namely (in the order named), the third, ninth, sixth, eighth, and seventh.

**Therefore shall the land mourn** (3); once again the suffering of nature is related to the sin of man. Even inanimate creation suffered from the moral depravity of the Israelites. The mourning of the earth, the languishing of the **beasts, fowls,** and **fishes** was the natural result of the drought in King Ahab's reign (I Kings 17:1-7). The drought may have actually continued longer during the continuing idolatry of the people (Amos 1:2; 8:8). Nature suffered because Israel sinned.

*a. Responsibility of the priests* (4:4-11). **Yet let no man strive, nor reprove another: for thy people are as they that strive with the priest** (4). This verse, an interjected clause, seems to indicate that reasoning and reproof are useless because of the desperate obstinacy and self-will of the people. It may be that one would have liked to blame the other; however, the right of reproof was the priest's and even the religious leadership was wicked in its works. Another interpretation[3] conveys a different sense: Let men not strive since it is God's controversy. He has forbidden man to speak in His name. He alone will plead His cause. *The Amplified Old Testament* renders it: "Do not waste your time in mutual recriminations—for with you is my contention, O priest."

"Priest-strivers" (4) seems to indicate that the people had lost confidence in the religious leadership to the point of contending with their priests.

The picture in 4-10 is a vivid description of a degenerate priesthood who will bring judgment from the hand of God. **Day** and **night** (5) do not indicate separate or special judgments, but

[2]Keil, *op. cit.*, p. 75.
[3]Pusey, *op. cit.*, p. 47.

that priest and prophet would fall under the hand of judgment at any time. The concluding phrase, **I will destroy thy mother,** announces the destruction of the whole nation (cf. 2:2). **Priest and prophet** come under special condemnation for not having shared the knowledge of God with the people. In fact, far from sharing, they themselves had **rejected** such **knowledge** and would suffer divine rejection of their office. "I reject you from being priest to me" (6, Phillips).

The terrible indictment against the priesthood continues. The priests are unworthy of their office, and **their glory** will be changed to **shame** (7). **The sin of my people** (8) refers to the sin offering: the flesh of the sacrificial animal offered to take away sin. Although it was legitimate to eat of the sacrificial offering, the priests' sin was in desiring an increase in the sins of the people so that they might enjoy a good supply of meat. "They feed on my people's sins and lick their lips over the guilt to come" (Phillips).

There is little to choose between priest and people. **Like people, like priest** (9). The priesthood shall suffer as the people (cf. 3, 5). God will **punish** them even as the common people are punished, **and reward them their doings.** The punishment is symbolized in v. 10. The priests will continue their indulgence and harlotry with the cult of Baal, but will neither be satisfied nor be able to enjoy the blessing of children because of their immoral practices with the temple prostitutes. This is **because they have left off to take heed to the Lord** (10). They have forgotten God. It is as though the Lord cannot understand their infidelity, or perhaps understands the reason all too well— "(Harlotry) and wine and new wine take away the heart and the mind *and spiritual* understanding" (11, Amp. OT). Lust and alcohol have deadened their sensibility.

*b. Responsibility of the people* (4:12-14). The prophet then turns from priest to people:[4] **My people ask counsel at their stocks** (12). God's chosen people were asking advice of a piece of wood (a practice called rhabdomancy) and seeking to foretell the future with a staff. This was a result of their false worship— idolatry. They had also gone back to sacrificing on **the tops of the mountains** and burning **incense** under the trees. In this form

---

[4]Authorities differ as to whether v. 11 concludes the indictment against the priests or introduces the one against the people.

of idolatry their **daughters** commit fornication and even **spouses** (brides) are guilty of **adultery.**

**I will not punish your daughters** (14) does not suggest that they will go unpunished for their **whoredom** and **adultery.** Rather it means that, instead of direct action by God, sin will be punished by more sin. "The spiritual adultery of parents and husbands would be punished by the carnal adultery of daughters and wives."[5] Keil takes a different view, suggesting that God would not punish the daughters and daughters-in-law because their parents "did still worse. 'So great was the number of fornications, that all punishment ceased in despair of any amendment' (Jerome.)"[6] **Therefore the people that doth not understand shall fall.** The nation had sunk so low that there was no hope and it must perish. **Shall fall** means to be cast headlong into destruction; "brought to ruin" (cf. Prov. 10:8, 10).[7]

c. *A warning to Judah* (4:15-19). These verses are a caution to Judah not to follow Israel. .**Though thou, Israel, play the harlot, yet let not Judah offend** (15). **Gilgal** and **Beth-aven** (Bethel) were the two chief shrines in southern Ephraim and easily reached by Judeans. Hosea ironically changed Bethel (house of God) to **Beth-aven** (house of iniquity). Judah would offend by making pilgrimages to the centers of idolatrous worship. Going to the seat of idolatry, **Gilgal,** and swearing as **the Lord liveth** were not compatible. Though swearing of this kind was commanded in Deut. 6:13; 10:20, yet the oath had its roots in "the fear of the Lord" and not in the practice of idolatry. Hosea is warning against hypocrisy and pseudo-piety.

The reason for the warning to Judah is found in a further description of Israel (16-19). Israel is as untractable as a **backsliding heifer** (16; stubborn cow). The RSV properly puts the last half of 16 in the form of a question: "Can the Lord now feed them like a lamb in a broad pasture?" No! **Ephraim is joined to idols: let him alone** (17). Israel is so bound up to her idols that there is no hope. Long addiction to sin has made reconciliation impossible. However, to interpret this passage as though God will utterly abandon Israel is not compatible with the ultimate teaching of the prophet. Hosea elsewhere writes of "the

[5]*Pulpit Com.,* XIII, 104.
[6]Keil, *op. cit.,* p. 81.
[7]*Ibid.*

valley of Achor for a door of hope" (2:15), and the great cry of God, "How can I give you up, O Ephraim!" (11:8, RSV; see also 14:4, 8). G. Campbell Morgan believes v. 17 was "the word of the prophet to the loyal to have no complicity with the disloyal. It was the word of warning to those who were still in greater measure maintaining their right relationship with God, not to imperil their own safety by coming into contact with Ephraim."[8] **Idols**—"idolatry is the worship of false representations of God."[9]

**Their drink is sour** (18) means that they have become derelict through their drinking. Their intoxication has led, then, to **whoredom continually.** The **rulers** (protectors of the people) came to the place where they loved their **shame.** "They love shame more than glory" (Berk.).

The conclusion in v. 19 is inexorable. "A wind has wrapped them in its wings" (19; RSV). **The wind** is the Assyrian invasion which Hosea sees on the horizon. Israel's doom is certain. Her shame will burst upon the kingdom like a tempest (cf. Ps. 18:11 ff.). Even **their sacrifices** shall not save them.

G. Campbell Morgan suggests that three truths arrest our attention in c. 4: (1) The thing forbidden, idolatry, 12; (2) The condition described, **Ephraim is joined to idols,** 17; (3) The warning uttered to Judah, **Let him alone,** 17.

### 2. *The Prophet's Warning* (5:1-15)

Chapter 5 constitutes an address to the priests, the people, and the royal court. The darkness deepens in the day of rebuke. Israel's conscience is dulled, her vision dimmed, her testimony destroyed, and her covenant with God severed. **Hear ye this, O priests** (1), indicates that the address was made directly to the religious leaders, but the people are also held accountable, and bidden to **hearken, ye house of Israel.** Neither are the princes absolved from guilt: **and give ye ear, O house of the king.** The **judgment** of God is upon all three classes because **ye have been a snare on Mizpah, and a net spread upon Tabor.** It is evident that the prophecy is related to the preceding one, for **Mizpah** and **Tabor** were notorious centers of Baal worship and **a snare** to Israel. **Mizpah** was located on the east side of the Jordan

[8]*Op. cit.,* p. 27.
[9]*Ibid.,* p. 28.

River (Judg. 10:17; 11:11, 34), while **Tabor** was located at the east end of the plain of Jezreel, west of the river Jordan (see map 2). Both were military strongholds where the princes of the royal house and the apostate priests "exercised their deadly hold on the people, waylaying them as birds and beasts are snared in the mountains of prey (Comp. 6:8, 9)."[10]

*a. God knows Ephraim* (5:1-7). Three ways to catch birds and beasts are mentioned: **snare, net,** and **pit.** These represent the manner in which seductions to idolatry were disguised. In the first half of v. 2 the Hebrew is uncertain and various interpretations have been given. It seems that Hosea is not speaking of sacrifice, but the depth of corruption to which **the revolters** had sunk. It clarifies the passage to translate it, "And they have made deep the pit at Shittim" (RSV), or, "The revolters are deeply sunk in corruption and slaughter" (Amp. OT).

There is no question about the second part of the verse: **I have been a rebuker of them all,** or, "I *the Lord God* am a rebuke and a chastisement for them all" (Amp. OT). The threat follows. Because of idolatrous conduct, judgment will come upon the nation. Verse 2 introduces vv. 3-4. The moral state of Ephraim is once again identified as **whoredom** (3), which has separated Israel from the knowledge of God (4; see Introduction). They cannot return to God since **they will not frame** ("contrive" or "manage") **their doings.** "Their doings will not permit them to return to their God; for with a spirit of harlotry in them, they cannot know the Lord" (Berk.). Idolatry has so monopolized their affection that knowledge of the true God is strangled.

**And the pride of Israel doth testify to his face** (5). The Septuagint renders it, "The haughtiness of Israel will be humbled." Robinson speaks of **the pride** of v. 5 as a sickness, "a diseased heart."[11] Israel was arrogant in striving to rival foreign powers as a great nation in its own right. The prosperity of Jeroboam was proving to be a snare in which "national honor was becoming synonymous with national whoredom."[12] Pride, then, is added to the list of evils which separated Israel from Jehovah. As a result, the nation would be destroyed by reason of its own sin.

[10]Reynolds, *op. cit.,* p. 420.
[11]*Op. cit.,* p. 23.
[12]*Ibid.*

**Judah also shall fall with them.** Arrogance led Israel to resent the superiority of Judah. This jealousy led to the initial rebellion of Jeroboam I. Now, once again, arrogance is to be the downfall of Israel, but Judah is also involved. Chapter 5 seems to have been delivered at a later time than c. 4 because there is in c. 5 the new note of prophetic utterance concerning the Southern Kingdom.[13]

There is pathos in v. 6 as the children of Israel go through the right acts of worship, but fail to discern the real nature of the experience and the Object of worship. To **go with their flocks and with their herds** (6) means to go with all their sacrifices (Berk.). They will come with impenitent hearts; therefore **he hath withdrawn himself from them.**

**They have dealt treacherously** (faithlessly) **against the Lord** (7); to act faithlessly (*bagad*) is frequently applied to marital infidelity. God, speaking as the Husband, introduces the second phrase, **they have begotten strange children;** they are an adulterous generation rather than children of the covenant. The threat of judgment again appears: **now shall a month devour them with their portions.** The RSV translates it, "The new moon shall devour them with their fields." This does not mean that they were to be destroyed by invasion in "the new moon" or the next month, but "any month may bring ruin to them and their fields" (Phillips). Keil explains the "new moon" as the festal occasion on which the sacrifices were offered (I Sam. 20:6, 29; Isa. 1:13-14); it stands for the sacrifices themselves. "The meaning is this: your sacrificial feast, your hypocritical worship, so far from bringing you salvation, will rather prove your ruin."[14] Reynolds believes this **month** speaks of the impending invasion by Tiglath-pileser (II Kings 15:29). This invasion was due in part to the alliance of Ahaz with Assyria against Pekah and Rezin. The involvement of Judah may explain the comment in v. 5, **Judah also shall fall with them.**

*b. Hosea warns Judah* (5:8-12). The prophet gives solemn warning in vv. 8-9. **Gibeah** and **Ramah** (8; see map 2) were on hilltops near the northern border of Benjamin, appropriately placed for the giving of such warning. The **cornet** (*shophar*) was made of the curved horn of the ram, while the **trumpet**

---

[13]Reynolds, *op. cit.*, p. 420.
[14]*Ibid.*, p. 89.

(*chatsotserah*) was straight, made of brass or silver and used on solemn occasions. (For **Beth-aven** see comment on 4:15.) The blowing of the horns was indicative of invasion of the land. Since **Gibeah** and **Ramah** were not of Israel, but Judah, it seems probable that the invasion of Israel had already taken place and the enemy had now moved to the very edge of Judah. **After thee, O Benjamin** is a difficult phrase to interpret. The Amp. OT translates it as a battle cry and warning: "The enemy is behind you *and* after you, O Benjamin (Be on your guard)!" This seems to be compatible with the emphasis of the verse.

Verses 9-10 give the explanation for 8. **Ephraim shall be desolate** (9) as a sign of the Lord's righteousness and the fulfillment of His prophecy. **The princes of Judah** (10) are really no different. Like "common land-thieves," they **remove the bound** or boundary markers. Upon them too, says Jehovah, **I will pour out my wrath.**

Israel is broken in pieces by the judgment of God. **The commandment** (11; *tzav*) is a human statute or commandment. It is found here and in Isa. 28:10, 13, where it occurs as an antithesis to the word or the commandment of God.[15] **The commandment** or human statute here spoken of is the worship of calves, the sin which brought about the destruction of the kingdom.

**Moth** and **rottenness** (12) indicate slow and quiet destruction: the moth feeding upon clothes (Isa. 51:8), the worm upon wood and flesh. Later the Lord is to come "as a lion" (14), but here **as a moth**, silently, slowly, and gradually.[16]

c. *The mystery of evil* (5:13-15). Both Judah and Israel could have cherished Jehovah, their divine Husband, but they chose otherwise. God himself becomes their Enemy working within until they are destroyed by their own "rottenness" and thus become an easy prey to the foreigner. Fearing Egypt, and knowing her own **sickness** (weakness), Israel, instead of turning back to Jehovah, turned **to the Assyrian** (13), who later destroyed them. **King Jareb** (*Jarebh*) means "warrior" or "great king." Apparently this was a title commonly used by Assyrian kings.

---

[15]Keil, *op. cit.*, p. 92.

[16]George Adam Smith, *The Book of the Twelve Prophets* (New York: Harper and Bros., 1928), I, 282.

If God is the Enemy within, He is also the Enemy without and will be **as a lion** (14), using the very nation (Assyria) to whom Israel and Judah had turned to tear and destroy. Hosea follows Amos in declaring Jehovah to be the God of all nations, controlling them as He will and using their evil to chasten His own people. **I will take away, and none shall rescue him.** Even as the lion withdraws to his cave, so shall the Lord withdraw to His own place[17] and "deprive the Israelites of His gracious, helpful presence until they repent, i.e., not only feel themselves guilty, but feel the guilt by bearing the punishment."[18] Thus, in the absence of God there is no rescue possible.

The thought is repeated in v. 15. God will retire until Israel acknowledges her **offence** and seeks His **face. Early** (15; *shachar,* cf. 6:3) is not used in the sense of "soon," but in the "morning dawn."

Alexander Maclaren treats "Physicians of No Value" in a textual exposition of 5:13: (1) Man's discovery of his sickness, 13*a*; (2) Man's mad way of seeking healing, 13*b*; (3) God's way of giving true healing, 13*c*. The conclusion is strengthened by reference to 6:1.

### 3. *Challenge to Repentance and Healing* (6:1-3)

The separation of 6:1-3 from c. 5 is unfortunate. There is an obvious connection between "I will go and return" (5:15) and **Come, and let us return** (6:1). It does not seem reasonable to interpret this section as the cry of the Israelites, as many commentators seem to do. It is rather the simple appeal of Hosea in the name of the Lord. (This interpretation requires a rapid shift in Hosea's thought, but such transition is typical of the literary style of the prophet.) God is the Source of all. It was God who had **torn**; it will be God who heals. **He hath smitten, and he will bind** (1). The national revival is to take place in a short period of time, figuratively indicated by **after two days** and **in the third day** (2). (Cf. Luke 13:32-33.) This is not a direct reference to the resurrection of our Lord. However, some look upon it antitypically as language which can refer to the Messiah, the "true Israel" (cf. Isa. 49:3; Matt. 2:15).[19]

[17]Not that He is inaccessible, but waiting for Israel's move. The book is full of figures to picture the tragedy.

[18]Keil, *op. cit.,* p. 93.

[19]Robert Jamieson, *et al., A Commentary on the Old and New Testaments* (Hartford, The S.S. Scranton Co., n.d.), I, 655; Keil, *ibid.,* p. 96.

Verse 3 reiterates the result of reconciliation as the knowledge of God. **Then shall we know, if we follow on to know the Lord.** Again this knowledge is not purely cognitive, but practical. Following on, or searching for this knowledge, brings God's blessings: **His going forth is prepared as the morning; and he shall come unto us as the rain, as the latter and former rain unto the earth.** Here are two lovely figures: the morning dawn and the life-giving rain. The going forth of Jehovah is looked upon as the dawn "which heralds the day" and as the rains in winter and spring—**latter and former**—which water the earth. The dawn is the herald of that salvation (Isa. 58:8; 60:2) which is represented as the rain of the "latter day" which waters the land (Lev. 26:4-5; Deut. 11:14; 28:12). Hosea speaks of the early and latter rain as blessings of the Lord in relation to obedience and wholehearted devotion. The fulfillment of the promise will take place through the Messiah (Isa. 35:6; 44:3; Ezek. 36:25-28).

## B. ISRAEL'S INFIDELITY AND ITS PUNISHMENT, 6:4—10:15

### 1. God's Case Against Israel (6:4—7:16)

*a. The divine lament* (6:4-6). God's *cri de coeur* (heart cry) is found in vv. 4-5. Many see in this passage evidence that the penitence of 5:15—6:3 is superficial, that Ephraim and Judah displayed no genuine repentance. "She relied on Yahweh's (Jehovah) *chesed* to be unshakeable; but her own GOODNESS 'chesed' was as short-lived as 'DEW' in the morning sunshine."[20] **Therefore have I hewed them by the prophets; I have slain them by the words of my mouth** (5). God was forced to discipline His bride by His prophets who were sent to destroy "her way of life." Hosea concludes the verse by adding, **and thy judgments are as the light that goeth forth.** Like the lightning God's judgment goes forth to cleave the heart. Thus, paradoxically, the divine light can bring darkness.

**For I desired mercy, and not sacrifice; and the knowledge of God more than burnt offerings** (6). "It is true love that I have wanted, not sacrifice; the knowledge of God rather than burnt offerings" (Phillips). *Chesed,* translated "mercy," is love for another that reveals itself in righteousness and has its roots in the knowledge of God. So **mercy** here would mean the

---

[20]**Knight,** *op. cit.,* p. 79.

affection for Jehovah which He longs for in the humble obedience of Israel. The heartless sacrifices to cover sin are rejected as an anathema to God. A similar declaration is given by Samuel in I Sam. 15:22: "Behold, to obey is better than sacrifice, and to hearken than the fat of rams" (cf. Ps. 40:7-9; 50:8-15; Isa. 1:11-17; Mic. 6:8).

b. *Man's failure* (6:7-11). The antithesis of Jehovah's yearning is found in the description of Ephraim and Judah in 6:7—7:16. They **have transgressed the covenant,** and have **dealt treacherously** (faithlessly) **against me** (7). The expression of locality—**there**—points to the place where the breaking of the covenant took place (probably Beth-aven). **They like men** (Adam) had broken their agreement with Jehovah, their God.

In citing a few examples of this faithlessness, the prophet mentions **Gilead,** a city[21] of evildoers **polluted with blood** (8). Gilead was notorious for homicides (II Kings 15:25). In v. 9, Hosea laments that, **as troops of robbers wait for a man, so the company of priests murder in the way by consent: for they commit lewdness.**

John Mauchline suggests that 9b should precede 9a, suggesting that the murders of 9b were attributed to the men of Gilead mentioned in v. 8. The priesthood, though charged with gross idolatry, was never before charged with murder. On the other hand, if it is spiritual murder that the priests are charged with, the meaning might follow the sequence of the text. Regardless, the priests are not freed from guilt. "The priests are banded together" (RSV) like robbers at Shechem (the Hebrew word translated **by consent**) and sin against the worshippers who visit the shrines for worship.[22]

It is assumed that **the whoredom of Ephraim** (10) refers to the idolatry of the priests, which is so far-reaching that the nation **is defiled.** Hosea does not forget Judah, for whom also "a harvest is appointed" (11, RSV).

Based upon the content of the message, it appears that 11b should be joined to 7:1. It would thus read, **When I returned the captivity of my people—when I would have healed Israel, then the iniquity of Ephraim was discovered.**

---

[21]Actually, Gilead was not a city but an area; probably all Israel east of the river Jordan. See Ramoth-gilead, i.e., Ramoth in Gilead, map 2.

[22]IB, VI, 630.

Chapter 6 identifies the resources of God in a very striking manner: (1) God is the Source of spiritual discipline, 1a; (2) God is the Source of reconciliation, 1b; (3) God is the Source of true knowledge, 3.

### 2. *Seeds of Destruction* (7:1-16)

Hosea clearly foresees the exile of Israel (722 B.C.), though he did not live to see the day. Yet even as Hosea loved Gomer by rescuing her from her harlotry, so would Jehovah bring His covenant people to himself and heal her diseases (Exod. 15:26; Ps. 103:3). "What pointed talk" Hosea had with his wife in those days of her exile from physical contact suggests in parallel the "pointed talk" Jehovah expressed in the face of **the iniquity of Ephraim . . . and the wickedness of Samaria.**[23] The prophet continues in c. 7 to list their misdeeds: **Their own doings have beset them about** (2).

*a. Internal turmoil* (7:1-7). The explanation in 7:1 is followed by a listing of the sins and crimes openly committed. Lying and highway robbery are rife, since men **consider not in their hearts that I remember all their wickedness** (2).

**They make the king glad with their wickedness** (3). The king is guilty because the sins of his people amuse him and entertain his court. Some commentators suggest the reading, "In their wickedness they anoint kings," suggestive of their rejoicing in a new king enthroned through intrigue (cf. II Kings 15:8-15). The text of v. 4 is difficult and believed by many to have been miscopied, yet it reveals the abject corruption of the age. The people are faithless and untrue to their covenant relations. *Living Prophecies* paraphrases 4 as follows: "They are all adulterers; as a baker's oven is constantly aflame—except while he kneads the dough and waits for it to rise—so are these people constantly aflame with lust."

In v. 5 the prophet speaks of those who make the unsuspecting king drunken when he unites with the **scorners** (plotters), in the day of festivity. **The day of our king** probably speaks of the annual celebration of the coronation. Ironically, the drunkenness of the king is preparing the way for his own murder.

Verse 6, though related to **the princes** of 5, picks up the figure of the oven once again: **For they have made ready their**

[23]Knight, *op. cit.*, p. 82.

**heart like an oven, whiles they lie in wait.** They profess loyalty
to their king, but wait until the expedient time. Their hearts
burn with intrigue **all the night.** And in the morning they blaze
like **a flaming fire** in the murder of their king. Regicide followed
regicide (cf. II Kings 15).

Even though the misery of the kingdom was extreme, **there
is none among them that call unto me** (7). "None sought the
true remedy and called upon Jehovah. For repentance itself the
capacity was gone."[24]

b. *Vacillation and deceit* (7:8-16). **Ephraim, he hath mixed
himself among the people** (8). The idea of mingling with the
nations does not here speak of exile, but the kind of mingling
in which the ten tribes had learned the works of the heathen
and served their idols. Because of this state, they were **a cake
not turned.** The pithy figure refers to bread baked upon red-hot
stones or ashes, which, not having been turned, is burnt on one
side and undone on the other, therefore good for nothing. The
apostate Israelites were fit only for rejection.

The indictment is continued in v. 9. **Strangers have devoured his strength ... Yea, gray hairs are here and there upon
him, yet he knoweth not.** Indications of old age apparent in
Israel are tokens of speedy decay; and she is ignorant of it all.

**The pride of Israel** (10) refers to her haughty demeanor and
is repeated from 5:5 (see comments on that passage).

As a consequence, **Ephraim also is like a silly dove without
heart: they call to Egypt, they go to Assyria** (11). Fluttering
about as an irresponsible dove, Ephraim vacillates in her cries for
help between Egypt and Assyria. All of the time, however, she
did not perceive that she had fallen to the power of Assyria
through the **net** (12) of Jehovah. God was using Assyria as a
means of judgment against His people **as their congregation hath
heard** (i.e., in accordance with the warnings already in the law—
Lev. 26:14-44; Deut. 28:15-68).

**Woe unto them! for they have fled** (flown) **from me** (13).
Fled (*nadad*), which is applied to the flying of birds, points back
to the figures of the dove in 11 and 12. **I have redeemed them,
yet they have spoken lies against me, and I will not now again
redeem them.**[25]

[24]Horine, *op. cit.*, p. 800.
[25]Keil, *op. cit.*, p. 109.

Hosea continues in vv. 14-16 to describe Israel's plight in the face of judgment. **They have not cried unto me with their heart, when they howled upon their beds** (14). The Lord accuses Israel of hypocrisy; their cry does not come from the heart. After crying in distress, they crowd together (*hithgorer*) for **corn and wine, and they rebel against me.** *Living Prophecies* paraphrases the meaning, "They worship heathen gods, asking them for crops and prosperity."

The Lord is not only speaking here of chastisement, but of instruction and help in the face of their **mischief** against Him (15). To bind and strengthen **their arms** is to instruct them and to give them the power to fight and gain victory over their enemies. The deceitful attitude of the nation is summed up in allegorical language in 16.[26] **A deceitful bow** is a bow upon which the archer cannot depend. Neither can God depend upon Israel. **The rage of their tongue** refers to the lies that they have uttered. Because of their falling **princes** they gained **derision in the land of Egypt.** They were ridiculed because they had boasted of their strength, only to fall before Assyria.[27]

God's judgment upon the sin of Israel lends itself to a suggestive exposition: (1) God's knowledge of sin, 2; (2) Sin's deadening impulse, 9; (3) Sin's self-condemnation, 10; (4) Sin's deceitfulness, 16; (5) God's spurned redemption, 13; (6) God's judgment upon sin, 12.

### 3. Israel Under Sentence (8:1—9:17)

*a. A backslidden nation* (8:1-14). Chapter 8 opens with a declaration of the foe which is to execute divine judgment upon Israel. In Hebrew, the first sentence is an exclamation with no verb. The summons from Jehovah is addressed to the prophet, **Set the trumpet to thy mouth** (1). He is to blow the warning. Here is the "brevity of urgency" (cf. 5:8).[28] The second sentence gives the message to be delivered: **He shall come as an eagle** (vulture) **against the house of the Lord, because they have . . . trespassed against my law.** The prophet, then, must play the part of the "watchman" (Ezek. 33:3), repeating the accusations against Israel in the face of invaders (the Assyrians).

[26]*Ibid.*
[27]Lange, *op. cit.*, p. 69.
[28]IB, VI, 643.

Two charges are made. First, Israel has **transgressed my covenant.** They have broken the original contract, the marriage agreement. They have declared that they are no longer Jehovah's people. Second, they have **trespassed against my law;** that is, they have committed the sin of disobedience as well as disloyalty. The accusations are particularized in v. 4.

The phrases in vv. 2 and 3 are given in staccato speech. The cry of Israel in 2 comes as a gasp without ordered utterance, and the reply of God in 3 is just as urgent and short. In spite of the divine accusation, the people cry, **My God, we know thee** (2). Keil puts it succinctly: "My God, we know thee, we Israel!"[29] as though they are surprised that God does not identify them as His people. Is the mere name **Israel** proof that they belong to Jehovah? God replies that it is not enough! Of itself, it cannot bring salvation. Why? Because **Israel hath cast off the thing that is good** (3). **They have set up** unauthorized **kings** (4) and **princes.** They **have made them idols** of gold and silver in the form of calves (5), an abomination in the eye of the Lord.

R. F. Horton in *The Minor Prophets*[30] reminds us that "during 253 years Israel had eighteen kings from ten different families and no family came to a close save by violent death. The rapid succession of usurpers in the closing years was only the final plunge of a disastrous career." The accusation in v. 4 indicates that the "charismatic election of the kings had given way to intrigue and power politics."[31] **Thy calf, O Samaria, hath cast thee off** is translated in the Amp. OT, "Thy calf-idol is loathsome, I have spurned it." Matthew Henry remarks that "God never casts off any till they have first cast him off."[32] The word **calf** seems to be a sarcastic diminutive for "bull." Samaria, Israel's capital city, had turned away from God. Now God spurns Samaria. Knight suggests that v. 5 might well read, "Thy calf stinks, O Samaria. What an *ersatz* or poor substitute for the living God a calf makes!"[33]

[29]*Op. cit.,* p. 111.
[30]P. 45 as quoted in IB, p. 643.
[31]*Ibid.,* p. 646.
[32]*Op. cit.,* p. 745.
[33]*Op. cit.,* p. 89. (Cf. I Kings 12:28-33. Jeroboam I had commanded the two golden calves to be built at Dan and Bethel. Jeroboam may have looked upon the bull as upholding the invisible *Yahweh* (Jehovah), but it was a dangerous innovation at best for peasants who could not distinguish between the cults of Baal and the worship of *Yahweh.*)

Jehovah cries, **How long will it be ere they attain to innocency?** (5) Since idolatry was fornication, innocence was purity. The "suffering God" cries out against the disloyalty of Israel "just as Hosea had known the pain which his wife's disloyalty had caused him."[34]

The prophecy follows that the **calf of Samaria shall be broken in pieces** (Heb., splinters). It is not of God; **the workman made it** (6; cf. Exod. 32:20).

Verse 7 represents both the climax and the theme of chapter 8: **They have sown the wind** and reaped **the whirlwind** (cf. Gal. 6:7). "The sources of national life are withered and the people count for nothing among the nations."[35] **The wind,** the passion and disloyalty of sin, brings **the whirlwind** of destruction both in crop and field and by Assyrian invasion—**strangers that swallow it up.** Hosea is declaring the world to be a moral universe in which judgment must follow upon sin.

Because **Israel is swallowed up** they shall be as an unclean vessel (8). The verse speaks not so much of the Exile as that the nation has already become despised **among the Gentiles as a vessel wherein is no pleasure.** This they have prepared for themselves. **For they are gone up to Assyria, a wild ass alone by himself** (9). The **wild ass** seems to be a pun in the Hebrew for *Ephraim.* **Gone up to Assyria** again does not speak of the Exile, but is rendered: "Israel went to Assur like a wild ass goes alone by itself."[36] She has **hired lovers,** i.e., bargained for her *amours;* she has given love-gifts for favors. "Political intriguing was . . . out of harmony with Israel's true mission. It tended to secularize the people, to make of them a nation like the other nations of the world, and so was equivalent to hiring lovers and speaking lies against Jehovah."[37]

**Yea, though they have hired among the nations, now will I gather them, and they shall sorrow a little for the burden of the king of princes** (10). This is a difficult verse, but seems to indicate that, although Israel has bargained for the favors of nations, Jehovah will **gather them** for disciplinary purposes. They will feel **the burden** of taxes by **the king of princes.** Phillips

---

[34]*Ibid.,* p. 90.

[35]T. Henshaw, *The Latter Prophets* (London: George Allen and Unwin, Ltd.), p. 98.

[36]*The Pulpit Commentary, op. cit.,* p. 240.

[37]Knudson, *op. cit.,* p. 116.

suggests that they will "diminish their gifts" because of the heavy burden of taxation.

The chapter closes with a description of worship without the "knowledge of God" (cf. 11:1-4). **Because Ephraim hath made many altars to sin, altars shall be unto him to sin (11).** Amos (4:4-5) had ironically suggested that Israel offer more and more sacrifices so that God would notice the quantity of their sacrifices and forget their quality (cf. Mic. 6:6-9). But Jehovah was not deceived; the nation was only multiplying its sin.

**I have written to him the great things of my law, but they were counted as a strange thing (12),** may be translated, "Were I to write for him my laws by ten-thousands, they would be regarded as a strange thing" (RSV). In the lust for foreign religions, the pure worship of Jehovah was forgotten and sounded strange to the insensitive ear of sinful Israel. The **law** (Torah) spoken of here is not just the Decalogue, but the revelation and instruction of Moses plus the declarations of the prophets.

**They sacrifice flesh for the sacrifices of mine offerings, and eat it (13).** The people loved to sacrifice in order to enjoy the feast of **flesh** that followed. No wonder Jehovah was wroth and accepted them not. Thus, **they shall return to Egypt.** Israel must learn the bitter lessons of her forefathers. **Egypt** represents the land of bondage, (cf. 9:3, 6) from which Israel had been redeemed, but which symbolized the suffering that the people were again to undergo.

In v. 14, the sin of Israel is once again traced to its source, **For Israel hath forgotten his Maker.** Forgetting God and parading her power before foreign nations brought judgment from the Lord upon Israel. The final phrase, **but I will send a fire upon his cities, and it shall devour the palaces thereof,** refers to both nations (Israel and Judah). "These castles of false security the Lord will destroy, the *armanoth* [fenced cities] answer to the *hokhaloth* [temples]."[38]

Chapter 8 offers a variety of possibilities for effective exposition. The character of sin is clearly represented: (1) The

[38]Keil, *op. cit.*, p. 114. The **fenced cities** are referred to by Sennacherib in the inscription relating to his campaign of 701 B.C. "Forty-six of his [Hezekiah's] strong cities, fortresses . . . I besieged and captured." They were built by Uzziah and Jotham (II Chron. 26:10; 27:4). For the allusion to Israel's **palaces** (temples) cf. Amos 3:11, 15. See Ellicott, *op. cit.*, p. 425.

deception of sin, 2, 11-12; (2) The reciprocal action of sin, 7; (3) The absurdity of sin, 9; (4) The burden of sin, 10; (5) The judgment against sin, 14.

An explanation of sin is given in a textual analysis of 8:1: (1) Sin is essentially a broken relationship, 1b; (2) Sin is a transgression of the law, 1c.

*b. Israel's distress and captivity* (9:1-17). Hosea follows the indictment of chapter 8 with a description in chapter 9 of the penalty of exile, the withering away of the nation. Israel has rejected Jehovah and must face the loss of king, children, places of worship, and country.

In vv. 1-9 the prophet gives a warning of judgment in spite of temporary prosperity. **Rejoice not, O Israel, for joy, as other people: for thou hast gone a whoring from thy God** (1). The Israelites are not to exult, for their faithlessness (harlotry) has been the cause of their separation from God. Israel's festivals were to be happy occasions, but the Baal feasts developed into licentious revelry. This was particularly true of the harvest festival, which was initiated as an occasion of thanksgiving and joy, but developed into a time of debauchery. "Hosea cannot stress too strongly that along with loyalty to *Yahweh* (Jehovah) goes the happy worship of a grateful people, while along with disloyal turning to a worship of the forces of nature goes a collapse of the moral life."[39]

**Thou hast loved a reward upon every cornfloor** (threshing floor; 1). Israel turned from regarding the blessings of harvest as from God to the worship of Baal, in which they rejoiced. Because of such "spiritual harlotry," **the floor and the winepress shall not feed them** (2). Corn, oil, and wine will not nourish nor satisfy them because they shall be far away in exile. Verse 3 explains 2. **Egypt** (3) is obviously a symbol for exile (8:13) as in the days of Moses. The reference to **unclean things in Assyria** shows that the food laws of the Pentateuch were known in Hosea's day. The eating of unclean things was associated with the Gentiles. God gave Israel His protection against degradation even at this time, but in exile no protection would be given. Their "badge of distinction" gone, their social boundaries and distinctions broken, were judgments that Israel felt keenly.[40]

[39]Knight, *op. cit.*, p. 95.
[40]*Bib. Illustrator, Minor Prophets,* I, 167.

The picture in vv. 3-4 is clearly descriptive of the exile to come. The Hebrew verbs are pure futures. In Assyria **they shall not offer wine offerings** (drink offerings) **to the Lord** (4), but **their sacrifices shall be unto them as the bread of mourners.**[41] **Their sacrifices** will not be pleasing to Jehovah. The expression **bread for their soul shall not come into the house of the Lord** means that there will be no temple to which they may bring an offering before eating their food.

**What will ye do in the solemn day, and in the day of the feast of the Lord?** (5) Israel will be unable to observe the feasts of the Lord while in exile. Or the meaning may be that sacrifices would be made, but that the joy of the festival occasion would be gone since it was unaccompanied by righteousness.

**For, lo, they are gone because of destruction** (6) means that the Israelites will be subject to exile. **Egypt** is mentioned symbolically as the place of this exile. **Memphis** was the ancient capital of Lower Egypt, now in ruins to the south of Old Cairo. Israel's treasure will be destroyed and her dwellings left desolate: "Nettles will inherit their treasures of silver and thorns will occupy their tents" (Phillips).

**The days of visitation** (7, cf. 2:13) are again spoken of and coupled with **the days of recompence.** The Hebrew root of the word suggests that **recompence** is the necessary fulfillment of Israel's harlotry. Then will Israel **know** that the professional **prophet is a fool.** These prophets of Israel predicted only prosperity for the nation (Ezek. 13:10). **The spiritual man** is identical to the foolish prophet. " '*Ish ruach* (a man of spirit) is synonymous with the *'Ish halekh ruach* (a man walking in the spirit) mentioned in Mic. 2:11 as prophesying lies . . . even the false prophets stood under a superior demonical power, and were inspired by a *ruach sheqer* (a lying spirit, I Kings 22:22)."[42] This in itself showed the depth of Israel's **iniquity** and **great hatred.**

God intended that Ephraim would be His **watchman** and a prophet to the surrounding nations, but there is a lack of confi-

---

[41]*Lechem 'onim,* bread of affliction. The bread eaten at funeral meals which was looked upon as unclean because the corpse defiled the house and all who were associated with the ceremony. The meaning, here, is that their bread would not be sanctified in the house of Jehovah, for they were far away from the point of revelation (shrines and temples).

[42]Keil, *op. cit.,* p. 122.

dence in those professional prophets, uninspired by God.[43] Thus, **the prophet is a snare of a fowler in all his ways** (8), and there are "enmity, hostility, and persecution in the house of his God" (Amp. OT).

Hosea reminds the readers of Israel's depraved behavior at **Gibeah** (9; cf. Judges 19) when "there was no king in Israel" (Judg. 19:1) and "every man did that which was right in his own eyes" (Judg. 21:25).

Once again we hear the pained cry of Jehovah: **I found Israel like grapes in the wilderness; I saw your fathers as the firstripe in the fig tree at her first time** (10). The Lord represents himself as a traveller in the wilderness delighted to find grapes to quench his thirst and the delicacy of the early fig, so dear to most Orientals (Isa. 28:4; Jer. 24:2; Mic. 7:1). So was He delighted to help Israel as His chosen people in Egypt. But Israel **went to Baal-peor**[44] and "they became abominable like the object of their love" (Vulgate).[45] They became in character like that which they loved.

A different but parallel figure is found in v. 11. The **glory** of Ephraim **shall fly away like a bird, from the birth, and from the womb, and from the conception.** *The Berkeley Version* translates the verse, "Ephraim's glory has flown away like a bird; no more births, no more motherhood, no more conception!" Sterility was looked upon with reproach in Oriental lands. "Ephraim" means "fruitfulness." The irony of the scripture is in the observation that the fruitful shall be unfruitful, and the term "fruitful" shall cease to characterize Israel.

The **glory** of Israel was her unique relationship to Jehovah; now she spurned that glory even as she spurned her election. No wonder God says, **Woe also to them when I depart from them!** (12) The glory will be gone because the later generations of Israel are gone: **there shall not be a man left.** The last clause of v. 12 gives the reason for the punishment threatened—the departure of the Lord. Luxury shall be punished by "diminu-

---

[43]Amos felt obliged to renounce the technical title of "prophet" because of the false prophecies of the professionals. He spoke of himself as a plain workingman (7:14). Hosea may have suffered from a similar situation.

[44]Baal-peor was the god of the Moabites in whose worship young maidens prostituted themselves.

[45]As quoted from Jamieson, *op. cit.*, p. 653.

tion of numbers" through barrenness. Even though children are born, **yet will I bereave them**—the men will be lost in battle.

The theme of the vanishing glory of Ephraim is continued in the descriptions of vv. 13-14. **Ephraim, as I saw Tyrus, is planted in a pleasant place** (13), yet the nation **shall bring forth his children to the murderer.** The word **Tyrus** means "rock." Israel was intended to be a rock, a symbol of power and glory. But now known for its apostasy, the Lord would give over its sons to death by the sword.

Hosea seems restless to get it over. "Give them their due" (14, Amp. OT), says the prophet. Jamieson interprets **a miscarrying womb and dry breasts** as suggesting, "So great will be the calamity, that barrenness will be a blessing though usually counted a great misfortune (cf. Job 3:3; Jer. 20:14; Luke 23: 29)."[46]

In v. 15, Hosea reverts to speaking for God. **Gilgal** was one of the shrines degraded by Baal worship (cf. 4:15; 12:11). Paradoxically, it was the first spot where worship to Jehovah had been offered after the crossing of the Jordan (Josh. 4:20; Mic. 6:5). It was there that Jehovah **hated them** (15). Like a wronged husband, He would **drive them out of mine house, I will love them no more,** for the **revolters** had rejected Him. Knight comments on v. 15, "The O.T. never uses the foolish language of some modern evangelists, who declare that God hates sin but loves the sinner. Sin does not exist apart from men sinning. That is why God in His purity and holy love, must hate the sinner himself."[47]

Ephraim, the fruitful, is now smitten with a blight: **Their root is dried up, they shall bear no fruit** (16; cf. Ps. 102:4). This may be a pun made by Hosea in bitter irony. "Ephraim, the fruitful, bears no fruit" (Phillips). The Hebrew indicates the certain execution of the prophecy.

The threatenings in vv. 11-12 are strengthened in 16 and concluded in 17 with a reason for that rejection: **My God will cast them away, because they did not hearken unto him: and they shall be wanderers among the nations** (17). The final clause carries a great deal of pathos. The word here translated **wanderers** is used of Cain in Gen. 4:14. (Cf. Deut. 28:65.) Since

---

[46]*Ibid.*, p. 568.
[47]*Op. cit.*, p. 100.

Israel has chosen wandering; it is God who now says, **They shall be wanderers among the nations.** "The light which God gives man, and particularly the light of love . . . may either enlighten the eyes, or it may blind the eyes. This is the belief of all the prophets."[48]

### 4. Review and Appeal (10:1-15)

Hosea has two burdens, Israel's sin and its punishment. These themes are repeated over and over. "Reiteration, not progress of thought, characterizes Hosea's fiery stream of inspired eloquence."[49] In c. 10 there is a fourfold repetition and a double reference to Israel's sin in (1) setting up unauthorized kings and (2) the establishment of calf-worship. The punishment parallels the sin in the destruction of the kingdom and its idols.[50]

Descriptive metaphors abound in this prophecy. Hosea has already spoken of the "backsliding heifer" (4:16), the treacherous dealer (5:7), a sick man (5:13), adulterers (7:4), "a silly dove" (7:11), and now an empty vine.

**Israel is an empty vine, he bringeth forth fruit unto himself** (1). The word **empty**[51] is misleading. Rather, "Israel is a luxuriant vine that yields its fruit" (RSV), or, Israel has "harvested" its fruit. The complaint of the Lord was not that they had prospered, but that they were selfish. Their prosperity, instead of increasing their gratitude to Jehovah, became the occasion of increasing the number of **altars** and **images** or Baal pillars[52] (cf. Exod. 23:24; I Kings 14:23).

**Their heart is divided** (2); "now they must bear their guilt" (RSV). Their affections were divided because of the nefarious influence of idol worship. Israel must atone for its infidelity, for God will destroy its **altars** and **images.**

Hosea announces that the day will come when they shall finally see that they have **no king, because we feared not the**

---

[48]_Ibid._

[49]Alexander Maclaren, _op. cit.,_ VI, 114.

[50]_Ibid._

[51]The participle _boqeq_ does not mean "emptying out," but "pouring out," overflowing (cf. Ezek. 15:6).

[52]The more prosperous Israel became, the more sacred pillars she carved with beauty and care.

**Lord** (3). The last clause seems to mean, "If we have no reverence for the Lord, what could the king do for us?" (Berk.)

Verses 4-7 carry still further the description of Israel's failure. **They have spoken words, swearing falsely in making a covenant** (4). While Israel divided its loyalties, it had also lost faith in its kings, who made and kept covenants only so long as they were personally advantageous. "There had been a dismal succession of rulers who played at foreign alliances abroad and at power politics at home and who did not rule in virtue of any charismatic gift which they possessed" (cf. 7:7; 8:4).[53] A ruler of this nature could do nothing more than "utter mere words" (RSV) and enter into empty compacts.

In these circumstances the only **judgment** (justice) that Israel knew was a bitter experience. **Hemlock** was the poison given to Socrates. Amos refers to it when he observes: "Ye have turned judgment into gall, and the fruit of righteousness into hemlock" (6:12, RSV).

Verses 5-6 are a graphic description of the people's relationship to their idols. If the relationship to Jehovah was to be one of joy, Israel's relation to the idols of **Beth-aven** (5) was one of mourning. In the face of impending judgment **the people** and **the priests** mourned for the safety of the golden **calves** (bulls). These **priests** were *kamar*, idolatrous ("priestlings," Berk.). Israel's true priests were *kohen*. Hosea points out that the golden calf will itself wander in exile: **It shall be also carried unto Assyria for a present** (tribute) **to king Jareb** (6). The word **Jareb** is not a proper noun. It means a "great king." **Ephraim shall receive shame** because of **its own counsel**, i.e., because of this idol from whom she took counsel. Thus "the puppet kings shall share the same fate as the puppet gods."[54] The king of Samaria shall be destroyed, like "a chip on the face of the waters" (7, Phillips).

Hosea identifies the chief sin of Israel with the image-worship at Beth-aven (Bethel). **The high places also of Aven** (Beth-aven), **the sin of Israel, shall be destroyed** (8).

These places of idolatrous worship were to be so utterly destroyed that **the thorn and the thistle shall come up on their altars** (8). When the kingdom is gone with the altars and shrines, the people will long for death and destruction, saying

[53]IB, VI, 670.
[54]*Ibid.*, p. 673.

**to the mountains, Cover us; and to the hills, Fall on us.** With the covenant broken and the idols gone the people looked to the mountains to hide them from the wrath of God (cf. Heb. 10:31; Rev. 6:16). In 9 the prophet returns to the sin of **Gibeah** as an example of Israel's utter sinfulness (see comments on 9:9).

The expression **two furrows** in v. 10 is to be distinguished from **furrows** in 10:4 and 12:11. It is better translated "double-iniquity" (RSV).[55] Thus, for its great iniquity the nation shall be chastened and put in bonds in the face of its enemies.

A comparison is made in v. 11 between the animal that is taught **to tread out the corn** and the one that is sent to **plow the field.** The Deuteronomic Code allowed the ox to eat while treading out the corn (cf. Deut. 25:4). The yoke that Jehovah had laid on Israel was light, but because of her sin He would now turn her into the fields to plow. God would now put a heavy yoke upon her neck rather than a rider upon her back. He would drive rather than guide. Here are figures of subjugation and bondage.[56] "Ephraim's hopes of escaping will be dashed to the earth. The Assyrians will prove themselves hard taskmasters."[57]

It is remarkable that, even in the zero hour before judgment, God once again offers His **mercy** (*chesed*) to Israel. She still has the chance to **sow to yourselves in righteousness, reap in mercy; break up your fallow ground: for it is time to seek the Lord, till he come and rain righteousness upon you** (12). **To sow . . . righteousness** implies right actions between man and man. If Israel would thus do God's will, she could reap **mercy** according to the compassion of Jehovah rather than reaping **iniquity.**

The word *nir* here and in Jer. 4:3 may mean either plowed soil or **fallow ground.** In either case, it had been neglected until it had become baked and thorny. Either interpretation indicates that the people are to work under difficult circumstances in a new course of life.[58]

---

[55]"Double-iniquity" is difficult to interpret in the light of the context unless it is translated "great." They are chastened for their "great" sin Keil, however, interprets the expression as two transgressions: "Their apostasy from Jehovah and the royal house of David" (cf. 3:5), p. 133.

[56]Keil, *op. cit.,* p. 134.

[57]S. Franklin Logsden, *Hosea* (Chicago: Moody Press, 1959), p. 86.

[58]*Ibid.*

The decisive moment is now here. It is God's will to **rain righteousness** upon Israel, but there is little if any response. The nation is so engrained in the disposition to idolatry that it is insensitive to the call of God.

Verses 13-15 once again identify the result of indifference and **wickedness.** There is a cumulative effect when men do evil: "You have cultivated wickedness and raised a thriving crop of sins" (13; *Living Prophecies*). They did not trust in Jehovah, but **in the multitude of thy mighty men.** Some translators link the last part of 13 to 14 as in RSV: "Because you have trusted in your chariots and in the multitude of your warriors, therefore the tumult of war shall arise among your people."

Nothing is known of the illustration given, in which **Shalman spoiled Beth-arbel** (14). **Shalman** is probably a contraction of Shalmaneser, the conqueror of Israel (II Kings 17:6). Logsden identifies **Beth-arbel** as a "pre-developed picture" of Bethel in which the prophecy of 14 later took place: **the mother was dashed in pieces upon her children.**[59]

**So shall Beth-el do unto you** (15) should read, "So shall I do to you" (Berk.). **Beth-el,** the seat of wickedness and idolatry,[60] shall be destroyed in **a morning** (*basshachar,* morning dawn). **The king of Israel** is to be identified as the monarchy in general rather than a specific king. Hoshea was on the throne at the time of the invasion.

Verses 11-15 offer an exposition in evangelism: (1) The false hope of Israel, 11a; (2) The loving appeal of God in the face of imminent judgment, 12; (3) The sure judgment of God, 13-15.

## C. THE LOVE OF JEHOVAH, 11:1—13:16

### 1. *His Magnanimity* (11:1-11)

The eleventh chapter of Hosea is one of the great chapters of the Old Testament. It is in this chapter that God adds the figure of a son to that of the bride. God loved Israel as a son (cf. Deut. 32:6, 18; Isa. 63:16; 64:8; Jer. 3:19; Mal. 1:6; 2:10).

---

[59]To destroy together "mother and children" is a proverbial expression in the Hebrew denoting inhuman cruelty and speaks of the fate of Israel at the hands of Shalmaneser (Keil, *op. cit.,* p. 136).

[60]The irony of Bethel, the place of calf-worship, was in the name itself, which was originally designated by Jacob as "house of God" (Gen. 28:19).

*a. God's concern for His people* (11:1-4). **When Israel was a child, then I loved him, and called my son out of Egypt** (1). This verse is based on Exod. 4:22-23. "And thou shalt say unto Pharaoh, Thus saith the Lord, Israel is my son, even my first-born: and I say unto thee, Let my son go, that he may serve me: and if thou refuse to let him go, behold, I will slay thy son, even thy firstborn." It is not a prophecy, but a description of Jehovah's relationship to Israel when they were elected of Him to be the covenant people. Snaith terms this the "election-love" of God.[61] Israel was the son of Jehovah because of his election as Jehovah's "chosen people" (Exod. 4:22). God's love was expressed in the adoption of Israel "as the son of Jehovah, which began with its deliverance out of bondage of Egypt, and was completed in the conclusion of the covenant at Sinai. [This] forms the first stage in the carrying out of the divine work of salvation, which was completed in the incarnation of the Son of God for the redemption of mankind from death and ruin."[62]

If Hosea's figure of the "bride" suggests that she was an individual prior to the marriage, it only indicates part of the significance of God's relationship to His people. A son "is dependent on his father's care right from the moment of birth, and even before birth. So this second figure supplements the first."[63]

Martin Buber, who as a Jew has enjoyed great influence upon the Christian community, attributes the relationship to the zeal of Jehovah in the desert: "I loved (11:1) and they betrayed me (9:10; 11:2; 13:6)."[64] Buber further suggests three kinds of love spoken of in Hosea, for "the prophet does not use the precious word 'love' lavishly." God's love (1) Is a demanding love, 11:1-4; (2) Is a wrathful love, 9:15; (3) Is a merciful love, 14:5.[65]

The phrase **called my son out of Egypt** means that Israel came from the service of Pharaoh to the service of Jehovah. This act of God, in the mind of the faithful Israelite, was one of the great moments of their history. But even though God had called them, they went away to sacrifice **unto Baalim, and burned incense to graven images** (2). *The Berkeley Version* renders 2 clearly: "But the more I called to them the more they deserted Me, offering sacrifices to the Baals and burning incense

[61]*Op. cit.*, pp. 131-42.      [62]*Ibid.*, p. 137.
[63]Knight, *op. cit.*, p. 108.      [64]*Op. cit.*, p. 45.
[65]*Ibid.*, p. 113.

to the idols." Now God speaks with great pathos and with the same figure of the son: "Yet it was I who taught Ephraim to walk, I took them up in my arms; but they did not know that I healed them" (3, RSV). This may have been because God so humbled himself that the son did not recognize the "God-likeness of such humility."[66]

In v. 4 the figure changes. It has been paraphrased, "As a man would lead his favorite ox, so I led Israel with my ropes of love. I loosened his muzzle so he could eat. I myself stooped and fed him" (*Living Prophecies*). The **cords** must be contrasted with the ropes by which beasts are controlled. They represent the compassion of the father to a child, guiding with **bands of love.** As when the day's work is done the farmer takes off the yoke from the oxen and gives them food, likewise did the Lord lift the bonds in the evening and lovingly feed His son.

*b. Israel's punishment* (11:5-7). Verses 5-7 point out once again that, because Israel rejected God's love (*chesed*), punishment must be his lot. **He shall not return into the land of Egypt** (5) seems to contradict 8:13 and 9:3. However, in these earlier references Egypt was spoken of symbolically as the land of bondage. Here it is used literally and is compared with Assyria. Although there was a longing to return in the sense of accepting help from Egypt, disappointment is to be their lot; **the Assyrian shall be his king, because they refused to return** to God.

The rebellious character of Israel and the punishment following is described further in vv. 6-7. **Abide** (6, Heb., "whirl over") suggests that the sword of Asshur shall "sweep around its cities" (Keil). **Branches** in all probability does not refer to the figure of the vine but to the "bars of their gates" (RSV). **Because of their own counsels** shows that this is Israel's doings, not God's!

The Hebrew in v. 7 is difficult in both translation and interpretation. The Septuagint renders it: "And God is angry with his precious ones, and will not exalt them." The RSV renders the same passage: "My people are bent on turning away from me; so they are appointed to the yoke, and none shall remove it." Either translation points to the inexorable ends of judgment in the face of the sinfulness of the nation.

[66]Adam C. Welch, *Kings and Prophets of Israel* (London: Lutterworth Press, 1952), p. 147.

c. *The yearning God* (11:8-11). Yet so great is the Lord's love for His people that He cannot allow them to go: **for I am God, and not man; the Holy One in the midst of thee** (9). Because of His holiness, revealed in His covenant love (*chesed*), He is "kinder than the kindest father and gentler than the gentlest driver."[67] In v. 8, God's warnings temporarily cease. The son has failed his Father; thus the Father must hand him over to Assyria and choose another instrument on earth to do His bidding. "But at Sinai God had set his *chesed* upon his son/bride forever."[68] Here is the cross in the heart of God. **Admah** and **Zeboim** (8) were cities of the plain that perished like Sodom and Gomorrah.[69]

Could God really destroy Israel? His yearning spirit says no, even while His justice says it must be. **Mine heart is turned within me, my repentings are kindled together.** His compassion burns within Him. "I will not again destroy Ephraim" (9, RSV). It is the disposition of man to finally despair, but not Jehovah. God does not allow disloyalty to affect His own compassion.

Thus, in one of the great, moving passages of the Bible, God reveals the pain which Israel has caused. Even though He is transcendent and apart from man, yet **the Holy One** (is) **in the midst of thee** (9, cf. Isa. 12:6). As an ancient rabbi put it, "God is Israel's heart."[70] The cry is in the "eternal now." **How shall I give thee up, Ephraim? . . . for I am God, and not man.**

In the next two verses the prophet continues God's promise of hope. **The Lord is like a lion** (10). The figure is not intended as a subject to terrify, but rather it is a call that the Lord can give for His children to hasten from all quarters of the globe. **And I will place them in their houses, saith the Lord** (11). In the day of Messianic promise, God will settle them in their inheritance forever (cf. Jer. 32:37, "I will cause them to dwell safely").

### 2. Inexorable Exile (11:12—12:14)

Representing Jehovah, Hosea once again justifies the approaching judgment because of Israel's apostasy: **Ephraim com-**

---

[67]Henshaw, *op. cit.*, p. 99.
[68]Knight, *op. cit.*, p. 110.
[69]IB, VI, 688 (cf. Deut. 29:23; Jer. 49:18).
[70]*Ibid.*

**passeth me about with lies, and the house of Israel with deceit** (12). The phrase **Judah yet ruleth with God** is difficult because the KJV suggests the contrary to the context. The Amp. OT translates the phrase consistently with the meaning suggested in 12*a*: "Judah is not yet steadfast with God, with the Holy One."[71]

*a. The Lord's controversy* (12:1). In 12:1, the lying and deceitfulness of Israel are more comprehensively described. Her vanity is like chasing after the parching **east wind** (1), which would destroy if caught. Unfaithful to the Lord, the Israelites seek **a covenant with the Assyrians** and export olive **oil . . . into Egypt.** By this, the Israelites expected to buy support against Assyria. Attempting to play one nation against the other, Israel was caught in between.

*b. A word to the Southern Kingdom* (12:2-6). **Judah** (2) is not guiltless. **Jacob** (all twelve tribes) shall receive the punishment he deserves. The prophet then cites the example of Jacob, who practiced deceit, was condemned for his hypocrisy, but repented of his sin. **By his strength** (3) is translated "in his manhood he strove with God" (RSV). Even as **Jacob prevailed . . . and made supplication** (4), so Israel can approach God. The reference in 4 is to Gen. 32:24-32, where Jacob wrestled with God in prayer. There his name was changed from Jacob to Israel, "Prince of God," in the sense of having power. Thus it was only by wholehearted striving that Jacob became Israel.[72]

**The Lord is his memorial** (5) may be translated "Jehovah (*Yahweh*) is His memorial name." The word is expressive of how God wished to be remembered—Everlasting, Never-changing, Israel's covenant God. It is to this God that Israel shall ultimately return; so the prophet pleads, **Therefore turn thou to**

---

[71]The meaning of *rud* (ruleth) in the Arabic is to "ramble about." It is used of cattle that have broken loose. *Niphil* is "to cause to ramble about" (Gen. 27:40); that is, to be unbridled or unruly. *Qedoshim*, Holy One, is used of God in Prov. 9:10, meaning firm, faithful, trustworthy, the opposite of *rud*. Thus Judah is "unbridled" toward the powerful God (El) (Keil, *op. cit.,* p. 145. Cf. F. W. Farrar, *The Minor Prophets,* New York: Fleming H. Revell Co., n.d., p. 93).

[72]*Yehovah zikhro* is to be spoken as the "God of Hosts" rather than of the patriarchs. This difference was important in Hosea's day, for He was not only the God of the patriarchs, but the God who ruled the heavens and the earth with unrestricted omnipotence (see Keil, p. 148).

thy God (6). "Come back to Me now," is the plaintive call. Moffatt translates the last part of the verse, "Ever be kind and just and in your God put your unfailing trust." As in Mic. 6:8, Jehovah calls once again to His people. The student of Hosea cannot help but be impressed by God's compassion and patience in His repeated offers of forgiveness and restoration.

c. *Israel's pride* (12:7-9). In 7, Israel is spoken of as a **merchant** (*canaan*) seeking advantage in deceit and oppression. Like a fraudulent trader, Ephraim finds no sin in this because he has **become rich** (8), as though wealth was a sign of innocency. But his gain is ill-gotten and punishment is at hand.

**The Lord thy God from the land of Egypt will yet make thee to dwell in tabernacles, as in the days of the solemn feast** (9). Is this punishment or restoration? The emphasis of the text is upon the latter, yet both ideas may be present. The nation is to be removed from the luxury and seduction of Baal worship to the simplicity and austerity of the wilderness it knew only by tradition. If this becomes the occasion of fitting the people for the Lord's service, it will be the consequence of the punishment rather than the purpose of the punishment.[73]

d. *Israel's guilt* (12:10-14). Jehovah now reminds Israel of who He is and what He has done. He has **spoken by the prophets,** given **visions** to reveal His will, and **similitudes** (10; parables) by the word of His servants. But in spite of this, the whole land is sunk in **iniquity** (11); specifically, calf-worship. Two famous centers of idolatry come under review, **Gilead** and **Gilgal.**[74]

Verses 12-14 speak of the punishment so well deserved: **Jacob fled into the country of Syria, and Israel served for a wife, and for a wife he kept sheep** (12). These words point to the distress which Jacob endured (Genesis 29—31) as a fugitive from Canaan. In **Syria** (Aram) he served as a common servant for his wife.[75] The purpose of the contrast between 12 and 13 is to

---

[73]IB, VI, 701.

[74]**Gilead,** east of the Jordan River, was busy manufacturing false gods. The term "gilgals" had become a pun for "heaps of stones" piled to the side of the furrows or plowed ground. Thus their altars are like "gilgals." Gilgal, in the heart of Ephraim, is spoken of continually as the seat of idolatrous worship.

[75]*Shamar,* the tending of cattle, was one of the most difficult of servitudes. Aram (Syria) is probably the Hebrew rendering of the Aramean *Padan-aram* (Gen. 28:2; 31:18).

help Israel remember the low estate from which they were called in Egypt. This they were to acknowledge each year in the festivals of the firstfruits (Deut. 26:5-10). **By a prophet (Moses) the Lord brought Israel out of Egypt (13) and by a prophet** was Israel **preserved.** In the face of such providential dealings, **Ephraim provoked (14)** the Lord. Instead of showing gratitude, his ingratitude stirred the Lord to anger.[76] **Therefore shall he leave his blood upon him, and his reproach shall his Lord return unto him (14).** The **blood** or "blood-guiltiness" refers to Ephraim rather than to Jehovah. It may refer specifically to the guilt of human sacrifice which was associated with the worship of Molech. God left them with the guilt of their sin and its punishment to follow.

In c. 12 we find: (1) The foolishness of sin, 1; (2) The measure of punishment—according to sins, 2; (3) The negligence of the sinful, 2-4. Also, (1) The character of God, 5, 10; (2) The long-suffering of God, 9; (3) The final wrath of God, 14.

### 3. *Eventual Outcome of the Exile* (13:1-16)

The first eight verses of c. 13 relate the arguments from which Hosea concludes that the conduct of Israel is suicidal. The people's ingratitude in the face of divine providence, their pride, and neglect of Jehovah justify the conclusion to which God comes. Because God has been their Helper and Deliverer all along, they are chargeable with their own destruction.[77]

To show in contrast how deeply Israel had fallen in her apostasy, the prophet points out the eminence that Ephraim held among the twelve tribes prior to her sin: **When Ephraim spake trembling, he exalted himself in Israel (1).** Even when Ephraim spoke in humility, he spoke with authority; **but when he offended in Baal, he died.** Through the introduction of Baal worship under Jeroboam I, in which Jehovah was symbolized by a golden bull (cf. I Kings 12:28), Ephraim was given up to destruction.[78]

---

[76]**Anger,** *tamrurim* in the Hebrew, is used as an adverbial expression meaning "bitterly" (Keil, p. 152).

[77]*Pulpit Commentary, op. cit.,* p. 395.

[78]Keil gives quite a different interpretation. V. 1a speaks of Ephraim raising itself to government at the rebellion of Jeroboam I. People trembled at the revolution and civil war, not the exaltation of the ten tribes (p. 153).

**And now they sin more and more** (2), and make their images of silver, the work of the craftsmen. The expression **let the men that sacrifice kiss the calves** refers to the young bulls, symbols of fertility. The people were kissing the idols made with their own hands. The absurdity of their action as an act of worship was painted with sarcasm by the prophet.

Israel's death is close at hand. The prophet uses four figures to emphasize the early destruction that is to come. Israel's life, he says, is like a **morning cloud** (3), **the early dew that passeth away, the chaff** driven by the wind, and **the smoke** that goes **out of the chimney.**

In vv. 4-8, God pleads with Israel to recognize that the very ground of his existence is in **the Lord thy God** (4). From **Egypt** to now, Israel has known no other God but Jehovah and has discovered no other **saviour** (true helper). Isaiah was later to make the same cry in 43:11: "I . . . am the Lord; and beside me there is no saviour." "But Israel had to learn first that God's 'strange work' involved the destroying of His people before He could save them, nay that destroying them was part of His saving activity."[79]

**Thou shalt know no God but me** (4). With the first commandment (Exod. 20:3), Israel must again learn the total claim that Jehovah held upon His people. It was Jehovah who gave them manna and water **in the wilderness** (5); but once they prospered, they forgot God and gave themselves to idolatry. Thus their Saviour is turned to be their Destroyer. **Therefore I will be unto them as a lion: as a leopard by the way** (7). They shall be torn as the prey of wild beasts. The figure is continued and emphasized in v. 8. The judgment is to be carried out **as a bear that is bereaved of her whelps** (young), tearing out the very **caul** (center) **of their heart.**

**O Israel, thou hast destroyed thyself; but in me is thine help** (9); or as the Septuagint renders it, "If I destroy you, O Israel, who will be your helper?" There is no salvation from destruction for those who serve false gods. The **king** cannot **save** you; the only saviour is Jehovah (10).

**I gave thee a king in mine anger, and took him away in my wrath** (11). Israel demanded a king (I Sam. 8:5) and Jehovah acquiesced. But this particular statement may refer

---

[79]Knight, *op. cit.*, p. 117.

to the succession of kings from Jeroboam I, the first king of Israel, to Hoshea, the king at the time of the invasion. The theocratic government of the house of David was replaced by a succession of self-determined kings which Jehovah in His **wrath** would allow to reign to their own destruction.

Nothing of the evil of Israel will be forgotten: **The iniquity of Ephraim is bound up** (12). The KJV expression **his sin is hid** suggests the wrong idea; Moffatt translates it, "His sin is kept in store for him." It will be kept in mind until the day of reckoning shall arrive.

The figure suddenly changes: **The sorrows of a travailing woman shall come upon him** (13). The judgments are here associated with the birth pangs of a woman in travail from which new life is born (Isa. 13:8; Mic. 4:9-10; Matt. 24:8). But Israel is a foolish son, for he will not break forth at the desired or right place: "He needs new birth, but makes no effort to acquire it" (Amp. OT). There is no change of figure. The mother and son are to be treated as one person. **He is an unwise son,** for he fails to come to the birth, or, like a stillborn infant, there is no life in him (cf. Berk., fn.).

Commentators differ radically as to the interpretation of v. 14. The KJV suggests a promise by its positive affirmations. The Hebrew, however, with its interrogatives seems to indicate that the idea of promise is at least secondary to that of threat. The RSV translates it: "Shall I ransom them from the power of Sheol? Shall I redeem them from Death? O Death, where are your plagues? O Sheol, where is your destruction? Compassion is hid from my eyes." The IB[80] observes that this last clause is the key to the meaning: **Repentance** (compassion) **shall be hid from mine eyes.** God can show no more mercy. Ephraim must stand in the hall of judgment. If the balance of the verse is to be interpreted consistently with such a clause, the interrogative clauses require a negative answer: "Ephraim is beyond the power of recovery."[81] He is spiritually dead.[82]

---

[80]IB, VI, 714.

[81]*Ibid.*

[82]Paul apparently took a more optimistic view in using the verse to his own design and purpose (I Cor. 15:55). "As spoken by Hosea, however, the words breathe defeat rather than defiance: Compassion is hid from their eyes" (*Ibid.*).

**OSCAR F. REED**

Professor of Religion and Philosophy, Bethany Nazarene College, Bethany, Oklahoma. A.B., Th.B., Bethany Nazarene College; M.Th., Ph.D., University of Southern California (School of Theology). Graduate studies at Pasadena College and Harvard Divinity School.

**ARMOR D. PEISKER**

General Editor, Pilgrim Holiness Church, and Editor of the *Pilgrim Holiness Advocate*. A.B. in Education, Colorado College; M.A., Butler University.

Verses 15-16 state again that the Lord plans utter destruction. The actual invasion took place twelve years later. Verse 15 opens with a play on Ephraim's name, which means "fruitful or double fruitful." **Though he be fruitful among his brethren,** tragedy shall come as an **east wind** to dry up **his spring** and **fountain,** the sources of power and stability. The last phrase is a threat: the Assyrian invader **shall spoil the treasure of all pleasant vessels.** He shall plunder the kingdom.

The chapter closes with a declaration that "Samaria must suffer for her guilt" (16; Phillips) or "bear her guilt" (RSV). The horrible details of the conquest and destruction of Samaria by Shalmaneser follow. Hosea foresees that **their infants shall be dashed in pieces, and their women with child shall be ripped up** (cf. II Kings 8:12; Ps. 137:9; Isa. 13:16).

Alexander Maclaren, in building a textual exposition from 13:9, notes: (1) The loving discovery of ruin; (2) The loving appeal to conscience as to the cause; (3) The loving forbearance which still offers restoration.

# Section III Repentance and Renewal

## A. FINAL APPEAL TO REPENTANCE, 14:1-3

After thirteen chapters of sin, judgment, and punishment, the Lord makes one last appeal in vv. 1-3. If God were not God, the reader would be overwhelmed by the unremitting uselessness of it all. "But I am God, and not man" (11:9), and that makes the difference.[1]

O Israel, return unto the Lord thy God (1). The reason for the call is identified as the iniquity of the people. Israel is exhorted not to return with idle words, but with the prayer, Take away all iniquity, and receive us graciously (2). "*Kashalta* (iniquity, or sin) is represented as a 'false step' which still leaves it possible to return."[2] Conversion must begin with a prayer for the forgiveness of *all* iniquity and simple trust in the mercy of God. The calves of our lips ("fruit of our lips," Berk.) would be sincere words issuing from penitent hearts.

In v. 3 there is continued confession. Asshur (Assyria) cannot save us, nor can Egypt with its war horses, nor can the gods made by the work of our hands bring salvation. The exclamation, Ye are our gods, will no longer be uttered by those now penitent. Both of Hosea's figures of the marriage and the son are involved in the statement, For in thee the fatherless findeth mercy. Israel was fatherless before he was adopted as the Lord's covenant nation, and two of Gomer's children would be fatherless unless Hosea took them through adoption.

## B. PROMISE OF ULTIMATE BLESSING, 14:4-8

The answer to the penitential prayer (1-3) is found in vv. 4-8, which represent the Lord's response. I will heal their backsliding, I will love them freely: for mine anger is turned away from him (4). God replies with a promise of salvation. The promise is to heal the injuries that came as a result of their apostasy. This includes both physical hurts and moral failures.

---

[1]Chapter 14 may be in the nature of a liturgy used to teach Israel the truths of God as expressed by Hosea.

[2]Keil, *op. cit.*, p. 164.

The Lord's promise is to **love them freely,** looking for no return for His love.[3] His **anger,** kindled at idolatry, is now **turned away from** Israel.

**I will be as the dew unto Israel** (5). This is the third time that Hosea has used the figure of dew. In the other instances he spoke of the duration of the morning dew (6:4; 13:3). Now "he employs the word as a picture of the gentle kiss of Yahweh's forgiveness, that brings new hope and life to the beloved."[4] Israel shall grow luxuriantly even **as the lily,** with **roots like** the cedars of **Lebanon.**[5] The expression **His branches shall spread** (6) suggests that Israel's prosperity shall abide.

As the cedars of Lebanon have a sweet aroma, so shall Israel be unto the Lord—a sweet-smelling savor. In regard to vv. 5-7, Rosenmuller suggests, "The *rooting* indicates stability; the *spreading* of the branches, propagation and the multitude of inhabitants; the *splendour* of the olive, beauty and glory, and that constant and lasting; the *fragrance,* hilarity and loveliness."[6]

The figures of speech continue in v. 7. **They that dwell under his shadow shall return.** They that sit under the shade of Israel shall **revive as the corn, and grow as the vine.** The scent, which **shall be as the wine of Lebanon,** has been renowned from time immemorial in Palestine.

The passage closes with v. 8: **Ephraim shall say, What have I to do any more with idols?** Some translations put the words in God's mouth: "O Ephraim, what have I to do with idols? It is I who answer and look after you" (RSV). The verse is partly promise and partly appeal. Actually, it suggests that the day of idolatry is over and God will have nothing to do with idols because Ephraim has freed herself from them.[7] Jehovah continues: **I am like a green fir tree,** the source where the nation shall find its **fruit** (strength and sustenance). The promise of the chapter is fulfilled in the Messianic age.

[3]This is the heart of God's *chesed* and the *agape* of I Corinthians 13.
[4]Knight, *op. cit.,* p. 125.
[5]The lily grows with profusion and beauty in Palestine, although its roots are weak. But Israel's root shall strike deeply, even as the cedars of Lebanon (5; cf. Ps. 80:10).
[6]Quoted from Keil, *loc. cit.,* p. 166.
[7]The promise seems to be the same as was fulfilled in Judah's return from Babylon, when images were never again used in worship.

## C. Epilogue, 14:9

The opening clause refers to everything that Hosea has laid before the people in his prophecy of warning: **Who is wise, and he shall understand these things? prudent, and he shall know them?** The chapter concludes with a great summary of the entire prophecy: **For the ways of the Lord are right, and the just shall walk in them: but the transgressors shall fall therein.**

Chapter 14 is a fitting climax to the Book of Hosea. In it is the secret of redemption: (1) The sincerity of the repentant, 2*a*; (2) The prayer for total renewal, 2*b*; (3) Faith in a merciful God, 2*c*; (4) The hope of the converted 4; (5) The growth of the converted, 5-6; (6) The end of the converted, 7.

Martin Buber fittingly concludes his study of the prophecy by speaking of "The Turning to the Future."

> YHVH promises Israel, rising to life again, a two-fold covenant (2, 20 ff.). First there is the covenant of peace that He makes for Israel with all living creatures and all the world of nations; and second there is the new marriage covenant, by which He betroths Israel to Himself forever in the great principles that make up the two-sided relationship between deity and humanity. This promise is fitted into a *dialogic* connection. In the wilderness where the inner change takes place and whence the change of all things proceeds, the woman "gratifies" her husband "as in the days of her youth" (17), and he "gratifies" (23 f.) not her alone, but the whole world, while a stream of gratification pours from Him to heaven, and thence to earth, and thence with all its productive blessing to Jezreel. Everything is changed: as *Lo-ruhamah* becomes *ruhamah*, and *Lo-ammi* becomes *ammi*, so Jezreel, formerly called by this cursed name after the place of a bloody deed, now becomes revealed according to the significance of this name, that is to say "he whom God sows," He stands here for a new generation. YHVH sows the land with a new seed. And at the end of the book the dialogic concept of "gratification" returns. YHVH heals the turning away of Israel, for His "anger is turned from them" (14:5). He wishes to be as dew to Israel, and they "will return to dwell in the shade of Lebanon (8) and to blossom "as the vine." For "I am He Who has gratified" (9).[9]

---

[9] *Op. cit.*, p. 125; YHVH, or Yahweh, or Jehovah.

*The Book of*

# JOEL

**Oscar F. Reed**

# Introduction

## A. NAME AND OCCASION FOR THE PROPHECY

The name Joel (Heb., *Yoel*) means "Jehovah is God." In all probability Joel was a Judean and an inhabitant of Jerusalem. Though there is no proof for the assumption, he may have been a priest, or at least a "Temple-prophet."[1]

The occasion of the prophecy was a time of national panic in the face of the ravages of an unparalleled locust plague. The prophet looked upon the plague as a solemn warning of judgment to come in the "day of Jehovah," which is the pivotal idea of Joel.

## B. TIME OF COMPOSITION

The date of the prophecy is a matter of much contention among biblical scholars. Since there are few, if any, external evidences, any conclusions must be drawn from the text itself. Joel does not date his prophecy according to the reign of a particular king, as do Hosea, Amos, Isaiah, and others; nor does he make any specific allusions to historical situations which can aid in designating a date.

It is quite evident that Joel either quotes from, or is quoted by, several other prophets. If the date of the prophecy is placed early, and Joel is original, the prophecy becomes the source of seed thoughts for much that follows. If it is placed late, Joel becomes a summary of much that was expressed before.[2]

An excellent defense of the conservative position, placing Joel about 830 B.C., during the minority of King Joash and the regency of Jehoiada, the high priest, is given by A. F. Kirkpatrick in the following arguments.[3]

---

[1] Joel speaks familiarly of Zion and the children of Zion (2:1, 23), of Judah and Jerusalem. He takes great interest in the Temple (1:13-17). He speaks objectively of the priests, however, in 1:13 and 2:17, which leads many to believe that he was not of the priesthood.

[2] A. F. Kirkpatrick, *The Doctrine of the Prophets* (New York: The Macmillan Co., 1897), p. 58.

[3] John A. Thompson, in his exposition on Joel in *The Interpreter's Bible*, VI, 729, places Joel as late as 400 B.C. because of the political and religious conditions described. This is quite typical of the more liberal perspective.

(1) The position of the book between Hosea and Amos indicates that Jewish tradition considered it to be ancient. The position in the canon gives strong evidence for an early date.

(2) There is clear evidence of "borrowing" between Amos and Joel (see Joel 3:18 and Amos 9:13. Joel 3:16 is used as a text by Amos in the beginning of his prophecy). If Amos is quoting from Joel, as he seems to be, the prophecy must have been earlier than 755 B.C.

(3) The type of government implied in Joel accords with a regency such as that of Jehoiada. Since a king is not mentioned, the priests and elders carry the "responsibility of national leadership."[4] II Kings 11:4 points out that Joash was crowned at the age of seven and his uncle, the high priest, "exercised a controlling influence in Judah to the day of his death."[5]

(4) The enemies of Judah are nations identified with an early date. The Assyrians, Chaldeans, and Persians are not mentioned. It is the Philistines, Edomites, Egyptians, and Phoenicians who play their parts in the drama painted by Joel. Evidently Assyria and Babylon were not then dangerous or Joel would have mentioned them. Egypt and the smaller nations threatened Judah. This would seem to indicate an earlier rather than a later date.[6] Archer concludes that the internal evidence for the composition of the prophecy agrees more closely with the period around 835 B.C. than with any other date. In addition to the arguments summarized, he adds: "The linguistic evidence perfectly accords with this early date, and makes a theory of post-Exilic composition quite untenable. It is fair to say that the arguments for a late date are largely based upon humanistic philosophical assumption rather than upon reasonable deduction from the data of the text itself."[7]

## C. The Pivotal Ideas in Joel

The teaching of Joel centers around the "day of Jehovah" in which the Lord in a great future crisis manifests His power and majesty in the destruction of His enemies and in the deliver-

---

[4]Gleason L. Archer, Jr., *Old Testament Introduction* (Chicago: Moody Press, 1964), p. 292.

[5]*Ibid.*

[6]Egypt was still to be feared in the day of Joash. On the other hand, Egypt had lost its world position after the Chaldean period. This would seem to eliminate the possibility of a date as late as 400 B.C.

[7]*Op. cit.*, p. 292.

ance of those who trust in Him. Its approach is marked by great convulsions and extraordinary phenomena in the sphere of nature. The character of the day, whether one of terror or blessing, will depend upon the attitude of heart and life toward Jehovah.[8]

A second principal teaching is found in the outpouring of the divine Spirit. Nowhere else in the Old Testament do we find a promise so comprehensive, the fulfillment of which would mean the realization of Moses' words: "Would that all Jehovah's people were prophets, that Jehovah would put his Spirit upon them!" (Num. 11:29, ASV) The Day of Pentecost marked the beginning of the fulfillment. Since then it has been and is being realized with ever-increasing fullness.

Joel is silent concerning the person of the Messianic King. In the final crisis it is Jehovah himself who interferes in judging the nations and delivering the Jews.

Because of his emphasis upon the externals of religion,[9] Joel has sometimes been accused of neglecting the "weightier matters of the law." That he entirely lacked interest in moral requirements is not true, for he promised deliverance not alone on external observances, but on the basis of "godly sorrow [that] worketh repentance to salvation."[10]

When the student of Joel transcends the "national particularism" of the prophet, he sees the abiding message of the book which had such a broad influence upon the New Testament. Joel is able under divine revelation to sustain a balance between the outward and the inward elements in religion. God reveals himself through His Spirit as well as through nature. While formal worship is given due regard, inner repentance and faith are looked upon as man's primary obligations. Although the Messianic promise points to the cleansing of the outward environment, the central emphasis of Joel is the presence of God in the midst of His obedient and faithful people. The most meaningful contribution of the prophet is found in the promise of the outpouring of the Spirit of God on all believers. "In fulfillment of this promise the truest Christian experience of God since Pentecost has been primarily spiritual and personal rather than formal and priestly."[11]

[8]1:15; 2:1-2, 11, 31; 3:14-21. See Frederick Eiselen, *Prophecy and the Prophets,* for a comprehensive discussion of the teachings of Joel, pp. 286-92.
[9]1:9, 13-14; 2:12-17.
[10]Cf. 2:12-13.
[11]IB, VI, 735.

# *Outline*

I. The Plague of Locusts and the Day of Jehovah, 1:1—2:11

    A. Superscription, 1:1
    B. The Devastation by the Locusts, 1:2-7
    C. The Invasion as a Type, 1:8-20
    D. The Day of Jehovah, 2:1-11

II. Joel's Call to Repentance, 2:12-19

    A. Appeal to Repentance, 2:12-14
    B. The Scope of Repentance, 2:15-17
    C. Promise of Mercy, 2:18-19

III. The Hope of Future Blessings, 2:20-32

    A. Destruction of the "Northern Army," 2:20
    B. Renewal of Spiritual and Earthly Blessings, 2:21-27
    C. The Coming of the Holy Spirit, 2:28-32

IV. The Day of Jehovah, 3:1-21

    A. Judgment upon Unbelievers, 3:1-17
    B. Triumph for Jerusalem and the Redeemed, 3:18-21

Section **I** *The Plague of Locusts and the Day of Jehovah*

Joel 1:1—2:11

## A. SUPERSCRIPTION, 1:1

Once again the Hebrew prophet begins with a reference to the divine source of his prophecy: It was **the word of the Lord that came to Joel** (1). Joel (*Yahu* or *Yahweh* is God) was the son of **Pethuel** or Bethuel (LXX). The meaning of the father's name is "openheartedness" or "sincerity of God." All else concerning Joel's life is conjecture based upon the internal evidences of the text itself.[1]

## B. THE DEVASTATION BY THE LOCUSTS, 1:2-7

By direct address, Joel gains the attention of his hearers. **Hear this, ye old men, and give ear, all ye inhabitants of the land** (2). The event is unheard of, an event unparalleled in preceding generations. Thus the prophet expects a negative answer to the question, **Hath this been in your days, or even in the days of your fathers?** The commandment follows so that the story shall not die! They were to tell their **children** (3), grandchildren, and great-grandchildren of the catastrophe. The persons addressed were the **inhabitants of the land** (Jerusalem and Judah; cf. 14; 2:1).

The view is generally held that the plague was real and not symbolic. Those who have observed the habits and destructive work of the locusts see in Joel's description an accurate picture of the occasion which the prophet uses to proclaim his burden.

The fourth verse contains a description of the locusts:
"What the *Gazam* left, the *Arbeh* hath devoured,
And what the *Arbeh* left, the *Jelek* hath devoured,
And what the *Jelek* left, the *Chasel* devoured."[2]

---

[1]W. Neil, "Joel," *The Interpreter's Dictionary of the Bible*, ed. George A. Buttrick, *et al.* (New York: Abingdon Press, 1962), p. 926.

[2]A. C. Gaebelein, *The Prophet Joel* (New York: Publication Office, *Our Hope*, 1909), pp. 31 ff.

Of the nine Old Testament Hebrew words used for **locust,** four are found in this verse. *Gazam* means "cutting locusts," *arbeh* "swarming locusts," *yeleq* or *jelek,* "hopping locusts," and *chasel* or *hasil,* "destroying locusts." These names do not represent four different species, but probably four different stages in the life of the locust. The Arabic has a name for each of the six forms of locust life.[3]

Most of the books and commentaries refer to the locust plague of 1915 in Jerusalem as a vivid description of what must have happened in the time of Joel.

> A loud noise was heard before the locusts were seen, produced by the flapping of myriads of locust wings and resembling the distant rumbling of waves (cf. Rev. 9:9). The sun was suddenly darkened. Showers of their excrements fell thick and fast, resembling those of mice. Their elevation above the earth was at times hundreds of feet; at other times they flew quite low, detached numbers alighting. "In Jerusalem, at least," Mr. Whiting said, "they inevitably came from the northeast going toward the southwest, establishing the accuracy of Joel's account in chap. 2:20." Tons were captured and buried alive; many were thrown into cisterns or into the Mediterranean Sea, and when washed ashore, were collected and dried and used for fuel in Turkish baths. . . .
>
> Mr. Aaronsohn, another witness of the plague in 1915, testifies that in less than two months after their first appearance, not only was every green leaf devoured, but the very bark was peeled from the trees, which stood out white and lifeless, like skeletons. The fields, he says, were stripped to the ground. Even Arab babies left by their mothers in the shade of some tree, had their faces devoured before their screams were heard. The natives accepted the plague as just judgment because of their wickedness.[4]

Joel interprets the calamity as the judgment of God and calls Judah to repentance. The prophet calls **drunkards** and **all ye drinkers of wine** (5) to sobriety, that they may understand the significance of the visitation. The price of wine probably soared astronomically as it has in times of more recent plagues that stripped the vines. Hence it is no wonder that drinkers would **howl** for **new wine** which was either unavailable or not within their reach financially.

The locusts are represented as a **nation** which is **strong** (6), numberless, and with **the teeth of a lion.** The expression, **The**

---

[3]Cf. IB, VI, 737.

[4]George L. Robinson, *The Twelve Minor Prophets* (New York: George H. Doran Co., 1926), pp. 34 ff.

**cheek teeth of a great lion** is translated "the fangs of a lioness" (RSV). The destruction by the locusts included fig trees and grapevines, leaving only the bare trunks and vines. Even the bark was shredded, so that the injury was not confined to a single year.

## C. THE INVASION AS A TYPE, 1:8-20

The call is now addressed to the whole nation, which is to mourn and lament as **a virgin girded with sackcloth for the husband** (the betrothed) **of her youth** (8; cf. Isa. 54:6). As soon as a woman was betrothed, her fiancé was known as her husband (Deut. 22:23-24; Matt. 1:19). **Sackcloth** was the sign of mourning.

**The meat offering and the drink offering is cut off** (9) because the **corn**, the **new wine,** and the **oil** (10) are destroyed at their source. Thus, **the priests . . . mourn in the house of the Lord.** Since the sacrifice is impossible, there is a "practical suspension of the covenant-relation—a sign that God had rejected his people."[5] The description of the desolation is continued in vv. 11-12. **Husbandmen** (11) are the tillers of the soil. Even the **pomegranate,** date **palm,** and **apple tree . . . are withered.** Thus, "all gladness fails from the sons of men" (12, RSV).

The ethical implications of the prophecy now come to the fore. There is a call to the **priests,** the **ministers of the altar** (13), to offer supplications day and night before the Lord. They, in turn, are to call **the elders and all the inhabitants of the land** to repentance in **the house of the Lord your God** (14). They are commanded, **Sanctify ye a fast;** that is, appoint a time of fasting as a service of prayer to the Lord in the absence of the morning and evening sacrifices.[6]

In verse 15, Joel introduces the pivotal idea of the book: the day of Jehovah. **Alas for the day! for the day of the Lord is at hand, and as a destruction from the Almighty shall it come.** With Amos, Joel interprets it in its present context as a time of judgment upon Israel.[7]

[5]C. F. Keil and F. Delitzsch, *Biblical Commentary on the Old Testament,* I, "The Twelve Minor Prophets" (Grand Rapids, Wm. B. Eerdmans Pub. Co., 1954), 184.

[6]*Ibid.,* p. 186.

[7]Cf. 2:1; 3:14; Amos 5:18, 20; also Ezek. 30:2-3; Zeph. 1:7, 14.

"The 'Day of the Lord' is so imminent that there is no time for anything except to make the people feel that the hand of the Lord has been laid upon them, that this visitation was an act of God calling for repentance and a return to Him whom they had forgotten."[8]

That day shall come like the devastation of the locusts—*Yom Yehovah* is the great day of Jehovah, **the Almighty,** who will destroy all who exalt themselves against Him.

Jehovah is the Lord of nature and expresses His righteousness through natural events. It was to be expected, therefore, that vv. 16-18 should describe these events as the expression of divine displeasure.[9] **Before our eyes** (16) indicates that the people witnessed the calamity. They were, however, helpless in the face of the onslaught which suspended the sacrifices in the Temple and thus cut off their **joy and gladness.**[10]

**The seed is rotten under their clods** (17), and "the storehouses are desolate, the granaries ruined" (RSV). The pastureland was destroyed, so that the **cattle** (18) were forced to wander seeking water and grass (I Kings 18:5). Even the **sheep** and goats suffered, though they needed little in comparison to the cattle.

The first chapter closes with a cry from the heart of the prophet for help from the **Lord** (19). Since both nature and **beasts** (20) are suffering, Joel cries to the Lord, who can aid both (Ps. 36:6). **Fire** and **flame** (19) are used to indicate the burning heat of the drought which followed the plague.[11]

Chapter 1 offers an opportunity to understand the conditions of national repentance: (1) The inevitable judgment of God upon the nation for its transgressions, 1:15 ff.; (2) The call to prayer, fasting, and repentance for the sins of the nation, 1:14; (3) The source of deliverance is in God alone, 1:19*a*.

---

[8]Raymond Calkins, *The Modern Message of the Minor Prophets* (New York: Harper and Brothers, 1947), p. 158. Joel probably shared in the idea that calamity of any kind was proof of sin.

[9]John Paterson, *The Goodly Fellowship of the Prophets* (New York: Charles Scribner and Sons, 1948), p. 259.

[10]Joel is speaking, in all probability, of peace offerings (Deut. 12:6-7); firstfruits (Deut. 26:10); weeks (Deut. 16:10); and tabernacles (Deut. 16: 13-15).

[11]Palestine is arid and dry. The streams dry up in the absence of rain. Severe drought only added to the problem.

## D. The Day of Jehovah, 2:1-11

Robinson believes that Joel must have coined the term **the day of the Lord** (1).[12] An eschatological phrase, it is found in Old Testament prophecy in its earliest times (cf. Isa. 2:12; Amos 5:18). "For, the idea of a great Judgment Day comes forth from his hand so perfect, that his successors have adopted it and been able to add to it hardly a single touch. It was the visitation of the plague of locusts which, first, suggested it to Joel's mind."[13]

The passage through v. 18 contains a renewed emphasis upon repentance in the face of Jehovah's great and terrible judgment day (1-11). To this is coupled an optimism regarding the Lord's mercy and compassion if the people will return with all their hearts (12).

The priests were instructed, **Blow ye the trumpet** (*shophar*) **in Zion, and sound an alarm in my holy mountain** (1). **Zion** is called the **holy mountain** (Ps. 2:6) because the Lord is there in His sanctuary, the holy of holies. The trumpet blast was to be relayed to other towns until **all the inhabitants** would **tremble** for the **day of the Lord,** which was **nigh at hand.**

The **day of darkness and of gloominess** (2) is an allusion to the locusts which darkened the land. They are likened to "a great and powerful people" (RSV) which the nation had not experienced previously nor would again in **the years of many generations.**

The description continues under the metaphor of **fire** (3) but the effects described could easily be attributed to the locusts as well. The contrast pictures a **garden of Eden** before the line of the plague and the **desolate wilderness** behind. Nothing is left.

Joel says the **appearance of them is as the appearance of horses** (4). The comparison is between the head of the locust and the head of a horse, which bears a strong resemblance to it.[14] In v. 5, the sound of the locusts' wings is **like the noise** (rumblings) **of chariots.** The locusts are also compared to a raging fire before the wind devouring **stubble,** and **a strong people set**

---

[12]*Op. cit.,* p. 38.

[13]*Ibid.*

[14]Locusts are called *heupferde,* hay horses, in Germany. In v. 4 their appearance is likened to advancing horses and like war horses rather than horsemen.

**in battle array.** It is no wonder that the people shall **be pained, and all faces shall gather blackness** (grow pale; 6).[15]

In vv. 7-10, the army of locusts is compared to a well-trained army, swarming upon the walls of Jerusalem, neither swerving nor breaking **their ranks** (7). Not jostling one another (8, RSV), each one takes his own way, not halted by **the sword** nor other weapons held against them. W. T. Thompson describes vain attempts to check locusts in Lebanon in 1845: "We dug trenches, and kindled fires, and beat and burned to death 'heaps upon heaps,' but the effort was utterly useless. Wave after wave rolled up the mountain-side, and poured over rocks, walls, ditches, and hedges, those behind covering up and bridging over the masses already killed."[16]

The locusts ran as horses, **upon the wall** (9). They climbed **up upon the houses** and crawled **in at the windows like a thief.** Nothing could contain them or resist them. Joel's description, **The earth shall quake before them** (10), was supported in the 1915 invasion when the army of locusts at times was so dense that it seemed the earth moved. The **sun** was darkened by their flights and the **stars** were obliterated from the sight of man.

**And the Lord shall utter his voice** (11). Only such displays of power as depicted in vv. 4-10 would befit **the day of the Lord.** Verse 11 is graphically paraphrased in *Living Prophecies:* "The Lord leads them with a shout. This is His mighty army and they follow His orders. The day of the judgment of the Lord is an awesome, terrible thing. Who can endure it?"

Joel's proclamation of "the day of the Lord" suggests the following exposition as a description of coming judgment: (1) It will be a day of darkness, 2:2; (2) It will be a day of desolation, 2:3; (3) It will be a day of the execution of God's word, 2:11.

---

[15]"All faces withdraw their redness" (Keil, p. 192)—in the sense that the face turns pale with terror (Jer. 30:6).

[16]IB, VI, 745.

# Section II   Joel's Call to Repentance

Joel 2:12-19

## A. APPEAL TO REPENTANCE, 2:12-14

Chapter 2:12-19 is a call to national repentance. Israel can avert judgment by a sincere turning to God in repentance and mourning.

The announcement of the day of the Lord (11) was to produce repentance in the face of threatening judgment. **Therefore also now** (12) may be interpreted as "yet even now" (RSV).

The nation was to turn **with all your heart.** Every element of true repentance is present: the confession of sin through **weeping, mourning,** and **fasting.** The prophet immediately balances the external evidences with the words of v. 13: **rend your heart, and not your garments.** God's primary requirement is always "a broken and a contrite heart" (Ps. 51:17). To such an attitude He always responds in love, **for he is gracious and merciful, slow to anger, and of great kindness, and repenteth him of the evil** (13; "suffers himself to repent of the evil"[1]).

**Who knoweth?** (14) may perhaps be understood as meaning God will repent of His judgment. To have been more confident of God's changed attitude would have been offensive to the divine sovereignty. A **blessing** in the form of a **meat** (cereal) **offering and a drink offering** would be a sign that He had restored the land, making the offerings possible. The restoration would also be a sign of the renewed covenant.

## B. THE SCOPE OF REPENTANCE, 2:15-17

Once again in v. 15 the call to **assembly** is made. In v. 1, the trumpet gives a warning; here it represents a summons to repentance. Note that it is in a context similar to 1:13-14 and that 2:15b is identical to 1:14a. The nationwide call to repentance is emphasized by a listing by age of the groups involved: the **elders** (16), **children,** and babies; even the **bridegroom** and **bride** are summoned from their nuptial **chamber.** No

[1]*Ibid.,* cf. Exod. 34:6 and Jonah 4:2.

95

age or rank is excepted—indicating the all-inclusive guilt of the nation. All are exposed to judgment before the Lord.

In 17 we find the source of a well-known figure of intercession. The **priests** as mediators are to **weep between the porch and the altar.** They are to stand between the porch of the Temple and the altar of burnt offering (brazen altar, II Chron. 4:1; see Chart B), and entreat the Lord in behalf of the people. Consistent with the context, Joel is not speaking in v. 17 of foreign domination, but the fear of scorn as a result of national calamity. The clause **that the heathen should rule over them** is translated, "make not thy heritage . . . a byword among the nations" (Berk.). The fear was not alone for the sake of Israel but that pagan nations might express doubt as to the existence or the power of Jehovah with the taunting words, **Where is their God?**

Joel is explicit in his demand for repentance as a condition of restoration: (1) The condition: the nation was to turn with all its heart, 2:12-13; (2) The response: the grace, mercy, and kindness of God, 2:13; (3) The conclusion: the restoration to the covenant relation, 2:14.

## C.  PROMISE OF MERCY, 2:18-19

The promise given in response to the prayer of the priests for the nation refers to both the present and the future. The destruction of the locusts will give assured anticipation of **corn, and wine, and oil** (19) because the Lord is **jealous for his land** (18) and pities **his people.** The taunt, "Where is their God?" in v. 17 is answered in v. 19, **and I will no more make you a reproach among the heathen.**

# Section III *The Hope of Future Blessings*

Joel 2:20-32

## A. DESTRUCTION OF THE "NORTHERN ARMY," 2:20

This verse does not find consistent interpretation among biblical scholars. If it refers only to the locusts, the prophet is speaking of the "northerner" (RSV) as the locusts coming from the north as they did in the plague of 1915. Keil argues that the "northern one" (**army** is italicized, indicating that it has been added to the text in KJV) furnishes no decisive argument in favor of an allegorical interpretation. The IB and other contemporary authorities concur in this view.[1]

In the minds of some scholars, **the northern army** is viewed as a human army since Israel's historic enemies are from the north. Both Archer and Ellicott[2] believe "him of the north" to be applied to the Assyrian hordes which were later to destroy Israel (Jer. 1:13 speaks of the Chaldean army pouring southward from the face of the north). Ellicott argues that the addition of the patronymic syllable to the Hebrew word indicates a "native of the North." Thus he believes that, under the image of the destruction of the locusts, the prophet points to deliverance from the northern invaders.[3]

In either case, the blessing of deliverance is promised to **land** (21), **beasts** (22), and people (23).

## B. RENEWAL OF SPIRITUAL AND EARTHLY BLESSINGS, 2:21-27

The **land** is now urged not to **fear**, but to **rejoice: for the Lord will do great things** (21). This promise is followed by

---

[1]Keil, *op. cit.,* p. 201; IB, VI, 749. According to this interpretation, God will drive the locusts **into a land barren and desolate** (20) and towards **the east sea** (Dead Sea). The **hinder part toward the utmost sea** speaks of the Western Sea (Mediterranean), where heaps of locusts washed upon the shores stink with an **ill savour** (foul smell). Vv. 21-23 rise to a climax as land, beast, and people are blessed with the promise of an abundant rainfall in the **former** (23) and **latter rain.**

[2]Archer, *op. cit.,* p. 294, identifies the invader as Sennacharib. Charles John Ellicott, *Old Testament Commentary* (London: Cassell and Co., 1897), p. 442.

[3]*Ibid.*

additional addresses to the **beasts of the field** (22) and the **children of Zion** (23), who are to be blessed with the **former rain, and the latter rain in the first month.**[4] As a result, the beasts are promised adequate pasture; the fruit tree and the fig tree, ravaged by the locusts, are now to be blessed by yielding **their strength** (fruit).

Verses 24-27 continue the promise of God's blessings of restoration. The drought has been broken, the rains have come in abundance. All that was lost through the plague will now be given back manifold to the **children of Zion.** The famine will be replaced by plenty, including **wheat . . . wine and oil** (24).

In v. 25 the same four stages of the locust are spoken of as in 1:4 (see comment there), though the order is reversed. And as in v. 11 the horde of locusts is spoken of as **my great army** used of the Lord in judgment upon the nation. The promise of restoration suggests that the plague continued for several **years.** Now, however, the blessings of the Lord are given as a response to penitential prayers and the **people shall never** (again) **be ashamed** (27). Keil adds the expression of duration—"to all eternity"—because Jehovah, the only true God, is present **in the midst of Israel** and **hath dealt wondrously** (26) with His people.

## C. The Coming of the Holy Spirit, 2:28-32

We now see the higher blessing set before the people of God as: (1) the outpouring of the Spirit of God upon all flesh; (2) the judgment of the nations; and (3) the glorification of the people of God. While these features are not kept strictly apart, nevertheless they are clearly indicated and closely related to one another.

Verses 28-32 are familiar to the New Testament student as

---

[4]The **former rain** indicates the early or first rains following the summer; it softens the soil and prepares for the sowing. The **latter rain** waters the seed. The interval between the two gives the farmer time to sow. (See James Hastings, *Dictionary of the Bible* [New York: Charles Scribner's Sons, 1909], p. 782.)

The **former rain** moderately is translated by the *Vulgate* as "Teacher of righteousness." If this translation is given, there is an intimation of the advent of the Messiah (Ellicott, p. 433). *Moreh,* translated "early rain" in the KJV, is translated "teacher" in the Chaldee and Vulgate. Keil has a full explanation in support of the position (*op. cit.,* p. 205).

the glorious promise quoted by Peter on the Day of Pentecost and identified as "spoken by the prophet Joel" (Acts 2:16-21).[5]

**And it shall come to pass afterward** (sometime in the future), **that I will pour out my spirit upon all flesh (28).** If the Lord had given the **early** and **latter rain** in material blessings, He was ready also to pour out (Isa. 32:5; Ezek. 39:29) spiritual blessing in the gift of His Spirit. In this respect, Peter is Joel's commentary.

If the first great teaching in Joel is repentance in the face of trouble, the second is the outpouring of the Spirit **upon all flesh.** The promise is an enlargement of Num. 11:29 and fulfilled, as previously observed, on the Day of Pentecost described in Acts 2. The whole promise is preeminently eschatological, yet meant "for the comfort of the people in the prophet's own time." Robinson continues that "it is akin to Jeremiah's promise of a 'new covenant' (Jer. 31:31-34). Though there is no prediction of the Messiah in the book of Joel, yet as Horton well observes, our study of this book should lead us to Christ and the baptism of the Spirit. Thus Joel begins to bridge the chasm to the Kingdom of Grace."[6]

The promise of the Spirit to **all flesh** is followed by a description of the phenomena accompanying the great event which Peter was later to identify with the Day of Pentecost. In Num. 12:6, **visions** and **dreams** are the two forms of prophetic revelation. This allusion in Joel means that **sons, daughters, old men,** and **young men** shall receive the Spirit of God with His gifts.

The promise is also extended to the **servants** and **handmaids** (29; men and women slaves). The gospel was to break the fetters of slavery, a conclusion which the Jewish expositors (LXX and Pharisees) were not able to accept.[7]

The promise of the Spirit is the high-water mark of Joel's prophecy. (1) The promise is universal, 28-29; (2) It is a promise of a new covenant, 32; (3) It is a promise to those who believe, 32.

**The great and the terrible day of the Lord** (31; cf. Mal. 4:5) is closely associated with the promise of the Spirit. The phe-

---

[5]In the light of the NT fulfillment Joel's prediction of spiritual illumination to all God's people is perhaps his most religious contribution" (IB, VI, 753).

[6]*Op. cit.,* p. 45.

[7]Keil, *op. cit.,* p. 211.

nomena spoken of in v. 31 are figurative descriptions of judgment in both the Old and New Testaments (Isa. 13:10; Mark 13:24; Rev. 6:12).[8]

Both Peter and Paul (Rom. 10:13) quote from Joel in applying the principle of salvation by faith to men of all generations. **And it shall come to pass, that whosoever shall call upon the name of the Lord shall be delivered** (32). There is the call to the Lord in the face of judgment and the promise of deliverance to those who repent. The last phrase of 32 implies that **the remnant,** those who truly believe, shall be saved. Even as early as Joel, human response in faith becomes the complement of divine election. God elects to deliverance those who call on the name of the Lord.[9]

---

[8]**Fire** (30) and **blood** (31) recall the plagues of Egypt (Exod. 7:17; 9:24). The **pillars of smoke** bring to mind the descent of Jehovah upon Sinai with the smoke of the mountain ascending to the heavens (Exod. 19:18). The darkening of **the sun** and the blood-red appearance of **the moon** also bring the plagues of Egypt to remembrance (Exod. 10:21).

[9]The full use of the prophecy is found in Peter's sermon in Acts 2:17-21, quoting Joel 2:28-32 with the exception of 32b. His reference in Acts 2:39, "For the promise is unto you, and to your children, and to all that are afar off, even as many as the Lord our God shall call," adds 32b. The fulfillment of the prophecy of Joel began at Pentecost and continues throughout the present dispensation to as many as call upon the Lord.

# Section IV  *The Day of Jehovah*

We have reached the finale of Joel's prophecy. The vision enlarges and embraces those broader experiences connected with "the day of the Lord." In cc. 1 and 2 we see the prophetic history of Israel; in the final chapter the judgment of the Lord upon all the earth is revealed, followed by the millennial triumph for Jerusalem and the redeemed.

## A. JUDGMENT UPON UNBELIEVERS, 3:1-17

**For, behold in those days, and in that time** (1) seems to refer directly to the period of Judah's restoration from the captivity in Babylon. However, the RSV translates it more generally: "I will restore the fortunes of Judah and Jerusalem." Along with most commentators this translation seems to include the broader promise of final restoration for Israel. This interpretation is verified in the gathering of **all nations** (2) to the **valley of Jehoshaphat** (Jehovah judges).[1]

The description of judgment, **I . . . will plead with them,** is not a picture of the Lord pleading in the modern sense of the term. Rather, God is contending **for my people and for my heritage Israel, whom they have scattered among the nations.** God will bring judgment in behalf of Israel upon the nations which have divided **His land.** (Joel uses **Israel** and **Judah** interchangably.)

Verse 3 points out that the enemies of Israel have shown no consideration for their captives, including the children, whom they have sold for a **harlot** and **for wine.** Casting **lots** refers to the dividing of the spoil in Jerusalem by the Chaldeans (Obad. 11).

Verses 4-16 constitute a direct address to the pagan nations. **All the coasts of Palestine** (4; the Philistines and Phoenicians)

---

[1]The valley of Jehoshaphat is probably the valley of Kidron on the eastern side of Jerusalem. (See Keil, p. 220, for full explanation.) It is here used, however, in its grammatical meaning as the scene of divine judgment rather than in its strict geographical meaning.

are added to **Tyre, and Zidon** as no less culpable. The question: **Will ye render me a recompence?** probably reflects a false claim by the enemies of Israel that they were only seeking justice. Jehovah very quickly "warns that their so-called 'recompense' will be repaid to them": **I return your recompence upon your own head.**[2]

The reasons for divine justice quickly follow: **Ye have taken my silver and my gold** (5). They had deposited God's treasures in pagan **temples.** Joel continues with the accusation of trade in slavery by selling **the children** (people) **of Judah** (6) to the Grecians (Ionian Greeks). Verses 7-8 follow with the punishment from the Lord returned **upon your own head** (7), i.e., by repaying in kind. The very people who were deprived (Israel) now sell the **sons** and **daughters** (8) of their enemies **to the Sabeans.**[3] The pronouncement is given divine verification: **for the Lord hath spoken it.**

In 9, Joel continues with the judgment to be visited on **the Gentiles,** first broached in v. 2 (cf. Zech. 14:2). The call is to all nations to prepare themselves for battle and to appear in **the valley of Jehoshaphat** (12). Their adversary, however, is not Israel, but the God of Israel: **for there will I sit to judge all the heathen round about.** It is to this end that He challenges the nations: **Beat your plowshares into swords, and your pruninghooks into spears** (10). Note that this is just the reverse of the later Messianic promise (cf. Isa. 2:4; Mic. 4:3). Even the **weak** are to be called into battle.

**Assemble yourselves, and come** (11) repeats the summons to doom. The RSV translates it, "Hasten and come" to the valley of judgment. In 13 the timeliness of judgment is represented in the figures of reaping ripened grain and treading out the grapes in the filled winepress. The same figures are used in 2:24 to describe conversely the fullness of God's blessings. Here the ripe harvest and the overflowing vats both indicate the degree of wickedness for which the nations shall be judged.

**Multitudes** (*hamonim*) means noisy or tumultuous crowds. Its repetition, **multitudes, multitudes** (14), here probably is in-

[2]IB, VI, 755.

[3]The Sabeans were famous slave traders. The "eye for an eye" philosophy can be understood only in the light of progressive revelation. This is another indication of the antiquity of Joel.

tended to suggest the great numbers **in the valley of decision** waiting for the imminent judgment of **the day of the Lord.**

In 15 the natural phenomena listed in 2:31 are repeated as signs accompanying the judgment; there shall be a darkening of **the sun, the moon,** and **the stars.** Then shall **the Lord . . . roar out of Zion, and utter his voice from Jerusalem; and the heavens and the earth shall shake** (16; similar imagery is used in 2:11; Jer. 25:30; Amos 1:2).

But it is only toward His enemies that the Lord roars **out of Zion.** To His own people He is a **hope** and a **strength.** From this, His people will learn that Jehovah is their **God** (17), sanctifying Jerusalem through His presence. It is apparent that Joel is here speaking of Armageddon as the valley of judgment and of Jerusalem as the heavenly Zion which shall appear in the "latter day."

### B. TRIUMPH FOR JERUSALEM AND THE REDEEMED, 3:18-21

In this section, with the exception of v. 19, judgment is broken off and the millennial vision forms the conclusion of the prophecy. In lovely symbolic language, Joel paints the glorious future of God's people. **The mountains shall drop down new wine** (18; cf. Amos 9:13). The streams which usually run dry **shall water the valley of Shittim**[4]—all from the **house of the Lord.**

Parenthetically, judgment is again threatened to **Egypt** and **Edom** (19; symbols of all the hostile nations). Their desolation shall come because of **violence against the children of Judah** and in the shedding of **innocent blood** (cf. I Kings 14:25-26; II Kings 23:29; Obad. 1-21).

On the other hand, **Judah shall dwell for ever, and Jerusalem from generation to generation** (20). Again and again Egypt or Assyria had crossed Judah to fight out their grievances in the quest for world power. Israel had been the battleground of all the great nations. Now, Jehovah was promising a perpetual peace in Jerusalem, the "glorified city of God."

The final verse combines both blessing and judgment—the themes of the entire prophecy. The rendering of the KJV may be misleading. The RSV translation is more accurate: "I will

---

[4]The Acacis valley, above the Dead Sea by the Jordan, was usually dry.

avenge their blood, and I will not clear the guilty."[5] This verse
does not announce a further punishment upon Egypt and Edom,
"but simply the thought with which the proclamation closes,
namely that the eternal desolation of the world-kingdoms . . .
will wipe out all the wrong which they have done to the people
of God, and which hitherto remained unpunished."[6]

The millennial blessings of the Lord in 3:18-21 suggest:
(1) The overabundant blessing of God in nature, 18; (2) The
balancing of the scales of justice, 21; (3) The final promise of
security from generation to generation, 20.

[5]This passage does not necessarily teach of the earthly renovation or
glorification of the earthly city of Jerusalem; for Zion is the "sanctified"
and "glorified" city of God in which the Lord shall eternally be united with
His redeemed, sanctified, and glorified Church (see *Pulpit Commentary,*
"Hosea and Joel," p. 53).

[6]Keil, *op. cit.,* p. 232.

*The Book of*

# AMOS

**Oscar F. Reed**

# *Introduction*

Amos lived and wrote in the first half of the eighth century during the reign of Jeroboam II of the Northern Kingdom. Perhaps 755 B.C. best fits the conditions which are reflected in the book. His teaching is of particular significance because it inaugurated a line of prophetic ministries through which the people of Israel were brought to a deeper insight concerning the character of Jehovah. Only the revelation of God in Jesus Christ goes beyond this understanding of the divine nature. It was through the teachings of Amos and the men who followed him that the Israelites were enabled "to survive the tragic ending of their career as a nation, and become the vehicle of God's distinctive revelation of himself to his world."[1]

## A. The Author and His Historical Background

A century ago, Amos was thought of as just one of the minor prophets; today because of exegetical and critical studies he is given an exalted position in biblical literature. His language is looked upon as one of the best examples of pure Hebrew style.

Amos was the first of the literary prophets who set themselves to eliminate those pagan elements which had crept into Israel's religious and social life. He, with others, was to revive the Mosaic ideal that God required holiness of life. These prophets "moralized" religion, and also universalized it. The God in whose name they spoke was not only their God, but the God of the whole world.

As in the case of Joel, we know very little about the man Amos except what can be gleaned from the internal evidence of his book. We know that he lived in the days of Jeroboam II (782-753 B.C.). Since a long period of prosperity seems to have preceded the prophet, we conclude that his ministry fell in the second half of Jeroboam's reign.

While Amos was a resident of Judah, his prophetic message was delivered in and to Israel. This fact raises an interesting question with reference to the relation of his message to Judah. Did Amos mean to except Judah from the doom pronounced on

---

[1]Hughell E. W. Fosbroke, "Amos," *The Interpreter's Bible*, VI, ed. by George Arthur Buttrick, *et al.* (New York: Abingdon Press, 1956), 763.

Israel and the neighboring peoples? Or did he mean to include Judah? The writer is inclined to believe the latter. Amos had no thought of sparing the Southern Kingdom. We must, therefore, hold that Amos meant to include Judah in the common doom that was to befall Israel and the surrounding nations. Why then did he choose Bethel instead of Jerusalem as the scene of his ministry? The probable answer is that he looked upon the two branches of the Israelitish people as essentially one and that, of the two, the Northern was the more important.

The center of national life was to be found in Bethel, the royal sanctuary of the northern realm, and it was the strategic place for a prophet to begin his ministry. His message would there produce the most immediate and powerful effect.

Amos disclaims the title of *nabi* (a professional prophet). By this he means that he did not belong to the prophetic order and had not received the training of a prophet. He designates himself as a man of lowly station who belonged to the poorer class. In view of this fact one naturally wonders how he acquired the degree of culture which he manifestly possessed. However, among the Hebrews, knowledge and culture were not peculiar to the wealthy and the professional classes. The early training of every Israelite equipped him religiously and culturally regardless of his social status.

Even so, Amos was a simple man, a herdsman who dressed sycomore fruit, the food of the poor. His father was not a prophet, nor did he possess a noble background as did Isaiah. His home was in Tekoa, twelve miles south of Jerusalem (see map 2), where genuine spiritual life and the pure worship of God survived in the rugged hill country.

His call was of God. Amos himself says that Jehovah "took" him from following the flock. This implies a sudden seizure by a power not of himself. Such is also the implication of 3:8, where the prophet says: "The lion hath roared, who will not fear? the Lord God hath spoken, who can but prophesy?" There was a burning fire shut up in his bones which compelled him to speak. Amos was a man who had a message from Jehovah and he had to be delivered of his burden.

Since his was a divine call, Amos was frank, courageous, and dynamic. He had a deep resentment against the social evils of his day and burned at injustice and dishonesty. He had a keen insight into the deeper things of God as well as into national and international relations. His tongue was like a whip to the oppressor and honey to the oppressed.

108

## B. Amos and His Message

The great fundamental conceptions underlying Amos' message of doom make him a significant figure in the history of religious faith. The people around him felt certain of the divine favor for two reasons: First, were they not the chosen of God? Second, they were attentive to all the details of worship. To Amos, however, these two pillars of popular confidence were broken reeds. Neither offered the slightest basis for any assurance of divine favor.

It was true that Jehovah had chosen Israel to be His peculiar people. He stood in an especially close relationship to the nation. But this did not mean, as they supposed, that they had a monopoly on divine favor or that Jehovah's protecting care was confined to Israel. His favor was universal, arising from a universal God who brooked no rivals.

Whatever preeminence Israel possessed was to be found in the special revelation which God had made to her of His character and will. This revelation, however, she had spurned. Israel, therefore, had no advantage over other nations. When she sinned she meant no more to Jehovah than the distant and despised Ethiopians. Such was the manner in which Amos dealt with the national pretension of his day.

With the popular trust in rites and ceremonies he was harsher still, but it is a mistake to suppose that Amos meant to condemn all rites and ceremonies as such. He was not so doctrinaire as to be blind to the fact that true piety needs its "days and seasons" and outward forms for its proper cultivation. What he objected to was the substitution of these external rites for the inner spirit of piety.

Against the popular trust in sacrifices, the unqualified election of a chosen people, and the special providence of God for the nation, Amos laid down the principle that the only hope of Israel was to be found in righteousness. And by righteousness he meant what was right in the absolute sense of the term, both objective and subjective: respect for personality in oneself and others.

Two evils which Amos expressly designated were the oppression of the poor by the rich, and the corruption of the judicial system in Israel. In these, human life was literally bartered away. To Amos this seemed the height of iniquity, and the very limit of folly. So he exhorted men: "Seek the Lord, and ye shall live"; and, "Seek good, and not evil, that ye may live" (5:6, 14). The prophet thus identified religion with the moral law. To seek Jehovah is to seek the good. There is no other way of entering into fellowship with Him. Religion then comes to be the chief conserving force in society and a most powerful stimulus to the development of man's highest faculties.

Our study of Amos' teachings can be completed however only with the addition of the words of hope found in 9:8-15. Evidently, in spite of all his dark forecasts, Amos was not without hope that Israel might be saved, and certainly was not without the conviction that some at least would "live." The prophet was a man of intense passion who saw purpose everywhere. The teleological element permeates the whole of his book. That such a man as he should not have reflected on what would take place after the destruction of Israel is incredible.

While Amos thus had his hopeful outlook into the future, it was subordinate to the mainstream of his teaching. His primary task was to assert the claims of the moral law as over against the unspiritual formalism and the national pretension of his time. His chief significance lies in the thoroughness with which he moralized the conception of religion in his demand for national and personal righteousness.

# *Outline*

I. The Approaching Judgment, 1:1—2:16

    A. Superscription and Theme, 1:1-2

    B. Oracles Against Neighboring Nations, 1:3—2:3

    C. Oracle Against Judah, 2:4-5

    D. Oracles Against Israel, 2:6-16

II. Sermons on Israel's Coming Judgment, 3:1—6:14

    A. Israel's Relationship to God, 3:1-8

    B. Samaria's Sinfulness, 3:9—4:3

    C. The Depth of Israel's Guilt, 4:4—5:3

    D. Exhortation and Condemnation, 5:4-15

    E. The Appearance of Jehovah, 5:16-25

    F. Invasion and Exile, 5:26—6:14

III. Visions and an Epilogue, 7:1—9:15

    A. Amos' Visions, 7:1—8:3

    B. Sin and Judgment, 8:4-14

    C. The Inexorable Judgment, 9:1-7

    D. Epilogue, 9:8-15

# Section I  *The Approaching Judgment*

Amos 1:1—2:16

The prophecy of Amos falls into three parts with a unity of plan which leaves no question as to its authorship and motivation. The prediction of immediate judgment is at the heart of Amos' ministry. He proclaimed that message skillfully starting with the non-Hebrew, moving toward the Judean, and concluding with Israel, the people he personally addresses. The "Israelite would listen with some inward satisfaction whilst his neighbor's faults, with the judgments that they would incur, were being pointed out."[1] However, he is measured by exactly the same standard applied to others with judgment no less severe.

## A. Superscription and Theme, 1:1-2

The author of the prophecy identifies himself as a herdsman[2] of Tekoa (1) in the reigns of Uzziah king of Judah and Jeroboam . . . king of Israel. Tekoa is a town located on the southern border of Judah (cf. II Chron. 11:6; 20:20). Amos affirms that he was a simple shepherd and a "gatherer of sycomore fruit" (7:14). Thus we view Amos, not as a prosperous sheep owner, but a modest shepherd and a "dresser of sycomore trees" who was determined not to be classed as a *nabi* (professional prophet). He was the very kind that Israel "insisted on silencing" (Amos 2:11-12).[3]

Students could date the prophecy more accurately if they could identify the earthquake (cf. Zech. 14:5) spoken of in v. 1, which evidently was well known at the time of Amos' ministry. However, we know that Amos was active during the

---

[1]S. R. Driver, *An Introduction to the Literature of the Old Testament*, (New York: Charles Scribner's Sons, 1891), p. 294.

[2]Herdsman (*noqedh*) is not the usual term for shepherd; but it is usually translated "sheepmaster." It was probably in the selling of wool that Amos had travelled to the Northern Kingdom and familiarized himself with conditions there (IB, *op. cit.*, p. 977).

[3]Bernard W. Anderson, *Understanding the Old Testament* (Englewood, N.J.: Prentice-Hall, Inc., 1957), p. 228.

112

height of the prosperous reign of Jeroboam II sometime before the king's death in 753 B.C. (see Chart *A*).[4]

Amos initiates his prophecy with the confirmation of a theme first declared by Joel (3:16): **The Lord will roar from Zion, and utter his voice from Jerusalem** (2). It was God himself who spoke through Amos. The figure was given to warn the covenant breakers who were at ease in their prosperity. They must know that the judgment of God would fall on Israel as well as the heathen world—even **the top of Carmel shall wither.**[5]

## B.  ORACLES AGAINST NEIGHBORING NATIONS, 1:3—2:3

This section is skillfully constructed to begin with a "burden" against foreign nations. It, of course, brings the applause of the people only to prepare them for the deep thrust to follow.

### 1. *Damascus* (1:3-5)

The first oracle is against **Damascus** (3; see map 2), the capital city of the Aramean (Syrian) kingdom, with which Israel had been at war for the greater part of the century. **Three,** the perfect number, is followed by **four,** which indicates a larger number of crimes in their worst form. The measure of iniquity was full, beyond all measure.

**Gilead,** the area most exposed to Syrian invasion (see map 2), was subjected to "threshing sledges of iron" (RSV). These **threshing instruments** were heavy, iron-shod rollers with jagged teeth, which had been used to destroy and mangle human flesh. The reference is to Hazael's destruction of Gilead in II Kings 10:32-33.

Verse 4 identifies the Syrian leaders who had sinned against Gilead (the story is told in II Kings 8—13). **Hazael** was the founder of the dynasty which **Ben-hadad** (Ben-hadah II), his son, represented. **The house of Hazael** represents the dynasty, **Ben-hadad** the specific ruler (cf. Isa. 17:1-3; Jer. 49:23-27;

---

[4]The contemporary reigns of Jeroboam II and Uzziah of Judah were marked by great prosperity in both kingdoms which covered a good part of the first half of the eighth century B.C.

[5]**Carmel** is the promontory at the mouth of the Kishon River on the Mediterranean and not Carmel of Judah  Thus **shepherds** (2) and **Carmel** represent Israel to Amos, the herdsman. Even the "head of the forest-crowned Carmel will fade and wither" (C. F. Keil and Delitzsch, *Biblical Commentary on the Old Testament,* "The Twelve Minor Prophets" [Grand Rapids: Wm. B. Eerdmans Pub. Co., 1954], I, 241).

**Zech. 9:1-4).** The concluding lines in v. 5 demonstrate the power of Jehovah in His judgment. The prophet hears the breaking of **the bar of Damascus** (the fortifications of the city) and he sees the massacre of the inhabitants of **Aven (5).** The balance of Syria will be taken to the remoteness of **Kir**—all of this through the word of the **Lord.**[6] This prophecy was fulfilled when Tiglath-pileser of Assyria (see Chart *A*) conquered Damascus during the reign of Ahaz, king of Judah (II Kings 16:9). The final word, **saith the Lord,** identifies the authority with which the oracle is given.

### 2. *Philistia* (1:6-8)

A like destruction is to overtake the Philistines (see comments on v. 3). **Gaza (6),** the principal city of Philistia, is used as a symbol of the whole nation. It was a key caravan center on the road between Egypt and Syria, situated on the southern border of Judah near the Mediterranean Sea (see map 2). The specific accusation against the Philistines is that **they carried away captive the whole captivity.** That is, they carried an entire people captive and delivered them to Edom, the archenemy of Israel. The reference is to the invasion of the Philistines in the time of Joram (II Chron. 21:16; cf. Joel 3:4). Verses 7-8 verify the fact that all of Philistia is included in the coming destruction. A similar judgment will fall upon all of her chief cities: **Gaza (7), Ashdod (8), Ashkelon,** and **Ekron.** All are included for extermination by the **hand** of **the Lord God.**

The irony of God's judgment is apparent. The very Edomites to whom the Israelites were sold will be those who will sell the Philistines into bondage. (The Edomites held a port on the Red Sea and were notorious as slave traders.)

### 3. *Tyre* (1:9-10)

The great sins of Tyre are symbolized again in **for three transgressions . . . and for four** (9; cf. comment on v. 3). The transgression is greater because Tyre **remembered not the**

---

[6]Keil points out that the "cutting off" of the inhabitants of Bicqath-Aven indicates "slaughter" rather than deportation. *Hikhrith* means to exterminate, "so that *galah* (captivity) in the last clause applies to the remainder of the population that had not been slain in war" (*op. cit.,* p. 243). Both prince and people shall perish. Valley-Aven and Beth-Eden were probably capitals of the nation. The Syrians originally emigrated from Kir (9:7), which was far to the east (Isa. 22:6).

**brotherly covenant,** i.e., the earlier alliance between Solomon and Hiram (I Kings 5:1, 12). Though the historical occasions cannot be confirmed, it seems to be indicated in the charge that Tyre delivered the Israelites to Edom in slave trade. There is no record that any king of Israel or Judah had ever warred against Phoenicia (Tyrus). Because of her sin, even the magnificent city of Tyre would not escape the judgment of Jehovah (10) as declared by Amos. (See Ezekiel 28 for a description of Tyre.)

### 4. *Edom* (1:11-12)

A rather special animosity existed between Israel and Edom even before the Exile. Amos did not condemn a particular sin, but pointed out Edom's implacable hatred in the pursuit of Israel **with the sword** (11), the utter lack of **pity,** and the continual spirit of **wrath** toward **his brother.**[7]

As in the former oracles, the judgment was to be by **fire upon Teman, which shall devour the palaces of Bozrah** (12). **Bozrah** was the capital of Edom, situated south of the Dead Sea. **Teman** was probably a district to the north of **Bozrah** (see map 2). Both symbolized the whole of Edom.

### 5. *Ammon* (1:13-15)

The territory of Ammon lay across the Jordan River to the east of Gilead. The specific charge, **They have ripped up the women with child of Gilead** (13), was only the climax of a succession of cruelties against Israel. However, Israel might also have been charged with a similar offense (II Kings 15:16).

As a punishment upon Edom, the capital city of **Rabbah** (14; "the great one") was to be burned **in the day of battle.** At that time the invader would seem like a **tempest** sweeping all before him. The prophecy closes with the oracle of doom against the **king** and **his princes** (15), who **shall go into captivity.**

### 6. *Moab* (2:1-3)

The final prophecy against the neighbors of Israel is directed toward **Moab,** situated between Edom and Ammon (see map 2).

---

[7]The Edomites were closely related to Israel through Esau (Genesis 36). They were strategically located at the head of the Gulf of 'Aqaba and wealthy in resources and trade. Having been subjected to Israel from the time of David, the opportunity for revenge was taken in 586 B.C. with the fall of Jerusalem. It is to this period that the judgment must be referred (George Adam Smith, *The Book of the Twelve Prophets* [rev. ed.; New York: Harper and Bros., 1940], I, 128-30).

The specific crime was against the **king of Edom** (1), whose bones were burned to **lime.**

Though there is no historical reference to the incident, it may refer to the war Jehoram of Israel and Jehoshaphat of Judah waged against the Moabites in which the king of Edom was an ally of Israel (II Kings 3).[8] Jerome reports a Jewish tradition that the Moabites dug up the bones of the king of Edom and heaped insult upon insult by burning the remains to dust.

As a punishment, Moab's chief city, **Kirioth** (2), was to be burned and the nation destroyed. The prophecies from 1:6 on are all fulfilled in the Chaldean invasions which carried off the inhabitants to captivity (Ezekiel 25).

At the time of Amos' prophecy, Assyria's threat (Tiglath-pileser III, 745-727 B.C.) was still a little cloud on the horizon. Amos, however, warns of the judgments to come, not because of Assyria's ambitions alone, but because Jehovah was at work in the political area. The prophet affirms that Jehovah is Sovereign over all nations of the earth. Those mentioned are only an indication of the scope of His sovereignty. In this, Amos did not claim to say anything new, but he certainly "spoke with a disturbingly new accent."[9]

### C. ORACLE AGAINST JUDAH, 2:4-5

Amos turns from the neighboring nations to the Southern Kingdom, **Judah.** Here is the second movement toward his final thrust against Israel.

With respect to Judah, Amos condemns the rejection of the **law of the Lord** (4; *Torah;* this "law" was the sum total of all the precepts given by Jehovah as a rule of life). **Commandments** (*chuqqim*) are the separate precepts of the *Torah,* including both ceremonial and moral commandments.[10] **Lies** (4) should

---

[8]Keil, *op. cit.,* p. 250. Since only crimes committed against the covenant nation are mentioned, there must have been some relation of the king of Edom with the Israelites as a vassal of Judah.

[9]Anderson, *op. cit.,* p. 230.

[10]IB and other authors believe Amos 2:4-5 to be a later insertion, Deuteronomic in emphasis, because of the legal vocabulary used. Whether valid or not, "the oracle against Judah represented the conviction that the closeness of its relationship to God did not exempt a people from that stern subjection to his righteous judgment of which Amos had spoken" (p. 786).

probably be translated "idols," or "their vanities which they made" (LXX).[11]

The punishment indicated in 5 was carried out by Nebuchadnezzar in 586 B.C. when he destroyed **Jerusalem** and carried away a greater part of the population to Babylon (see Chart *A*).

## D. Oracles Against Israel, 2: 6-16

Amos finally turns to Israel. One can imagine the chagrin of the people in the marketplace. If they had cheered him for his prophecies against their enemies, and murmured of his prophecies against Judah, their hostility was made plain as he declared the truth against Israel. In precisely the same language that he had been using, he announced that God's judgment against Israel was just as irrevocable.

### 1. *The Rebellion of Israel* (2: 6-8)

The first charge is that **they sold the righteous for silver, and the poor for a pair of shoes** (6). This phrase is usually interpreted as the custom which condemned the innocent through bribes and gave the poor to the creditor (for the merest trifle) as slaves. This was done on the strength of the law described in Lev. 25: 39 (cf. II Kings 4:1).[12] The rich thus showed callous disregard for the righteous (*tsaddiq*). Those who **pant after the dust of the earth on the head of the poor** (7) are men who "trample the head of the poor into the dust of the earth" (RSV). The address is phrased in participles as though they "panted" in their eagerness to humiliate the poor. In addition, they turned **aside the way of the meek**, i.e., kept them from their natural way of life, turning them to destruction.

The third accusation was profanity of the Lord's holy name by the gross immorality of **a man and his father** having intercourse with a **maid**. "The meaning is, to one and the same girl; but *achath* [**the same**] is omitted, to preclude all possible misunderstanding as though going to different prostitutes was allowed.

---

[11]Amos calls idols lies because they are only fabrications and ·non-entities, having no reality in themselves.

[12]Keil, *op. cit.*, p. 252. "Recent commentaries (cf. Arthur Weiser, *Die Profetie des Amos*: Alfred Topelmann, 1929, pp. 90-91) have pointed out that the verb here (sell) employed is most often used of selling into slavery (Gen. 37:27-28; Exod. 21:16)" (IB, *op. cit.*, p. 786).

This sin was tantamount to incest, which according to the law, was to be punished by death."[13]

The fourth accusation concerned **the house of their god** (8). They drank wines purchased by the fines of the **condemned**. The **clothes** they slept on beside their altars profaned the holy name of Jehovah, since a pawned garment was to be returned before night came on (Exod. 22:26).

### 2. *The Revelation of God* (2:9-12)

Privilege brings corresponding responsibility. Amos cannot refrain from pointing out that, since Jehovah favored Israel above all other nations, He would hold them accountable for their sins.[14] It is this revelation of God in history that provokes the rehearsal of His destruction of **the Amorite** (9, pre-Israelite inhabitants of Canaan) as a preparation for the migration of Israel from Egypt (10) **to possess the land of the Amorite** (cf. Josh. 3:10). The expression, **I destroyed his fruit from above, and his roots from beneath** (9), is a figure to indicate complete devastation.

Jehovah's care was not only expressed by His protection on the journey from Egypt to Canaan, but through the raising of **prophets** (11) and **Nazarites** to reveal His holy will to Israel. The Nazarites were men of holy calling who were pledged to abstain from (1) strong drink, (2) eating meat, and (3) cutting the hair. Samson, Samuel, and probably John the Baptist were Nazarites. In the face of this divine providence, and against divine law, the Israelites tempted the **Nazarites** with **wine to drink** (12) and attempted to silence the prophets: **Prophesy not.** The word of the Lord was not wanted by them.

### 3. *The Anticipated Judgment* (2:13-16)

Because of their gross transgressions, the Lord now warns of a judgment which no one will escape. It will be an oppression in which the strongest shall suffer. "Behold, I will press you

---

[13]There is some difference in judgment as to the significance of the passage. While some commentators (IB, p. 787) seem to indicate that it refers to temple prostitution in which the old and young frequented the shrine for this purpose, Amos does not use the term *queheshah* (sacred harlot). He simply states that "they resort to a girl." In either case the practice is condemned as profanity against the holy name of Jehovah.

[14]John A. Sampey, *The Heart of the Old Testament* (Nashville: Broadman Press, 1922), p. 152.

down in your place, as a cart full of sheaves presses down" (13, RSV). Israel is to feel the grinding pressure of the heavily laden cart. Other expositors, with a slight change in the Hebrew verb translated "press" (a change supported by the LXX), get the meaning "to totter." Thus, "I will make (everything) totter under you as a cart totters."[15]

Verses 14-16 describe the inability of Israel to **flee** from the Lord. **The swift** (14) shall not be able to escape. **The strong** "shall not retain his strength nor the mighty save his life" (RSV). Neither the archer, the footman, nor the horseman shall be able to withstand the judgment of the Lord (15). The word **naked** (16) suggests the utter helplessness of a man "stripped of all the resources on which he counts to maintain himself when he faces the final catastrophe."[16]

Amos startles his listeners by bringing his judgments to Israel after his monologue against the neighboring nations. Here are the reasons for "God's Judgments Against His People": (1) They despised the law of the Lord, 4b; (2) They tried to deceive their Maker, 4c; (3) They sacrificed their God-given integrity, 6; (4) They oppressed the poor, 7a; (5) They fell into immorality, 7c; (6) They profaned that which was sacred, 8, 12. Therefore God will destroy those who have broken His covenant, **14-16.**

[15]*Ibid.*, p. 790; W. K. L. Clarke, *Concise Bible Commentary* (New York: The Macmillan Co., 1954), p. 599.
[16]IB, VI, 790.

## Section II Sermons on Israel's Coming Judgment

Amos 3:1—6:14

In the second section of the prophecy, Amos particularizes the charges made in the first two chapters and emphasizes the finality with which he speaks of judgment to come. The sermons begin with **Hear this word** (3:1; cf. 4:1; 5:1), which identifies the authority of the prophet and the Source of his utterances.

### A. ISRAEL'S RELATIONSHIP TO GOD, 3:1-8

Israel is reminded again of God's deliverance of the nation from **the land of Egypt** (1). The figure of the bride is not used in Amos as it is in Hosea. Yet Amos must have had the same comparison in mind when he used the expression, **You only have I known**[1] **of all the families of the earth** (3:2). The reason for God's choice in establishing His unique relationship with Israel through "election-love" (see Introduction to Hosea) is as inscrutable as the choice of a bride.[2]

#### 1. Election (3:1-2)

Since Israel is specially chosen, she bears a special responsibility. The judgment of God must lie heavier on her because of her election (cf. II Chron. 36:16; Isa. 1:2-4). **Hear this word that the Lord hath spoken against you, O children of Israel** (1).

It is the relationship described in v. 2 that sets Israel apart for a special role among **the families of the earth** and also for a special responsibility. Their sin calls not for any compromise on

[1] The verb *yadha* (to know) and its noun *daath* refer not only to the cognitive aspect of knowledge (see introduction to Hosea), but knowledge gained through the emotions as well. Such an aspect of "knowledge" is found in a man "knowing" his wife. Amos' use of the verb in 3:2 is consistent with the use of the term in Hos. 2:14; Jer. 3:14; 31:32; Isa. 54:5-6 (Knight, *op. cit.*, pp. 177-78).

[2] George F. A. Knight, *A Christian Theology of the Old Testament* (Richmond, Virginia: John Knox Press, 1959), pp. 200-201.

the part of Jehovah because of that covenant relation, but rather
for judgment on **all** their **iniquities.**

### 2. *The Authority of the Prophet* (3:3-8)

In spite of Israel's election, she is rebellious and arrogant.
The nation will not hear the prophet (cf. 2:4; 7:10-13). Amos
therefore established his right and duty to prophesy from a series
of similes drawn from life itself.[3]

Verses 3-6 illustrate the causal relation between the utterances of the prophet and their source in God. **Can two walk together, except they be agreed?** (3) suggests not the relation
between Jehovah and His people, but Jehovah and His prophet
who was sent to Samaria and Bethel to declare judgment against
the chosen people.

The **lion** (4) is Jehovah (cf. 1:2; Joel 3:16), who does not
roar without a cause.[4]

**Can a bird fall in a snare upon the earth, where no gin is
for him?** (5) The **gin** (*moquesh*) is a net with a stick for a
spring which is sprung only when the prey is there.[5] The punishment is as deserved as it is certain. As in Joel, the sinner has set
his own trap.

Amos continues in v. 6 with the same causal argument. **Shall
a trumpet be blown in the city, and the people not be afraid?**
(6) In his climax, the prophet compares the coming judgment of
God with the blowing of the trumpet. It brings warning of the
approaching enemy with the consequent anxiety and dread to
the people. The judgment is from Jehovah, who uses the enemy
as an instrument of destruction. Thus, **the Lord hath . . . done it.**
The similes in vv. 1-6 are made perfectly clear in vv. 7-8, where
the thought is explained. Jehovah carries out His purposes of
judgment only after He has warned His people through His
prophets. "Surely the Lord God does nothing without revealing
His secret to His servants the prophets" (7, RSV).

[3]Keil, *op. cit.*, p. 259.

[4]*Kephir* is the lion that goes in pursuit of his prey, to be distinguished
from *gur* (the young lion), which cannot as yet hunt, thus crying **out of
his den** (4). The two similes have similar meanings, "that God not only
has before Him the nation that is ripe for judgment, but that He has it in
His power" (*ibid.*, p. 261).

[5]W. J. Dean, "Hosea" (Exposition), *The Pulpit Commentary, Amos to
Micah,* ed. H. D. M. Spence and Joseph S. Exell (New York: Funk and
Wagnalls Co., n.d.), p. 40.

Amos has vindicated his call. He has the right to represent God in His judgments. **The lion hath roared . . . the Lord God hath spoken** (8). Amos can do nothing **but prophesy.**

## B. Samaria's Sinfulness, 3:9—4:3

Now that the foundation is laid for an authoritative utterance, Amos proceeds to reveal what the Lord has resolved to do to His sinful nation.

### 1. *The Sin of Oppression* (3:9-10)

Verses 9-10 are a summons to **Ashdod** (9; given as Assyria in the LXX and RSV) and **Egypt** to assemble to see the oppressors in **Samaria** that they may witness against God's people. Again Jehovah is using foreign nations as an instrument of judgment. It is the inhabitants of the palace who would pronounce just judgment upon the sins within the **palaces** (10) of Samaria. Verse 10 carries pathos as well as condemnation: "They do not know how to do right" (Berk.). The people of Samaria lost all sense of moral reality, honesty, and integrity.

### 2. *The Destruction to Come* (3:11-12)

An enemy shall attack **round about the land** (11) i.e., on all sides. He will possess it by plundering the **palaces** ("strongholds," RSV) and will **bring down** (hurl down) the splendor of Samaria. Thus the enemy attacking from the hills overlooking the city shall destroy both its fortifications and its beautiful buildings.

The prophet concludes with a simile in answer to an assumed question: Will the destruction be complete? Will there be any who escape? Amos replies with irony. "Yes, a few!" like a **shepherd** (12) saving **two legs, or a piece of an ear** (shinbone and lappet of the ear). The last half of v. 12 is another illustration of the same truth. When **the children of Israel** are taken captive they shall have left only **the corner of a bed.** The ivory and costly fabric came from **Damascus.** Smith-Goodspeed renders the figure as "the corner of a couch and the leg of a bed." Samaria is to be utterly destroyed!

### 3. *Bethel's Fate* (3:13-15)

The words, **Hear ye** (13), consistent with v. 9, are addressed to the heathen, who will **testify in the house of Jacob** (the whole of Israel) and learn a lesson from the destruction of Samaria. The

122

name **the Lord God, the God of hosts** is to strengthen the declaration that Jehovah is the God of all peoples and has the adequate resources to carry out His threats.

The punishment is to extend to the **altars of Beth-el** (14), seat of idolatry. The destruction will include **the horns of the altar**, i.e., the place of refuge, as well as the elaborate **houses** (15) of king and nobility. **The horns of the altar** were projections from the corners of the altar somewhat like the horns of an ox. They possessed special sanctity as a place of refuge (I Kings 2:28). The fulfillment of the prophecy took place when Shalmaneser took Samaria (II Kings 17:5-6).

Chapter 3 offers at least "Three Great Spiritual Insights": (1) Personal privilege brings greater responsibility, 1-2; (2) God does not rebuke or convict men without cause, 3-8; (3) Unfaithfulness to God brings divine judgment, 13-15.

### 4. *The Greed of Selfish Women* (4:1-3)

To Amos, the infidelity of Israel was shockingly evident in the evils that flourished in an urban society. He was so striking in his words that Amaziah, the priest, looked upon his prophecy as high treason and insisted that "the land is not able to bear all his words" (7:10). The symptoms of sickness were apparent in the sleek, sophisticated ladies who were likened by the prophet-herdsman to the **kine of Bashan** (1). **Bashan** was famous for its fine cows and productive land (Numbers 32). Amos accused the women "in high Samaria" (Moffatt) of pressuring their husbands for riches, who in turn oppressed the people. Thus the women were equally responsible. They also continually asked **their masters** (husbands) "to procure for them the means of debauchery"[6]—**Bring, and let us drink.**

Verses 2-3 identify the judgment to be meted out because of the women's sin. Verse 2 begins with an unusually solemn oath suggesting the extreme severity of the evil. **The Lord God hath sworn by his holiness.** The Holy One cannot tolerate the unrighteousness of the rich (tyrannical oppression of the poor). Judgment is pronounced: **Lo, the days shall come upon you** when the enemy shall **take you away with hooks, and your posterity with fishhooks.** The conqueror shall drag the corpses away to the refuse pile outside the city with the hooks normally used to

[6]Keil, *op. cit.*, p. 267.

dispose of the carcasses of dead animals (a current Oriental custom).

Verse 3 has been translated in *The Berkeley Version:* "You shall go out at the breaches, each of you going straight ahead; and you shall be driven to the fortress" (*harmon*).[7]

## C. THE DEPTH OF ISRAEL'S GUILT, 4:4—5:3

The prophecy now turns again to the nation as a whole. The irony of the prophet is apparent. "Carry on with your doings, knowing full well what you are doing and what it inevitably means!"

### 1. *Sin Within the Sanctuary* (4:4-5)

Amos lashes out: **Come to Beth-el, and transgress; at Gilgal multiply transgression** (4). **Beth-el** was an established city of worship (see map 2). **Gilgal** means "the circle." This particular place of worship was either not far from Jericho (Josh. 4:19-20) or that associated with Elisha (II Kings 2:1; 4:38) somewhat north of Bethel. There could be many Gilgals as places of worship.[8] One would have expected the sacrifice to be made for reconciliation, but it was used in the worship of idols and thus widened the separation between Jehovah and His people.

The whole picture is one of great zeal, with **sacrifices every morning, and . . . tithes. Years** probably should be translated "days," as *The Berkeley Version:* "Bring your sacrifices every morning, your tithes every three days." The irony was that with exaggerated zeal they turned their sacred traditions to idolatrous worship. **Thanksgiving with leaven** (5) refers to the leavened loaves of the praise offering. These were used when the unleavened bread of the sin offering should have been brought.

**For this liketh you, O ye children of Israel** may be rendered, "For so you love to do, O people of Israel" (RSV). The whole act of worship centered on themselves. It evidenced greed, injustice, and oppression which Amos denounced with fervor. He knew that God was more concerned with their spirit than He was with the mechanics of their worship.

---

[7]The meaning of the Hebrew text is quite obscure. The word translated **palace** is *hermonah* or *harmon.* All commentators agree that the meaning of *harmon* is not known. Its etymology denotes a high land, but it cannot be taken in the sense of *armon* (a citadel or palace). This word appears only the one time in sacred literature (*ibid.,* p. 269).

[8]IB, VI, 804.

### 2. *Indifference to Chastening* (4:6-12)

Five times in verses 6-11 Amos represents the Lord as saying, **Yet have ye not returned unto me** (6). The phrase depicts the continuing love of God in the face of indifference. Amos rehearsed the visitations of the past by which the Lord had attempted to restore His people within the covenant. **Cleanness of teeth** is explained by the **want of bread** (6). The thought is reiterated when Jehovah withheld rain (7) **three months** before harvest, allowing it to rain selectively on the cities and fields. The heavy rains usually ceased in February. Amos interprets the capriciousness of the season to be the work of the Lord forcing a search for water as in the time of drought.

The prophet next turned to the **gardens** (9) and **vineyards.** The Lord smote the corn with blight; the **fig** and **olive trees,** the locust devoured. In all this Amos enumerates a series of judgments through which the Lord endeavored to awaken the people from the deceit of their sinning. But we have only the repeated refrain, **Yet have ye not returned unto me.** The judgment is freighted with pathos.

Amos repeats the same truth in the fourth chastisement, **I have sent among you the pestilence after the manner of Egypt** (10). The combination of pestilence and sword (cf. Lev. 26:25; Isa. 10:24, 26) is typical of warfare. The slaying of **young men** in warfare by **the sword** would bring painful memories to the Israelites (cf. II Kings 8:12; 13:3, 7). From the slain men with their horses came **the stink** of the camp. The very stench was a reward for their sins. Even in the face of death, **have ye not returned unto me, saith the Lord.**

Progressively moving toward greater chastisements, the Lord now refers to the overthrow of Israel even as **Sodom and Gomorrah** (11), which He had destroyed by fire in the days of Lot (Genesis 19). *Living Prophecies* renders the first part of 11, "I destroyed some of your cities, as I did Sodom and Gomorrah." "The verb *haphakh*, 'overthrow,' is also used in the destruction wrought by an invader (cf. 2 Sam. 10:13), and Marti . . . may be right in his contention that the text refers to the critical situation . . . in the time of Jehoahaz (2 Kings 13:7)"[9] when Israel indeed was as a **firebrand plucked out of the burning.**

---

[9] IB, VI, 808.

After a recital of all the punishment that Israel had suffered because of her transgressions, the Lord repeats His determination to chasten the nation with judgment in the absence of national and personal repentance. **Prepare to meet thy God, O Israel (12)**.

### 3. *The Doxology* (4:13)

The doxology that follows is different in form from the oracles which precede it. God, in the glory of His majesty, is depicted in contrast to that which was created. It is **the God of hosts (13)** who formed **the mountains** and created **the wind.** The word **createth** (*bara*) suggests the sovereign power of God totally beyond creative power in man. **He declareth unto man what is his thought, that maketh the morning darkness, and treadeth upon the high places of the earth.** All of this is a description of God's sovereignty, a revelation of the God of hosts.

Amos in chapter 4 beautifully describes the integrity of God: (1) He hath sworn by His holiness, 2; (2) He hath warned His people, 12; (3) He hath identified His name, 13.

### 4. *The End of a Nation* (5:1-3)

Verses 1-3 are an elegy over the fall of Israel. The **lamentation** mentioned in v. 1 is found in v. 2. Israel is spoken of as a **virgin** who **is fallen** (2). The expression **she shall no more rise** implies death from which there is no redemption. There is an inexorable finality to the prophet's words. For Amos, this was no dramatization. His heart was torn with the vision of his nation prostrate before him as in death. The pronouncement is the more real when one remembers that Amos prophesied at the height of Israel's prosperity. No wonder he and his words were rejected as nonsense. Verse 3 interprets and emphasizes v. 2. Israel is to perish in war. "For the Lord God says, 'The city that sends a thousand men to battle, a hundred will return. The city that sends a hundred, only ten will come back alive' " (*Living Prophecies*).

### D. EXHORTATION AND CONDEMNATION, 5:4-15

#### 1. *True Religion* (5:4-6)

**For thus saith the Lord unto the house of Israel, Seek ye me, and ye shall live (4)**. The exhortation expresses clearly the central element of Amos' teaching. He identifies true religion with righteousness (keeping the moral law). When the people seek Jehovah they are seeking the good. "When a religion busies itself with rites and ceremonies, with signs and omens, it is of slight value to the world. Indeed, it usually acts as a bar to progress. It is guided by no rational principle, and so tends to sanctify the inconsistent, absurd, and often harmful usages and beliefs of the past. But when religion is identified with the moral nature, all this is changed."[10]

It was absolutely necessary that Amos set down the moral dictum that the only way to seek Jehovah was to seek the good, rather than the evil which was represented by the shrines at **Gilgal, Beth-el, and Beer-sheba** (5).

Fosbroke points out that an effective play on two distinct meanings of the verb **seek,** *darash,* is used in 4-5. In early times it was used in regard to the seeking of the will of a god through a seer or prophet. Later the word came to be used of turning Godward and of "longing for God himself rather than something he could bestow (Deut. 4:29)."[11]

The word **live** (6) also means more than the prolongation of existence. "It speaks rather of the life lived richly in the right relationship to God as in the familiar passage, 'Man does not live by bread alone' (Deut. 8:3)."[12]

In some degree the concept of personal responsibility had been apprehended centuries before. But Amos seems to have been "the first to differentiate it from popular religion, and to make it the one fundamental principle of all true religion. He thus stands out in history as the great prophet of moral law."[13]

The KJV rendering of 5-6 scarcely gives the rude force of the text. **And Beth-el shall come to nought** (5) is originally, "And Bethel becomes *Beth-aven.*" *Aven* (idolatry) also means wickedness. George Adam Smith suggests "that we should not exaggerate the antithesis if we employed a phrase which once was not vulgar: and Bethel, house of God, shall go to the Devil."[14]

[10]Albert C. Knudson, *The Beacon Lights of Prophecy* (New York: The Methodist Book Concern, 1914), p. 83.

[11]IB, VI, 811.

[12]*Ibid.*

[13]Knudson, *op. cit.,* p. 84.

[14]*Op. cit.,* p. 169. Hosea uses the term *Beth-aven* (house of idolatry) more than he does *Beth-el* (house of God).

In 6, Jehovah once again identifies His energy as **like fire** which shall consume **the house of Joseph** and purge His land from the unrighteousness of **Beth-el** (*Beth-aven,* house of idolatry).

### 2. *Sins of the Wealthy, and a Second Doxology* (5:7-13)

Amos is fond of participial construction (cf. 2:7; 4:13). He therefore offers the thoughts of 7-8 without close logical connection. **Wormwood** (7; *haanah*), a bitter plant, is a symbolic term suggesting "bitter wrong" (cf. 6:12). **Leave off righteousness in the earth** suggests the trampling under feet of the goodness required by Jehovah. Verse 7 is to be linked with 10-13, the doxology of 8-9 representing an interpolation which identifies the **Lord** who can bring destruction on those who **leave off righteousness** (7).

The doxology identifies the name of Him who is responsible for the mystery of created nature. "He made the stars also" (Gen. 1:16) was familiar to Amos. This declaration of God's creation of the stars was probably a reaction to Assyrian starworship. The whole verse points to the rule of Jehovah over the earth. The allusion to the Flood—**that calleth for the waters** (8)—suggests the terrible power of judgment which no man can defy. **The Lord is his name** is again a call to recognize God as God, and turn to Jehovah, the God of all peoples. Verse 9 has been made clearer by Smith-Goodspeed: "The Lord is his name— He who causes ruin to burst forth upon the strong, and brings destruction upon the fortress."

The prophet's condemnation of social injustice as practiced by the wealthy is detailed in 10-13. It opens with an introductory statement of the people's attitude toward anyone who lifted his voice in protest **in the gate** (10; **the gate** was the lawcourt of the city). **Him that rebuketh** should not be limited to the prophet, but would include any voice that is lifted against evil.

Verses 11-13 point to the punishment for unjust oppression. The very possessions that came as a result of the oppression shall be useless. The oppressors **shall not dwell** (11) in houses built **of hewn stone** (in striking contrast to the houses of the poor, built of wood and stubble). They **shall not drink** of the **wine** of **pleasant vineyards.** God knows those who **afflict the just** (12), **take a bribe,** and ignore **the poor** in their right of justice in the courts.

The mood of 13 is one of resignation. **Therefore the prudent shall keep silence in that time; for it is an evil time. The prudent** (*hammaskil*) man is one who keeps his silence, not because one should not speak, but only because warnings seemed to have been of no avail before. The judgments of God were coming upon a people who seemed impervious to counsel.

### 3. *The Penitent Spirit* (5:14-15)

Israel seemed incorrigible, and swift judgment was about to overtake her. Nevertheless a sincere repentance will follow for **the remnant of Joseph** (15). The prophecy of doom continues in 16-17, indicating that Amos seems to think the appeal in vain. Yet the Lord's integrity will not allow Him to proceed to judgment and destruction without an oft recurring plea. Hence the prophet pleads: **Seek good, and not evil, that ye may live** (see comments on 4-6): **and so the Lord, the God of hosts, shall be with you, as ye have spoken** (14).

Amos addresses **the remnant** (15), the fragment left of a nation after a desolating catastrophe. He points out once again the only possible manner in which they can escape judgment: **Hate the evil, and love the good, and establish judgment in the gate.** Amos does not designate a promise, but a possibility: **it may be.** Northern Israel was reduced to a remnant in 734-31 B.C. when Tiglath-pileser (see Chart *A*) left only Ephraim after sweeping Gilead and Galilee into exile. Smith observes that it is rash to deny to Amos "so natural a mitigation of the doom he was forced to pass on a people which had so many good elements in it that it shortly produced a prophet like Hosea."[15]

"The Secrets of Spiritual Life" are suggested in chapter 5 as: (1) Discover the good, 14b; (2) Hate the evil, 15a; (3) Be consistently honest, 15c; (4) Trust the Lord, 15d.

## E. THE APPEARANCE OF JEHOVAH, 5:16-25

### 1. *Lamentation* (5:16-17)

These two verses picture the **wailing** (16; lamentation) of the people over the dead in the time of judgment. **Alas! alas!** indicates the death wail (cf. Jer. 22:18). While the mourning will take place in the towns, the **husbandman** (farmer) shall be called into the towns to weep for the deceased of his own house. The **skilful** (professional mourners) shall also be hired to wail for the dead (cf. Jer. 9:17-18; Matt. 9:23). Even the **vineyards**

---

[15]*Op. cit.*, p. 172.

(17), usually scenes of rejoicing, shall be places of **wailing**. Amos has borrowed from Exod. 12:12 in quoting, "I will pass through the midst of you" (RSV). As the Lord passed through Egypt to take the firstborn, so now He will pass through Israel and destroy the ungodly. Israel, the covenant nation, has become Egypt, the pagan nation.

### 2. *Darkness* (5:18-20)

The threat begins with **woe** (*hoi*) to those who have represented their "election" as insuring deliverance in spite of their sins. Amos shared the expectation of the **day of the Lord** (18). However he knew that it was not a day of privilege for Israel. It could be only a **day . . . of darkness** (judgment) to a people who had broken their covenant with Jehovah. The truth is enforced by the picturesque description of a man fleeing **from a lion** (19), but meeting **a bear**; or another leaning against an unmortared **wall** and being bitten by a poisonous **serpent**. Whoever should escape one danger would only fall into another. For men who know not God, there is danger in all places on the **day of the Lord** (18).

Amos reemphasizes the judgment in v. 20. **Shall** (*nonne*) equals "assuredly." *Living Prophecies* renders the verse: "Yes, that will be a dark and hopeless day for you."

### 3. *Repudiation of Feast and Ceremony* (5:21-25)

Instead of speaking about the Lord, Amos now represents the Lord as speaking: **I hate, I despise your feast days, and I will not smell** ("take delight," RSV) **in your solemn** cere- monial) **assemblies** (21). Since the covenant is broken, the Lord takes no pleasure in their religious ceremonies. "Their outward, heartless worship, does not make them into the people of God, who can count upon his grace."[16]

Verses 22-24 reiterate in Hebrew style the thought of 21. In cutting off the virtue of feasts and sacrifices,[17] the foundation of "false reliance" was swept away. **I will not hear** (23) brings to a finality the rejection of the cultus.[18]

---

[16]Keil, *op. cit.*, p. 287.

[17]**Burnt offerings** (*zebhachim*) and **meat offerings** (*minchah*) are mentioned to denote sacrifices of all kinds (Keil, *op. cit.*, p. 291).

[18]Amos lists the essential offerings which in all represented "the sacred means of friendship between God and man" (IB, VI, 819).

"But let justice roll down like waters, and righteousness like an overflowing stream" (24, RSV). Because the Lord will not accept hypocritical worship, **judgment** shall run like a mighty flood over the land (cf. Isa. 28:2). As Keil observes, *mishpat* is not the judgment practiced by man, but God.[19]

**Have ye offered unto me sacrifices and offerings in the wilderness** (these) **forty years, O house of Israel?** (25) is equivalent to denial. Ye have not! Apostasy had continued over the forty years in the wilderness even though they outwardly carried on a portion of their ritual sacrifices and offerings.[20]

## F. INVASION AND EXILE, 5:26—6:14

### 1. *The Self-deceit of Idol Worship* (5:26-27)

Verse 26 is attached to 25 by way of contrast. "While you were faithless in your sacrifices," **ye have borne the tabernacle of your Moloch and Chiun your images** (26). Although the verse is difficult, the intent is apparent. The Assyrian deities were made by the hand of man; they were helpless before **the Lord, whose name is The God of hosts** (27). The RSV translates v. 26: "You shall take up Sakkuth your king, and Kaiwan your star-god, your images, which you made for yourselves." Because of this gross apostasy, the nation will be taken **beyond Damascus,** a banishment already prophesied in v. 24.

### 2. *The Self-sufficiency of Israel's Leaders* (6:1-7)

The evil engendered by formal worship was the false confidence it gave to the people concerning their covenant relation to Jehovah. In chapter 6, "we are taken from the worship of the people to the banquets of the rich, but again in order to have their security and extravagance contrasted with the pestilence, war and exile that are rapidly approaching. The ease which is condemned means a proud overweening ease."[21] Those revelling in wealth "were completely indifferent to the ruin threatening the people."[22]

---

[19]*Op. cit.*, p. 289.

[20]Amos is not implying that Jehovah was not pleased with worship, but that He was displeased with the hypocrisy of that worship.

[21]Smith, *op. cit.*, p. 178.

[22]Frederick Carl Eiselen, *Prophecy and the Prophets* (New York: The Methodist Book Concern, 1909), p. 46.

Verses 1-6 demonstrate the "flaunting flamboyant luxury of the rich" and the "bacchanalian orgies of debauched men and women who forgot the simple pieties and elementary decencies of life."[23] These were the leaders in Israel, called **chief of the nations** (1).

Verse 2 seems to be an interpolation pointing out that **Israel** (1) is no better than **Calneh** of northern Syria, **Hamath the great** on the Orontes in Syria, and the important city of **Gath** in Philistia, all of which fell to Assyria (see map 2).

After the warning of v. 2 the description is continued of those that **are at ease in Zion** (Jerusalem). They have their winter and summer houses (3:15), and **lie upon beds of ivory** (4) from Damascus. They devour **the lambs out of the flock,** and sing idle songs **to the sound of the viol** (5).[24] These self-indulgent leaders **drink wine** (6) irreverently from ceremonial **bowls** (or by the bowlful) **and anoint themselves with** "the finest of oils" (RSV) as a sign of gladness. As leaders, they should have been concerned over the symptoms of the moral sickness of their nation, **but they are not grieved for the affliction** (ruin) **of Joseph.**

The conclusion to the description is found in v. 7, which prophesies that the nobility of the land shall find themselves **the first that go captive.** They shall head the procession of captives and "the shout of the revelers shall pass away" (Smith-Goodspeed). The government shall come to an end.[25] Amos said this about 760 B.C., when Jeroboam II reigned over a prosperous people. Less than forty years later northern Israel was conquered by Assyria and all but the poor were exiled.

Sellin lists five forms of Israel's sin as denounced by Amos: (1) The exploitation of the poor and oppression of the needy, 2:6; 3:10; 4:1; 5:11; 8:4-6; (2) The lack of justice and the partiality of the judges, 5:7-12; (3) The flaunted luxury of the rich in the face of imminent disaster, 6:1-6; (4) The substitution of mechanical and magical relations for the personal relations with

---

[23]John Paterson, *The Goodly Fellowship of the Prophets* (New York: The Methodist Book Concern, 1909), p. 46.

[24]The phrase **invent to themselves instruments of musick like David** (5) is a difficult phrase and is interpreted variously. IB suggests: "shouting, they imagine to be singing" (p. 824).

[25]See George L. Robinson, *The Twelve Minor Prophets* (New York: George H. Doran Co., 1926), p. 54, for a fuller explanation.

Jehovah, 4: 4; 5: 5; 6: 3; 8: 14; (5) The arrogance that dares to flaunt itself in the face of promised judgment, 4: 2; 9: 7.[26]

### 3. *The Horrors of Siege* (6: 8-11)

As in 4: 2, Amos introduces 6: 8 with **The Lord God hath sworn by himself** (*nephesh*), i.e., His innermost being or His holiness. He will **deliver up the city** because of the "pride of Jacob" (RSV). In this pride the nation had depended upon its own self-sufficiency rather than upon God.

The horror of siege is realistically detailed. No one shall escape death even if there remain only **ten men in one house** (9). The Israelites buried their dead, but in a time of plague they would sanction burning the bodies. Verse 10 pictures such a time of devastation, and a great terror of Jehovah's further judgment. "A man's uncle will be the only one left to bury him, and when he goes in to carry his body from the house, he will ask the only one still alive inside, 'Are any others left?' And the answer will be, 'No,' and he will add, 'Shhh . . . don't mention the Name of the Lord—He might hear you' " (*Living Prophecies*).

### 4. *The End of Israel* (6: 12-14)

Examples of impossibilities in v. 12 highlight the certainty of Israel's fate. Can **horses run upon** rocks? (12) "Does one plow the sea with oxen"? (RSV) Israel had turned justice into **gall** (bitterness) and goodness into **hemlock** (poison).

Amos follows with a play upon the names of *Lodebar* (a **thing of nought**, 13) and *Karnaim* (horns). **A thing of nought** is in the Hebrew *lo dhabhar,* the consonants of which are the same as those of Lodebar, a town east of the Jordan. *Karnaim,* which the KJV translates **horns**, is also a town in the same region. They were taken by Jeroboam II in his successful campaigns to the east. The two are relatively insignificant—thus the play on their names.[27] Moffatt renders the verse: "You are so proud of Lo Debar, you think you captured Karnaim by your own strength."

The final word of judgment returns to the thought of v. 11. The **nation** that the Lord shall **raise up against** Israel (14) will

---

[26]John Paterson, *op. cit.,* p. 33, quoting from Ernest Sellin, *Kommentar Zum Alten Testament XII; Das Zwolfprophetenbuch Erste Haefte,* 1929, p. 184.

[27]IB, VI, 827.

**afflict** (oppress) them **from the entering in of Hemath** (the pass between the Lebanon Mountains in the north) to "the brook Arabah" (RSV), the southern limit of Israel near the Dead Sea.

An intriguing list of the "woes" of Amos is found in chapter 6: (1) Woe to those who depend on ritual rather than on faith and obedience, 1; (2) Woe to those who really do not obey God's word, 3; (3) Woe to those who enjoy their riches, but are not concerned with national and personal transgression, 4-6; (4) Woe to those who transform the fruit of righteousness into the gall of bitterness, 12.

# Section III *Visions and an Epilogue*

## A. AMOS' VISIONS, 7:1—8:3

The account of Amos' visions is found in cc. 7—9. There are five of them clearly identified. The first is found in 7:1-3, and the second in 7:4-6. The third and fourth visions are to be distinguished sharply from the "fragmentary messages" which are attached to them; the visions themselves are recorded in 7:7-9 and 8:1-3. The fifth vision is decidedly different in form and character and probably should be viewed as including 9:1-4.[1]

**Thus hath the Lord God shewed unto me** (1) is an introduction common to the first four of the five visions. The fifth begins with "I saw the Lord" (9:1). Another common element of each of the first four visions is the word **behold,** followed by the content of the visions.

### 1. *Locusts* (7:1-3)

The first vision describes a "brood of locusts" **in the beginning of the shooting up of the latter growth** (1). This would be just as the rains were preparing the crops for final growth and harvest. They could not have come at a more disastrous time. **The latter growth after the king's mowings** seems to imply that the tribute (tax) paid to the state came from the first **mowings.** Failure of the second growth would destroy the farmer's personal income.[2]

Amos saw the expected famine as a judgment on Israel. When the locusts had **made an end of eating the grass of the land** (2), they would leave it stripped, bare of fruit, produce, and crop.

The description of the plague is followed by the dialogue between Amos and the Lord. **I beseech thee** is a "participle of entreaty," the equivalent of "please!" Thus Amos speaks for

[1]John D. W. Watts, *Vision and Prophecy in Amos* (Grand Rapids, Mich: Wm. B. Eerdmans Publishing Co., 1958), p. 28.

[2]Norman Snaith points out that no such tribute was known to Israel and interprets the passage as meaning "shearing," which is the usual meaning of the term rendered **mowings** (quoted, IB, VI, 831).

135

Israel, not as they saw themselves, a "proud, self-sufficient nation, but as God saw them, a little, helpless people."[3] "How can Jacob stand? For he is so small" (Smith-Goodspeed).

The answer to Amos' plea is evident in the assurance that the disaster could be avoided. **The Lord repented for this: It shall not be, saith the Lord** (3).[4]

### 2. *Fire* (7:4-6)

The devouring **fire** (4) represents the second and more severe judgment of God against Israel. **To contend by fire** means "the Lord God was calling for a trial by fire" (Berk.). While **fire** is one of the figurative symbols of the wrath of God, the prophet possibly saw the judgment as a continuing hot wind sweeping across the land from the desert. It was so intense as to devour the great deep, "the underground reservoir of waters, from which the springs were supplied (cf. Genesis 49:25, 'the deep that coucheth beneath')."[5]

Again Amos intercedes in the same words found in v. 2 and the Lord alters His threatened action: **This also shall not be, saith the Lord God** (6).

### 3. *Plumbline* (7:7-9)

In the third vision God asked the question, **Amos, what seest thou?** (8) The plumbline was used for testing the straightness of a mold, and the figure thus describes God's righteous demands upon His people. Sidney Lovett observes succinctly that famine and drought are seasonal occurrences beyond the power of man to control; therefore Amos' intercession was to the only One who could intervene. However, "A wall is the labor of man's hands. If it buckles, for whatever reason, its deviation is inexorably marked by the plumbline. And from that verdict there is no appeal."[6] One can vision Amos standing silent before the judgment of God. There was nothing more to say. Judgment was inevitable because the building was of man's own doing. God declares, **I will not again pass by them any more** (8).

[3]*Ibid.*

[4]Keil interprets vv. 1-3 as Amos interceding before the Lord after the vegetables (Gen. 1:11, "grass of the field") were eaten by the locusts and before the consumption of the second crop. This would save Israel from complete destruction (*op. cit.*, p. 307).

[5]Clarke, *op. cit.*, p. 601.

[6]IB, VI, 834.

Verse 9 describes the judgment to come as including **the high places of Isaac** (the shrines of the hills), **the sanctuaries of Israel** (sacred buildings), and **the house** (dynasty and family) **of Jeroboam.**

### 4. *The Conflict with Amaziah* (7:10-17)

In the visions Amos has been speaking in the first person. In this passage, however, we have an account of the conflict between Amos and Amaziah. Amaziah was the high priest of the sanctuary of the golden calf in Bethel. This shrine had been set up to keep the worshippers from going to Jerusalem to worship.

The daring announcement of judgment upon both priest and king caused **Amaziah** (10) to advise Jeroboam II of Amos' supposed conspiracy. His judgment was that **the land is not able to bear all his words.** Amaziah's charge indicated that he associated Amos with subversion and that his preaching was having a marked effect on the nation. It is clear that Amos was a prophet to be feared because of the influence of his message.

The dramatic confrontation between prophet and priest (vv. 11-17) brought the career of Amos to a crisis. His "stern unpalatable prophecies of national doom" now faced ecclesiastical and royal rebuke. The acrid clash in Bethel "is a landmark in the great debate between priest and prophet, the fierce conflict between state and church, whose bitter entail infests all subsequent history."[7] There was not only the conflict between two strong personalities, but a conflict of vocation and institution. As a result, Amaziah presented a formal charge of treason, **Amos hath conspired against thee** (Jeroboam, 10), having said that the **king shall die by the sword, and Israel shall surely be led away captive out of their own land** (11).

Amaziah turned from his charge of treason to direct a command to Amos: **Flee thee away into the land of Judah** (12). In other words, "Go back where you belong and prophesy professionally there to earn your bread." Then the priest continued with a prohibition, **But prophesy not again any more at Beth-el: for it is the king's chapel** (13), a sanctuary founded by the king (I Kings 12:28). **The king's court** (*beth mamlakhah*) is the house of the kingdom, i.e., the principal seat of the worship which the king had established for his kingdom. Thus no one

---

[7]IB, VI, 834.

could be allowed to prophesy against the king there.[8] The fact that the high priest gave these orders to Amos probably indicates that Jeroboam did not take the charge seriously and left the matter in the hands of Amaziah.

Amos immediately replied to the insinuation that he was a professional prophet (*nabi*). He declared: **I was no prophet, neither was I a prophet's son** (14, a member of the prophet's guild), but **an herdman, and a gatherer of sycomore fruit** ("a dresser of sycamore trees," RSV). He continued by appealing to his call by the Lord, who took him from his **flock** and said, **Go, prophesy unto my people Israel** (15).

Dramatically Amos confronted Amaziah with his own words and proceeded to prophesy even as the Lord had commanded: **Now therefore hear thou the word of the Lord** (16). Amaziah's tragic punishment was then described: **Thy wife shall be an harlot in the city** (17); i.e., when Bethel was taken by invasion, she would be raped, his children slain, and his land given to new settlers. What was to happen to Amaziah would also befall the whole of the nation, **and Israel shall surely go into captivity forth of his land.**

An exposition from chapter 7 might be entitled "When God Can Use Man": (1) Though from humble circumstances, he hears and follows God, 14-15; (2) He is willing to proclaim the word of the Lord in the face of opposition, 12-13; (3) He is not afraid to prophesy of judgment to come, 17.

### 5. *Basket of Summer Fruit* (8:1-3)

The fourth vision is like the others in form and points back to the preceding three (7:1-9). Its message is similar and confirms the former judgments. The **What seest thou?** (2) of the Lord is followed by the vision of the **basket of summer fruit.** This would be fruit that ripened in the summer and was gathered in the fall. In Hebrew there is an alliteration where ripe fruit (*qayits*) is followed by **the end** (*qets*). The figure points to a nation that is ripe for judgment and destruction—**the end is come upon my people.**

Evidently these visions appeared over a period of a year; the locusts associated with the spring, the devouring fire with the summer, and the fruit with the autumn. Their repetition and

---

[8]Keil, *op. cit.,* p. 312.

138

growing severity must have impressed upon Amos the immediacy of judgment and the urgency of his prophecy.

Amos represents the Lord once more as stating, "I will not defer their punishment again" (2, *Living Prophecies;* cf. 7:9). All the joy shall be turned into **howlings** (3; mourning or wailing). **There shall be many dead bodies in every place.** Keil translates the final phrase, in "every place hath He cast them forth; Hush!" The interjection "Hush!" is not a sign of despair, but "an admonition to bow beneath the overwhelming severity of the judgment of God, as in Zeph. 1:7 (cf. Hab. 2:20 and Zech. 2:17)."⁹

## B. SIN AND JUDGMENT, 8:4-14

Amos 8:4 begins a group of oracles which are rather obscure in their relations to each other, but reiterate the prophet's concern over Israel. They deal in general with the sins of the nation and the judgments to come.

### 1. *Oppression of the Poor* (8:4-7)

The oppression of the poor is denounced in an address to the greedy. **Hear this, O ye that swallow up the needy** (4). Both the day of **the new moon** (5)¹⁰ and **the sabbath** were days of rest from business, days prized by the workman but begrudged by **the merchants.** "The interests of the Sabbath are the interests of the poor; the enemies of the Sabbath are the enemies of the poor. And all this illustrates our Saviour's saying that the 'Sabbath was made for man.'" **Making the ephah small** was to give less than full measure. Making **the shekel great** was overcharging the buyers. The **balances** were made deceitful by using false weights.

It was the purpose of the wealthy to make **the poor** poorer, so that they would be forced to sell themselves into slavery for **silver** (6) or be handed over to their creditors because of inability to pay debts no greater than the price of a **pair of shoes.** The greedy merchants would sell for a profit even **the refuse of the wheat** ("mouldy wheat," *Living Prophecies*).

⁹*Ibid.,* p. 314. Fosbroke takes the view that silence refers to the "silence of despair brooding over the scene." In either case, the seriousness of the occasion was apparent to Amos (IB, VI, 389).

¹⁰**The new moon** (*chodesh*) was a holiday on which all trade was suspended, just as it was on **the sabbath** (cf. Num. 28:11 and II Kings 4:23).

Verse 7 represents a burning sense of indignation over the character of these crimes. God is God of the poor as well as the wealthy, and **hath sworn by the excellency of Jacob, Surely I will never forget any of their works.**

God swears by the **excellency** or "pride" (RSV) **of Jacob** as He does by His own holiness. As surely as He is what He is, He will bring judgment on the greedy.

### 2. *Earthquake, Darkness, and Mourning* (8:8-10)

The feeling of God's anger is shared by Nature herself. **Shall not the land tremble?** (8) refers to earthquakes. On all sides there will be mourning. **It shall rise up** refers to the destruction which is also likened to the flood of Egypt, or the Nile when it rises to flood stage. Though the action is not as sudden as the shock of an earthquake, yet the flood is just as devastating and as irresistible. The same type of judgment is described in 9:5-6.

The threat of earthquake is followed by the prediction of eclipse (9).[11] In the terror of that unnatural night **songs** shall be turned into **mourning** and **lamentation** (10). The wearing of **sackcloth** and the shaving of the bald place on the head were signs of mourning (cf. Isa. 3:24). The sorrow will be severe, like mourning after the death of **an only son** (cf. Jer. 6:26; Zech. 12:10). **And the end thereof as a bitter day** suggests that the judgment was not to be of short duration. *Living Prophecies* renders it, "Bitter, bitter will be that day."

### 3. *Famine and Thirst* (8:11-14)

The judgment of God becomes progressively more severe. The **famine in the land** (11) and the **thirst** were not famine for food and drink, but a famine for **the words of the Lord.** This **word of the Lord** (12) is identified as the light of His revelation. Those who do not now cherish His Word will then have a hunger and thirst for that which was formerly ignored and rejected.

Their desire is depicted in v. 12. **They shall wander** ("reel," RSV) from one end of the earth to the other. From **north** to south and from **east** to west, **they shall run . . . to seek the word of the Lord, and shall not find it.** Even **the fair virgins and**

---

[11]Smith points out that there were eclipses in 803 B.C. and 763 B.C., the memory of which probably inspired the symbolism of this passage (*ibid.*, p. 191).

young men (13) shall swoon away from their **thirst** for the Word. These represent the strongest of the nation. What of the weak?

Verse 14 is difficult to interpret. It is now generally agreed that **the sin** (guilt) **of Samaria** (*ashmath shomeron*) was the golden calf of Bethel, the chief idol of Samaria placed at the national sanctuary (cf. 4:4-5).[12] Reference to Dan in the extreme north as well as to Beersheba in the far south reveals the widespread infection of idolatry throughout the land.

**The manner of Beer-sheba** (14) speaks of the pilgrimage for the sake of worship rather than the act of worship itself. This worship was probably an idolatrous worship of Jehovah rather than the worship of pagan idols. Amos declares of all such worshippers, **They shall fall, and never rise up again** (14). The fulfillment of this prophecy commenced with the exile of the ten tribes. It continues to this day for those who are still looking for the Messiah.

## C. THE INEXORABLE JUDGMENT, 9:1-7

### 1. *The Fifth Vision* (9:1-4)

Amos declares: **I saw the Lord standing upon the altar** (1). This fifth vision in Bethel recalls the inauguration of Isaiah (Isa. 6:1-13). God is seen already in the midst of His judgment in which "completeness and inescapableness are emphasized."[13] In Isaiah's vision the Lord was seated upon a throne, but Amos saw Him standing alone with the final word, **Smite.**

Verses 1-4 are made up of five stanzas of four lines each, with each couplet carrying a thought of its own. But the entire prophecy carries with it the finality of judgment upon the whole of the covenant nation to which Israel still belonged, though now divided from the house of David.[14]

The Lord appears at **the altar** before the whole nation gathered at the sanctuary. His judgment will shatter the Temple

[12]Keil, *op. cit.,* pp. 318-19.

[13]Watts, *op. cit.,* p. 47.

[14]"Though the article before *hammizbeach* points to the altar of the sanctuary in Bethel, and seems to attach itself in an explanatory manner to 8:14, there is no evidence that Amos' prophecy is directed against Israel alone. . . . The Lord roars from Zion to Zion and from Zion He utters His voice (1:2), not only upon the nations who have shown hostility to Judah or Israel, but also upon Judah and Israel on account of their departure from His law" (cf. 2:4, 6 ff.) (Keil, *op. cit.,* p. 321).

to its foundations and bury the people. **The lintel of the door** would be "the capitals" or tops of the pillars, so from top to bottom the place would fall in ruins. (Possibly a severe earthquake was envisioned as an instrument of judgment.) The smiting of the posts until the "threshold" (RSV) shakes rhetorically represents the finality of the destruction of the national life. *Living Prophecies* says, "Shake the temple until the pillars crumble and the roof crashes down upon the people below." None shall escape, "and what are left of them I will slay with the sword" (RSV).

Verses 2-4 point out the inexorable completion of God's judgment upon His covenant-breaking people. The language of God's omnipresence is reminiscent of Ps. 139:7-9. Neither **hell** (2, sheol), the grave, nor **heaven** (the heavens), nor **the top of Carmel** (3; a high mountain), nor **the bottom of the sea,** nor **captivity** (4; residence in a foreign land) can save them from the omnipresent vengeance of God. **The serpent . . . shall bite them** has been interpreted, "I will send the sea-serpent ['Dragon,' Moffatt] after them to bite and destroy them" (*Living Prophecies*). Amos summarizes the passage: **And I will set mine eyes upon them for evil, and not for good.** "They are more richly blessed than the world, but they are also more severely punished."[15]

### 2. Third Doxology (9:5-6)

The transcendent majesty of Jehovah is again declared (cf. 4:13; 5:8-9) in the third doxology of Amos' prophecy, which is reminiscent and partially repetitive of 8:8. Moffatt renders 5, "'Tis the Eternal, Lord of hosts, at whose touch the earth trembles." The "earthquake" is once again looked upon as punitive. **It shall rise up** seems to refer to God's sovereign action of judgment and mercy. **And shall be drowned** would refer to the effect of God's judgment on the people. Verse 6 declares again the universal power of God over all the nations. The first part of the verse has been paraphrased, "The upper stories of His home are in the heavens, the first floor upon the earth" (*Living Prophecies*). **The waters of the sea** represent the nations of the earth which shall pour over Israel in judgment. **The Lord** (*Yahweh*) **is his name** identifies the **Lord God of hosts** (5) and reemphasizes the One who can bring all this to pass.

[15]*Ibid.,* p. 325, as quoted from Hengstenberg.

### 3. *The Lord of All Nations* (9:7)

The famous seventh verse climaxes Amos' teachings concerning the universality of God. Once more, but in a more articulate way, he emphasizes the truth of the unity of God (cf. Deut. 6:4). There is no other God. All others so named are false. While Amos insisted that it was Jehovah who had redeemed Israel from Egypt, he was equally insistent that the Lord had also brought the **Philistines from Caphtor, and the Syrians from Kir.**[16] He even places **the Ethiopians** on a similar plane as the children of Israel, "Are ye not like the Ethiopians to me?" (RSV) Thus Amos completely undercuts Israel's carnal security in reliance upon its standing as the chosen people.

## D. EPILOGUE, 9:8-15

### 1. *Purging Judgment* (9:8-10)

The judgment of God predicted in v. 8 was consummated in the fall of Samaria in 722 B.C. and the destruction of Jerusalem in 586 B.C. (see Chart *A*). This passage may at first seem redundant, but it opens a new vista which is climaxed in the promise of restoration in 14.

**The house of Jacob** (8) is to be understood not merely as Judah contrasted with the kingdom of Israel. Jacob here represents the whole of Israel. Amos is pointing out that after Israel has been shaken **as corn is sifted in a sieve** (9), faithful servants of God will be preserved. This remnant will be a "holy seed" from which the kingdom of God shall grow. The distinction is here made between the evil nation and faithful persons, of whom there must have been at least a few. This distinction calls forth in v. 10 a solemn warning to **sinners** not to deceive themselves by thinking that they shall escape the Lord's judgment.

### 2. *Restoration* (9:11-12)

The prophecy closes with the promise of the restoration of the faithful remnant and the establishment of the kingdom of God. **In that day,** when judgment is meted out, **will I raise up**

---

[16]**Caphtor** is generally associated with Crete, **Kir** somewhere far to the northeast. Jehovah is designated Lord of Damascus (1:3-5), and Tyre (1:9-10) as well. "Thus Amos offered Israel a new depth to the so-called First Commandment . . . without anywhere explicitly declaring that Yahweh was the only God" (Knight, *op. cit.*, p. 63).

the tabernacle of David (11). In this oracle there sounds forth a note of hope in the face of despair. Deep in the hearts of the people lingered "the memory of the golden age of David."[17] That a renewal of that age was possible, even when the strength of David's reign had **fallen**, revealed the hand of Jehovah in "governing the course of history. 'He who had smitten could heal.' "[18] Verse 12 promises that the surrounding nations, including **Edom** (see map 2), shall be reconquered. The phrase **called by my name** indicates only that these nations also are under the power of the Lord. There is no question but that **the tabernacle of David** refers to the rule of the Messiah. The Jews formed a name from this passage as a designation of the Messiah, *Felius cadentium,* "He who had sprung from a fallen hut."[19]

### 3. *Nature's Blessing* (9:13)

The closing oracle is a "pleasant piece of music, as if the birds had come out after the thunderstorm, and the wet hills were glistening in the sun."[20] In the Messianic kingdom the people will enjoy the promises of Moses (Lev. 26:5): **The plowman shall overtake the reaper.** While one is plowing, the other shall be reaping because of the rapid growth of the grain. The work of the **treader of grapes** shall overlap with **him that soweth seed.** This marvelous age will make it seem as though the God of all nations, the Lord God of hosts, is making the **mountains** to **drop sweet wine** and **the hills** to "flow with it" (RSV). Israel will at last enjoy the fruit of her inheritance.

### 4. *Return of the Remnant* (9:14-15)

Smith-Goodspeed renders the opening statement of 14, "And I will restore the fortune of my people Israel." George Adam Smith has it, "I will reverse the captivity of my people Israel." Thus, because the land shall be blessed with the greatest of fertility (13), the faithful remnant shall enjoy the blessings of continuing peace and prosperity. They shall have again all that was taken from them. **They shall build the waste cities, and inhabit them; and they shall plant vineyards, and drink the wine thereof; they shall also make gardens, and eat the fruit of them** (14).

---

[17]IB, VI, 851.                     [18]*Ibid.*
[19]Keil, *op. cit.,* p. 331.        [20]Smith, *op. cit.,* p. 202.

There is no apparent reason in the text for the appearance of this beautiful Messianic prophecy. It is a vindication of the righteousness of Jehovah that such a Messianic promise comes from a prophet who spent most of his time predicting the absolute and final ruin of a sinful people. Even out of prophetic destruction arises prophetic hope. This hope is as permanent as the preceding judgments. **They shall no more be pulled up out of their land which I have given them, saith the Lord thy God (15)**.

Two expositions might be developed from the final chapter of Amos. The first is "The Awesome Presence of God": (1) His omnipotence, 1; (2) His omniscience, 2; (3) His omnipresence, 4. The second would be God's wonderful restorative powers: (1) The rebuilding of the fallen, 11; (2) Under God, there are better days ahead, 13-14; (3) The eternal promise of God, 15.

It is in this confidence that we are to leave Amos in Tekoa. "The passing days served only to authenticate his prophetic word." The God who destroys because of sin will in the "wilderness of despair and destruction move to the fulfillment of all that is partial,"[21] as long as man's probation lasts. We can expand the words of St. Paul to point out the sovereign and eternal purpose of God, "He which hath begun a good work in you will perform it until the day of Jesus Christ" (Phil. 1:6).[22]

[21]IB, VI, 852.
[22]*Ibid.*

*The Book of*

# OBADIAH

**Armor D. Peisker**

# Introduction

"Tell that fox . . . I finish my course." With these words Jesus met the Pharisees' warning that He had better leave the area, because Herod Antipas was planning to arrest Him (Luke 13:32, RSV).

Facing the murderous plot of Herod, the Edomite, in this bold manner, Jesus incidentally pointed up the bitter, centuries-old hostility which had existed between the two peoples from whom each had descended: the sons of Esau, the Edomites, and the sons of Jacob, the Israelites. Herod's Edomite forebears are the principals in Obadiah's prophecy.

Jesus' words also stamped Herod as clever, ruthless, and scheming. History indicates that these were general characteristics of Esau's sons.

The New Testament writer to the Hebrews describes Esau as a "profane" man; or, as we say today, as irreligious, materialistic, secularistic. His offspring seem also to have followed that same pattern. Writing of this, George Adam Smith cites the fact that in the Old Testament we never read of Edomite gods. He goes on to say that, although they had their gods, the Edomites "were essentially irreligious, living for food, spoil, and vengeance—a people who deserved even more than the Philistines to have their name descend as a symbol of hardness and obscurantism."[1]

Jacob and his descendants have been known for their cunning, but they have also been deeply religious men with spiritual vision and faith, essentially the opposite of the Edomites. In this divergence of interest and purpose lie the roots of the Edom-Israel antagonism.

These hereditary foes of Israel are mentioned first in the Old Testament in Gen. 25:30 and last in Mal. 1:2-5. The long record in between is an account of tragic relations between Israel and Edom. Several Israelite prophets foretold Esau's doom: Isa. 34:5-8; 63:1-4; Jer. 49:17; Ezek. 25:12-14; 35:1-15; Amos 1:11-12. The fact that Edom was a constantly recurring theme with the Hebrew prophets helps to account for the similarity

[1]*The Book of the Twelve Prophets* (New York: Harper and Brothers Publishers, 1938) II, 182.

between Obad. 1-9 and Jer. 49:7-22. While it is possible that Obadiah could have taken his thought from Jeremiah, it may be that both were using the work of another earlier prophet. Obadiah is unique among the prophets, however, in that he concerns himself only with the nation of Edom.

Who Obadiah was we are not told. A dozen or so men appearing in Old Testament history bore this name, which means "worshiper of the Lord" or "servant of the Lord." None of them, however, can be identified with the author of this book.

Obadiah does not state when he delivered his scathing denunciation. Dating this, the shortest book in the Old Testament, therefore, has been a problem. Verse 11 would seem to be a key, but scholars have disagreed as to just what event in Jerusalem's history is here referred to. Most likely, it appears, Obadiah delivered his message soon after Jerusalem fell at the hands of Nebuchadnezzar in 586 B.C. and therefore his prophecies relate to that occasion.

## *Outline*

I. Edom's Judgment, 1-9

II. Reasons for Judgment, 10-14

III. The Day of the Lord, 15-21

# Section I Edom's Judgment

The book opens with the title, **The vision of Obadiah** (1). The term translated **vision** is the word most commonly used to describe the content of a divine revelation to one of the prophets (Isa. 1:1; Jer. 14:14; Ezek. 7:26; Nah. 1:1). By referring to a **rumour**—a report or tidings—**from the Lord,** Obadiah may suggest that he is quoting from another of God's prophets—words which he felt were particularly relevant at the time (cf. Jer. 49:14). The **ambassador** or messenger **sent among the heathen** may have been a subversive person or persons sent by some king to stir up the surrounding nations against Edom. But it is also possible that the prophet was referring to a mounting spirit of general unrest, envy, and ill will toward Edom (see map 1) among her neighbors which had resulted from political causes. Whatever the situation may have been, it was as a messenger from the Lord, for God was using it to bring about His purposes of judgment toward the Edomites.

That God was not intervening in Edomite affairs in some strikingly miraculous manner, but was working through the conspiracy and treachery of the surrounding nations, reminds us that "there are historical forces operative in the world which make the position of any nation, however strong it may appear, actually precarious. Obadiah is therefore peculiarly fitting as a prophetic utterance which every powerful, wealthy, and well-established nation does well to heed."[1]

**I have made thee small . . . thou art greatly despised** (2) is better translated as prophetic, "I will make you small . . . you shall be very despised." The Hebrew text refers to something already determined in the mind of God, but still in the human future (cf. RSV, Amp. OT, Berk.).

The land of Edom stretched along the sides of the rocky ridge of Mount Seir extending from the Gulf of Akabah nearly to the Dead Sea. The territory varied from fertile areas where

---

[1]Norman F. Langford, "Hosea" (Exposition), *The Interpreter's Bible* (New York: Abingdon Press, 1956), VI, 861.

wheat, grapes, figs, pomegranates, and olives flourished to high mountain peaks separated by deep gorges. Midway in the country's main ridge Mount Hor rose high and dark above the surrounding terrain only a short distance from Sela or Petra, the capital city. The capital itself was located in a deep valley surrounded by 200-foot cliffs and was accessible only through a narrow rift 12 feet wide.

Thus the Edomites very literally dwelt high **in the clefts of rocks** (3), their position practically impenetrable and impregnable. For many generations they had lived here secure. No enemy had been able to enter the narrow canyon defiles which led to their chief cities hewn out of the rocky mountain walls. In such positions a small company of Edomites could defend a mountain pass against a whole army of invaders. Their lofty position also enabled them to observe the activities of the peoples about them. Like a lion crouched and ready to pounce upon its prey, the Edomites were always alert to make plundering forays against their neighbors whenever the time was opportune.

Shrewd people that they were, the Edomites had developed a much higher civilization than the tribes who roamed the surrounding deserts. From their lofty home they controlled the trade routes from Akabah and Egypt (see map 1), which gave them access to commodities and riches unknown to their neighbors. As a result they had grown proud, disdainful, and defiant (3).

They lived secluded, alone like the eagle, their homes high in the mountain fastnesses—as it were, **among the stars** (4). But they would in their pride be brought down in keeping with the principle of life expressed in Prov. 16:18: "Pride goeth before destruction, and an haughty spirit before a fall." Edom's boasting is also condemned in Ezek. 35:13.

God's judgments were to be severe. The prophet reminds the Edomites that when a band of robbers makes a night raid, or when grape harvesters go through a vineyard, they always leave something. But it will not be so with the despoilers who will come against Edom. The nation will be utterly desolated. Edom, the descendant of **Esau** (6), will be brought to nothing. Her treasured goods and wealth, hidden in the most secret, inaccessible caves and stored in the most formidable fortress cities, will be searched out and confiscated (cf. Jer. 49:10). G. A. Smith's translation of vv. 5-6 is helpful:

"How art thou utterly undone!
Had thieves of a night come into thee,
Would they have stolen more than their need?
Had vine-croppers entered thee,
Would they not have left gleanings?
How ransacked is Esau,
How rifled her treasures!"[2]

The Edomites sought shelter and safety in the cleft of the rocks. Laughing, perhaps at Obadiah's prophecy, they were confident that their rocky homeland, never yet penetrated, would protect them even from God's vengeance of which the prophet spoke. However, their hope of refuge was vain, as is the hope of all who resist God. Only in Him is there safety. There is One of whom Isaiah wrote who is "as an hiding place from the wind, and a covert from the tempest . . . the shadow of a great rock in a weary land" (Isa. 32:2). In our Lord Jesus Christ all men who will can find a sure refuge from every blast of coming judgment. W. O. Cushing rejoiced in this and wrote:

*Oh, safe to the Rock that is higher than I,*
*My soul in its conflicts and sorrows would fly.*
*So sinful, so weary, Thine, Thine would I be.*
*Thou blest "Rock of Ages," I'm hiding in thee.*

The Edomites took great pride in their treasures, as do men and nations today. But the Bible has much warning against putting one's trust in earthly riches. Suggestive of these divine teachings are Ps. 62:10; Prov. 23:5; I Tim. 6:5-11.

The destruction of Edom would be the more bitter because it would come at the hands of friends: **The men of thy confederacy . . . the men that were at peace with thee** (7). Nations which have been allies will trick the Edomites. Those who as intimate friends have shared their food will use this seeming friendship to conspire against them. The Edomites, long eminent for their wisdom and prudence (Job 4:1; Jer. 49:7), had become foolishly infatuated with the security of their geographical position, with their vast stores of wealth, and with their political situation. They would not sense what was going on as their supposed friends set traps to ensnare them. These same friends and

[2]*Op. cit.,* p. 175.

allies would finally drive the Edomites out of their own land, thus **even to the border.**

Worldly wisdom cannot be relied upon (I Cor. 1:18-19, 27). "Pride and self-confidence betray man to his fall. When he is fallen, self-confidence betrayed passes readily to despair. . . . Men do not use the resources which they yet have because what they have valued, fails them. Undue confidence is the parent of undue fear."[3]

**Wound** (7) is better rendered "snare" (ASV) or "trap" (Berk.).

The tragic situation described by Obadiah developed in Edom quite soon after this prophecy. In the sixth and fifth centuries before Christ historical records show that the Edomites, under Arab pressure, were driven from their country and settled in southern Palestine.

**The mount of Esau** (8) was Edom's principal stronghold, consisting of the prominent high points of the Sela or Petra area. **Teman** (9) was a chief Edomite city about five miles from the capital. **Thy mighty men . . . shall be dismayed**—the dismay of these warriors is further described in Jer. 49:22.

Edom's attitude is a remarkable illustration of the tragic "Fruits of Pride": (1) Pride of heart is deceptive, 3*a*: in commerce, in intellectual matters, and in moral values; (2) Pride of heart is presumptive, 3*c*; it presumes upon material advantages, upon man's own ability with no thought of divine intervention; (3) Pride of heart is destructive, 4; cf. Prov. 16:18; Luke 14:11; God may use various means to bring low the proud—economic difficulties, physical incapacity, bereavement, domestic conflict, slander, or even death.

---

[3]E. B. Pusey, *The Minor Prophets* (Grand Rapids, Mich.: Baker Book House, 1963 [reprint]), I, 358.

# Section II Reasons for Judgment

Obadiah 10-14

God never acts in judgment without good reason. He here tells the Edomites why destructive judgment is coming to them. Their chief offense against Him was their cruel treatment of their own brethren in the hour of tragedy and suffering. **Thy brother Jacob** (10) is probably used here to highlight the relationship that existed between the Edomites as the sons of Esau and the men of Judah, sons of Esau's twin brother, Jacob.

The Old Testament here foreshadows the New Testament's solemn statements regarding our attitude toward all men, each of whom is to be regarded as a brother. Whatever we do for or against him we do for or against God himself (Matt. 25:31-46; I John 3:10-15; 4:20-21). Is there any doubt that many of the social distresses we now suffer, such as the problems of the race issue, come to us largely as a harvest of the generations of bad seed sowing? No one can escape the unalterable law: "Whatsoever a man soweth, that shall he also reap" (Gal. 6:7).

The acts of antagonism for which judgment was coming on Edom went back to her refusal to grant Israel passage through her borders during the exodus from Egypt to Palestine (Num. 20:14-21). These acts reached a climax in Edom's treatment of Judah when Nebuchadnezzar sacked Jerusalem in 586 B.C. On that occasion, Edom apparently stood aloof, offering no assistance until they saw how the tide of battle would turn. But this made them as part of the invader's army (11). *The Amplified Old Testament* rendering is clear: "On the day you stood aloof from your brother Jacob, on the day that strangers took captive his forces and carried off his wealth, and foreigners entered into his gates and cast lots on Jerusalem, you were even as one of them."

It would appear from vv. 12-14 that the Edomites actually gave aid to the Babylonians when they saw that Nebuchadnezzar would be victor. The prophet graphically details some of the ways in which they did this. **Looked on the day** (12), i.e., "gloated over the day" (RSV). **Looked on their affliction** (13) would be "looked with delight on their misery" (Amp. OT). We have

155

no information from history as to the exact ways in which the Edomites collaborated with the invaders. It would seem that they joined in plundering the stricken nation (**laid hands on their substance**), blocked the escape of refugees (**stood in the crossway, to cut off those of his that did escape, 14**), and even betrayed fleeing Israelites into Babylonian hands (**delivered up those of his that did remain**). Apparently Edom sought by these means to put herself in favor with the victorious Babylonian invaders, but her actions were without excuse before God. Jer. 49: 7-22 and II Kings 25 are probably parallel scriptures to this portion of Obadiah.

# Section III *The Day of the Lord*

Obadiah 15-21

Obadiah indicates that judgment for Edom will not end simply by her being soon driven out of her long-cherished homeland. He goes on to make reference to **the day of the Lord** (15), one of the great Old Testament themes (Joel 1:15; 3:14; Zeph. 1:7). Although it is often spoken of as being **near,** that is, surely approaching and imminent, the exact time of its coming is not stated. Nor do we know just the manner and methods of the day. We do know, however, something of its character. In that day the Lord alone shall be exalted (Isa. 2:11), and all the nations that forget God will receive retribution (Ps. 9:17).

Edom will be among those godless nations to be finally judged. Obadiah tells them, **As thou hast done, it shall be done unto thee** (15). This suggests the New Testament teaching in such passages as Matt. 6:14-15; 18:21-35; Luke 6:31; Jas. 2:13.

The prophet reminds the Edomites of their drunken orgy in Jerusalem at the time of its plunder by Nebuchadnezzar. Obadiah says that similarly **all the heathen** (16)—all nations who live without God—will drink of His wrath and their destruction will **be as though they had not been** (cf. Jer. 25:15-28).

In contrast, **upon mount Zion** (17) in Jerusalem, the site of the holy Temple, there will be **deliverance** (escape, RSV) from divine wrath. And **there shall be holiness.** Holiness here is only partially related to the moral quality so stressed in the NT. Obadiah refers to freedom from defilement from the godless nations, and so suggests safety from any assault (Joel 2:32; 3:17). The **house of Jacob,** i.e., Judah, shall recover the territories which God had of old given them. The Septuagint puts it interestingly: "The House of Jacob shall take for an inheritance those that took them for an inheritance" (17).

**The house of Joseph** (18) refers to the northern kingdom of Israel, which had been overthrown by Sargon in 721 B.C. In accord with the prophecies of Hos. 1:11 and Ezek. 37:16-22, Israel is to join with Judah, the southern kingdom, and together they, like a **flame** burns **stubble,** shall destroy Edom (cf. Isa. 11:13-14).

Verses 19 and 20 speak of the extent of Israel's inheritance. History recounts that during the exile of Israel the Edomites occu-

157

pied towns in **the south (19)** of Judah, the Negeb, an area south of Hebron toward the wilderness of Paran. After the Exile, **they of the south,** i.e., the men of Judah who return from exile, will possess Edom, **the mount of Esau. The plain** would be the lowlands lying west of Hebron toward the sea. **They** who possess **Ephraim, and . . . Samaria** probably refers to the men of Israel who had formerly possessed the hill country of Palestine. These conquests were accomplished in the second century B.C. when the Jews under the Maccabees pressed out into the areas indicated.

**The captivity (20)** refers to the exiles. **This host of the children of Israel** would be the Jews deported from the northern kingdom by Sargon after Samaria's fall in 721 B.C. **The Canaanites** were the Phoenicians. **Zarephath** was a city between Tyre and Sidon (see map 1), the Sarepta of Luke 4:26. **The captivity of Jerusalem** was the Jews of the Southern Kingdom taken off by Nebuchadnezzar in 586 B.C. to **Sepharad,** probably Sardis in Asia Minor.

The two main themes of the Book of Obadiah are summarized in the final verse. The prophet says that Israelite **saviours,** wise men of spiritual insight and faith, will rule over Edom, the territory once occupied by the irreligious, fleshly sons of Esau. God's plan is that the spiritual shall at last rise above the profane. **And the kingdom shall be the Lord's:** the Lord shall rule over all (Ps. 22:28; 103:19; Zech. 14:9; Rev. 11:15).

*The Book of*

# JONAH

Armor D. Peisker

# Introduction

"The Lord is merciful and gracious, slow to anger, and plenteous in mercy" (Ps. 103:8). Poignantly, succinctly, this is the message of Jonah.

To read this book is to see the world through God's eyes. All men in every land, of every color appear as persons, individual souls, each with an eternal destiny. Each is precious in God's sight, one as precious as the other.

"The book of Jonah," says W. W. Sloan, "comes closer to New Testament teachings than any other book in the Hebrew Scriptures. Its central theme is that God is interested in all people whatever their nationality or race and expects those who know him to dedicate themselves to sharing that knowledge."[1]

Never in history has the Book of Jonah had greater relevance than now. There is tremendous urgency for every Christian to feel and heed this message, to involve himself in the Church's world mission.

The message comes through to us as we watch Jonah—narrow, vindictive, nationalistic, bitterly exclusive—clutching his faith to his bosom while God seeks to get him to share it in His broader purpose of redemption. Jonah, struggling under the divine dealings, reminds us at times of the prodigal's despicable elder brother. And like the forgiving, rejoicing father, the Lord finally entreats Jonah to leave his withered gourd and sun-beaten booth to come and share the joy of the spared city. Again, Jonah reminds us of the unmerciful servant in another of Jesus' parables. We can almost hear the Lord pleading with the prophet: "O thou wicked servant, I forgave thee all that debt, because thou desiredst me: shouldest not thou also have had compassion . . . even as I had pity on thee?" (Matt. 18:32-33)

The historicity of Jonah's prophecy was not questioned until quite recently, when incredulous scholars refused to "swallow the whale." Since then other miraculous factors in the account have also come in for discussion. By some it is looked upon as a myth. Others see it as an allegory of the Exile and mission of Israel based upon Jer. 51:34. Still others look upon

[1]*A Survey of the Old Testament* (New York: Abingdon Press, 1957), p. 304.

it as a parable. But there are good reasons why we accept it as a historical narrative.

The prophet Jonah was without question a historical figure. He was a resident of Gath-hepher, the son of Amittai, and ministered as a true prophet of the Lord in the northern kingdom during the reign of Jeroboam II about 786-746 B.C. (II Kings 14:25). He was, therefore, an early contemporary of Hosea and Amos. What Jonah did after preaching in Nineveh the Bible does not relate. The tradition that he was buried in Nineveh on a site now marked by a mosque lacks historical support.

Jesus speaks of Jonah's three-day experience in the "belly of the whale," as prefiguring His own experience between His crucifixion and His resurrection. And our Lord seems to regard the repentance of the Ninevites as a historical fact. Jonah, in fact, is the only Old Testament prophet with whom Jesus compared himself and that in respect to His resurrection (Matt. 12: 39-41; Luke 11:29-32).

Jonah's mission to Nineveh with its miraculous features was not unique. It is paralleled by those of Elijah and Elisha to Sidon and Syria (I Kings 17:8-24; 19:15; II Kings 8:7-15). Nor was the perilous voyage of the Apostle Paul to Rome in New Testament times unlike Jonah's in its miraculous implications (Acts 27:1—28:14).

The Book of Jonah is in the form of a straightforward historical narrative and contains no indication that it is to be interpreted otherwise. Both Jews and Christians generally have, until the last century, regarded the book as a factual account.

As Robinson suggests: "It may be urged that the whole force of Jehovah's self-vindication to Jonah demands an actual mission to a heathen city with an actual repentance and 'sparing' of it. It is not easy to believe that the challenge, 'Should not I spare Nineveh?' was presented to the people of Israel through the inspired writer as a purely hypothetical consideration."[2]

Authorship and the dating of the Book of Jonah are uncertain. The book is about Jonah, but not necessarily by him. We have no information as to who made the record. Neither are we told when the story was first written. It would seem probable, however, that the writing occurred before the fall of the northern kingdom of Israel in 721 B.C. or at latest before the fall of Nineveh in 612 B.C. It may well be that the book was not put into its

---

[2]"Jonah," *The New Bible Commentary* (Grand Rapids, Michigan: Wm. B. Eerdmans Publishing Co., 1963), p. 714.

present form until after the latter date. This conclusion is sometimes drawn from the fact that the past tense "was" is used in describing Nineveh (3:3).

It would seem that in Jonah's lifetime Assyria (see map 1), of which Nineveh was the capital, was in a period of decline. A succession of three weak kings had lowered its prestige and power in the world. Babylon, in the lower Tigris-Euphrates valley, was again gaining strength and was a threat to be reckoned with. To the northwest, Urartu—ancient Armenia—also threatened Assyrian supremacy. Western dependencies were aware of Assyria's decline, and the success of Damascus and Arpad in resisting the Assyrian monarchs encouraged others. There resulted a succession of calamities that left the empire greatly impoverished.

It appeared to be an appropriate time for the Spirit of God to move upon the capital. The mood of the people was one of uncertainty and insecurity, which provided a ripened harvest. The Lord sought a reaper in the person of Jonah.

The importance of the circumstances is suggested by S. C. Yoder when he writes of fleeing Jonah: "Here was a man running away from an opportunity that comes perhaps once in a lifetime and more rarely yet in the history of a nation, to bring a people to repentance, and now the messenger who was called to represent God in this mission is unwilling to face the issues, whatever they may have been, and assume the responsibility which the opportunity afforded."[3]

[3]*He Gave Some Prophets* (Scottsdale, Pa.: Herald Press, 1964), pp. 80-81.

# *Outline*

I. Jonah Commissioned but Disobeys, 1:1-3

II. God Interposes, 1:4—2:10
- A. The Storm, 1:4-14
- B. Jonah Cast Overboard, 1:15-17
- C. Jonah in the Deep, 2:1-9
- D. Jonah Delivered, 2:10

III. Jonah Recommissioned and Obeys, 3:1-10
- A. The Commission, 3:1-2
- B. The Obedience, 3:3-4
- C. The Result, 3:5-10

IV. God Reasons with Jonah, 4:1-11
- A. Jonah Displeased, 4:1-3
- B. God Counsels, 4:4-9
- C. God's Concern for All, 4:10-11

# Section I Jonah Commissioned but Disobeys

Jonah 1:1-3

From II Kings 14:25 we learn that **Jonah the son of Amittai** was an experienced, trusted prophet to whom **the word of the Lord came** (1). He was a man to whom God spoke and revealed His will. We learn from the Kings passage also that he was a native of Gath-hepher in Galilee, a site later known as Cana (see map 2). This town, situated some three miles northeast of Nazareth, was most likely visited numbers of times by Jesus during His thirty years of obscurity at Nazareth. We know surely that it was here He attended a wedding feast and performed His first recorded miracle (John 2:1-11; cf. also 4:46; 21:2). The Pharisees who said to Nicodemus, "Out of Galilee ariseth no prophet" (John 7:52), must have forgotten Jonah.

At Cana, Jonah's tomb was probably pointed out to Jesus, as it was to visitors in Jerome's day. And it seems, as Robinson suggests, that "it may have been here as a youth that Jesus began to realize something of the significance of Jonah's mission and of His own."[1] (See Introduction for further comments regarding Jesus' knowledge of the prophet.)

Jonah, whose name means "dove," is said by tradition to be the shy, young prophet of II Kings 9:1-11. His father's name, Amittai, means "true"; and he is traditionally reported to have been among the 7,000 of I Kings 19:18 who did not bow to Baal.

A commission to prophesy in **Nineveh** (2) must have surprised Jonah, and he looked upon it fearfully as a most distasteful prospect. It would require an arduous overland journey of some five hundred miles (see map 1). But even worse, Nineveh was a **great city**: the metropolis of the Gentile world located on the left bank of the Tigris River some forty miles north of the Zab junction. It was the magnificent capital of the mighty Assyrian Empire, a constant and dreaded enemy of Israel. During Jehu's times Israel had been forced to pay tribute to the Assyrian king, Shalmaneser III. Jonah was also aware of the sufferings Syria had endured in repelling recent Assyrian attacks. The

[1]*Op. cit.,* p. 715

Assyrian atrocities which later terrorized the Western nations under Tiglath-pileser III may already have been practiced during Jonah's time. And Nineveh's general **wickedness, which God declared is come up before me,** was no less well-known than its might and grandeur (Nahum 3).

That God was concerned about Nineveh's wickedness indicates that from the very outset His love reached beyond the bounds of those people widely proclaimed as His chosen ones, even though they considered themselves alone within the reach of His care (2).

Jonah, overcome by fear, finally concluded that the assignment was just not for him. He felt it was indeed the command of God, but withal there were to him too many imponderables. He later confessed (4:2) that it was not physical hardship or danger that deterred him. Rather, he feared that Nineveh would indeed repent and that God would forgive and spare the city. He then would be considered a false prophet. To be so discounted by his countrymen might well have been particularly objectionable to Jonah, for it would appear that he was a popular, highly esteemed prophet in Israel. In a time of oppression he had promised prosperous days. This, as Schultz reminds us, "was most welcome. . . . Undoubtedly the fulfillment of his prediction, in the extension of Israel's territory under Jeroboam, enhanced his popularity in his homeland. There is no indication that he had a message of warning or judgment to deliver to his own people. II Kings 14:25."[2]

Furthermore, should Nineveh repent, that powerful enemy of his own nation would be spared. To his limited faith and narrow nationalism this was unbearable.

The conflict within him became so severe that he hoped to escape it by getting away from home and the surroundings where the call had come to him. So it was that he **rose up to flee . . . from the presence of the Lord** (3). He chose to go in the opposite direction from Nineveh just as far as he could, to **Tarshish,** probably Tartessus, a Phoenician colony in Spain near the Straits of Gibraltar, the most westerly point to which ships were likely to sail from Palestine. The place is also mentioned in Isa. 23:1-12 and Ezek. 27:12, 25.

[2]*The Old Testament Speaks* (New York: Harper and Brothers, 1960), p. 379.

To understand Jonah's point of view, "it is necessary," G. Campbell Morgan tells us, "to remember the national prejudice of the Hebrews against all other people in the matter of religion. Believing in Jehovah as a loving God, they yet thought of Him as their God exclusively. The charge to deliver a message to a city outside the covenant, and one moreover which was the center of a power which had been oppressive and cruel, must have been a startling one to Jonah."[3]

From our vantage point it is easy, certainly, to censure Jonah. Surely, we say, a man of his position and experience should have known better. It may give us more sympathy and understanding, however, if we recall that centuries later, even after the blazing light of Pentecost, the outstanding Jewish apostle of our Lord, Simon Peter, had a similar period of bewilderment. Peter had preached so powerfully at Jerusalem that multitudes of his fellow Jews had believed in Christ. Yet when, during an especially intimate period of prayer, he was instructed by the Lord himself to preach the gospel to the Gentiles, he was adamant against it. "Not so, Lord," he said. It took a special revelation and some almost miraculous, providential circumstances to get this apostle to fulfill his appointment at Cornelius' house (Acts 10). Also, the whole Book of Galatians reflects the struggle among early Christians before the Gentiles were admitted into the Church on equal terms with the Hebrews.

There is need for each of us even now to consider his own life in the light of these events. As one has written: "Every man of us is either in the caravan to Nineveh or on the boat to Tarshish . . . going God's way or his own. . . . Some of us go to Tarshish religiously. We sing and pray while going our own way and straight across the grain of God's way for us."

Jonah apparently left his hometown in Galilee and made his way west and south to the seaport city of Joppa (see map 2), the only good port on Palestine's Mediterranean coast. Here it was that some eight centuries later the Lord spoke to the Apostle Peter about preaching to Gentiles (Acts 10). Here Jonah **found a ship going to Tarshish: so he paid the fare thereof, and went down into it.** Seeking to rationalize his action, the runaway prophet may have concluded his findings to be providential.

[3]*The Analyzed Bible* (New York: Fleming H. Revell Co., 1908), p. 212.

Here was a ship bound for the place he wanted to go, and he had the money for a ticket! This was not, however, a situation arranged by divine providence. God never encourages disobedience. It was rather a temptation of which Satan took advantage.

When Jonah paid his shekels to the purser, he little realized the full cost of this trip. He had been unwilling to pay the price to go to Nineveh, but the Tarshish journey proved far more costly. The way of disobedience is always most expensive. To serve God may cost us dear, but not to serve Him is the utmost in reckless extravagance.

Jonah 1:4—2:10

## A. THE STORM, 1:4-14

God does not withdraw His call nor change His purposes for men (Rom. 11:29), nor does He easily turn His called ones over to disobedience. He seeks by all possible means to bring them around to walk in His way. In the case of Jonah, He "who hath gathered the winds in his fists" (Prov. 30:4) **sent** (lit. "flung") **a great wind into the sea** (4), so that there **was a mighty tempest** which threatened to break the ship to pieces.

Rough weather was nothing new to seamen of the Mediterranean, but the sudden gale was so severe that **the mariners** (lit., "salts," experienced seamen) **were afraid** (5). In mortal terror, they each prayed desperately to his own god. Things looked so hopeless that they were panic-stricken. They began throwing overboard equipment and perhaps even cargo in order to lighten the ship so that it would ride higher. Jonah, meanwhile, had **gone down into the sides of the ship** (the hold of the vessel), where he **was fast asleep** and snoring (Septuagint).

The snoring apparently called the shipmaster's attention to the suspicious passenger. He awakened Jonah, saying, **What meanest thou, O sleeper? arise** (6). The term here rendered **sleeper** refers to one in a deep sleep, a sleep of unconcern (cf. Rom. 11:8). The captain demanded to know why Jonah was sound asleep in such an extreme hour. He besought him: "Get up and cry to your God, and see if he will have mercy on us and save us!" (*Living Prophecies*) The word used here for **God** is the generic name applied to all divine beings. It is the Old Testament word which refers also to imaginary deities as "the gods of the nations." This use would reflect the religious understanding of the sailors, not Jonah's concept of God.

Feeling that this was no ordinary storm, the sailors were determined to find the reason for it. They said, therefore, **Let us cast lots, that we may know for whose cause this evil is upon us. . . . The lot fell upon Jonah** (7). The casting of lots was a common means among the ancients for deciding uncertain issues (Num. 26:55; Josh. 7:14; I Sam. 10:20-21; Acts 1:26).

Upon the sailors' inquiry, Jonah identified himself as a **Hebrew** who feared Jehovah, **the God of heaven, which hath made the sea and the dry land** (9). All Scripture bears out the fact that God is the Creator of the heavens, seas, and land (cf. Ps. 8:1-4; 65:5-7; 107:23-32; 139; 7:12; Mark 4:35-51). Jonah also acknowledged his guilt. The sailors, convinced of the greatness of Jonah's God, were astonished at how he could be false to Him. They asked: **Why hast thou done this?** (10): "What is this you have done!" (RSV) It is probable that Jonah now began to realize something of the enormity of what he was doing. The rebuke of the ungodly men may well have added to his condemnation and remorse.

Convinced that the storm was a divine judgment upon himself, the prophet saw that his sin had involved and endangered others. This increased the conviction upon him. Without hope of escaping judgment, he was willing to be thrown overboard and drown, if this would but save the lives of his shipmates (11-12).

In a very real sense Jonah became their sacrifice. "There is [in our Lord's death] a spiritual parallel to the picture of Jonah cast into the sea, as well as a spiritual contrast. The fiercest of tempests is that of the wrath of God against sin; *that* storm gathered about the Person of our Lord and could only be stilled by His death on the cross. Jonah's experience was terrible, but only the Lord Jesus Christ Himself completely experienced the words of Jonah's prayer, 'All thy billows and thy waves passed over me' 2:3b."[1]

It is possible that other boats were endangered by the storm which Jonah's sin provoked. Sin always hurts others—oftentimes many others—besides the actual offender.

Jonah's experience here is striking proof that God is inescapable—a fact proclaimed in Ps. 139:7-10. The disobedient prophet had gone to sleep thinking he had successfully escaped from the Lord. He did not realize that God was indeed present and was at work to frustrate his self-determined plans.

The seamen **rowed hard** (13) to bring the vessel to safety and spare Jonah. When they could not, they themselves prayed to the prophet's God lest He hold them responsible for Jonah's death. They cried out: "Oh Jehovah, don't make us die for this

[1]Leon J. Davis, *Bible Knowledge*, edited by Henry Jacobsen (Wheaton, Ill.: Scripture Press, 1956), V, 355.

man's sin; and don't hold us responsible for his death, for it is not our fault—You have sent this storm upon him for your own good reasons" (14, *Living Prophecies*). It is interesting to observe here that the sailors no longer spoke of Jonah's God with the common generic term, but rather as the **Lord,** Jehovah, the only true and living God.

## B. JONAH CAST OVERBOARD, 1: 15-17

Despairing of saving themselves in any other way, the sailors reluctantly followed Jonah's suggestion. They picked him up and **cast him forth into the sea (15).**

The waters immediately quieted. The phrase rendered **ceased from her raging** can be translated, "The sea stood from its anger." The storm stopped so suddenly that the sailors were awed before the Lord. The witness of the prophet and the miraculous manifestations of God's power filled their hearts with fear and reverence. They worshiped before Jehovah (15-16). So it was that Jonah became a missionary in spite of his first failure. So it was that God's judgment upon the disobedient prophet revealed to the heathen sailors His compassionate concern (Ps. 76:10). So it was in these sailors that Jonah "sees heathen turned to the fear of the Lord. All that he has fled to avoid happens before his eyes and through his own mediation."[2]

In an act of merciful discipline **the Lord had prepared** (appointed, RSV; commanded, LXX) **a great fish to swallow up Jonah** (17). We are not told what kind of fish it was. Nor does the fact that Matt. 12:40 speaks of "a whale" help us much, for the Greek word used there literally means "a huge fish" or sea monster.

It is interesting to observe, however, that J. D. Wilson recounts a modern analogy to Jonah's experience. He tells of an incident in which a sperm whale near the Falkland Islands swallowed a ship's crew member, who was rescued three days later, revived from unconsciousness, and subsequently lived in good health.[3]

The prophet remained inside the fish for **three days and three nights.** This expression of time appears to be a colloquial term implying simply an indefinite, short period, as in Josh. 2:16.

[2]G. A. Smith, *op. cit.,* II, 508.
[3]*Princeton Theological Review,* XXV (1927), 636.

Jesus used it in this sense in Matt. 12:40, since the New Testament repeatedly declares that His resurrection took place on "the third day" (Matt. 16:21; Mark 9:31; Luke 9:22; I Cor. 15:4).

In Jonah's "Flight from Duty" we see that: (1) Flight from duty is not a flight from God's control, 1:4; (2) Favorable circumstances in flight do not provide excuse, 1:3; (3) Flight from God and duty is more expensive than obedience—in bitter experience, in moral loss, 1:15.

### C. JONAH IN THE DEEP, 2:1-9

This passage, composed after the prophet's release from the fish, records how he **prayed unto the Lord his God out of the fish's belly** (1). It is written in poetic form. Although it includes a confession of sin and a promise to obey God, it is largely a psalm of praise and adoration for divine deliverance from death by drowning in the depths of the sea.

The fact that Jonah prayed in such an unlikely place and received an answer reminds us that we can make anyplace—anyplace at all—a chapel. Prayer and praise are nowhere amiss.

Out of Jonah's **affliction,** his anguish of spirit, his distress of body and mind, he **cried . . . unto the Lord** (2). Effective calling upon God is not necessarily with the voice, but with the heart. **The belly of hell** would be the innermost part of Sheol or the depths, the region of darkness and death, the grave. The deep waters were as a grave to him who was counted as among the dead (cf. Ps. 88:3-12). Various of the psalms begin in a similar strain, for example: Ps. 18:5; 120:1; 142:1. Lam. 3:55-58 also speaks of prayer during deep distress.

The prophet graphically rehearses the horrors of his frightening experience as he sank "deep, into the heart of his seas" (3, RSV; cf. Ps. 42:7-9). But he begins this rehearsal by acknowledging that he did not come to such extremities by chance. All came to him by God's own action. He acknowledged to the Lord, **Thou hadst cast me into the deep** (3a). It should encourage us to realize that all things—even afflictions and distresses—come either by the direct moving of God or by His permissive will. He has a design in them for us, a design which holds future good for us and glory for himself.

> *Oft the cloud which wraps the present hour*
> *Serves but to brighten all our future days.*

Jonah had booked passage to Tarshish purposely to get away from God's presence. But in the face of death, he was of a different mind (4). Part of his fears arose from the very fact that he knew he was indeed out of God's sight, out of His will, and out of His favor. He declared, "I am cast out of thy presence" (LXX). This rendering suggests that he despaired of ever looking again toward the Temple, which symbolized to a pious Jew the very presence of God: "Shall I indeed look again toward the holy temple?" The KJV suggests repentance and a sincere purpose to again worship God wholeheartedly: **I am cast out of thy sight; yet I will look again toward thy holy temple.** The Berkeley translation implies even more. Jonah declares, "I have been driven away from Thine eyes," but he seems to have had faith that he would be delivered, for he proclaims, "I shall again behold Thy holy temple."

Which of these translations more exactly expresses the prophet's feeling in the watery deep we cannot know. But from any of them it is clear that Jonah had changed his mind and regretted running from the divine call. "God's presence, which once he regarded as a burden, and from which he desired to escape, now that he has got his desire, he feels it to be his bitterest sorrow to be deprived of. He had turned his back on God, so God turned His back on him, making his sin his punishment."[4]

How desperate his plight was! "Waters encompassed me, threatening my life," he said; "Seaweed was wrapped around my head" (5, Berk.; cf. Ps. 69:2). He utterly despaired. "I sank to the very roots of the mountains, to a land where bars shut behind me for ever" (6, Moffatt). But he rejoices that God in His mercy delivered him: **yet hast thou brought up my life from corruption, O Lord my God** (6). This testimony has a striking parallel in Ps. 16:10, quoted by Peter in Acts 2:27.

The Septuagint gives a glimpse of the anguished penitence which filled Jonah's heart: "Yet, O Lord my God, let my ruined life be restored" (6c). The backslider may take courage. The waves of evil desire have engulfed him. But if he, like Jonah, will humble himself, turn from sin to God, from disobedience to obedience, he may be assured God will again come to him. His ruined life also can be restored.

[4]A. R. Fausset, *A Commentary on the Old and New Testaments* (Grand Rapids, Michigan: Wm. B. Eerdmans Publishing Co. [reprint], 1948), IV, 576.

**When my soul fainted within me** (7) may mean that the prophet passed into unconsciousness. Then reviving, instinctively he prayed (cf. Ps. 139:18). Now he is grateful that God answered that prayer. He is mindful that to follow after anything apart from God is to **observe lying vanities** (8) or idols. They cannot perform what they promise and they only separate the soul from God, our Source of mercy. Many a man has made a god out of intellect, pride, ambition, covetousness, or self-will. Jonah would warn us: "Those who revere worthless idols give up the grace that might be theirs" (8, Berk.). The RSV translates it, "Those who pay regard to vain idols forsake their true loyalty." Jonah, who had set up an idol of self-will, tore it from his heart and promised henceforth to worship and obey only Jehovah, for in Him alone is **salvation** (9).

From the experience of Jonah recorded here we may learn a great deal about "Effectual Prayer": (1) *When* to pray, 1; (2) *Where* to pray, 2-6; (3) To *whom* to pray, 7-8; and (4) For *what* to pray, 9.

### D. JONAH DELIVERED, 2:10

Following Jonah's confession of sin and his recognition of God as his only means of deliverance and salvation, **the Lord spake unto the fish, and it vomited out Jonah upon the dry land.** Just where the prophet was released we are not told, but he was now free again to do God's work. He had learned the hard way that to flee from God's will through a desire to avoid difficult tasks always involves us in even greater difficulties.

By this experience in the sea Jonah became "the prophet of Christ, not in words, but in personal sufferings, the typical significance of which, though probably unknown to himself (I Pet. 1:10-12), is revealed to us by the Holy Spirit. His passing from the ship into the dark though living tomb, and thence into the light again after three days, sets forth the Lord's descent from the cross of wood into the dark sepulchre, and His ascent thence into life again after the same number of days, more vividly than if he had foretold the same in words."[5] Matt. 12:38-41 should be considered in this connection. It indicates that the only sign God gives to the sinful world is the resurrection of

---

[5] A. R. Fausset, *op. cit.*, IV, 578.

Jesus Christ from the dead (cf. Rom. 4:25; I Corinthians 15; I Thess. 4:14).

The whole episode of Jonah in the sea and the stomach of the fish, as related in this chapter, seems to some people so utterly incredible that they do not accept the account as history (see Introduction). There is no question but that God's discipline, preservation, and restoration of Jonah was a miracle. But if one recognizes God as the Creator and Sustainer of the universe, His intervention by a miracle is to be expected. Indeed, "Miracles themselves were a part of redemptive revelation. Through them the true God of heaven and earth manifested His superiority over the gods of the nations and His full control over His creation."[6]

The Bible relates many incidents—even events vital to our salvation—which cannot be explained by human philosophy and science. Read without faith, the whole message of God's Word is lost. But if we through faith grant what the Bible teaches about the postulates of creation, providence, sin, and salvation, miracles become a veritable necessity, a necessity of grace.

But among those who accept the Book of Jonah as history, some become so intent upon the details of the unique fish story that they miss the real message God has intended to convey. To avoid this we need to keep in mind that the major purpose of miracles as related in the Bible is not just a display of power to prove the existence of God. Rather, their purpose is to show the attitude of God toward men and to indicate the consequent response men should make to God. Gillett has said, "As religious phenomena, miracles are not to be viewed as proof of God; but as revelations about God."[7]

---

[6]E. J. Young, *Christianity Today*, "Jonah," Sept. 28, 1959, p. 12.

[7]*A New Standard Bible Dictionary*, edited by Jacobus, Lane, Zenos, and Cook (New York: Funk and Wagnalls Co., 1936), p. 582.

# Section III *Jonah Recommissioned and Obeys*

Jonah 3:1-10

## A. THE COMMISSION, 3:1-2

With mercy toward His prophet and with determination to accomplish His purpose toward Nineveh, **the Lord came unto Jonah the second time** (1). The chastened, penitent prophet was given a second chance. Jesus' parable recorded in Matt. 21:28-31 is apropos here.

A New Testament parallel is found in the experience of Peter. The apostle's first commission is recorded in Mark 1:16-17 and Luke 5:10. After his failure and restoration, he was recommissioned as recorded in John 21:15-17. Most of us praise God for the fact that we were allowed to hear the call of God more than once.

Christian brethren are frequently not so considerate toward each other as the Lord is toward those who fail. Even Paul shrank from permitting John Mark to accompany him on a second missionary journey after the young man failed on the first trip (Acts 15:36-40). It is to the apostle's credit, however, that he later recognized Mark's true worth and earnestly desired his help (II Tim. 4:11).

The Heavenly Father longs to be gracious and ever deals with His difficult children in whatever way is most likely to obtain their obedience and trust. The writer to the Hebrews speaks of God's chastening (12:7-12), and encourages those who might be hopeless: "Wherefore lift up the hands which hang down, and the feeble knees." Nevertheless, God continues to call us back to begin again at the places of our failures. The command to Jonah was still, **Arise, go unto Nineveh . . . and preach unto it the preaching that I bid thee** (2).

Jonah had been forgiven of God, but he must take up his cross where he laid it down. There is no alternate Tarshish of human proposal for Nineveh, nor is there any substitute service for that which God asks us to perform in making known His saving grace to others. This is emphasized by the Septuagint rendering: "Preach in it according to the former preaching which I spoke to thee of."

To maintain God's restored favor and blessing, we must face up to the same issue we sought to escape. God is tender, understanding, patient, and forgiving; but He is also firm. Samuel's admonition to Saul is always true: "To obey is better than sacrifice, and to hearken than the fat of rams" (I Sam. 15:22).

God's insistence upon Jonah's going to Nineveh speaks to us who are parents. We sometimes correct and discipline our children, only to let them go on and please themselves afterwards. The results of discipline are thereby lost. Punishment brings its God-intended result when it is administered so as to produce obedience.

### B. The Obedience, 3:3-4

It would seem that Jonah's inward feelings toward the Ninevites had not changed greatly. However, the disciplines through which he had passed convinced him that it was impossible to escape God's mandate. **So Jonah arose, and went unto Nineveh, according to the word of the Lord** (3).

Nineveh is referred to as **an exceeding great city of three days' journey**. The inner city walls, according to ruins examined by archaeologists, were only some eight miles in circumference. The author doubtless had in mind here the populous administrative district of Nineveh, which was some thirty to sixty miles across. The Greek historians Ktesias and Diorus claim that Nineveh had a circumference of 480 stadia, a little over 60 miles. The meaning of the text is clarified in the paraphrase: "Now Nineveh was a very large city with extensive suburbs—so large that it would take three days to walk around it" (*Living Prophecies*).

A footnote in the ASV calls attention to the fact that **exceeding great city** is literally "a city great unto God." This is a common Hebrew form of expressing the superlative. But the phrase suggests another thought. Jonah and the Israelites, who considered themselves the specially elect of God, saw Nineveh as a wicked heathen city to be hated and destroyed. The city was, however, "great unto the Lord," an object of His compassionate concern. It is true, the Ninevites were vile, idolatrous, and merciless; but God yearned for their salvation and regeneration. The Lord is not interested in exterminating evil men, but in changing

**177**

them into God-fearing, upright persons. He meets man's sin with offers of salvation. He will have recourse to retribution only when the offer of His grace has been rejected.

God's redemptive concern reaches to all men. As Purkiser has pointed out: "The door of salvation has been opened to all who will enter in. Not only does the Book of Jonah speak against racial exclusiveness; it also protests against any sort of theology which would limit salvation to an elect few chosen by God in such a way as to shut out all others not so chosen. The Bible joyfully proclaims to all men everywhere that God has elected to salvation all who savingly believe on the Lord Jesus Christ. He has predestined to eternal life all who accept the provisions made beforehand for their redemption. If any are excluded, it is because of their unbelief and disobedience rather than because of a sovereign decree of God. No one dares whittle down the gospel which declares that 'God so loved the world, that he gave his only begotten Son, that whosoever believeth in him should not perish, but have everlasting life' (John 3:16)." [1]

**A day's journey** (4) here probably refers to the length of time which Jonah spent in preaching rather than the distance traveled. He doubtless stopped at various vantage places to proclaim God's message, the purpose being to reach the greatest number of people rather than to cover the greatest possible distance.

Jonah may earlier have been a disobedient prophet, and even as he made his way through Nineveh he may have been reluctant, but he was never a false prophet. He preached God's word just as it had been given to him: **Yet forty days, and Nineveh shall be overthrown.**

This kind of faithfulness must characterize every worthy servant of God. We must beware how we try to recast God's message to fit our hearers. Some instructors would tell us that we should not preach of divine judgment, as did Jonah, lest we frighten our hearers, and so add to their guilt complex. Too often, however, our hearers are actually guilty and need to repent. The Ninevites were moved Godward through fear. And we read that it was through fear that Noah prepared an ark for the safety of himself and his family (Heb. 11:7).

[1]*Aldersgate Biblical Series,* "Jonah" (Winona Lake, Ind.: Light and Life Press, 1963), pp. 25-26.

In our preaching or teaching relative to God's judgment we need to be sure, however, that we avoid Jonah's spirit of retaliation. He unconsciously joined his own passions to the divine threatenings. We need always to preach about God's judgment with the compassion manifest by Jesus when He wept over the doomed city of Jerusalem (Matt. 23:37-39). It is too easy to be like the preacher who, although he was scriptural in presenting God's warning against sinners, acted as though he were glad his hearers were on their way to hell. Adam Clarke writes, "He who in denouncing the word of God against sinners, joins his own passions with the divine threatenings is a cruel and bad man and should not be an overseer in God's house."[2]

The forty-day delay in divine judgment upon Nineveh gave the people time to repent. Had sudden destruction been proclaimed, they might well have been so confounded and terrorized that they could not have weighed the issues at hand.

Jonah by his presence and preaching was a sign to the Ninevites (Luke 11:30). In this we see "What God Can Reveal Through a Man." (1) He was a sign of God's mercy toward men: in forgiving sin, in restoring a backslider, and in reinstating a runaway prophet. (2) He was a sign of God's inflexible justice toward men: God's servants must be disciplined and corrected; the city must forsake its sin. (3) He was a sign of God's unchanging purpose toward men: God's plans are made in wisdom, not subject to caprice of men; pleas and excuses are vain. God gives work for all to do, and expects it to be done.

C. THE RESULT, 3:5-10

Jonah could not but have been impressed by the marvel that was Nineveh. The inner city was surrounded by a wall 100 feet thick, wide enough for 3 chariots to drive abreast upon it. The walls had 1,500 towers 100 feet in height. Colossal lions and bulls carved out of stone guarded its 27 gates. Lovely gardens surrounded the public buildings, which were ornamented with alabaster and sculptured figures. Fields of growing crops were maintained within the city proper to save the inhabitants from famine in case of siege. Notwithstanding, in Jonah's day Assyria's national fortunes were at a low state (see Introduc-

[2]*A Commentary and Critical Notes* (New York: Mason and Lane, 1837), IV, 707.

tion). The depression prevailing might well have contributed to the willingness of the people to listen to the Hebrew prophet.

The Assyrians probably did not fully comprehend that Jehovah, whom Jonah represented, was the only true and living God, for they worshiped many gods. But they feared lest they should offend the God of this prophet. The situation was comparable to that which Paul encountered at Athens when he spoke of the altar to the "unknown god" (Acts 17:22-31). There seems, nevertheless, to have been some recognition that Jonah's God was indeed the Lord God. The modern translations (RSV, Berk., *et al.*) agree with KJV in capitalizing the word where used by the Ninevites. In their pagan darkness and corruption, these people **believed God** and called upon His name. In deep contrition for their evil ways, they **proclaimed a fast, and put on sackcloth, from the greatest of them even to the least of them** (5).

Sackcloth was a coarse fabric made of goats' hair. Throughout the Semitic world garments of this material were worn as a sign of mourning: mourning for the dead, sorrowing over personal or national disaster, grieving over sins for which deliverance was being sought (cf. I Kings 20:31; Isa. 15:3; Jer. 49:3; Ezek. 27:31).

The desperation wrought among the Ninevites by Jonah's preaching is evidenced by the extreme decree proclaimed by **the king and his nobles** (7). They repented thoroughly, and they did so in hope with faith. **Who can tell,** the king declared, **if God will turn and repent, and turn away from his fierce anger, that we perish not?** (9) To declare that God might **repent** means that, if His warnings are heeded, God might alter His present course of action. The significance of the passage is clear from the rendering, "Who can tell, God may turn and revoke His sentence against us (when we have met His terms) and turn from His fierce anger, so that we perish not?" (Amp. OT; cf. Num. 23:19; Jer. 18:6-10; Joel 2:13-14).

With mercy **God** listened to the cry of the praying Ninevites and He **saw** that **their works** showed the sincerity of their repentance, for **they turned from their evil way** (cf. Matt. 3:8); Jas. 2:18). Repentance done with hope and faith always brings God's attention. **And God repented of the evil, that he had said that he would do unto them; and he did it not** (10). **Evil** as here used in connection with the work of God refers to the judgment which was to come upon the people for their disobedience. The

Old Testament on several other occasions speaks of God repenting or changing His mind. God is unchanging in His ultimate purpose for mankind, and He is unchanging in His nature. But as men change in their response to Him, it becomes necessary for Him to change His methods in dealing with them. He must in such cases take a different course of action to be true to His unalterable purpose and nature.

The Ninevites did not always continue in the fear of the Lord; Nahum and Zephaniah (2:13-15) prophesied against the city and predicted its fall, which actually occurred at the hands of the Babylonians and the Medes in 612 B.C.

God's forgiving grace toward the repenting Ninevites reminds us that He calls all men to repentance and promises His grace to all who will do so. "Come now, and let us reason together, saith the Lord: though your sins be as scarlet, they shall be as white as snow; though they be red like crimson, they shall be as wool" (Isa. 1:18). This call to repent and the assurance of forgiveness is indeed at the very heart of the Christian message. Jesus declared: "I came not to call the righteous, but sinners to repentance" (Luke 5:32). And again on the Emmaus road, He said, "Thus it is written, and thus it behoved Christ to suffer, and to rise from the dead the third day: and that repentance and remission of sins should be preached in his name among all nations, beginning at Jerusalem" (Luke 24:46-47).

The repentance of the Ninevites brings us face-to-face with our own responsibility toward the gospel of Christ. Jesus declared to the people of His day: "The men of Nineveh shall rise up in judgment with this generation, and shall condemn it: because they repented at the preaching of Jonas; and, behold, a greater than Jonas is here" (Matt. 12:41). Still today the measure of light and opportunity determines our responsibility. Jesus' words are all the more searching for us because our light and opportunity are even greater than of those in the first century.

Jonah's preaching was divine in its content; He spoke as an **oracle of God** (I Pet. 4:11). That preaching was in serious earnestness and it was practical in its aim—to move the hearts of men. The prophet's message brought desired results—penitent Nineveh illustrates the power of God to move even the most **unlikely** people.

## A. JONAH DISPLEASED, 4:1-3

Jonah's self-esteem and nationalism made him unwilling to accept God's merciful intentions for a repentant people. They caused him to resent deeply the forgiveness shown toward Nineveh. To see thousands of Israel's enemies seeking God actually enraged him.

From his low point of view all he could see was that his prediction was proved false and Israel's national enemy would be spared. He was **displeased . . . exceedingly, and he was very angry** (1). Literally: "It was evil to Jonah" and "it [displeasure] burned to him."

The prophet felt that if Assyria, the predicted destroyer of Israel (Hos. 9:3; 11:5, 11; Amos 5:27), were destroyed as he had prophesied, Israel would be relieved of her greatest danger. She would be free from heavy tribute, and would then be able to develop into a stronger and more influential nation. Now it seemed that, through the salvation of Israel's enemies, Jonah was announcing the destruction of his own people.

But Israel could not have been spared simply by the destruction of Nineveh. Her own sins were destroying her (cf. Matt. 7:4-5).

In spite of his bad spirit, Jonah considered himself to be a faithful believer and **he prayed unto the Lord** (2). It is sadly true that it is not uncommon for those who observe the forms of piety and count themselves as believers to manifest unkind attitudes and reject God's will.

"Some persons suppose that the gifts of prophecy and working miracles are the highest that can be conferred on man; but they are widely mistaken, for these gifts change not the heart. Jonah had the gift of prophecy, but had not received that grace which destroys the old man and creates the soul anew in Christ Jesus. This is the love of which St. Paul speaks, which if a man have not, though he had the gift of prophecy, and could miraculously remove mountains, yet in the sight of God, and for any good himself might reap from it, it would be as sounding brass and a tinkling cymbal."[1]

[1]Adam Clarke, *op. cit.*, p. 708.

The petulant prophet blamed the Lord, not only for sparing the enemy capital, but for his own personal, disobedient flight to Tarshish. He dared to say: **I fled ... for I knew that thou art a gracious God ... and repentest thee of the evil** (2). Thus he defended his own failure by blaming God's loving-kindness. He might well have had in mind Exod. 34:6 (cf. Joel 2:13).

Jonah felt personally discredited and humiliated. Overcome with self-pity, he wanted to die rather than face the embarrassment of being a laughingstock among his own people when he returned home. He felt sure that they would judge him by the result of his prophecy. He prayed therefore: **O Lord, take, I beseech thee, my life from me; for it is better for me to die than to live** (3). His reputation and prestige among narrow-minded friends and fellow countrymen were of more importance to him than the preservation of thousands of innocent people.

Elijah, on one occasion, when he saw the unfavorable outcome of events in which he was involved, also asked that he might die (I Kings 19:4). He was, however, jealous *for* God and distressed because so few sought God. Jonah, on the other hand, was jealous *of* God and distressed because so many people sought Him (cf. Num. 11:15; Job 6:8-9).

Shortly before (2:6), the prophet was full of joy and gratitude over the preservation of his life. At that time he spoke eloquently of God's mercy. Now he despises life because that same divine mercy has been shown to others. It is tragically true that men often do not realize of what spirit they are (cf. Luke 9:55). Jonah's angry displeasure showed a lack of self-control, a lack of reverence toward God, and a lack of love for men.

How different was the attitude of Paul toward life and death! He had a desire "to depart, and to be with Christ," but he was also willing to live, if by living he could be used of the Lord to extend His mercy to others. While death would be gain to him personally, living would be to the greater honor of Christ (Phil. 1:20-26).

## B. God Counsels, 4:4-9

God, who had rescued Jonah from death in a time of flagrant disobedience, now reasoned with him in his displeased, angry state of mind. **Doest thou well to be angry?** (1; cf. Jas. 1:20). The question was really: Why was Jonah angry? What ground did he have for it? The Lord was displeased with the prophet's attitude, but He did not openly rebuke him. Instead, He tried to present the situation so that Jonah would see for himself how childishly he was conducting himself and so come to change his attitude.

"What the Lord says to Jonah, He says to all who in their office of the cure of souls are angry. . . . If they are angry, not with men but with sins of men, if they hate and persecute, not men but the vices of men, they are rightly angry, their zeal is good. But if they are angry, not with sins but with men, if they hate, not vices but men, they are angered amiss, their zeal is bad."[2]

Whether Jonah's conscience was awakened to secretly acknowledge his wrong attitude, we are not told; but it would seem that he was not deeply affected. Still sulking, he went a safe distance outside the city to see what would happen. He seemed to be hoping against hope that, even though the forty days were now past, the city might yet be destroyed. So he built himself a **booth (5)** or shelter of branches and leaves and sat down to watch.

Having spoken verbally, the Lord now used some "visual aids" to reach the slow-to-learn prophet. First He provided further shade against the sun's heat by preparing a **gourd, and made it to come up over Jonah . . . So Jonah was exceeding glad of the gourd (6).** God knows how often our discouragements and shortcomings are due to physical weariness; and in His mercy He provides relief for us (cf. I Kings 19:1-8; Ps. 103:13-14). The exact nature of the plant which God gave Jonah is not clear from the Hebrew term, but it is commonly thought to have been either a castor oil plant or a variety of melon. Its miraculous speed of growth is another evidence of God's care for this reluctant prophet.

Jonah was glad for the gourd. But gladness is not necessarily gratitude; and it would seem that Jonah lacked this. His gladness was entirely selfish and sensual. He was glad for the gift, but he had no thought for the Giver. When the gift was gone, he was angry and complained to God.

Carrying the object lesson still further, **God prepared a worm . . . and it smote the gourd that it withered (7).** The boughs of the prophet's booth were probably wilted by this time too, so

---

[2]E. P. Pusey, *The Minor Prophets* (Grand Rapids, Michigan: Baker Book House, 1963), I, 423.

that he was left quite at the mercy of the sun's beating rays. To impress Jonah still more, **when the sun did arise . . . God prepared a vehement east wind; and the sun beat on the head of Jonah, that he fainted, and wished** (Heb., requested) **in himself to die (8).** The wind referred to may well have been the sirocco, which brings both scorching heat and suffocating dust from the desert and makes life miserable, even indoors.

Jonah's mental and spiritual frustration was now augmented by further physical distress. The Lord again spoke to the prophet, who continued selfish and unfeeling, angry and unbending. In his preoccupation with himself he did not get the point that God was trying to show him. If he regretted the destruction of a mere plant which shaded only him, should he not much more regret the destruction of a whole city?

## C. GOD'S CONCERN FOR ALL, 4:10-11

When the Lord spoke to Jonah, He explained what He had been demonstrating, reasoning from a lesser case to a greater. He said: **Thou hast had pity on the gourd, for the which thou hast not laboured . . . which came up in a night, and perished in a night . . . should not I spare Nineveh, that great city, wherein are more than sixscore thousand persons that cannot discern between their right hand and their left hand; and also much cattle? (10-11)**

There is varying opinion as to how to interpret the statement regarding the city's population. Some scholars understand the 120,000 people mentioned to refer only to small children, and so place the total population at some 600,000. Others, however, understand the 120,000 to refer to people who were ignorant of God's moral law (see similar terminology in Deut. 5:32; Josh. 1:7; etc.). If this is the case, 120,000 would represent the total population. Be that as it may, God expresses His concern for the suffering of those who cannot help themselves.

The Lord was attempting to show Jonah just how blind his religious exclusiveness had made him. He was saying to him: You had nothing to do with the origin or growth of the short-lived gourd, but you grieve over its destruction. You are displeased at the loss of the transient plant which was for the temporary enjoyment of only one individual and over which you had no control. Should I not much more pity a great and ancient city filled with immortal souls of whose being I am the Author and of whose lives I am the Preserver?

This passage linked with Luke 19:41 helps us to see God's attitude toward cities. We know they are the centers of crime and iniquity. Cities are centers of poverty and degradation. But God loves them. He yearns over them. This seems particularly relevant in view of the continued urbanization of our world. Perhaps the tendency of the evangelical Church to shun the city and seek the suburbs is not in keeping with the compassionate concern of our Lord. G. Campbell Morgan wrote: "God has not forsaken the city. He is still sending His prophets, His messengers, His Son. Moreover, He is, by His Holy Spirit, the actual and ever-present force for the relieving of every condition of evil and sorrow. No problem is too complex for His wisdom, no opposing force too mighty for His power, no darkness too dense for His light, no trifle too trivial for His notice. He is working for its regeneration. What, then, is the responsibility of the city? What does the Church of Christ exist for? For the select few who today worship within the buildings called by His name? Then in God's name close the doors! Such churches have no mission, and should cease to exist. The Church of Christ exists to reveal God and to act in concert with Him."[3]

Most of us at times are inclined, like Jonah, to overvalue the less important things of life, those which are temporal. We are also inclined, even when thinking about spiritual things, to do so in their relation to ourselves, our loved ones, our friends, our social group. But God's concern, which includes both the temporal and the spiritual, reaches out to the last person in all the world. It is not the will of our Father "that any should perish" (II Pet. 3:9).

The knowledge of this divine attitude prompted Paul to cry out: "O the depth of the riches both of the wisdom and knowledge of God! how unsearchable are his judgments, and his ways past finding out!" (Rom. 11:33) A more recent poet has written:

> ... the love of God is broader
> Than the measure of man's mind;
> And the heart of the Eternal
> Is most wonderfully kind (F. W. Faber).

[3]"Jonah," *Biblical Illustrator,* ed. J. S. Exell (New York: Fleming H. Revell Co.), p. 80.

**H. RAY DUNNING**

Chairman, Department of Philosophy and Professor of Philosophy and Biblical Literature, Trevecca Nazarene College, Nashville, Tennessee. A.B., Trevecca Nazarene College; B.D., Nazarene Theological Seminary; M.A., Vanderbilt University.

**WILLIAM M. GREATHOUSE**

President and Professor of Biblical Theology, Trevecca Nazarene College, Nashville, Tennessee. A.B., Lambuth College; Th.B., D.D., Trevecca Nazarene College; M.A. in Theology, Vanderbilt University Divinity School. Additional graduate studies at Vanderbilt University.

God's love constrained the apostle to leave his all that he might be an ambassador for the King of Love (Phil. 3:8). He would fully agree with the words recently written by S. C. Yoder: "To have been an effective preacher in Jonah's time, in the early church, the middle ages, or in modern times, one like Jonah must die to the lusts, the attractions, allurements, emoluments, and rewards which man has to offer and be content with the compensations that God has to give."[4]

The love of God in our hearts will constrain us to that full commitment which God sought from Jonah and which He received so joyfully from Paul. It will attune our ears to His voice so that we shall hear God's call to a worldwide witness to His salvation. We shall hear His call to a solemn, sacred stewardship of life and possessions. Our measure of response to God's call is, in fact, the measure of our love for Him.

---

[4]*He Gave Some Prophets* (Scottdale, Pa.: Herald Press, 1964), p. 82.

*The Book of*

# MICAH

**Armor D. Peisker**

# Introduction

The people to whom Micah prophesied were deeply religious. They attended well-programmed, colorful services in a magnificent Temple. Their activities included observance of divinely appointed holy days intended to remind them of God's long faithfulness and of their continuing duty to serve Him. They participated in numerous sacred rites pointing forward to the Christ.

Micah's contemporaries were, however, not godly. They felt confident in merely taking part in the ceremonies. It did not occur to them that it might matter how they conducted themselves outside the Temple.

This situation of being religious and at the same time ungodly disturbed Micah. Against such an attitude he cried out. In doing so he speaks pointedly to our own day.

He faithfully warned of divine judgment; but Micah is remembered most for his positive, comprehensive definition of true religion. In a single terse statement he includes Amos' emphasis on justice (Amos 5:24), Hosea's concern for mercy (Hos. 6:6) and Isaiah's plea for a humble walk with God (Isa. 2:11; 6:1-8). He declared: "He hath shewed thee, O man, what is good; and what doth the Lord require of thee, but to do justly, and to love mercy, and to walk humbly with thy God?" (Mic. 6:8) Thus he taught that true religion brings one into an intimate fellowship with God, and that out from that fellowship flows righteous conduct toward one's fellowmen.

Micah, living in the last half of the eighth century B.C., was one of that century's brilliant galaxy of prophets, among whom Isaiah was the most notable. The messages of the two men of God are in harmony. Some have suggested that Micah was a disciple of Isaiah, and it is interesting to note the similarity between Mic. 4:1-5 and Isa. 2:1-4. But the two prophets are very different. Isaiah was a member of the aristocracy. Micah was a commoner. Isaiah was polished, familiar with the manners of the capital, and moved in royal circles. Micah was a rough man of the countryside, a prophet of the humble.

His own background probably made Micah sensitive to the burdens of the poor. He was doubtless aware of corrupt politics in the capital, of which Isaiah spoke. He must also have known something of the luxury and hidden vices in the Northern Kingdom against which Amos and Hosea, two of his contemporaries, protested. He was aware of the religious apostasy of the land. But it was the suffering of the oppressed poor which wrung his heart.

He was a native of Moresheth, a foothill town some twenty miles west of Jerusalem on the edge of the maritime plain between the Judean hills and Philistia by the sea.[1] While the area was well watered and fertile, a place of grainfields, olive groves, and grasslands, the farmers among whom Micah grew up were almost always in economic distress. Debt-ridden, they were forced to mortgage their farms to rich men of Samaria and Jerusalem, who finally dispossessed them of their land. So it was that they became tenant farmers, oppressed by greedy absentee overlords. This exploitation of the poor was in the eyes of Micah one of the most heinous crimes of his day, and he fiercely denounced the exploiters (Mic. 2:2).

Micah's world was in revolution. And the prophet was acquainted with the ominous situation. He lived in a region of small villages remote from the political activities of the capitals, but his broad, open valley must bear the brunt of any attack from an invader who would undertake the conquest of Judah. So it was that he saw and felt the terrors of his world's grim drama.

The secure, prosperous half-century enjoyed by the Northern Kingdom ended with the death of Jeroboam II and the westward advance of the Assyrians. Damascus, the capital of Syria, fell in 731 B.C. (II Kings 16:9). Samaria, the capital of Israel, was overcome by the Assyrian armies under Shalmaneser and Sargon in 721 B.C. (II Kings 17:5-6). The fall of the northern capital left Jerusalem and Micah's beloved countryside exposed to the attackers who swept all before them in their determined advance upon Egypt. The prophet must have suffered unspeakable anguish of spirit as he saw the Assyrian king Sennacherib invade Judah and in 701 B.C. lay siege to Jerusalem (II Kings 18:13—19:37).

The prevailing ungodliness and the tragic deterioration of Israel and Judah did not, however, cause Micah to despair. He knew full well that the last word would not be spoken by the cruel moneylenders who kept him and his neighbors in bondage, nor even by the heartless pagan kings and their armies who

[1] "Called Moresheth-Gath, vs. 14, probably near Gath but inside the Judah boundaries" (Berk. footnote on 1:1; see map 2).

swept high-handedly across his world. He was sure that Jehovah still had a final word. He looked forward to a purified and restored nation. Micah saw the fulfillment of the Lord's purpose in the coming of the Messiah. And it must have delighted him to learn that the Anointed One would be raised up from the humble Judean hill country, out of the little village of Bethlehem.

## *Outline*

I. God's Judgment Is Coming, 1:1—3:12

    A. What Judgment? 1:1-16

    B. Why Judgment? 2:1—3:12

II. God's People Have a Future, 4:1—5:15

    A. The Coming Glory of the Lord's House, 4:1-8

    B. The Sorrows of the Present, 4:9—5:1

    C. The Coming of Christ to Redeem, 5:2-15

III. God's Controversy with His People, 6:1—7:20

    A. God Makes a Supreme Appeal, 6:1-8

    B. God Condemns Evil, 6:9-16

    C. Micah Laments the Nation's Corruption, 7:1-6

    D. Micah's Faith in God, 7:7-13

    E. Micah's Prayer for His People, 7:14-20

# Section I God's Judgment Is Coming

## A. WHAT JUDGMENT? 1:1-16

### 1. *God Himself Appears* (1:1-5)

Like all true prophets in Israel, Micah, under divine inspiration, spoke forth God's message to his contemporaries. He felt himself under direct authority of God, whom alone he must obey, for **the word of the Lord** (1) came to him. Having thus been made aware of God's holy will and purpose, Micah was impelled to share with his people these solemn counsels. With confidence in God and with the assurance that he spoke the words of truth, the prophet in delivering his message was fearless and utterly without regard for personal consequences.

Micah was in this respect a model for preachers of all time. The preacher should be a man of God and of God's Word. He must be confident that he has a divine revelation. He must be a man courageous to speak the truth in a manner which is assured and convincing. Only a man who, like Micah, feels compelled by God should engage in the business of preaching. But the man who feels this compulsion dares not tarry.

A native of Morasheth or Moresheth (see Introduction), Micah prophesied during the reigns of three successive kings in Judah: **Jotham, Ahaz, and Hezekiah** (1; see Chart A). This fixes the date of his labors between 750 and 687 B.C. Although he lived in Judah, his message pertained to both **Samaria,** the capital of Israel, and to **Jerusalem,** the capital of Judah. Since Samaria was destroyed in 712 B.C., it is evident that the early section of the prophecy must be dated previous to that year.

This chapter which trembles with imminent judgment begins with a graphic, figurative description of the Lord God coming down from His holy dwelling place to judge a rebellious people. The whole earth is summoned. All men everywhere are commanded to stop and listen to what God has to say **from his holy temple** (2). God had come to deal primarily with the **transgression of Jacob** (5; the Northern Kingdom) and of its capital city, **Samaria,** and with the wickedness of **Judah,** which centered in its capital at **Jerusalem.** But Jehovah is the God of all the earth. God is not remote from our world. He is concerned about the affairs of men. His word is more urgent than anything else which may claim our attention. So all need to stop and pay attention. "Where God has a mouth to speak we must have an ear to hear; we all must, for we are all concerned in what is delivered." [1]

**The Lord . . . will . . . tread upon the high places (3).** God is here pictured as using the mountaintops for stepping-stones as He approaches His people. Under His majestic stride, the mountains disappear and the earth becomes a level plain: "Beneath him the mountains melt and flow into the valleys, as wax melts before the fire and pours like water" (4, Phillips). Moffatt translates v. 5:

> *And all this for Jacob's transgression,*
> *for the sins of the house of Judah!*
> *Jacob's transgression? Is it not in Samaria?*
> *Judah's sin? is it not in Jerusalem?*

To this day God continues to enter into the affairs of men and nations. Whenever He comes into a situation, we may expect change. No circumstance is beyond His concern nor will any escape His judgment.

### 2. *What God's Judgment Is to Be* (1:6-7)

Speaking in the first person, God declares that Samaria is to be razed. **I will make Samaria as an heap (6).** She will be as a pile of stones in a field. *The Berkeley Version* interprets **an heap of the field** as the rock terraces common in hilly, grape-growing areas. The once-proud city will become an empty place for the planting of vineyards. **I will discover the foundations,** i.e., the stone walls of the buildings and the battlements of the city will be thrown down into the valley below, leaving the foundations naked and exposed for all to see—a tragic memorial to her disobedience and ungodliness. **All the graven images thereof shall be beaten to pieces (7).** The idols of heathen deities whose worship had been practiced in Israel would be broken up and the gifts given to those idols would be burned.

---

[1]Matthew Henry, *Commentary on the Whole Bible* (New York: Fleming H. Revell Co., n.d.), IV, 1304.

This desolation will come upon the city because Samaria had forsaken the true God and committed spiritual harlotry. As an unfaithful wife goes off after other men, so Israel had gone off after other gods. Furthermore, much of the apparent prosperity of the city had been brought about through the fees of religious prostitutes attached to the heathen temples' precincts. The Septuagint translates 7d: "because she has gathered of the hires of fornication, and of the hires of fornication has she amassed wealth."

The judgment here foretold was brought about by the Assyrian armies under Shalmaneser and Sargon (II Kings 17:4-6). When Hoshea, Israel's king, withheld tribute from Assyria, Shalmaneser ravaged the land, threw Hoshea into prison, and besieged the city. After a three-year siege, Sargon (by this time king of Assyria) in 721 B.C. reduced the city to rubble and made Samaria a vassal state ruled by a provincial governor in the former royal city. Sargon claims in his inscription to have at this time deported 27,290 Israelites. Most of these were settled in Media. To supplement the poorer classes remaining in the land, Sargon imported foreigners from various Assyrian dominions.

### 3. The Prophet Laments (1:8-16)

Micah mourns not only the mortal blow to fall upon Israel, but the fact that the corruptions of the Northern Kingdom had also swept over Judah, even into Jerusalem. God's judgment could be expected, therefore, to reach into his very homeland. Indeed Sargon's successor, Sennacherib, did invade Judah and lay siege to Jerusalem itself. It may well be that it is this of which Micah spoke when he declared: **He is come unto the gate of my people, even to Jerusalem (9)**.

The moral and spiritual breakdown among any people, Micah knew, was a fatal wound which could not be cured by any means other than a turning to God for His salvation. **Her wound is incurable**; literally, "She is grievously sick of her wounds." That the wages of sin are always death was very clear to the prophet.

It is a solemn fact that obstinacy in sin among any people always brings divine judgments. It is a wound which only God himself can cure.

To dramatize his tremendous concern and to impress his people with the destitution sure to come, Micah gives public expression to his grief in a manner common in his time. **Therefore I will wail and howl, I will go stripped and naked** (8). He goes barefoot and stripped of his upper garment. So deeply was the prophet affected by what he saw coming upon his people that he felt he "would make wailing like the jackals, and a lamentation like the ostriches" (8b, ASV). The jackals' **(dragons, KJV)** terrifying night calls and the sad, mournful sound of the ostriches **(owls, KJV)** seemed to express the emotions of fear and grief which throbbed uncontrollably within him.

Men of God who would be effective must share in Micah's understanding concern for the suffering saints and for the judgment coming upon sinners. The minister must himself be affected by the word of the Lord which comes to him. He must be moved by the truth he gives to his people; for only as he speaks out of a concerned heart can he expect his message to move the hearts of his hearers. Preaching to be meaningful must be heart-to-heart communication.

Micah not only grieved over the sad plight of his people; he was angered as he recalled the sins which had brought this catastrophe. He thereupon spoke of the destruction to come upon Judah in sharp satire by means of a series of puns (10-15) built upon the names of the cities in his own southwest section of Palestine. His dramatic play upon words is apparent in J. B. Phillips' translation:

> *So then, in Gath where tales are told, breathe not a word!*
> *In Acco, the town of Weeping, shed no tear!*
> *In Aphrah, the house of Dust, grovel in the dust!*
> *And you who live in Shaphir, the Beauty-town, move on,*
>     *for your shame lies naked!*
> *You who live in Zaanan, the town of Marching, there is no*
>     *marching for you now!*
> *And Beth-ezel, standing on the hillside, can give no foothold*
>     *in her sorrow,*
> *The men of Maroth, that town of Bitterness, wait tremblingly*
>     *for good,*
> *But disaster has come down from the Lord, to the very gate*
>     *of Jerusalem!*
> *Now, you who live in Lachish, the town far-famed for horses,*
> *Take your swiftest steeds, and hitch them to your chariots!*

*For the daughter of Zion's sin began with you,*
*And in you was found the source of Israel's rebellion.*
*So give your farewell dowry to Moresheth of Gath!*
*The houses of Achzib, that dried-up brook, have proved a*
    *delusion to the kings of Israel,*
*And once again I bring a conqueror upon you, men of*
    *Moresheth,*
*While the glory of Israel is hidden away in the cave of Adul-*
    *lam.*

Micah speaks of Lachish as **the beginning of the sin to the daughter of Zion** (Jerusalem, 13). He probably had in mind that it was here that the idolatrous corruptions of the Northern Kingdom found their first foothold in the south. He indicates (14-15) that the people of this place might want to send gifts to his hometown, **Moresheth-gath** or Mareshah, and the adjacent city of **Achzib** in order to secure their support against the enemy. But such aid, the prophet says, will not be forthcoming, for **an heir** (15, an enemy or conqueror) will also overcome those towns. In the words **Adullam the glory of Israel,** Micah recalls that Judah's plight is like that of David, who in a desperate moment of flight found refuge in the cave of **Adullam,** located near Mareshah. He sees the glory of the once proud Hebrew nation facing a new Adullam of despair.

Micah's sad lament concludes with a call for the people to mourn the impending loss of their children. These children whom they had brought up with loving care are doomed to a hard life of servitude in an enemy's land. In speaking of this mourning, Micah uses a common symbol of grief: **Make thee bald, and poll thee** (16). They should **poll** (cut or shave) their heads (cf. Amos 8:10; Isa. 22:12; Jer. 16:6). **Thy delicate children**—"your darling children" (Phillips). In their mourning, Micah says, they will resemble **the eagle,** or better, the vulture (margin, ASV), the head of which, unlike the eagle, is "bald," having down but not feathers.

As suggested above, the judgment Micah saw coming upon Judah here involved the siege of Sennacherib in 701 B.C. By comparing this passage with Isa. 10:28-32 we see something of the panic and havoc which spread from town to town with the approach of the Assyrian armies. Micah's reproofs were, however, seriously heeded by King Hezekiah (Jer. 26:18-19) and Isaiah's complementing message brought the king further hope and faith. Through penitence and trust in God, judgment was delayed (II Kings 18:14-16; Isa. 37:36-37).

### B. Why Judgment? 2:1—3:12

#### 1. *Injustice* (2:1-5)

God continues His case against His disobedient people. Through His prophet, He lays bare specific evils in their social and religious life which were responsible for their undoing. Micah makes it clear that sins against people are in reality sins against God. In this he anticipated the teaching of our Lord (Matt. 25: 31-46; Luke 11:39-42; 16:13-15).

Injustice was rampant in Judah. Men who could do so were quick to take advantage of their fellows. Among those particularly guilty were rich city dwellers eager to obtain extensive land holdings (see Introduction). They were infected with that covetousness which God condemned at Sinai (Exod. 20:17). To covet is the root of various kinds of evil. From it springs that sinful desire which prompts men to break many of the other nine commandments.

These men were so intent upon their greedy pursuits that they would **work evil upon their beds** (1)—lie awake nights scheming how to acquire more and more land. Then, **when the morning is light,** they arise with no recognition of God or of His laws ("for they have not lifted up their hands to God," LXX). Shamelessly, not shrinking from the light of day, they deliberately set about executing their selfish designs. In league with equally corrupt authorities, with bribes and other illegal procedures, they evicted farmers from desirable fields and houses. In Micah's day, wealth consisted largely in real estate. These men were so gripped by a mania for land that they ruthlessly "plundered orphans" (LXX) and oppressed entire households, giving no regard to the owners' sacred inheritance rights (2). Micah is not condemning wealth *per se,* but he condemns the dishonest acquisition of it and the selfish use to which men put it.

Wicked thoughts led these men to wicked deeds of seizure, theft, and violence. From thought to deed, this is the way evil develops. The passage suggests, then, the need to resist the first attacks of sin, to cast out the first thoughts of evil. It is bad enough to be suddenly tripped into error or sin quite unawares, but it is much worse deliberately, with design, to follow an evil course. The testimony of the Psalmist (63:5-6) and the admonition of Paul (Phil. 4:8) give us God's guidance in this area.

Not only do acts of sin develop from evil thoughts, but sinful acts increase in their sinfulness. Those who devoured widows' houses in a later generation plotted against Him who had rebuked this evil practice (Matt. 23:14). It was they who cried, "Away with this man" (Luke 23:18).

The situation of which Micah speaks is a striking illustration of what happens when men are ruled by selfishness. They plan and work for their own interests. Because they are godless they depend upon their own scheming and ability to carry through and they disregard or circumvent any established law which might hinder their purposes.

The oppression which God hates is not limited to taking material goods. It involves all social wrongs. All men are created in the divine image with equal rights before God. Each is precious in His sight. None is to be oppressed or taken advantage of in any matter.

Paul points out further (II Cor. 5:15-16) that we as Christians should look upon all men as potential children of God. We are not to see them merely from a human point of view and evaluate them by their outward appearance. Even though they may be the vilest sinners, Christ died to make them saints. We are therefore to look upon all men with deep compassion as lost souls to be loved and prayed for, to be won to our Lord.

Micah is not alone in his condemnation of injustice. The Psalmist (36:1-4) speaks out in a similar manner, as do also Isaiah (5:8-12; 32:7) and Amos (8:4). Elijah faced Ahab and condemned him severely for demanding Naboth's vineyard (I Kings 21). Jesus much later condemned some of the most religious men of His day for injustices prompted by covetousness (Matt. 23:14; Mark 12:38-40; Luke 20:46-47). We need to keep always in mind that justice and goodwill toward our fellowmen are still "musts" in Christian living.

In Micah's day the altars ran red with the blood from thousands of bullocks, rams, and lambs purchased by the rich men of Jerusalem who paid the priests lavishly for their services. It is possible today to participate in public religious exercises in quite an approved manner but be far from meeting the Christian standards of proper worship. To be unfriendly, to drive a sharp bargain, to divorce creed from practice disqualify one before the Lord.

God is the Judge between man and man and avenges the innocent. Therefore, because of the oppression Micah cites, God devises a humiliating judgment upon **this family** (3; the Israelites) from which they will not soon be able to escape or to "shake themselves" (Phillips). Disastrous days were upon the people, and they would be so humiliated by their enemies that they would no longer be able to walk proudly erect. **Ye shall not remove your necks**—they who had refused to bend their necks to the easy yoke of God's commandments must now bow low under the heavy yoke of His judgment, the awful bondage of slavery in exile. **This time is evil**—evil times were upon them, times similar to those spoken of by Jeremiah (18:11) and Amos (5:13).

It is true today that those who refuse Christ's easy yoke of obedience cannot escape the heavy yoke of judgment. Those who through pride will not bow their necks willingly to carry Christ's yoke will sooner or later have their necks forcibly bent low (Rom. 14:11-12; Phil. 2:9-13).

Judgment in keeping with their sin was about to fall upon the covetous rich. The lands which they had wrenched from others would in due course be taken over by their captors. They would mockingly be reminded of their distasteful fate by their enemies reproachfully putting this song into their mouths: **We be utterly spoiled** (4)—"We are utterly ruined and laid waste! God changes the portion of my people. How He removes it from me! He divides our fields to the rebellious—our captors" (4, Amp. OT; cf. Hab. 2:6).

The fields which they had so gleefully seized from the helpless would be taken from them. **Thou shalt have none that shall cast a cord** (5) means none of them would be able to take up an allotment of land in Israel. There would be no restoration at the time of Jubilee, for there would be no congregation of Jehovah left. These men who had taken possession of the land would be carried into captivity while only the few poor who remained and the imported strangers would benefit from their fields.

It is ever true, as Matthew Henry points out, "The more there appears of a wicked wit in the sin, the more there shall

**201**

appear of a holy wisdom and fitness in the punishment; for the
Lord will be known by the judgments He executes."[2]

### 2. *Desire for Soft Preaching* (2:6-11)

Some of his hearers, indignant because Micah had publicly
exposed their crimes and asserted that God's judgment would
surely come upon them, interrupted him and indicated that
they would no longer tolerate such talk—**Prophesy ye not** (6).
The confused cries of these galled hecklers might be interpreted:
"Stop your prophesying! They are prophesying (at us)! They
shall do no such thing! Will their reproaches never cease!"[3]

Honest teaching was not wanted. Like many people of our
own day, the men of Judah desired new things; things invented
by man, not things revealed by God. It was popular to disbelieve
what had been revealed and what had been proved true by their
fathers.

The attitude faced by Micah is similar to that met by Isaiah
(30:10), Jeremiah (5:30-31), and Amos (2:12). Those who
heard Micah were like the listeners with "itching ears" of whom
Paul writes (II Tim. 4:3-5). In another place the apostle also
speaks of the tragic results of refusing to hear the word of God
(II Thess. 2:8-12). It is a sad day indeed when, as Pusey says,
"men teach their teachers how they wish to be mistaught, and
receive the echo of their wishes as the voice of God."[4]

Micah is not, however, intimidated, nor does he "pull his
punches." He seeks faithfully to create a proper concept of righteousness in the minds of the people. And we today need to
consider the basis for true righteousness. For now as in Micah's
day, commercialism and materialism are supplanting ethical and
spiritual values. We need to be reminded that "an act is not
righteous because it has legal sanction or not necessarily so
because it has the sanction of the church, or of one's conscience.
Nations, as well as lesser organized bodies, have at times given
legal status to acts that were not only unmoral but even immoral.

[2]*Op. cit.,* IV, 1308.

[3]A. Fraser and L. E. H. Stephens-Hodge, "Micah," *The New Bible Commentary,* ed. F. Davidson (Grand Rapids: Wm. B. Eerdmans Publishing Co.,
1953), p. 722.

[4]*The Minor Prophets* (Grand Rapids: Baker Book House, 1962), II, 35.

People in groups or as individuals have subordinated their consciences to justify evil in order to gain certain ends."[5]

Micah tries further to reason with the people. He poses four principal questions (7): (a) "Should this be said, O house of Jacob?" (7a, RSV). Are you really justified, he asks, to talk the way you do? (b) **Is the Spirit of the Lord straitened** (restricted)? Can you by silencing me, Micah probes, silence also God's Spirit? Can you by your unbelief and disobedience frustrate the divine counsels? Can you make God your Prisoner and Servant? (c) **Are these his doings?** Can you really blame God for the judgments coming upon you? Micah reminds them, Are they not your own fault? (d) **Do not my words do good to him that walketh uprightly?** No upright man needs to fear anything that I say. If you will, then, walk uprightly. My words, which are actually those of God, are for your instruction and comfort rather than to cause distress.

Opposition to God's word as portrayed in vv. 6 and 7 suggests that men may oppose God's truth as it is faithfully and constantly spoken. They may oppose it, but the divine purposes will continue; the Holy Spirit cannot be restrained. To oppose that ongoing divine word deprives one of the unmeasured blessings of a faithful ministry. It offends God's Spirit, and robs men of all gospel privileges.

Micah goes on to confront his antagonists with more of their cruel exploitations against innocent people of the land. These men, perhaps hiring robber bands to waylay unsuspecting travelers, plundered their victims even as an invading army. They stole the very clothes from well-meaning people who were quietly going about their business. "You rise against my people as an enemy," Micah declares. "You strip the robe from the peaceful, from those who pass by trustingly with no thought of war" (8, RSV).

**The women of my people have ye cast out** (9). They had caused women and children to be turned from their homes and carried into captivity away from their rightful heritage under God, away from the Temple and its ordinances whereby they came to learn about God and to see His glory. Micah urges his erring countrymen, therefore, to arise and change their ways.

[5]S. C. Yoder, *He Gave Some Prophets* (Scottsdale, Pa., Herald Press, 1964), p. 145.

He warns them that they can expect no rest, for their sin which has polluted the land is sure to **destroy** them (10).

This prophetic statement brings all of us face-to-face with the sad fact that it is man who has polluted and continues to pollute the world, not the world which pollutes man. And it is a law of life that those who pollute the world about them will sooner or later find themselves destroyed by the corruption which they themselves promulgated. "Don't be misled," Paul said. "Remember that you can't ignore God and get away with it: a man will always reap just the kind of crops he sows! If he sows to please his own strong desires, he will be planting seeds of evil and he will surely reap a harvest of spiritual decay and death" (Gal. 6: 7-8a, *Living Letters*).

The people of Judah, however, did not want a prophet of integrity. They were determined to listen only to those who, claiming to be God's prophets, would condone their unprincipled, undisciplined living, preaching to them **of wine and of strong drink** (11). "This was one of those days," Rolland Wolfe declares, "when the pew ruled the pulpit, and the chief criterion in choosing a prophet or minister, was that he should say what pleased people's ears, dispensing cheerful lies rather than ofttimes bitter truth."[6]

The faithful man of God is often less popular than he who willingly compromises the issues of truth which disturb sinful men and simply echoes the opinions of the day. Proclaiming the true gospel which demands repentance, forsaking of sin, and living justly not infrequently meets with opposition.

False cults today often promise to provide the favor of God without demanding obedience to many of His righteous teachings. Why such cults attract so many people is suggested by Pusey:

> Man wants a god. God has made it a necessity of our nature to crave after Him. Spiritual, like natural hunger, debarred from or loathing wholesome food, must be stilled, stifled with what will appease its gnawings. Our natural intellect longs for Him; for it cannot understand itself without Him. Our restlessness longs for Him, to rest upon. Our hopelessness longs for Him, to escape from the unbearable pressure of our unknown futurity. Our imagination craves for Him; for being made for the Infinite, it cannot be content with the finite. Aching affections long for Him; for no creature

[6]"Micah," *The Interpreter's Bible* (Nashville: Abingdon Press, 1956), VI, 915.

can soothe them. Our dissatisfied conscience longs for Him, to teach it and make it one with itself. But man does not want to be responsible nor to owe duty; still less to be liable to penalties for disobeying. . . . The natural man wishes to be well-rid of what sets him ill at ease, not to belong to God. And the horrible subtlety of false teaching, in each age and country, is to meet its own favorite requirements without calling for self-sacrifice or self-oblation, to give it a god, such as it would have, such as might content it.[7]

### 3. *Preview of Deliverance* (2:12-13)

Micah, like other Old Testament prophets, saw the future as a whole, without time perspective. He saw significant coming events in God's dealing with His people, but he was not given insight as to their timing. He was not aware that long years or even millenniums might in some cases separate one from the other. His vision was like our view of the stars as we gaze into the night sky. We see the heavenly bodies there, but lacking space perspective, we see nothing to suggest that some of them are vastly more remote than others.

It should not be surprising, then, to find that Micah's record of the things he saw does not run as a chronological narrative. It should not disturb us, therefore, to have him recount a future restoration in the midst of his forecast of God's more immediate judgments. Nor should we think it strange that verses dealing with Christ's coming to redeem are mingled with those which speak of His coming to reign in cc. 4 and 5.

While Micah was telling of soon-coming judgment, he was aware also that a remnant of God's people would return to Palestine. He speaks of this in 2:12-13, declaring that true believers from among the twelve tribes will be gathered from their captivity and again settled in their homeland. Speaking for the Lord, Micah says: "I will surely gather all of you, O Jacob; I will surely collect the remnant of Israel; I will bring them (Israel) together as sheep in a fold, as a flock in the midst of the pasture. They (the fold and the pasture) shall swarm with men and hum with their much noise" (12, Amp. OT). Their divine King, **the breaker** (13; "the breachmaker," Berk.), would not only fling wide the gate, but make a breach in the prison wall of their exile to hasten their escape. Like a flock of troubled sheep they would "rush" (LXX) noisily through the openings made for

[7]*Op. cit.*, p. 35.

them. God, their Good Shepherd, would go before them, leading them homeward to their own fold.

This forecast doubtless referred directly to the restoration of a considerable number of the captives under the edicts of Cyrus and Artaxerxes in the sixth and fifth centuries B.C. respectively. It may also be a foreshadowing of the thousands of both Jews and Gentiles who, believing in Christ, became the true children of Abraham (Gal. 3:7), and have been gathered within the one fold of the Church (Rom. 11:1-5). It may perhaps also be a fore-view of that still more glorious day which John saw wherein "a great multitude which no man could number" unite in one voice of praise to the Good Shepherd who has brought them to the safe fold in God's immediate presence (Rev. 7:9-10).

**All of thee** (12) does not mean that every captive in Babylon will return. **All** means, rather, both Israel and Judah. God is saying that those desiring to return, whether originally from Israel or Judah, will be gathered together as one group. No longer will they be two nations. "I will most surely gather you all together again, O Jacob; I will most surely bring home the survivors of Israel" (12, Phillips). **Bozrah** means "sheepfold" and is perhaps better translated so, as it is in some of the more recent versions (cf. Amp. OT, Berk., Phillips).

Micah had shattered the false hopes of the people resulting from the wrong teaching of the false prophets who had said there was no need to fear. But he is also faithful to show them that after their chastisement God purposes to show mercy to His people.

### 4. Unworthy Leaders (3:1-12)

Judgment is coming, Micah declared, because of gross injustice in the land and because the influential people, who were especially guilty, wanted it that way. The leaders were taking advantage of their privileges and responsibilities.

*a. Rulers denounced* (3:1-4). The responsible political leaders of God's people—**heads of Jacob, and ... princes of the house of Israel** (1)—were supposed to **know judgment** and to practice it. They were to be guardians of justice, understanding protectors of the people. If they were ignorant of any aspect of their duty, they had means at hand to ascertain the right, that they might administer impartial justice. So they were without excuse (I Kings 3:9-12; Jer. 5:3-5).

But instead, Micah complains, they are evil men **who hate the good, and love the evil** (2). Instead of being good shepherds who feed the flock, they fleece and eat the sheep. Heartless and unfeeling, they, as it were, tear off the skin and cut the flesh from the people. They "break their bones, and chop their bodies into pieces as for the pot, like meat in a big kettle" (2, Amp OT; cf. Ezek. 34:2-4).

It is bad enough when ordinary citizens plunge onward in ignorant or careless opposition to the righteous will of God, but it is much worse when leaders do so. With no sense of sacred stewardship they knowingly removed appointed checks to corruption, and so encouraged their people in unrighteousness. Micah sternly warns that there will be a radical reversal in fortunes. There is coming a day when the rulers will find themselves in a situation like that in which they have placed their victims. Desperate days lie ahead for them, and when they come, the rulers will cry to God for help. But He, remembering the ruthless treatment they meted out to others, **will not hear them** (4). With the froward (disobedient, perverse) God will show himself froward (II Sam. 22:27; Ps. 18:26). The hardest punishment for these rulers will not be the wrath of their mistreated people, nor even the cruelties of their victorious foes. It will rather be the impenetrable silence of the God they have outraged. Prayer offered unworthily always remains unanswered. "Whoso stoppeth his ears at the cry of the poor, he also shall cry himself, but shall not be heard" (Prov. 21:13). And James warns, "He shall have judgment without mercy, that hath shewed no mercy" (Jas. 2:13; cf. Isa. 1:12-15).

*b. False prophets denounced* (3:5-8). Those men who profess to be called and enlightened to speak God's message to the people should be outstanding examples of commitment and devotion to His cause and to His people. They should champion justice and mercy. But prominent prophets in Micah's day led the people astray. No error is so hopeless as that which is taught in the name of God.

These prophets were described by Isaiah when he lamented, "O my people, your leaders mislead you, and confuse the course of your path" (Isa. 3:12, RSV; cf. Jer. 9:16). They were as greedy as the political leaders; yes-men, mercenary in their motives. Their pronouncements carried a price tag, and they trimmed their oracles according to the fee. When paid well, when they have good food to **bite with their teeth** (5), they promise the people **peace** and safety, "but declare war against him who puts nothing into their mouths" (5c, RSV). They were unscrupulous racketeers. (See Ezek. 13:19, 22-23.) The servant of God is to live by the gospel (I Cor. 9:13-14), but is not to luxuriate by it, nor modify his message according to his support.

Micah exposes the false prophets for what they really are. He says that their **vision** (the revealed word of the Lord to them) will be taken away (6). They who had misguided others for hire will be left to their own dark delusions. Because they themselves would be in spiritual night, they would be unable to **divine** or make God's will known. As a result, spiritual darkness would plague the whole nation. Such darkness comes upon every man, or group of men, who for unworthy, selfish ends close their eyes to the truth. To play fast and loose with righteousness causes men to lose all sense of principle; "right" and "duty" become only empty words. See Matt. 7:22-23; I John 1:7.

It is bad enough to be under ungodly rulers, but it is worse to be guided by false teachers. Jesus spoke of them when He referred to blind leaders of the blind (Matt. 15:14) and of the necessity of walking in the light lest it be taken away (John 12:34-36). If for monetary gain, or for any other unworthy motive, leaders of the church distort the gospel, when men ask for counsel these leaders will have no answer from the Lord for them. And how great is that darkness! (Matt. 6:19-23; cf. Isa. 5:20-21.)

Those prophets or **seers** (7; cf. I Sam. 9:9) and **diviners** (men who by casting lots and other such means tried to determine future events) had abused the people's trust for selfish ends. Although God had deserted them, they professed to give His message. But they would be **confounded** because their words were not valid. That they were only shams and impostors would soon be evident to the people. The Septuagint says, "The seers of night-visions shall be ashamed, and the prophets shall be laughed to scorn: and all the people shall speak against them, because there shall be none to hearken to them." **Cover their lips** refers to putting their beards up over their heads to hide their faces in embarrassment and shame. This was required of lepers (Lev. 13:45). It was a sign of mourning (Ezek. 24:17, 22). The false prophets had lied with their lips; now they should cover them as men that are speechless and ashamed.

Micah, in contrast to the false prophets whom he had just exposed, was assured of the divine favor. He therefore could testify, **Truly I am full of power by the spirit of the Lord** (8). It was because of this that he had light to judge rightly and had the moral courage to reprove the wickedness of the people. He found his sufficiency in the Lord (cf. Ezek. 2:7-8; II Cor. 3:4-6). Micah also manifested here the qualities of godly leadership of which Paul wrote to Timothy: courage, power, love, and self-control (II Tim. 1:7, RSV). Like Micah, those who act honestly may always act boldly; and they who are sure that they have a commission from the Lord need not fear the opinions and oppositions of men.

c. *Leaders further denounced* (3:9-12). The leaders of the nation, secular and religious alike, had lost their sense of equity and justice. Covetousness so consumed them that any means which secured them desired gain was looked upon as acceptable. Micah challenges them, **Hear this,** you rulers who **abhor judgment, and pervert all equity** (9). They hated any right demand which might thwart their practices, and they twisted laws to meet their crafty designs.

**Jerusalem** (10) and the nation of which it was the capital were being built up through the zeal and religious pretense of the wealthy swindlers. In a very real way the bread of the needy was the life of the city. Like Habakkuk (2:12) and Isaiah (22:13-19), Micah knew that this was an unstable foundation. Jerusalemites, mistaught by the false prophets, had all the while maintained a sense of security. They thought of their city as old and sacred, therefore impregnable. They had just enough religion to think that God would fight for them in a pinch. They had, therefore, been unheeding toward the warning message of God's true prophet. But godlessness always brings judgment; no one is exempt. Without God, all of the high-sounding political and social schemes with which men seek to establish security will fail. The Lord still rules the affairs of men. With Him faith, integrity, and love rank high.

Things were in such a bad state that even the older men of the community, **the heads** (11), who served as judges and who in other periods could be implicitly trusted, now were being influenced with bribes. **Priests** and **prophets** also had their price. They were tools of the unscrupulous rich, rather than spiritual and moral mentors of the people. They had used their offices as opportunities for exploitation instead of as channels for service. Covetousness entered into all they did. Gain was their chief end, and so became their god.

In spite of all their perverted ethics, these leaders had the effrontery to pretend to **lean upon the Lord.** In their spiritual blindness and moral stupor, they blandly claimed that all was well. God, they said, was in the midst of His people, so no misfortune could befall them.

In the face of this blatant hypocrisy, Micah boldly declared that it was the corruption which these pious-talking leaders had brought upon the people that would result in the nation's destruction. **Therefore shall Zion for your sake be plowed as a field** (12). "Though that which is wicked can never be consecrated by a zeal for the church, yet that which is sacred may be, and often is, desecrated, by the love of the world. When men do that which in itself is good, but do it for filthy lucre, it loses its excellency, and becomes an abomination both to God and man."[8]

Micah and others of God's early prophets amaze us with their courage. As Raymond Calkins says, "They did not seem to care what might happen to themselves. They uttered their message in sublime disregard for consequences. They are models in this respect for the modern preacher. They sober him. They make him ask himself whether or not he is true to his calling as they were to theirs, or whether he simply echoes, more or less unconsciously, the opinions of the day."[9]

Jerusalem, the once prosperous city, once blessed of God, would **become heaps**—a "heap of ruins" (RSV). Its most sacred precinct, **the mountain of the house,** the very height where the glory of God had shined forth in Solomon's Temple, would be but "a tangle of scrub on the top of a hill" (Phillips).

The words of James Wolfendale are always true: "When teachers corrupt doctrine, and preachers withhold the gospel; when rulers and princes pervert equity, and neglect special duties for the defence of which they are put in office; they poison the stream of life and turn it into deadly fountains."[10]

---

[8] Henry, *op. cit.,* 1316.

[9] *The Modern Message of the Minor Prophets* (New York: Harper and Brothers, 1947), p. 57.

[10] "Minor Prophets," *The Preacher's Homiletical Commentary* (New York: Funk and Wagnalls, 1892), p. 411.

It is interesting to observe that this verse was remembered a century later. At the trial of Jeremiah, who had been preaching a similar message, it was quoted by those defending him against charges of treason (Jer. 26:18). It is evident there that this prophecy of Micah was delivered by him during Hezekiah's reign, and was so impressive that true repentance followed. It is also clear that the Lord had spared the city until Jeremiah's time. The passage not only resulted in a revival in Judah, but was a means of sparing Jeremiah's life a hundred years later during the reign of Jehoiakim. The city was, however, finally destroyed as Micah had prophesied.

By contrast, this chapter points up some qualities of the godly leader: (1) He serves. He gives of himself rather than demands to receive from others (cf. Matt. 20:26; John 13:14-17). (2) He serves in light. His mind is enlightened by a personal knowledge of and communion with God. Christ's apostles were first to be "with him" and then to go for Him (Mark 3:13-14). Paul also stressed this principle among his co-workers (II Tim. 2:2). (3) He serves in power. Filled with the Holy Spirit, he labors with might beyond his own. (4) He serves with courage. He knows that his directives are from the Lord, not from even influential human persons. He knows he speaks, "Thus saith the Lord." He is not speaking mere human philosophies or seeking to call attention to himself (II Pet. 1:16). (5) He serves in love, not greedy of filthy lucre (I Tim. 3:3; Titus 1:7).

Micah's rebuke of unworthy leaders of his day suggests the importance of leaders really leading. A true leader may often lack the flamboyancy of a politician, but he is characterized by insight, wisdom, magnanimity, courage, and integrity. He discerns the actual needs of the people. He knows where these needs may be met. He places the good of his people above personal wants. If occasion requires, he dares to oppose even the majority in order to direct the whole group toward the proper ends. He honestly faces up to the issues involved. His transparency begets confidence, so that he inspires the people to come to grips with their problems and follow through even though it cost them "blood, sweat, and tears."

The situation in Israel points up the mutual responsibility between leaders and people, who become like leaders. The community was corrupted by the evil example of the leaders of Micah's day. Blind leaders of the blind, they "ditched" the whole nation. But it is also true, especially in our day, that people can demand that their leaders be just and righteous. It is clear from Micah's prophecy that the people shared the responsibility involved in the judgments brought upon the land.

This mutual responsibility is clear in the work of the church. A false man in the pulpit who leads his congregation astray will be judged before God. But on the other hand, the people in the pew can exert a great deal of influence over their minister. They will be judged by the Lord as to whether they make him better or worse. Some churches make preachers. Others break them. Indifference, inertia, pettiness, and fussiness can take the life out of a man. "You cannot," as someone has said, "put icebergs in the pew and then ask the minister to perspire!" Better ministers make better people. But it is also true that better laymen make better preachers. Like priest, like people. Like people, like priest.

# Section II God's People Have a Future

Micah 4:1—5:15

## A. The Coming Glory of the Lord's House, 4:1-8

In an evil day of strife and warfare, Micah was able to speak of a time of peace among nations. For he saw the coming of Christ to establish His earthly kingdom among men. In contrast to the sordid situations about him, in spite of the present fear of the judgments to overtake God's people, Micah lifts his eyes and sees a bright picture of future glory.

### 1. A Glorious Future (4:1-4)

**In the last days** (1) he says that God's people, now destined for captivity, will be free, happy, and preeminent among the nations. With this vision he encourages his countrymen to look ahead toward a future golden age wherein righteousness and peace will prevail throughout the earth.

Micah declares that in these "latter days" (ASV), in the age of the Messiah, **the mountain of the house of the Lord** (Mount Zion), the site of the holy Temple in Jerusalem, should "be established as the highest of the mountains" (RSV). At that time the nations of the earth will turn to that exalted city. There they will seek the guidance of God's law. Mountains are symbols of great nations, while **the hills** are symbolic of smaller ones. The essential idea is that the worship of Jehovah, the one true God, will be established as supreme throughout the earth.

There is a double emphasis in the words **He will teach us . . . and we will walk in his paths** (2). It is one thing to be taught and to learn about God's will. It is another thing to do that will in all of our daily living.

Zech. 8:20-23 is a commentary on this passage. Zion will be, not only the place of universal worship, but also the center of international instruction. To some extent this prophecy has been fulfilled through the spread of the gospel from the tiny country of Palestine to all parts of the world. But the passage also has definite Messianic connotations reminiscent of the picture of the millennium drawn in Revelation 20. That day is still in the future. We look forward to the fulfillment of these things

213

when Christ comes to perfect His just and righteous kingdom upon earth and personally to reign among men.

When Christ reigns, **the law shall go forth of Zion.** Disputes will no longer be settled by the sword but in the light of God's truth. Even strong nations will be held in check by His righteous judgments, for **he shall judge** (3; "decide," ASV) the issues which concern them. Size and force do not change God's decisions. The Lord is not influenced by marching armies. He judges men by the rightness of their cause. War will be no more. Armaments will be turned into implements of peace. Time, energy, and wealth once devoted to the making of war will be turned to more constructive occupations.

This passage in Micah is almost identical with Isa. 2:2-4. Whether or not one of these contemporary prophets quoted the other, we do not know. The fact, however, that it is recorded twice under the inspiration of the Holy Spirit suggests its significance.

In that glorious day of which Micah writes, the Word of God is to be so universally obeyed that individuals will dwell safely at all times in all places. There will be no predatory interests, no predatory nations. Without fear of molestation, law-abiding citizens will be able to enjoy their homes and possessions—**they shall sit every man under his vine and under his fig tree (4).** Security and contentment will characterize the period. The basis for this is private property—not communism—amid a God-fearing people. The prosperity and blessing which came to Israel in Solomon's reign (I Kings 4:25) foreshadowed what is in store, but in Solomon's day sin was still abounding. In the millennium here forecast, Satan will be bound and Christ and His people will reign in righteousness. Man cannot do this in his own strength. This is a condition which God himself will bring about. **The mouth of the Lord of hosts hath spoken it.**

### 2. Courage for Today (4:5-8)

Because of this future glory that Jehovah is preparing for His people, Judah is encouraged to walk on with the Lord. She will not be diverted even though the other nations follow the way of their gods: "For all the peoples now walk every one in the name of his god, but we will walk in the name of the Lord our God for ever and ever" (5, Amp. OT).

God's people who were at the time being afflicted and oppressed could take heart. **In that day** (6), the day of the Lord's reign, they will be comforted and exalted, ruled by an understanding, loving Shepherd-King. The Hebrew idiom here suggests sheep who are weary and lame after a difficult journey. Doubtless the Lord applied this to the Israelites, who are so often referred to as His sheep. In punishment for disobedience Israel would suffer greatly. But these verses seem to imply that **a remnant** (7) of the Jews will during the millennium be given special attention, restored to divine favor under Jehovah's fatherly care. See also Isa. 40:9-11; Ezek. 34:11-16; 37:24-28; Zeph. 3:19; Rom. 11:26-29.

The city of Jerusalem, though doomed to destruction, is therefore exhorted to lift up its head in hope. In that future day it will again be highly exalted among the nations of the earth. Micah says:

> And you, O tower of the flock,
>   hill of the daughter of Zion,
> to you shall it come,
>   the former dominion shall come,
>   the kingdom of the daughter of Jerusalem (8, RSV).

### B. The Sorrows of the Present, 4:9—5:1

Before the day of deliverance comes, the people of God must pass through the fires of judgment. In 9-10, Micah makes further reference to the captivity which will come as judgment upon his people, and of God's dealings with them there. He speaks of the trouble through which the inhabitants of Jerusalem were passing and must continue to pass. They have rejected the rulership of Jehovah; they have refused His counsels, so in reality they are without king and counselor. "Broken to pieces" (9, Phillips), they are no longer a strong, united people, and so are at the mercy of their enemies. So great will be their pain and distress that Micah likens their condition to **a woman in travail** (10). In their anguish they would **go forth out of the city,** i.e., be driven from the shelter of their cherished, holy city. They would be forced to **dwell in the field.** There, without the conveniences and protection of the city, they would endure the elements and the treachery of their enemies' designs. They would be taken **even to Babylon.** But, Micah said, there in that strange land, God would work among them. In due time they would be delivered, rescued out of the hands of their oppressors. This reference to Babylon as the place of exile by Micah, who lived during the days of Assyrian supremacy with the capital at Nineveh, is an interesting example of the divine inspiration and prophetic insight in which he carried on his ministry. The captivity in Babylon which he forecast did occur some one hundred years later.

Judah is now harassed. Jerusalem is under pressure from the strong nations about her, eager to **look upon** (11) her downfall. But those opposing forces do not know **the thoughts of the Lord** (12) for His people. They are not aware that they too are in the hands of Judah's God, and after He has used them in bringing judgment upon the chosen nation, they must likewise come under His righteous judgment. Micah writes of this judgment, "The Lord will gather the enemies of His people like sheaves upon the threshing floor, helpless before Israel. Rise, thresh, oh daughter of Zion; I will give you horns of iron and hoofs of brass and you will trample to pieces many people; and you will give their wealth as offerings to the Lord, the Lord of all the earth" (12-13, *Living Prophecies*).

But before this redemption of Israel comes, there is danger. The prophet, therefore, again warns his people of the imminent invasion by the Assyrians, and exhorts them to set themselves to withstand the onslaught.

*Now call up your troops, you daughter of troops!*
*For the siege is laid against us,*
*And in the insult they will take a stick,*
*And strike the judge of Israel on the cheek!* (5:1, Phillips)

C. THE COMING OF CHRIST TO REDEEM, 5:2-15

1. *Messiah's Birthplace* (5:2-5a)

Micah saw God dealing with a captive people whom the Lord would ultimately deliver, but he also caught a glimpse of the long-promised Saviour-King. This was He for whom God-fearing men had longed and waited since Adam's loss of paradise (Gen. 3:15). The prophet saw that Messiah would not be born in the stately and royal environs of Jerusalem, but rather in **Bethlehem** among the insignificant clans **of Judah** (2). **Ephratah**, here identified with Bethlehem, was really an older settlement which

216

became absorbed into that city (Gen. 35:19). This was the original home of David, Israel's first conquering king, who frequently is referred to as a foreshadowing of Israel's greater King (Ps. 89:19-37). David's family is called Ephrathites in Ruth 1:2; I Sam. 17:12.

Micah's prophecy had a literal as well as a spiritual fulfillment in the birth of Jesus. And this detailed forecast helped to keep hope alive in the hearts of God's people through the long centuries while they waited for a Messiah. The Jewish leaders of Herod's day had this passage well in mind and cited it promptly to him when he inquired concerning where Israel's king was to be born (Matt. 2:4-6). See also Isa. 7:14 and 9:6-7.

God, speaking through Micah, declared that the Messiah was coming "forth for me" (RSV) as a **ruler in Israel**. This special Servant of Jehovah would spring from the ancient line of David. But the promised King is to be no ordinary earthly man, for "his goings forth were from the beginning, even from eternity" (LXX). This speaks to us of the Incarnation, for only God himself is from eternity.

Of v. 3, Adam Clarke writes: "Jesus Christ shall give up the disobedient and rebellious Jews into the hands of all the nations of the earth, till **she which travaileth hath brought forth;** that is, till the Christian church, represented in Rev. 12:1 . . . as a *woman in travail,* shall have had the fulness of the Gentiles brought in. **Then the remnant of his brethren shall return;** the Jews shall also be converted unto the Lord; and thus *all Israel shall be saved,* according to Rom. 11:26."[1]

**He shall stand** (4) implies "carefulness, confidence and strength." In ASV **feed** is rendered "and shall feed his flock." The meaning is, "He will nourish His people, leading them in pastures of tender grass and beside the waters of quietness, through the grace and power of God. He shall be regarded with awe and reverence, because He is kingly, and bears the name of the Lord, and His form shall spread abroad unto the ends of the earth."[2]

The first part of v. 5, **And this man shall be the peace,** rightly belongs to this prophecy according to Adam Clarke and *The Berkeley Version.* And it reminds us that the angels announcing the Saviour's birth sang of peace and goodwill (Luke 2:14). This

[1]*Op. cit.,* p. 720.
[2]Fraser and Stephens-Hodge, NBC, p. 724.

may well have reference to the peace of heart and mind which individuals in all generations know who make Christ their trust. It was the Lord himself who declared: "Peace I leave with you, my peace I give unto you: not as the world giveth, give I unto you. Let not your heart be troubled, neither let it be afraid" (John 14:27). Such peace of mind and spirit is referred to often throughout the New Testament. See especially Acts 10:36; Rom. 5:1; 14:17; Phil. 4:7.

The peace of Christ may well speak also of the goodwill created as men live worthily. For true Christians are people of goodwill, and wherever they go they change the environment for good. It is a fact proved by history that social justice and peace prevail to the degree that individuals in the social order accept Christ and live with His peace in their hearts and according to His righteous teachings. Wherever Christ goes, in the lives of His believing people, He displaces injustice and all forms of evil.

Not only so, but the fears which beset the masses are largely eliminated through vital Christian faith. The strong democratic nations of the earth which have influenced the whole of mankind so favorably have been established on Christian principles by men who valued highly the rights of individuals. Only upon such principles can true democracy flourish. So long as they are disregarded our world will be a jittery, uncertain place. Thomas Melton wrote truthfully when he said, "We cannot be at peace with ourselves because we are not at peace with God." Efforts to negotiate world peace and to legislate international justice have been ineffective largely because consideration of God and the Christian gospel have been ignored. This gospel with its simple formula of individual peace and righteousness is conspicuously and tragically lacking in the strategic talks of the upper echelons of present-day politicians and statesmen who seek the path to peace.

Micah's reference to the Christ as the Source of peace may also have reference to a universal peace which He purposes to establish among all men. But that "reign of peace" will not come until the Prince of Peace himself comes to earth to reign. Of this event Micah also spoke.

### 2. *Deliverance from the Enemy* (5:5b-6)

The prophet describes the deliverance that is to come by saying that **seven . . . and eight** (5) leaders competent to meet the powers of their enemies would be raised up against the invaders. **Seven** or **eight** is here used to mean an indefinite number, as it is used on other occasions. (See Eccles. 11:2; Job 5:19.) **They shall waste** ("tend," LXX; or "rule," RSV) **the land of Assyria with the sword, and the land of Nimrod** (synonymous with Assyria, Gen. 10:9-11) **in the entrances thereof** (within the gates where the city's council and court held sessions, 6). Thus it was that He, the Lord God, would deliver His people.

Whether this passage refers to a single specific incident or to a series of events over a period of time, we cannot know certainly. We do know, however, that during the invasion of Sennacherib late in the eighth century B.C., Judah, then ruled by righteous Hezekiah, was miraculously delivered. Jerusalem was given a new lease on life and continued on for another century. In the meantime the Assyrians with their capital at Nineveh were defeated by the Babylonians, and the city of Babylon became the new world capital.

### 3. *The Purging of the Remnant* (5:7-15)

Micah tells his countrymen that in the future which God has prepared for them they will be a blessing upon the earth **as a dew from the Lord** (7) and like summer rain: gentle, refreshing, sparkling, and elusive. **The remnant of Jacob** (8) shall also be a ruling force: strong, kingly, and irresistible. **Her enemies shall be cut off** (9).

The two comings of Christ are merged and described in alternating passages by Micah—His coming as Redeemer, and His coming as King to reign. In similar fashion these two are clearly set forth in Heb. 9:26-28. Those who take advantage of the blessings of His coming to redeem look forward confidently to enjoying the benefits of His coming to reign. But it is also true that, regardless of one's interest in the Second Coming, he will not be permitted to share its good things if he has neglected the redemption of Christ and failed to live uprightly in His strength.

There is for us today then great hope in Micah's prophecy. Conditions are serious in many respects. The religious, political, and social life all about us seem at times to fall under the warning judgments of Micah. Personal evils destroy men and women. International and interracial tensions fill the world with fear and insecurity. But we have faith to believe God's prophet and the sure words of our Lord, who declared, "Heaven and earth shall pass away; but my words shall not pass away" (Mark 13:31). We know that God and right will ultimately prevail. Who of us, then, will mind the journey since the road leads home?

The prophet forecasts (10-15) that the people of Judah will be carried into Babylonian captivity, but he asserts that even there God will be dealing with them. In captivity they will be cut off from the very things they had come to trust in: **horses** and **chariots** (10), **cities** and **strong holds** (11), **witchcrafts** and **soothsayers** (12), **graven images** and **standing images** (13), **groves** (14; wooden poles used in worship of the Canaanite baals). Even the heathen people, whose manner of life the Israelites had sought after, would be brought to nought (15).

Only as God's people were separated from the love of these things could He work His purposes in and through them. So it was that, in the absence of the material items in which backslidden Israelites had placed their hope, many of the people were brought back to trust alone in Jehovah. After the Captivity they never served idols or engaged in evil heathen practices which had so offended the Lord. God thus used Israel's enemies to purge His people of their idolatry and unbelief. He often turns man's evil intentions to His own good purpose and glory (Ps. 76:10).

# Section III *God's Controversy with His People*

Micah 6:1—7:20

## A. God Makes a Supreme Appeal, 6:1-8

Using legal terminology, Micah here calls upon God to arise and plead His cause against a guilty and rebellious people. The Lord had a controversy with sinning Judah, for sin always brings tension between God and man (cf. Isaiah 1). God is, however, always faithful to make clear what sins are involved. He waits to reason, and He tenderly pleads for the return of sinners, that they may be justified and brought again into fellowship with himself.

### 1. *The Witnesses and the Charge* (6:1-5)

**The mountains** (1), nature's loftiest realities and common symbols of permanency, along with **the hills** and the very **foundations of the earth** (2), are summoned as jurors. God pleads His case before these natural objects which had witnessed the long history of Jehovah's relations with His people. With words full of pathos He inquires, **Wherein have I wearied thee?** (3) He asks what He may have done to make His will irksome and to set them so against His ways. Cf. Jer. 2:5-8.

In His own defense, the Lord recounts the mighty acts He had mercifully wrought to redeem His people from slavery in Egypt. Here we see God's main ground of appeal to His people for their trust and obedience. He has redeemed them. They are not their own. They are His. The Lord then cites His appointment of faithful, God-fearing shepherds—**Moses, Aaron, and Miriam** (4)—to lead them forward in His loving will and purpose.

Intent upon demonstrating the righteous way He had handled their interests, God uses the expression **the righteousness of the Lord** (5). The Hebrew term appears elsewhere only in Judg. 5:11. It suggests that each act of mercy was a separate manifestation of God's righteousness.

He chose the episode in which He, through Balaam, changed to a blessing what their enemy, **Balak king of Moab,** designed as a curse (Numbers 22—24). To move their minds and hearts, He recalled the notable events which transpired between the en-

221

campment of Israel at **Shittim,** just east of Jordan in the Plains of Moab immediately northeast of the Dead Sea, and that at **Gilgal,** across Jordan in Canaan (Numbers 22—27; Joshua 1—4).

God's appeal to His people here illustrates the reasonableness of true religion. It

> emphasized religion as rational and moral, and at once preserved the reasonableness of God and the freedom of man. God spoke with the people whom He had educated: He pled with them, listened to their statements and questions, and produced His own evidences and reasons. Religion—such a passage as this asserts—is not a thing of authority nor of ceremonial nor of mere feeling, but of argument, reasonable presentation and debate. Reason is not put out of court: man's freedom is respected; and he is not taken by surprise through his fears or his feelings. . . . But it is not till the earthly ministry of the Son of God, His arguments with the doctors, His parables to the common people, His gentle and prolonged education of His disciples, that we see the reasonableness of religion in all its strength and beauty.[1]

### 2. *What Does God Require?* (6:6-8)

Verses 7-8 have been given two interpretations. One is to the effect that the prophet is enquiring of the Lord concerning the basis of acceptance with Him. The other view represents Israel as answering the Lord with a counter challenge. "What worship and what service does the Lord really require? Does He desire a meticulous observance of the Levitical law? (6b) Does He wish it to be fulfilled in an excessive and lavish manner by holocausts of herds and **rivers of oil?** (7a) Does He desire the people to show a frenzied and non-moral devotion to Him comparable to the fanaticism of some of the heathen peoples round about, such as moved the worshippers to offer human sacrifices? (7b) . . . The controversy is closed by the Lord's own declared answer (8)."[2]

Like many others since their day, the people of Judah hoped to obtain divine favor by performing external duties. They were willing to purchase their pardon upon any terms but that of reforming their lives. The people, obsessed with doing outward religious acts, overlooked "the weightier matters of the law" (Matt. 23:23). God was, however, saying to them: "It is not

[1] George Adam Smith, "The Book of the Twelve Prophets," *The Expositor's Bible* (New York: A. C. Armstrong and Son, 1889) I, 421.

[2] A. Fraser and L. E. H. Stephens-Hodge, *op. cit.,* p. 725.

yours I seek, but you." He was more concerned about their spirit than about their substance. He was much more anxious about their hearts than about their sacrificial bulls and goats.

Micah, then speaking for the Lord, answers their questions. In a single sentence he sums up the legal, ethical, and spiritual requirements of true religion and points up the principal teachings of Isaiah, Amos, and Hosea (Isa. 30:15; Amos 5:24; Hos. 2:19-20; 6:6). These requirements of true religion are those which every man can meet if he will. Men are inclined to make religion "too complicated, too involved, too mysterious," as Raymond Calkins reminds us. "But this verse sets us straight. The Lord requires of us nothing that we are not able immediately to render. No man, whatever his intellectual difficulties may be, but can enter at once, wholly and with entire conviction, into the blessedness of the life of real religion."[3]

**He hath shewed thee, O man, what is good** (8). The term for **man** here refers to all mankind, and so this passage has universal significance. God himself had through His law and prophets made known earlier what was actually essential regarding worship. He had made clear His ultimate requirement for gaining and maintaining divine favor (Deut. 1:12-13; 30: 11-14).

These moral and spiritual requirements are even more meaningful for us now than for the men of Micah's day. For through God's further revelation of himself in Christ as recounted in the New Testament, we are more fully aware of God's will than were they. Amid the current confusion of voices regarding what God demands, it is good to know that He himself has spoken. In the complexities of a multitude of propounded theologies and philosophies, we take confidence in that He has made our duty simple and plain. All can understand.

John Knox expressed this on one occasion when speaking before Mary, Queen of Scots. The royal lady was greatly moved upon by the Holy Spirit, but confused as to what to believe. "You teach one thing," she complained to Knox, "and the church of Rome teaches another. Which shall I believe?" Knox answered, "Ye shall believe neither, madam: ye shall believe God who speaketh in His Word. And save as we agree thereto, ye shall believe neither of us."

[3]*Op. cit.,* p. 63.

The Word of God is, indeed, the basis and final authority for our faith. We do not consult ourselves, nor need we depend upon supposition and fancy. The great God might well have spoken in language too exalted for us to understand. But in loving consideration He has come down, as it were, from the mountains of eternity, meeting us at the foot of the hill to assure us that He will speak our language until we are able to speak His.

Through the ages there have been times of great darkness, and other periods when men have been blinded by false lights, but we are now greatly blessed with sure means of spiritual instruction. Today it is largely through negligence or obstinacy that men remain unacquainted with their duty toward God.

The Scripture declares that we are to **do justly.** We are to be truthful, honest, and sincere toward ourselves, toward God, toward our civil and business obligations, and in all other relationships with our fellowmen (cf. Prov. 21:3; Amos 5:23-24; Zech. 8:16).

We are to **love mercy.** This is a higher quality than justice. While to be just means to give everyone what is due him, mercy implies kindness, compassion, and love for even those to whom we may not be directly indebted. To be sure, it includes such matters as practical consideration and help for the poor, the oppressed, the handicapped, and underprivileged. But it involves much more than simply giving our possessions. In mercy we give ourselves to lift and redeem our fellowmen.

Mercy must always temper justice. In fact James tells us that judgment is without mercy to him that hath showed no mercy (Jas. 2:13). We may expect God's mercy only in proportion as we show kindness and consideration to others.

Shakespeare reflected these scriptural sentiments when he wrote in his *Merchant of Venice:*

> *The quality of mercy is not strained;*
> *It droppeth as the gentle dew from heaven*
> *Upon the place beneath:*
> *It is twice blest;*
> *It blesseth him that gives and him that takes.*

In these first two requirements, which deal with our relationships to our fellows, we have a summary of the second table of the Decalogue. Now in a third requirement, **Walk humbly with thy God,** we have the summary of the first table of the Ten Commandments, which deals with our relationships to God.

This requirement is higher than the other two. It is the motive out of which the others spring. The Hebrew literally says, "Bow low to walk with God." To "bow low" implies that the first step in any life of fellowship with God is to acknowledge our own iniquity and insufficiency. We must bring down every high thought into submission to the divine will, and by faith depend upon the love and grace of God for salvation. To walk with God requires agreement and fellowship with Him (Amos 3:3).

Any amount of mere human justice and mercy is not enough. "The best of men are but men at the best." Men must have a divine life implanted in their hearts through Christ. Jesus indicated the significance of this when He said that such a walk is based upon faith and is manifested by love (Matt. 23:23; Luke 11:42; cf. Jas. 1:27).

This triple command **to do justly, and to love mercy, and to walk humbly with . . . God** must not be dismembered. It is possible to execute stern, inflexible justice without mercy. There may also be mercy without justice, as when a man endows worthy enterprises with money dishonestly acquired. And men have been both just and merciful only to set aside the claims of God in Christ. Furthermore, men too often profess even a Christian walk with God, but give justice and mercy but little place in their lives.

The three demands must surely be considered together. When they are, they provide a splendid description of true religion, surpassed only by Jesus' summary of "the law and the prophets" as recorded in Matt. 22:36-40.

Teaching the futility of merely ritualistic worship, Micah is saying that God's demands are both moral and spiritual. Acceptable worship, he says, involves a life lived in obedience to both of those demands. Even divinely appointed ritual and form, though a proper part of worship, must be accompanied by the sincere movement of the heart Godward. The forms of true worship must be the expression of a man "ready to walk with the Lord" (LXX). This reminds us of Jesus' call recounted in Matt. 11:23-30, and of His declarations found in Matt. 7:21-23

225

and John 4:23-24. True religion is not found in a treadmill of duty, nor in a bewildering maze of ritual, costly though it may be. Cf. Ps. 51:16-19.

"The prophet is simply putting first things first and showing that, after all, a holy walk with God is the best evidence of genuine religion. The sacrificial system was never meant to be an end in itself, but was intended to assist the inner resolution of a man's mind by a series of specific, overt acts which must have their significance interpreted in terms of actual holy living to make them effective. . . . Along with Christ's teaching, this word of Micah is a sufficient rule of life for Christian men."[4]

Samuel Chadwick summarizes some special implications in all this pertinent to our own day. "The solution of our modern problems, as those of Micah's day, will not be found in legislation or machinery, but in realizing the sufficiency of God. No great and permanent solution of social problems has ever been reached without religious influence. The only way is to get back to God, to go to the house of the Lord and there find the power to do justice, love mercy, and walk humbly with our God. Then will be found the true bond of brotherhood."[5]

In 6-8 we find the question—and answers to it—"What Does the Lord Require of a Man?" (1) Not a formal religion of either sacrifice or works, 6-7; (2) Justice—observing God's laws for human relationships, 8; (3) Mercy—being kind as well as just, 8; (4) Walking daily under the leadership of God's Spirit, 8 (A. F. Harper).

## B.  God Condemns Evil, 6:9-16

Micah here announces that God is about to speak a final urgent word to His unrepentant people. The prophet therefore counsels the inhabitants of Jerusalem, especially the leaders of the city, to attend earnestly to what the Lord has to say to them. **See thy name** (9) is rendered "fear thy name" in the modern translations. The meaning thereby becomes clearer. In the Septuagint it reads: "The Lord's voice shall be proclaimed in the city, and he shall save those that fear his name; Hear, O tribe; and all who shall order the city."

---

[4]Fraser, Stephens-Hodge, *op. cit.*, p. 725.

[5]*The Expositor's Dictionary of Texts,* ed. W. R. Nicoll, Jane T. Stoddard, and James Moffatt (New York: George H. Doran Company) I, 748.

### 1. *The Sins of Judah* (6:9-12)

Through the rough country prophet, God comes to condemn Jerusalem's sophisticated city dwellers, for they are at the center of the nation's sins. "He did not refer to idolatry alone, but also to the irreligion of the politicians, and the cruel injustice of the rich in the capital. The poison which weakened the nation's blood had found its entrance to their veins and the very heart. There had the evil gathered which was shaking the state to a rapid dissolution."[6]

In announcing God's approach, Micah reminds his hearers that "it is sound wisdom to fear" (RSV) the Lord. Men who are wise discern the hand of God in the providences of life. They profit by corrective judgments. It was only by such a return to sincere reverence for the Lord and obedience to the divine moral demands that they could expect salvation. But if, even now, they come back to acknowledge and fear Him, He remains gracious to save.

In solemn words of judgment, God himself now speaks, "Hear this, you people and council of the city!" (Phillips) He continued by asking some sharp questions which immediately highlighted their evil practices. He asks, In spite of all My warnings and long-suffering, **are there yet the treasures of wickedness in the house of the wicked, and the scant measure that is abominable?** (10) Cf. Deut. 25:13; Prov. 11:1; 16:11; Amos 8:5.

God would not forget nor overlook the hoarded wealth that Jerusalem's **rich men** (12) had heaped to themselves. It had been acquired through oppression, through cheating by means of dishonest weights and measures, by arrogant blustering, and by lying (11-12). Micah earlier had described these evils in greater detail (3:1-3), but they were still prevalent.

The sins rebuked here are most prominent now in countries without the transforming benefits of the Christian gospel. It is nevertheless true that these evils are too common in our own morally enlightened Christian civilization. We crave personal material security and insist upon having physical comfort, and leisure to enjoy ourselves. Our set purpose to maintain a high standard of prosperity at almost any price creates an ofttimes pitiless rivalry among us in which we tend to disregard the rights of others and to engage in subterfuge and intrigue. Workmen too often seek

*Smith, op. cit.,* p. 426.

the highest wage for the smallest amount of labor, and employers become intent on giving the smallest wage their laborers will accept. The words of the prophet are indeed currently relevant. And it is a pertinent fact that the people addressed were, like us, a professedly religious society.

### 2. *Punishment Promised* (6:13-16)

In these verses the Lord proclaims the unchanging principles that gain gotten by wickedness is loss, that prosperity built by injustice cannot endure, that comforts obtained through oppression cannot be long enjoyed. The happiness and power sought by sinners will always elude them, because the means by which they seek them are not congruent with the end. Divine judgment is an inevitable consequence. See Lev. 19:35; Jas. 5:1-6. "What they minish from the measure, that they add to the wrath of God and the vengeance which shall come upon them; what is lacking in the measure shall be supplied out of the wrath of God."[7]

Not only would the men of Jerusalem not be permitted to benefit from their accumulated possessions (13-15) but, even worse, they are told, "There will be famine in your heart" (14, Phillips; cf. Ps. 106:15).

God tells the people of Judah that they have so degenerated in their spiritual and moral lives that they are actually following in the ways of that notoriously wicked and apostate dynasty of Israel headed by the conspirator **Omri** and his son **Ahab** (16), against which Elijah had battled some two hundred years before (I Kings 16—22). They were surely following Ahab's procedures, as illustrated in his heartless seizure of Naboth's vineyard.

Because this was true, Judah could expect nothing but desolation at the hands of their enemies. God warned them again: **Ye shall bear the reproach of my people.** The very fact that they were God's people would only increase the gravity of their sin. "Your being God's people in name, whilst walking in his love, was an honor; but now the name without the reality is only a reproach to you."[8] They could expect only to "bear the scorn of the peoples" (16, RSV) among whom God had intended them to be honored and exalted. See Deut. 28:1-14.

---

[7]Pusey, *op. cit.,* p. 85.

[8]A. R. Fausett, *A Commentary on the Old and New Testaments* (Grand Rapids: Eerdmans Publishing Co., 1948), IV, 606.

### C. MICAH LAMENTS THE NATION'S CORRUPTION, 7:1-6

Micah, after faithfully delivering God's message, looks in
vain for signs of repentance and reformation in Judah. What he
sees fills him with sadness. Little, if any, favorable response
appears to have resulted from his preaching. He likens his eager
but disappointing search for righteousness to that of a man who,
hungry for fresh fruit, goes to the vineyard after the harvest
hoping perchance for some remaining fruit. He finds a show
of leaves, but **there is no cluster to eat** (1). Judah, he discovers,
is morally barren. The poignancy of his distress is conspicuous
in the Septuagint, which reads: "Alas for me! for I am become
as one gathering straw in harvest, and as one gathering grape-
gleanings in the vintage, when there is no cluster for me to eat
the first ripe fruit; alas for my soul!"

Like Diogenes in Athens and like Jeremiah in Jerusalem
(Jer. 5:1), Micah looks for an honest man in Judah. But he
finds none. **The good man** (2) has apparently utterly vanished.
All men are filled with hate and are utterly selfish in their intentions. Each man is for himself, and seeks to ensnare his fellow—
**they hunt every man his brother with a net.** Even murder is
winked at if by it a man but gets what he wants.

**The prince** and **the judge** (3), who should be trustworthy,
have lost all sense of responsibility in guiding and protecting the
people. They have sunk to the level of seeking bribes and cater-
ing to the whims of the flatterer. These leaders do not just occasionally yield to temptation, but deliberately make dishonesty
their policy. They are in collusion against the common people.
**They . . . do evil with both hands earnestly.** Moffatt interprets
it, "They have quick fingers for foul play."

The officials of the land had no sooner expressed their evil
desires, Fausset says, than venal judges were ready to decide
their cases according to their instructions.[9] Thus "between them
they baffle justice" (Moffatt).

The men who should be most trustworthy prove to be hard
and sharp in their dealings—**the best of them is as a brier** (4).
Mutual confidence is no longer possible. Even one's closest
friends and family cannot be trusted. Confusion prevails throughout the nation. The whole social order is disintegrating. The
wages of sin are being collected and death for the nation seems

[9]*Ibid.*, p. 607.

inevitable. "The day which the watchers foresaw, the day of punishment has come; now follows utter destruction" (4, Phillips). These relationships between sin and judgment are elsewhere set forth in such passages as Ps. 37:35-38; Prov. 14:34; Isa. 5:15; Jer. 17:10-11. The principle of moral cause and effect applied to men and nations in Micah's day applies in ours, too, and will be true for all time to come.

Jesus referred to this passage from Micah (Matt. 10:34-36; Luke 12:51-53) to show that the preaching of His gospel may be expected often to produce the same hostility that the prophet describes. Such is the evil of the unregenerate heart that the declaration of God's truth often evokes only hatred and persecution toward those who proclaim it.

For every family man and for every young man looking forward to having a family, there is particular significance here. Just as family confidences in Micah's day were destroyed by evil practices outside the family, so today no man can engage in dishonesty and selfishness anywhere and expect his family to be untouched. Even wife and children lose respect for the husband and father who is unfaithful in his relationships with others. How do they know when they themselves can fully trust him? Parents who desire the honor of their children must first see that they themselves are honorable.

## D. Micah's Faith in God, 7:7-13

Viewing the state of his nation, Micah sees a gloomy prospect. But he refuses to be overcome by the sordid corruption about him. **I will look unto the Lord,** he says (7). "And confident in Him I will keep watch" (Amp. OT). Men cannot be relied upon, but God can be completely trusted. Like the Psalmist, Micah was aware that, when even fathers and mothers can no longer be counted on, God can be (Ps. 27:10). In this the prophet took heart.

Even in the darkness he would continue to watch. **I will wait** with hope and expectancy **for the God of my salvation: my God will hear me.**

All men of God should make Micah's threefold resolution, especially in trying times. His was (1) A resolution of faith: **I will look;** (2) A resolution of patience: **I will wait;** (3) A resolution of hope: **God will hear.**

Because Micah believed that God would yet manifest His steadfast love toward His people, he dared to speak out in the name of his nation. He bravely faced the enemies who waited to destroy them, and strongly affirmed his belief that God's light would yet shine through. Judah would see and respond obediently to the truth and so arise to match God's faithfulness (8). Bunyan's Christian, facing Apollyon, who had thrown him to the ground in the Valley of Humiliation, thrusts his sword at his assailant, the while quoting Micah's confident words, **Rejoice not against me, O mine enemy; when I fall, I shall arise** (8). So may every believer meet the enemy in the dark hour of temptation and trouble.

It appeared at the time that Micah had lost the battle in his effort to build the kingdom of God. But it became evident to him that God had not lost the war. Men who seek to fight God's battles even now can take heart in Micah's discovery. The lines by Maltbie Babcock are true:

*This is my Father's world. Oh, let me ne'er forget*
*That, though the wrong seems oft so strong, God is the Ruler*
*    yet.*
*This is my Father's world, the battle is not done;*
*Jesus, who died, shall be satisfied, and earth and heav'n be*
*    one.*

The Lord Jesus while on earth demonstrated again and again the divine ability to bring deliverance when men reach the end of their strength. Disciples, storm-tossed on the sea, rejoiced to have Him come to their rescue (Mark 6:48). The apostle, imprisoned and fearing for his life, heard assuring words, "Be of good cheer, Paul" (Acts 23:11). One dark night while Peter languished in prison, an angel stood by him (Acts 12:5-10). And today in life's darkest hours, God's people can testify, **The Lord shall be a light unto me.**

Micah identifies himself with his people in this section and acknowledges the justice and purposes of God's chastisements. He penitently bears them until the day that God shall **bring me forth to the light, and I shall behold his righteousness** (9). He declares that Judah's mocking enemies will in due time be put to shame (10). He even sees the day when Jerusalem's **walls are to be built** (11) and the exiled people who have been scattered to many parts of the earth will be gathered again to their homeland

(12). They shall come "from Assyria and from Egypt even to the River," Euphrates (12, ASV; see map 1), and from all lands to which they may have fled or been taken as exiles.

But before that day things will be difficult—**the land shall be desolate** (13). The people will still be reaping the fruits of their iniquity. For then, as now, sins may be forsaken and forgiven, but even God cannot halt the consequent harvest that follows every seed sowing (Gal. 6:7).

E. MICAH'S PRAYER FOR HIS PEOPLE, 7:14-20

### 1. A Petition for Loving Care (7:14-17)

As a farmer, Micah knew how essential a faithful shepherd was to the welfare of the flock. He prays, therefore,

> Shepherd thy people with thy staff,
>   the flock of thine inheritance,
> who dwell alone in a forest
>   in the midst of a garden land;
> let them feed in Bashan and Gilead
>   as in the days of old (14, RSV).

**Carmel** was known for its vineyards, while **Bashan and Gilead** were proverbially fruitful pasturelands.

With the restoration of Israel, Micah anticipated manifestations of God's power and leadership like those at the Red Sea, at Sinai, and other sites along the Exodus route **out of the land of Egypt** (15). In the face of these events, the surrounding **nations shall see and be confounded** (16). They would humble themselves and acknowledge Israel's God. To **lay their hand upon their mouth** was a common gesture of conviction and assent.

The thought of these marvelous events causes Micah to rejoice, and he expresses his elation in a psalm of praise for God's mercy and faithfulness.

### 2. Praise for God's Steadfast Love (7:18-20)

**Who is a God like unto thee?** (18) This question is repeated numerous times in Scripture (Exod. 15:11; Ps. 89:6; Isa. 40:18-25; 46:5), but usually in acknowledgment of the divine power and glory. Here, however, the prophet speaks of God's boundless grace and mercy toward sinners.

Wolfendale comments on the phrase **that pardoneth iniquity** as follows: "The forgiveness that there is with God is such as is suitable to His greatness, His goodness, and all other excellencies of His nature; such as that therefore by which He will be known to be God. It is not like that narrow, difficult, halving, and manacled forgiveness, that is found among men; but it is full, free, bottomless, boundless, absolute; such as becomes His nature and His excellencies."[10]

Micah's psalm is both timeless and timely, for it speaks of the very essence of salvation, past, present, and future. Godly men of all ages can join the prophet in his glad refrain of redemption. His psalm speaks an evangelical message of hope which was fulfilled in the salvation provided by the Babe of Bethlehem of whom Micah had spoken earlier in 5:2. All men of faith unite in Micah's firm confidence, **Thou wilt perform the truth . . . which thou hast sworn unto our fathers from the days of old** (20).

Here is a matchless view of "Our Incomparable God." **Who is a God like unto thee?** (1) Pardoning iniquity and transgression, 18; (2) Proving His mercy and compassion, 18-19; (3) Providing power over sin, 19; (4) Performing His ancient promises, 20 (W. T. Purkiser).

[10]*Op. cit.,* p. 461.

*The Book of*

# NAHUM

**H. Ray Dunning**

# *Introduction*

## A. The Prophet

Nahum is one of that group of prophets who are bereft of a biography. One scanty reference (1:1) is the only record which is given of his life; and his name, as such, appears nowhere else in the Old Testament. There are, however, other similar names to which it probably is related (cf. I Chron. 4:19; Neh. 7:7), and its meaning is nearly identical to Nehemiah. It is conjectured, based on inscriptions discovered on potsherds found in southern Palestine, that Nahum was of a hereditary family of potters.

Nahum is called the "Elkoshite" (1:1), which apparently means that he was from a place named Elkosh. No such place is known in Palestine; some scholars believe that it was located in Mesopotamia and that the man himself was a descendant of Israelite captives.[1] The fact that Nahum was so familiar with the city of Nineveh gives credence to this view (see map 1). Cases have also been made for a Galilean and Judean location based on certain noncanonical references.[2] Capernaum has been suggested as the city in question, since its name means "city of Nahum."

The prophet's name means "full of comfort," being formed by the Hebrew word similar to other words meaning "full of grace" and "full of compassion." Some have failed to see the appropriateness of this designation since Nahum proclaims a message of doom and devastation. But a closer look will reveal that the nature of his prophecy is of the essence of comfort— to God's people.

## B. The Book

The prophecy of Nahum has been criticized in these days on the basis of certain presuppositions about God. There are those who say the book lacks value and that its message is ethically and theologically deficient. This judgment is based upon

[1]Julius A. Brewer, *The Literature of the Old Testament* (N.Y.: Columbia University Press, 1962), p. 147.

[2]Walter A. Maier, *The Book of Nahum* (St. Louis: Concordia Publishing House, 1959), pp. 24-26.

a view of God which excludes any sense of wrath or justice and which declares that the nature of God is non-punitive. The biblical view, however, presents the antagonism to and punishment of sin as being compatible with the divine nature, in fact of its very essence.

In addition to the above criticisms, Nahum has also been scored as being blindly patriotic and nationalistic in ignoring the sin of Israel; as manifesting gloating hatred and malicious joy at the doom of Nineveh; as being a prophet of incipient Judaism; as being a false prophet opposed to other prophets; and as reflecting "pan-Babylonian" eschatology.[3]

The accusation concerning Nahum's ignoring the sins of his own people is implicitly in 1:12 and is also involved in a consideration of the date of the book.

## C. The Date

There are three factors to be taken into account in attempting to fix the date of Nahum's prophecy. These facts also provide us with a historical setting for the book. None of them, it must be stated in advance, will put the chronological question beyond doubt.

There is, first, a reference in 3:8-10 to the destruction of the Egyptian city of Thebes (called **populous No** in KJV and *No-amon* in other translations) by the Assyrians. It is clearly spoken of as a past event. The date for its fall was 663 B.C. This would put the oracle subsequent to that date.

The major consideration is the fall of Nineveh, which it is the main purpose of the book to predict. Nineveh was the powerful capital of the Assyrian Empire. It achieved great glory when Sennacherib reestablished it as his capital. Esarhaddon and Ashurbanipal, his two successors, continued its development. It was surrounded by a system of fortifications that was practically impregnable. Three chariots were supposed to have been able to drive side by side along the top of its wall. Within the wall were beautiful buildings, massive friezes and monuments, a great library, roads, and gardens. There is little disagreement on the date of its fall. Archaeological records have firmly established it as 612 B.C.

Assyria was both conqueror and terror of the nations. Its wickedness, especially under Ashurbanipal, was aggravated, as its own records attest. "Its victims were shut up in cages, ex-

---

[3]See Maier, *op. cit.*, pp. 70-84, where these criticisms are examined and refuted.

posed to the derision of jeering spectators, forced to carry in procession the heads of their former comrades in arms, their homes burnt and treasures plundered."[4] It is no wonder that Nahum concludes his prophecy with the words, "All who hear the news of you clap their hands over you" (3:19, RSV).

Such wickedness carried with it the seeds of dissolution. This certain knowledge along with the rising power of the Babylonians and Medes gave external support to Nahum's prophetic insight. Another herald of approaching doom was the fall of the city of Asshur to the Medes in 614 B.C. On the site of this ruined city the Medes and Babylonians joined in alliance. These events could possibly have precipitated Nahum's declaration. He could see visions of God beginning to act and his own people the recipients of the benefits involved. Discovery of some of the annals of Nabopolassor, king of Babylon at the time, reveals the fact that he and Cyaxares, king of the Medes, were already in open conflict with Assyria as early as 616 B.C., though separately. The city of Nineveh itself was actually attacked in 614 B.C. by the Medes under Cyaxares, but they were defeated.[5]

The third factor, previously mentioned, is Nahum's silence concerning the sins of his own people. If this is not just a reflection of his preoccupation with other matters, it could well indicate a hopeful outlook in the face of the religious reforms of King Josiah. These reforms took place in 621 B.C., and Josiah was on the throne continuing the reformation until his death in 609 B.C. Nahum may not have detected the temporary character and covert problems of the movement as did Jeremiah. A comparison of Nah. 1:15 with II Kings 23:21 lends some support to the view that Nahum was optimistic about Josiah's efforts.

At any rate, Nahum was the contemporary of Jeremiah and Zephaniah. Likewise the tenor of the letter seems to put it on the very threshold of the event it predicts, thus giving credence to the later date, between 616 and 613 B.C. If this date is adopted, Nahum also becomes the contemporary of Habakkuk.

## D. Literary Style

The Book of Nahum is an example of Hebrew literature at its best. It is poetic to an extremely brilliant degree. Professor Bewer, who fails to appreciate the message of the prophet, never-

[4]S. M. Lehrman, "Nahum," *The Twelve Prophets,* ed. A. Cohen (London: The Soncino Press, 1948), p. 191.

[5]C. J. Gadd, *The Fall of Nineveh* (Department of Egyptian and Assyrian Antiquities, British Museum, 1923).

theless extols his poetic ability in glowing terms: "His word pictures are superb, his rhetorical skill is beyond praise. In the description of the attack, destruction, and plundering of the city he exhibits a vivid imagination and a great power of poetic expression."[6]

Nahum's poetic style is better seen in a modern-language translation such as the RSV than in the prose format of the KJV.

Any attempt to discuss the literary structure of the book would raise problems beyond the scope of this work.[7] Hence a literary outline is impractical and recourse is taken to a highly generalized material division of the work.

## E. VALUE

Is this brief prophecy only an item of historical interest? Is it merely a reminder that God can reveal events to His prophets before they transpire? Or is there some further enduring message which we may glean from this oracle of vengeance?

It is perhaps partly true that Nahum was so concerned with politics that his message reflected more his political interests than the religious and theological convictions which underlay them. Nevertheless there were certain fundamental prophetic truths which shaped his utterances. At least two are evident. One is the final sovereignty of God over history. The other is that the universe is so morally structured that those who violate its constitution are broken by it. Those who choose to live by the sword shall die by the sword (Matt. 26: 52).

[6]*Op. cit.,* p. 148.

[7]Several highly technical monographs have been written on the problem of the text, its corruption and nature. E.g., Alfred Haldor, *Studies in the Book of Nahum* (Uppsala: A. B. Lundequistreka Bokhandeln, 1946).

# *Outline*

I. The Government of God, 1:1-6

    A. Superscription, 1:1

    B. God's Nature, 1:2-3a

    C. God's Power, 1:3b-6

II. The Application of God's Sovereignty, 1:7—2:13

    A. Varying Applications, 1:7-8

    B. Addresses to the Recipients of Justice, 1:9-15; 2:2

    C. The Fall of Nineveh, 2:1, 3-13

III. God Shall Destroy the Evil, 3:1-19

    A. The Wickedness of Nineveh, 3:1-4

    B. God's Opposition to Wickedness, 3:5-7

    C. Inevitability of Evil's Overthrow, 3:8-13

    D. The Dirge of Death, 3:14-19

# Section I The Government of God

## A. SUPERSCRIPTION, 1:1

This introductory statement was more than likely added by an editor for the purpose of identification. It is composed of two parts, the first giving the intent of the message, the second identifying the author. It is suggested that part two was specifically stated for purposes of cataloging the book among the Temple scrolls. It was undoubtedly used in the Temple worship in later times, and also perhaps in the year 612 B.C. However, the book was not primarily a liturgical production, as several have seriously contended.[1]

One opinion states that the basic portion of the writing (1:9—2:13) was a public message or debate in which the prophet contended with persons of opposite opinions on the momentous events of the time.[2] If this is correct, it was probably delivered in Jerusalem.

**Burden** (1) is more generally translated "oracle," a technical term denoting the message of a priest-prophet in the name of a god. It means literally "the lifting up" of the voice. Obviously the oracle was *about*, not *to*, Nineveh, the capital of the Assyrian Empire. For nearly two centuries this tyrannical power had been the great political and military force in the world known to the Hebrews. It was under Sargon II that Israel (Northern Kingdom) was eclipsed in 722 B.C. Later under Sennacherib, through Ahaz' foolishness, Judah was subjected to Assyria's dominion and annually paid heavy tributes. Ashurbanipal was the last great ruler of the empire, and lesser rulers were on the throne at the time of Nahum's prophecy. But Judah was still in subjection to the vast empire. The capital city of Nineveh was located on the Tigris River (see map 1).

The second superscription (1b) is unique in literature, since only one was customary. It is also unique in its use of the word

---

[1]E.g., Paul Haupt, *The Book of Nahum* (Baltimore: Johns Hopkins Press, 1907).

[2]Wm. C. Graham, "Nahum," *Abingdon Bible Commentary*, ed. Frederick Carl Eiselen, *et al.* (N.Y.: Abingdon-Cokesbury Press, 1929), p. 798.

**book. Vision** is a technical word, indicating that the source of the prophetic inspiration was divine insight. **Nahum,** meaning "the comforter," is so appropriate to the message when rightly understood that some have thought it to be a fictional addition, but there is little basis for this view.

Most scholars have found evidence of an acrostic poem beginning at v. 2, using the first half of the Hebrew alphabet. This is a literary form which in no way involves the content of the message. However there is much disagreement since the acrostic is incomplete—leading many of those who wish to hold to this theory of the poem to consider the text itself to be very corrupt. Likewise there is considerable disagreement as to the length of this particular construction. Rabbi Lehrman says, "The attempts at restoring the missing letters do not justify the many emendations proposed."[3]

## B.  GOD'S NATURE, 1: 2-3a

Verse 3 may be considered the key verse of the book. It is most clearly rendered in the American translation: "The Lord is slow to anger and great in power, but the Lord will by no means leave guilt unpunished."

The prophet does not speak of a petulant anger that is aroused over incidental matters. Rather he is indicating the full holiness of God which holds both love and justice in creative tension. The patience of God is remembered, but Nahum knows that His inevitable retribution must come. The nature of God demands that He punish sin because the nature of sin demands that it receive punishment. This does not indict the goodness of God. Rather His holiness would be indicted if He failed to oppose evil.

Paul proclaims the same message in Rom. 2:3-5: "And thinkest thou this, O man . . . that thou shalt escape the judgment of God? Or despisest thou the riches of his goodness and forbearance and longsuffering; not knowing that the goodness of God leadeth thee to repentance? But after thy hardness and **impenitent heart** treasurest up unto thyself wrath against the day of wrath and revelation of the righteous judgment of God." This is the way God governs the world: He rewards righteousness, is patient with wickedness, but eventually punishes it.

[3]*Op. cit.,* p. 194.

It is appropriate to remember here that at an earlier time God had sent a prophet to Nineveh to preach. Under the reluctant ministry of Jonah, the Ninevites repented in sackcloth and ashes (Jonah 3:5-10). How long this lasted we do not know but they had now repented of their repentance. If Jonah is extolled as the missionary prophet, Nahum should not be exorcised for proclaiming judgment upon the receivers of the missionary message, especially since he bases the proclamation upon such a fundamental view of the nature of God.

Three characteristics of God are mentioned which may need to be explained. **God is jealous** (2), avenging, and full of wrath. These are not human emotions. If modern theology has taught us anything, it is that there is no univocal language about God. The attributing of human passions to God is at best using an analogy. The transcendence of God voids any attempt to fully understand Him in human terms. Consequently, criticism on the basis of this language fails to sense the meaning of the scriptural references to Deity.

The word **revengeth** (*nokem,* avenging) is used three times in this passage, suggesting perhaps that Assyria had exiled Israel thrice and would receive three punishments fitting to its crimes.

### C. God's Power, 1:3b-6

Man has always been awed by the forces of nature. It is natural to associate the power of Deity with the display of nature's majesty. It was to be expected that sin-darkened humanity should even exalt the powers of nature to the stature of gods and offer worship and sacrifices of appeasement. Here God is not considered to be a part of nature (in the sense of a nature deity); rather the prophet speaks of Him as dominating the powers and entities of the natural order. He is Lord of the sea, the river, the mountain, and the people. There are two movements symbolizing Jehovah's power: a hurricane on the sea and a simoom[4] on the land.

Possibly 4a refers to the rolling back of the Red Sea and the parting of the river Jordan. This is the most natural interpretation and is adopted by Adam Clarke. **Bashan, Carmel,** and **Lebanon** (4) are some of the most fruitful areas of Palestine, the last

---

[4]A hot, dry, violent wind laden with dust, that blows occasionally in that part of the world.

to be affected by drought. In 5-6 the wrath of God is pictured in the language of earthquake, volcano, and violent and devastating storm.

> *Oh, worship the King, all glorious above,*
> *And gratefully sing His wonderful love:*
> *Our Shield and Defender, the Ancient of Days,*
> *Pavilioned in splendor, and girded with praise.*
>
> *Oh, tell of His might, and sing of His grace,*
> *Whose robe is the light, whose canopy space.*
> *His chariots of wrath the deep thunderclouds form,*
> *And dark is His path on the wings of the storm.*

—ROBERT GRANT

Section **II** *The Application of God's Sovereignty*

Nahum 1:7—2:13

A. VARYING APPLICATIONS, 1:7-8

After having spoken of the nature of God which underlies His government of the world, the prophet proceeds to show its twofold application. These passages are "theological, affirming those general principles of Divine Providence, by which the overthrow of the tyrant is certain and God's own people are assured of deliverance." [1]

1. *A Stronghold to the Faithful* (1:7)

Jehovah is declared to be **good.** This is not capricious favor just as His wrath is not petulant judgment. Rather the prophet means that God is faithful in the administration of justice. To those who serve Him, **the Lord is . . . a strong hold in the day of trouble.** There could possibly be a reference here to the cities of refuge (cf. Exod. 21:13; Num. 35:9-14; Josh. 20:7-9) but more likely, in the circumstances of the times, the prophet intends to convey the idea of protecting ramparts. If this is the case, he could be intending to make a contrast with the walls of Nineveh. Impregnable as they appeared, they would provide little protection in the day of visitation for those who trusted in them. On the other hand, God is a Stronghold who will not fail those who put their trust in Him.

This was a wonderful promise to the small nation of Judah, in those days of crisis. A great empire was on the verge of crumbling, and other mighty forces were rising. A battle of giants was impending, and it was a **day of trouble** for tiny vassal nations.

It is true that the fulfillment of this promise is not seen in the subsequent history of Judah. For after the reformation of Josiah (see Introduction) the people of Judah turned again to idolatry. But the general nature of the assurance is such that one need not argue for material prosperity as a sign of God's favor. Nevertheless it is a comfort to remember that **the Lord . . . knoweth**—that He takes care of **them that trust in him.**

[1]George Adam Smith, "The Book of the Twelve Prophets," *The Expositor's Bible*, ed. W. Robertson Nicoll (N.Y.: A. C. Armstrong and Son, 1903), II, 91.

### 2. *Vengeance on His Enemies* (1:8)

The **overrunning flood** is so clearly a reference to the circumstances surrounding the fall of Nineveh that some scholars
have questioned the text. But, aside from the textual analysis,
one who believes in divine inspiration finds it no more difficult
to believe in such specific prediction than to believe that Isaiah
could predict the preservation of Jerusalem with the Assyrian
forces under Sennacherib standing at the gates (Isa. 37:33-34).
Devastation by flood is frequently mentioned in the Old Testament both literally (Job 38:25; Ps. 32:6; Isa. 54:9) and figuratively (Isa. 8:7; Dan. 9:26; 11:22).

**The place thereof,** in the original Hebrew, is "her place."
Once again this is so specific that the more universal terms have
been adopted in most translations, especially since the LXX, *et al.*,
render it "adversaries." J. H. Eaton suggests the better translation as "her sanctuary" and makes an incisive comment:

"The suddenness of this allusion to a specific female enemy
causes surprise and has led many scholars to avoid the obvious
meaning of the traditional text. Yet the reference, in substance
and in manner, is typical of Nahum; it prepares us for the direct
address to the same female enemy in verse 11; and it corresponds
exactly to 2:5-7 where her temple is swept away by flood while
she herself is made captive."[2]

It is further suggested that use of the feminine gender
points behind the capital city itself to Nineveh's goddess, Ishtar.
This raises the conflict to a war between opposing deities. Such
a meaning also underlies 11 and 14 (see comments there).

The completeness of the annihilation is declared in the last
two phrases of this verse and is reinforced by the succeeding
passage. **Darkness shall pursue his enemies** is more correctly
and poignantly translated, "He . . . will pursue his enemies into
darkness" (RSV).

In vv. 1-8 we have a striking picture of the "God of Wrath
and Mercy." (1) The wrath of God: (*a*) expresses His justice, 3;
(*b*) His power, 4-6; (*c*) His awesome sovereignty, 2, 8; (2) The
mercy of God is revealed in goodness, protection, and concern
for those who trust Him, 7 (W. T. Purkiser).

[2]*Obadiah, Nahum, Habakkuk and Zephaniah* (London: SCM Press,
1961), p. 60.

B.  ADDRESSES TO THE RECIPIENTS OF JUSTICE, 1:9-15; 2:2

Beginning with 9, there is an abrupt change and the address is leveled at the Ninevites. A series of direct statements ensue which are somewhat difficult to follow because they shift so rapidly. First to Nineveh, and then to Judah, back and forth the speaker surges in fiery eloquence. The rapid succession of addresses in these verses has led many to believe that the recitation of this poem was accompanied by dramatic action so as to make the meaning clear to the listeners.

### 1.  *Challenge to Assyria* (1:9-11)

To the Assyrians the prophet throws down a challenge, **What do ye imagine against the Lord?** (9), perhaps meaning, "Who do you think God is?" It is a cry of derision, as "the prophet mockingly asks them what they can do in the face of God's decree of doom."[3]

Verse 10 presents difficulty for translators, but the substance is reasonably clear. Nineveh is compared to thorns, difficult to clear from the land, hard to burn while wet, but burning as stubble before the fire of God's judgment. This was a figure easily understood by the agriculturally-minded Israelites.

The full import of this passage is that the destruction of the city would be complete. Nahum declared, **Affliction shall not rise up the second time.** There would be no need for a second visitation. History has verified its truth.

The KJV translators take a more specific view of 10 as is indicated by their phrase, **while they are drunken as drunkards.** The phrase is an enlargement of the text which involves an interpretation as well as a translation. Most other translations omit it, and render the entire verse simply, as e.g. the RSV: "Like entangled thorns they are consumed, like dry stubble." Lehrman and Maier, however, agree with the KJV in their interpretation of the Hebrew. As to exactly what it means, Maier offers two alternatives. First, the Ninevites may feel so secure behind their defenses that they drink and carouse and forget their danger. Rabbi Lehrman agrees with this view. Second, the prophet may be predicting the impotence of the Assyrians, declaring them to be as helpless as an intoxicated soldier. Maier himself seems to

[3]Lehrman, *op. cit.*, p. 196.

hold to this interpretation and states, "According to tradition, Nineveh was taken when the defenders were engaged in riotous drinking."[4]

The **one** referred to in 11 is generally applied to Sennacherib, who was the most aggressive foe of Judah and invaded her when Hezekiah was king (II Kings 18:13 ff.). The Hebrew for **come out** is a technical word used of military expeditions and invasions (cf. I Sam. 8:20; Isa. 42:13; Zech. 14:3). These invasions were seen as directed against Jehovah himself since He was associated with the people in covenant relationship. Also the deportation struck a terrible blow at the Temple and its worship. Compare also the ridicule of God by Rabshakeh, Sennacherib's general, in II Kings 18:29-35.

There seems, however, to be a more sinister reference in the background. **Wicked counsellor** is variously translated. The word is *Belial* and is repeated in 15, where it is rendered "the wicked." This is often interpreted to mean a figure corresponding to Satan or the devil in Christian thought, a personification of evil. Behind the power of Assyria stands the power of darkness. Its impotence will be made evident in the face of Jehovah's omnipotence.

### 2. *Consolation to Judah* (1:12-13)

The Hebrew of these verses is uncertain but once again the word is comforting to the oppressed who have been long trodden underfoot by the enemy. The puzzling phrase **Though they be quiet, and likewise many,** has been rendered, "Although they are strong and many" (Berk.). Despite the enemy's strength, this yoke of bondage is to be broken. The prophet sees the events of history to be the workings of God, and the affliction of Judah to be under His direction—**Though I have afflicted thee, I will afflict thee no more** (12).

### 3. *Annihilation of Assyria* (1:14)

Once more attention is called to the religious nature of the conflict and Jehovah will triumph over the **vile** gods of Nineveh. The Assyrians had bestowed particular attention upon their temples, which abounded in stone figures and sculptured bas-reliefs.[5]

---

[4]*Op. cit.,* pp. 191-92.
[5]*Ibid.,* p. 212.

The finality of the destruction is predominant in the prophecy. **No more of thy name be sown** can be translated, "Your name shall no more be remembered" (Moffatt).

### 4. *Anticipations of Deliverance* (1:15; 2:2)

Nahum here borrows a beautiful and well-known passage from Isaiah; **Behold upon the mountains the feet of him that bringeth good tidings, that publisheth peace!** (15) The prophet pictures the messengers treading the mountain paths bringing to the inhabitants of Jerusalem the good news of the enemy's destruction. He optimistically sees this to be the foregleams of a golden age with the restoration of the whole nation to a working relationship with Jehovah and the establishment of peace. Verse 2 of the second chapter apparently goes with this address but to so associate it involves an interpretation and translation quite different from the KJV rendering. Maier advances a lengthy defense of a position which would be in accordance with the KJV, but the weight of scholarship rests on the other side. The American Translation is a representative rendering and 2:2 is placed in that version immediately following 1:15, reading as follows:

> For the Lord will restore the vine of Jacob
> likewise the vine of Israel;
> Though devastators have devastated them
> and laid waste their branches.

"Good News from Above" is the theme of vv. 12-15. The gospel is, by definition, **good tidings,** 15 or good news of (1) Deliverance, 13; (2) Comfort, 12; (3) Peace, 15; and (4) The vindication of righteousness, 14, 15*b* (W. T. Purkiser).

### C. THE FALL OF NINEVEH, 2:1, 3-13

#### 1. *The Destruction* (2:1, 3-9)

Like the sound of a mighty orchestra, Nahum's message rises to a thundering crescendo in his description of the impending battle. Even though it is an anticipated event, it is pictured in all its terrible color and gory detail. How accurate was it? Certainly it was a typical picture of warfare in those times with chariots and foot soldiers in predominance. As to the actual description of the fall of the city, there is little record in contemporary literature. The Babylonian Tablet, discovered by Mr. C. J. Gadd of the British Museum, is the most authoritative source of information. It supplies the date of the destruction of Nineveh in 612 B.C., and relates the fall of other Assyrian strongholds.

Unfortunately, only two lines of the text on the Babylonian Tablet are devoted to the victory over Nineveh and these are greatly mutilated. The siege lasted from the beginning of June until sometime in August, about two and one-half months.[6] There is nothing in the chronicle to either substantiate or disprove the stories which have been connected with the defeat of the city, and Gadd suggests that there is nothing improbable about these accounts.

The story goes that the capture of the city was made possible by a great storm of rain and thunder, which caused the river to flood and sweep away a large portion of the wall (cf. 1:8). The time of the invasion is easily in accord with such an occurrence. The heaviest rainfall in the Tigris district occurs normally in March, and coupled with the melting of the Armenian snows, results in the river attaining its greatest volume in April and May. "The truth doubtless is that Cyaxares simply took advantage of the devastation caused by an abnormally high Tigris in the preceding spring to press home his assault upon the only place in the walls which accident had rendered vulnerable."[7]

We shall see, however, that it may not have been the Tigris River which was the instrument of victory and further that the flooding may not have been accidental (cf. below).

What Nahum has given is not an ordered account of the siege, but rather pre-invasion "impressions," as G. A. Smith suggests.[8] There are three of these impressions—2:5 ff.; 3:2 ff.; and 3:12 ff.

*a. Taunts at the besieged* (2:1). **He that dasheth in pieces** is literally "the shatterer" and is sometimes identified with the word meaning "a hammer." Nahum evidently has in mind Cyaraxes, who had led the earlier siege against Nineveh, which had failed (see Introduction). On this anticipated occasion the Medes, under Cyaxares, joined forces with the Babylonians and moved in for a three months' siege, which was to result in the

---

[6]Gadd, *op. cit.*, p. 17.
[7]*Ibid.*, p. 18.
[8]*Op. cit.*, p. 103.

virtual end of the Assyrian Empire.[9] "The Besieger of the world
is at last besieged; every cruelty he has inflicted upon men is now
to be turned upon himself."[10]

With faith in a successful conquest, Nahum calls out in
derision for the Ninevites to prepare for the assault, using a
form of the verb which expresses its force with maximum emphasis.

> *The shatterer has come up*
>   *against you.*
> *Man the ramparts;*
> *watch the road;*
> *gird your loins;*
>   *collect all your strength* (RSV).

See the discussion of 2:2 in connection with 1:15.

b. *Description of the invader* (2:3). The invaders are pictured in exquisite battle array, clothed **in scarlet,** as was the
practice. Their shields were covered with skins dyed **red.** Herodotus pictures part of the army of Xerxes as wearing brightly
colored clothing; some "painted their bodies, half with chalk,
and half with vermillion."[11]

The text in this section and following is rather difficult and
innumerable variations in translation are the consequence. The
reference here to **flaming torches** is uncertain. The most likely
suggestion is that the description refers to the "burnished plates
of metal with which the chariots were mounted or mailed, and
the glittering weapons hung on them."[12] These polished surfaces
gleamed like torches in the sun.

**The fir trees shall be terribly shaken.** Two possible alternatives present themselves. Rather than **fir trees,** the word may be
more literally rendered "cypresses" and so may refer to the

[9]The capital was moved to another place by some who escaped the
siege, but the empire was broken.

[10]Smith, *op. cit.*, p. 102.

[11]*Hist.*, VII, 61, 69.

[12]A. B. Davidson, *Nahum, Habakkuk and Zephaniah*, "The Cambridge
Bible for Schools and Colleges," ed. J. J. S. Perowne (Cambridge: University
Press, 1896).

shafts of the spears, which were made out of cypress wood. However, "ancient classical authors often refer to spears as 'firs' and 'ash-trees.' "[13]

The interpretation which receives the greatest support is based upon the Septuagint, which renders the word "cypress" as "chargers" or "horsemen." In this case the reference would be to the cavalry charge. Following an Arabic root, the phrase **be terribly shaken** is rendered "mustered in array," or if left as it is, refers to the horses that quiver with impatience. Hence:

> *The shields of his heroes are crimson,*
> *the soldiers are clad in scarlet,*
> *His armoured chariots gleam like fire,*
> *And their horses prance at the muster* (Moffatt).

c. *The charge through the suburbs* (2:4). First, let us look at a picturesque but adequate translation of this scene:

> *His chariots tear through the*
> *open country*
> *and gallop across the broad*
> *spaces,*
> *flashing like torches,*
> *darting like lightning* (Moffatt).

Nineveh lay along the eastern bank of the Tigris River, where the Tigris is met by the Khoser, which crosses the city proper (see map). Low hills descend to the very north corner of the fortress, continue around the walls to the east and south, and return to the river at the south of the city. On the east there is a large, level plain about two and one-half by one and one-half miles. The exterior walls of the city were seven and one-half miles in circumference and estimates of the population it could accommodate range

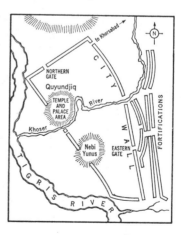

CITY OF NINEVEH

---

[13]Lehrman, *op. cit.*, p. 200.

from 175,000 to 300,000. Around the walls, except on the western side, about sixty feet distant, ran moats some one hundred fifty feet broad. Water was supplied by the Khoser to the moats south of it, and those to the north by a canal entering the city at the north corner.

These moats were controlled by dams and sluices. Past the moat on the eastern side were two outworks, one north and one south of the Khoser. The one on the south was in the form of a segment of a circle and was composed of two lines of fortification. In front of this was a third line of fortification which was closed on the south by a large fortress.

The Medes approached from the east and north so as to avoid known strong fortresses; they captured other fortresses which Nahum had predicted would fall into their hands like ripe figs (3:12). It is the opinion of military authorities that they attacked the city on the northeastern corner, where the ground height placed them on a level with the wall. Here they could also command the waterworks by which most of the moats were fed. Also their flank would be protected by the ravines of the Khoser on the northeast.

Verse 4 refers to the fighting in the suburbs which Nahum described as taking place before the walls were assaulted. It was on the northern approach that the famous suburbs of Nineveh are alleged to have lain, along the canal and the road to Khorsabad. Having been defeated there, the Assyrians would withdraw to the great walls and the waterworks would be yielded to the attackers.

d. *The assault on the wall* (2:5). After the suburbs had fallen, the **worthies** (best military units) were called to the attack. There is some disagreement as to whether this verse applies to the attackers or to the defenders. It seems more likely to be the former, as most modern translations render it:

> *Then he masses the picked men,*
> *they charge ahead,*
> *they rush to the wall,*
> *and the mantelet is fixed* (Moffatt).

These are the men who bear the battering rams and hence perhaps really **stumble in their walk** as they come to ram the gates. It is suggested that after having captured the sluices and waterworks they did not destroy them immediately, and therefore had to lay strong dams across the moats. The eastern moat was actually found to be filled with rubbish in front of a great breach in the wall.

Since the KJV obscures the meaning by turning its translation in favor of v. 5 as being a description of the defenders, the phrase **The defence** (Heb., "cover") **shall be prepared** is poorly rendered. All other translations speak of the "mantelet." This was a wooden framework covered with skins to shield the warriors as they operated the battering rams.

e. *The city falls* (2:6-8). Nineveh, which used the siege in its own military operations so successfully, is now to feel the force of its own weapon. And Nahum senses the exultation of the world that had lived in horror of her assaults. "He hears the very whips crack beneath the walls and the rattle of the leaping chariots; the end is slaughter, depression and a dead waste."[14]

The breaches in the wall could have been caused by the battering rams but also perhaps by directing the waters of the canals against the wall, which was made of mud bricks and earth. **The gates of the rivers** (6) may refer to the Khoser itself in its spring floods. It may have been confined and then released upon the sluices which channelled its passage under the eastern wall, thus breaching the wall. The flood of water would undermine the foundations of the buildings and **the palace** itself **be dissolved.**

Verse 7 is difficult as it stands in the KJV. There are several possibilities of interpretation, the most prominent one being that Nahum refers to the queen. If the interpretations suggested for 1:8, 11, 14 be correct, that there is an underlying spiritual conflict involved, the view that interprets the name **Huzzab** to be another name for Ishtar, the goddess of Assyria, has much credence. It had been Assyria's custom to lead away captive the gods of her victimized nations. Now her own chief goddess is to **be brought up** and carried away without dignity. In this case **her maids** would be the "sacred" harlots moaning as **doves** and beating their breasts in anguish.

The people, more particularly the soldiers, **flee away** (8) in undisciplined confusion. The calls of their officers, **Stand, stand,** go unheeded. Hence the defeat is complete.

[14]Smith, *op. cit.*, p. 102.

*f. The sack of the treasures* (2:9). Nineveh's great treasures, spoils of Assyria's own conquests, become the spoils of the victors. The verse has been translated dramatically: "Loot the silver! Loot the gold! There seems to be no end of treasures. Her vast uncounted wealth is stripped away" (*Living Prophecies*).

2. *The Desolation* (2:10-13)

In poetic language v. 10 describes the sacked city.

> *"Desolate! Desolation and ruin!*
> *Hearts faint and knees tremble,*
> *anguish is on all loins,*
> *all faces grow pale!* (RSV)

Nahum then pictures the city as **the dwelling of the lions** (11). **The old lion** had brought in his victims, mangled and bleeding, but in abundance to feed the hungry family. He had **filled his holes with prey, and his dens with ravin** (torn flesh, 12). Now they stand desolate, "cleaned out." Great fear and convulsions of terror are present on every hand. It is the Lord who stands over the scene—**Behold, I am against thee** (13). His word is bringing it to pass. The lions shall be cut off and Nineveh shall be no more.

# Section III God Shall Destroy the Evil

Nahum 3:1-19

In chapter 3 the passionate description of the fall of the city gives way to a reasoned explanation of why it was necessary.

## A. THE WICKEDNESS OF NINEVEH, 3:1-4

Nineveh is condemned for three things: her plundering, her destructiveness, and her wicked influence. The Assyrians were among the most cruel people in history. The chronicles of Ashurbanipal II (885-860 B.C.) tell of his own atrocities:

> I flayed all the chief men (in the city of Suru) who had revolted, and I covered the pillar with their skins; some I walled up within the pillar, some I impaled upon the pillar on stakes, and others I bound to stakes around the pillar, many within the border of my own land I flayed, and I spread their skins upon the walls; and I cut off the limbs of the officers, of the royal officers who had rebelled. Ahiababa I took to Nineveh. . . .
>
> . . . In the midst of the mighty mountain I slaughtered them, with their blood I dyed the mountain red like wool, with the rest of them I darkened the gullies and precipices of the mountains.[1]

Nahum rightly called Nineveh **the bloody city** (1). She had stripped other nations of their wealth and pillaged many towns, thus manifesting "no end to plunder."

Verse 3 refers to the cruel habit of cutting off the heads of the captives and heaping them up with other bodies before city gates. Again from the royal chronicle we read: "I formed a pillar of the living and of heads over against his city gate and 700 men I impaled on stakes. . . . Their young men and their maidens I burned in the fires."[2]

Nineveh is personified as **the wellfavoured harlot** (4), who entices her victims to their ruin by her displays of power and fair-seeming proposals. They respond to her charms only to fall prey to her greed. What she did not take by force she took by **witchcrafts** (deceit).

---

[1]Quoted in Maier, *op. cit.*, p. 291.
[2]*Ibid.*, p. 292.

### B. God's Opposition to Wickedness, 3: 5-7

The metaphor of the harlot is carried through in these verses. The condemnation described refers to the practice of exposing a woman convicted of unchastity to public gaze (cf. Ezek. 16: 37-39; Hos. 2:3). **Discover** (5) means to uncover, to remove that which served as a covering. Since Nineveh has played the harlot, she must suffer the fate of being displayed in disgrace. There are none to feel pity; rather the nations rejoice because of her destruction.

### C. Inevitability of Evil's Overthrow, 3: 8-13

Assyria herself, under Ashurbanipal, had overthrown **populous No** (Thebes, the Egyptian capital), thus extending her borders to the southernmost limit of the inhabited world. Why should this city be mentioned? First, because it too had been a great capital city; and second, because Nahum perhaps thought of it as depending on the Nile for protection just as Nineveh looked to the Tigris. The Nile, like other large rivers in the Bible, is called **the sea** (8).

Ashurbanipal's own account speaks of the fall of Thebes: "The entire city . . . my hands captured—silver, gold, precious stones, the contents of his palace, all that there was . . . coloured [raiment], cloth, horses and people, male and female."[3]

The two countries **Ethiopia and Egypt** (9) were closely allied, along with other helpers who increased the military might of Thebes. However, Eaton is right in observing that "Nahum did not regard the fall of Thebes as testimony to Assyrian strength, but to the fragility of all human empire. In the last analysis, Thebes had fallen because God had decreed her end."[4]

Verse 11 describes the shock of the invader's attack on Nineveh:

> You also will be drunken,
>   you will be dazed;
> you will seek
>   a refuge from the enemy (RSV).

**All thy strong holds** (12) refers to the outlying fortresses, which fell like **firstripe figs** into the hands of the invaders as they marched toward the city itself.

[3]Quoted in Lehrman, *op. cit.*, p. 205.
[4]*Op. cit.*, p. 75.

We need to be reminded that Nahum was not writing a history of a past event but was anticipating an impending crisis. Even though he is not making a pretense at detailed prediction, it is remarkable how exactly the events paralleled his descriptions. The defenders of the city fought desperately. But despite their courageous stand they were as helpless as **women** (13) before the onslaught. Nahum's emphasis again is that, when God's judgment falls, men are powerless to stand against it.

### D. THE DIRGE OF DEATH, 3:14-19

Once again—and finally—Nahum turns to the actual attack. Again he pours out his derisive invectives against the doomed city. He reverts to the same verb forms as before in giving terse, poignant instruction to prepare for their inevitable fate.

He exhorts them first to **draw thee waters for the siege** (14). Some archaeologists maintain that the water of the Khoser River was controlled by a large dam outside the city, thus both creating a means of flood control and a reservoir. This reservoir was contained by a magnificent double dam with massive river walls. Traces of the original dam gates or sluices were found in the ruins.[5] At this point, possibly Nahum envisions that the invaders will close these gates, thus cutting off the water supply to the city, since the water of the Tigris was undrinkable.

The prophet next calls upon them to make bricks to repair the crumbling fortifications. **Make strong the brickkiln** is usually translated, "Lay hold of the brick mold" (Berk.). But this preparation will be of no avail. **The fire** and **the sword** (15) are to prevail. The city was actually razed by fire, as the excavations show. According to tradition, the king, Sardanapalus, recognizing his destiny, burnt himself alive in his palace.[6] While the city is being destroyed by flames, the inhabitants are to be slaughtered by the sword.

The multitude of the Assyrians, **many as the locusts**, will not diminish the destruction, but rather like a plague of locusts they shall be annihilated. The destruction is seen to be complete, the silence of death reigns, the city is desolate. The words of the Babylonian Chronicle in its broken remains tell the final story and write a fitting epitaph for the mighty city:

[5]Maier, *op. cit.*, p. 253.

[6]F. W. Farrar, *The Minor Prophets* (New York: Fleming H. Revell Co., n.d.), p. 152.

38. [In the fourteenth year] the king of Akkod mustered his army . . . the men (?) of the king of the Umnan-Mandu to meet the king of Akkod
39. . . . they met one with the other
40. The king of Akkod . . . and [Cyaxa]res . . . he made to cross
41. By the bank of the Tigris they marched . . . against Ni[neveh] . . . they . . .
42. From the month of Sivan to the month of Ab three battles (?) . . .
43. A mighty assault they made upon the city, and in the month of Ab, [the . . . day the city was captured] . . . a great [havoc] of the Chief [men] was made.
44. At that time Sin-shan-ishkun, king of Assyria . . .
45. The Spoil of the City; a quantity beyond country they plundered, and [turned] the city into a mound and a ru[in] . . .'

But the recorded events of history are scarcely more exact than Nahum's inspired vision:

> *Assyria, your rulers are asleep,*
>   *your lords slumber in death!*
> *Your people are scattered all over the hills,*
>   *with none to rally them.*
> *You are shattered past repair, wounded to death.*
>                     (18-19, Moffatt)

'*Ibid.*, pp. 39-40.

*The Book of*

# HABAKKUK

H. Ray Dunning

# Introduction

## A. THE PROPHET

Actual knowledge about Habakkuk is very slight. Only his name is mentioned in the book, and in the Bible only here. There are traditions which are largely fanciful but perhaps with some grain of historical truth. Even the derivation of his name admits of several possibilities.

First it is very similar to an Assyrian word (*humbakuku*) which is the name of a flower. It is further related to a Hebrew word which means "to clasp or embrace." This was favored by Jerome and followed by Martin Luther, who turned it to an interesting interpretation: "He embraces his people, and takes them to his arms, i.e., he comforts them and holds them up, as one embraces a weeping child or person to quiet it with the assurance that if God will it shall be better soon."[1]

Jerome interpreted the name as indicating the prophet's love for God or that he wrestled with God in argument. The Rabbinic tradition also favors "embrace" as the root meaning of his name, and presents Habakkuk as the son of the Shunammite woman whom Elisha restored to life (II Kings 4:16-37). This is partially based on the possibility that the abstract form of his name may mean "darling." But here we are in the realm of fancy.

It is conjectured from 3:19 that Habakkuk was officially qualified to take part in the liturgical singing of the Temple, i.e., was a member of the Temple choir. The musical arrangement of c. 3 adds support to this view. If this is the case, he belonged to one of the Levitical families who were charged with the maintenance of the Temple music.

Habakkuk is an example of the rare occurrence in which one of the prophets is actually called "the prophet" (1:1; *nabi*). This leads one to believe that he was recognized as a professional prophet.

There is one further source of information entitled *Laws of the Prophets*. It dates from about the latter part of the fourth century, but its authorship is uncertain and it is considered

---

[1]Quoted in Keil & Delitzsch, *The Commentary on the Old Testament*, II, 49.

quite unreliable. This work relates that, when Nebuchadnezzar came up against Jerusalem, Habakkuk fled to a place called Ostrakine on the Egyptian coast. After the Chaldeans had left, it continues, Habakkuk returned to his own land, where he died and was buried, two years before the Jews returned from Babylon in 537 B.C.

## B. His Period

Habakkuk's message is timeless, yet his time provokes the questions he asks. He was a contemporary of the great prophet Jeremiah and his book is traditionally dated around 600 B.C., not long before the Babylonian captivity in 586 B.C. The question of date is far more important in the study of this book than many others. In fact it is intimately bound up with the interpretation of the message. If we could determine definitely who the peoples actually were who caused Habakkuk's concern, we could more accurately locate it historically. This turns out to be one of the knotty problems of the Old Testament. There are no extra-canonical sources by which one can pinpoint who the enemies were, so the student must depend entirely on the content of the prophecy itself, and this is far from decisive. The major problem here is identifying the "wicked" whom he denounces in the first paragraph (1:4). The only general agreement about the date seems to be that the book falls sometime between 697 and 586 B.C.

The Dead Sea Scrolls, a collection of writings discovered in 1947-48 near the Dead Sea, have been highly influential in much Old Testament study. Included is a commentary on the Book of Habakkuk. This commentary is considered to be the earliest "witness to the text of Habakkuk perhaps by many centuries."[2] It is dated by scholars in the first century B.C. Consequently it would have considerable bearing on the more modern interpretations of Habakkuk.

Taylor points out[3] three matters which he claims the Scrolls have confirmed:

(1) Chapter 3 was not an original part of the book. It was not included in the commentary which dealt only with cc. 1—2. The manner in which it was rolled prohibited the objection that c. 3 might have been torn off. However this does not say that

[2]C. L. Taylor, Jr., "Habakkuk" (Exegesis), *The Interpreter's Bible,* ed. George A. Buttrick, *et al.,* VI (New York: Abingdon Press, 1956), 974.
[3]*Ibid.,* p. 977.

Habakkuk was not the author of c. 3. In fact, the position of J. H. Eaton is that Habakkuk composed it later as a liturgical psalm and it was subsequently added to the original work. This seems sound.

(2) The use of the name "Chaldeans" in 1:6 is genuine. This has been one of the major points of discussion. By using a word closely related as a substitute (*chittim*) some scholars have endeavored to interpret the avengers which the Lord was using as the Greeks of Alexander the Great. The Dead Sea Scrolls commentary would have had every reason to use this substitute word but rather retained the traditional reading. This seems quite decisive in limiting the interpretation of the passage to the period of the Chaldeans.

(3) The Book of Habakkuk appears to have had a number of variant texts up until the first century B.C. This allows for a great deal of assumed composition over the years which many scholars have exploited to the full. It is clear that the text of Habakkuk has varied in copying, but much of the shifting of passages to fit various theories is quite arbitrary and imaginative.

## C. His Problems

Two problems face the prophet. Both have to do with the ways of God with men. Habakkuk is one of the few men who have been bold enough to wrestle and argue with God. Perhaps the key verse is 2:1—"I will stand upon my watch, and set me upon the tower, and will watch to see what he will say unto me, and what I shall answer when I am reproved."

The crucial answer is in 2:4b—"But the just shall live by his faith."

# *Outline*

# Section I  Habakkuk's Complaint

## A. Superscription, 1:1

Although Habakkuk is clearly called a **prophet** (*nabi*), he is not a prophet in the traditional sense. Ordinarily it was the prophet's function to speak to men for God, to proclaim the divine will which was received in a special revelation. In the case of this man, we see just the reverse: the prophet speaks to God for men. He is carrying on a discourse with God and that in such a manner as to classify him as almost a skeptic rather than a prophet. "This is the beginning of speculation in Israel."[1]

It is possible that what we really have here is an insight into the inner life of a prophet, the hidden struggles prior to proclamation. In a different sort of way we have the same thing in the case of Hosea, whose marital problems prepared his heart for the message he was to preach. With Habakkuk it may be the hammering out on the anvil of life of a theological foundation for his public preaching. This would accord with the contention of Davidson, who maintains that the real subject of the book is the destruction of the Chaldean, found in c. 2.[2]

**Burden** is usually translated "oracle" and implies revelation. It refers many times to future events and is also often used in connection with the pronouncement of doom (cf. Obad. 1).

## B. The Prophet's Problem, 1:2-4

It is at the point of identifying the occasion of this complaint that the greatest diversity of interpretation arises. There are at least five clearly different opinions, each with an elaborate defense of its position. The view that requires the most juggling of the text is the one that identifies **the wicked** (4) with the Chaldeans themselves. But the establishment of the veracity of the reading in v. 6 as future reasonably eliminates this identifica-

---

[1] G. A. Smith, "The Book of the Twelve Prophets," *The Expositor's Bible*, ed. W. Robertson Nicoll (New York: A. C. Armstrong & Son, 1896), II, 131.

[2] *Op. cit.*, p. 48.

tion. A more likely candidate, yet still with little probability, is Egypt. If the writing is placed during the early reign of Jehoiakim, there is a good case to be made for Egypt's being the object of Habakkuk's complaint. Jehoiakim was a vassal of Egypt under Pharaoh-necho, who had only recently killed King Josiah and established a foothold in Asia east of Palestine.

Another more probable answer, and one which receives considerable support, is the identification of **the wicked** with Assyria, which had occupied the attention of Nahum. This terror of the nations was oppressing Judah and exercising great influence in her internal affairs. Likewise it was the Chaldeans who put an end to this great and fearful nation.

One argument in favor of the view that the complaint is directed at alien interference is that there is no exhortation to repentance. It is supposed that such an exhortation would certainly follow if it were directed toward "native misdoing."[3] To follow this line of reasoning would lead to the conclusion that the prophecy was written during Josiah's days when idolatry was banned, and that the prophet was speaking a lament for his people over their undeserved oppression by the foreigners.

However, it seems most probable that this complaint is occasioned by evil within the prophet's own nation of Judah. This is the traditional interpretation and makes the most sense out of the total picture, as the nature of the second complaint reveals.

**How long?** (2) The prophet has cried out but it seems that God does not hear his cry. Therefore he questions God. Why is it that God does nothing? Here is the classic problem of "Truth forever on the scaffold, Wrong forever on the throne." The excruciating situation arises out of the vast discrepancy between faith and fact. If God is just and sovereign, why do the righteous suffer while the wicked prosper? Here is a question raised by multitudes of people in every age. In Habakkuk it is the same problem at a national level that the Book of Job deals with in the personal sphere. It is more easily dealt with however on the personal level and therefore the test to Habakkuk's faith is really the more severe.

Only those who have faith in a good God have any problem with regard to the government of the world. If one believes in polytheism, or in an indifferent or wicked deity, he has no prob-

[3]F. W. Farrar, *The Minor Prophets* (New York: Fleming H. Revell Co., n.d.), p. 161.

lem with the apparent injustices in the world. It is monotheistic faith that must wrestle for its very life in the face of facts that challenge it.

Many have supposed it to be audacious to question the working of Providence. This position is shown to be false by the inclusion of Job's and Habakkuk's complaints in the Bible. If further evidence is needed, one may remind himself of the cry from Calvary, "Why hast thou forsaken me?" (Matt. 27:46; Mark 15:34) It is probably more wrong to stifle one's sincere doubts than to give vent to them in an earnest effort to find a clue to the meaning of life. G. A. Smith was right when he observed in one of his incisive comments, "It is not the coarsest but the finest temperaments which are exposed to skepticism."

There are two words translated cry in v. 2. The first is used especially as a cry for help; the second means to cry out as one does in sudden alarm. Both words are also used in Job 19:7.

Civil wrongs abound (3), a situation which likewise prevailed in the eighth century, in the days of Amos and Hosea, who also cried out with vehemence against such perversions. There are three pairs of nouns used to point up the situation: **iniquity** and **grievance** (perverseness), **spoiling and violence,** and **strife and contention** (cf. Isa. 58:4). *Living Letters* renders the verse: "Must I forever see this sin and sadness all around me? Wherever I look there is oppression and bribery and men who love to argue and to fight."

**The law** (4) is the Torah, the Jewish term for the law of Moses. **Judgment** (*mishpat*) refers to an established practice or custom.[4] The Torah was the fountainhead of all legal justice, but here the people were deprived of its benefits chiefly because the **wicked . . . compass about the righteous.** The word **slacked** means "numbed" or "paralyzed" (cf. Gen. 45:26, where it is translated "fainted"). Such a situation evidently prevailed under Manasseh, with a godless ruling party in power. True liberty and justice are firmly based on godliness and righteousness; where these are absent, justice is perverted. Habakkuk infers that even where a semblance of justice is maintained, **wrong judgment proceedeth**—it "goes forth perverted" (Smith-Goodspeed). The wicked are able to twist a "right" judgment to their own ends.

[4]Taylor, *op. cit.*, p. 981.

Section **II** *God's Answer*

Habakkuk 1:5-11

## A. God's Work, 1:5

God's answer to Habakkuk is the comforting assurance, I am working. The place where God is working is indicated by the phrase, **Behold ye among the heathen.** This is translated by others, "among the nations." The same word is translated in 13, "them that deal treacherously." Several suggest that 5 should read, "Behold, ye faithless ones" (i.e., ye faithless Judahites;[1] cf. Acts 13:41, where the LXX is followed).[2]

The admonition, **Wonder marvelously,** may be translated, "Wonder and be astounded" (RSV). There are in Hebrew two forms of the same verb which Taylor suggests may be reproduced in English by "Shudder and be shocked."[3]

The prophet declares, **Ye will not believe** what God will do. This may have been because it was incredible that the iron colossus of Assyria in fact had feet of clay and would soon come crashing to the ground.[4] Or perhaps it would be unbelievable to the Judeans that God would give them into the hands of a foreign nation—them who had the Temple, the sacrifices, and the city of David.

The phrase **in your days** limits the prophecy to the lifetime of the hearers if we maintain the integrity of the book.

## B. The Instrument of God's Work, 1:6-11

**Chaldeans** (6) is from the Hebrew word *Kasdim,* which is the Babylonian and Assyrian word *Kaldu,* mentioned in Assyrian inscriptions from about 880 B.C. The Kaldu had their home in lower Babylonia. In 721 B.C., Merodach-baladan became king and ruled twelve years (Isa. 39:1). According to inscriptions he was called king of the land of Kaldu. Under Nabopolassar and

---

[1]S. R. Driver, *The Minor Prophets,* II, "New Century Bible" (New York: Oxford University Press, 1906), 67.

[2]*Ibid.,* p. 67, n.       [3]*Op. cit.,* p. 982.

[4]J. H. Eaton, *Obadiah, Nahum, Habakkuk and Zephaniah* (London: SCM Press, 1961), *loc. cit.*

Nebuchadnezzar the Kaldu became the ruling class in Babylon. At first Nabopolassar seems to have been viceroy of Babylon under Ashurbanipal of Assyria and his successor. However, during an uprising of southern subject peoples, probably in 612 or 611 B.C., he joined forces with the rebels and declared his independence from Assyria.

By the time of the traditional date of Habakkuk, Nabopolassar had been on the throne twenty years and was well known in Judea. This dating would limit the predictive import of the first vision. In an effort to provide for this, Driver maintains that the expression **raise up** means, "I am raising up so as to establish and confirm," meaning that Babylon was not yet in a position to challenge the dominion of Assyria.

Habakkuk now proceeds to give a descriptive account of these Chaldean invaders:

### 1. *Their Character* (1:6)

The Chaldeans were **bitter and hasty**—"a fierce nation swayed by violent impulses, which will commit terrible deeds without forethought."[5]

### 2. *Their Arrogance* (1:7)

The statement, **Their judgment and their dignity shall proceed of themselves,** is better translated, "Their justice and dignity proceed from themselves" (RSV). The Chaldeans became a "law unto themselves," assuming political superiority. **Judgment** is *mishpat*, found in v. 4 (see comments there); here it implies both legal and moral right. International law was not a concept for such barbarous tribes, nor was there any idea of natural law such as would dictate universal canons of justice. Might made right in their eyes, and upon their own military supremacy they erected their standards of justice.

### 3. *Their Warfare* (1:8)

**Leopards** are considered among the swiftest of animals and also lie in wait for their prey, upon whom they spring with suddenness. **Evening wolves** are referred to twice in scripture (cf. Zeph. 3:3). They were symbols of fierceness "on account of the sudden ravages which, in the keenness of their hunger, they com-

[5]Lehrman, *op. cit.*, p. 215.

mit on the flocks at that time of day."[6] **Their horsemen shall spread themselves** has been interpreted, "Their horsemen press proudly on" (RSV). **The eagle** refers to a vulture but not a carrion vulture; rather one that sweeps down from the heavens to capture its live prey.

### 4. *Their Conquests* (1:9)

This is one of the most difficult verses in the book. The first phrase is rather clear but the next clause is obscure and the text is uncertain. The RSV rendering, "Terror of them goes before them," is admittedly an emendation of the text. Some commentators give it the meaning of so hastily and eagerly conquering territory that they seem to swallow it up. This interpretation rests on the word which is translated in the KJV as **sup up.** It is related to a verb in Gen. 24:17 translated, "Give me a drink," or literally, "cause one to swallow." Like the east wind with its drying power so effective that it seems to drink the moisture, they "swallow up" their victims.

The most consistent view would appear to be to interpret the passage as referring to their conquests, which resembled the strong east wind driving irresistibly forward.

### 5. *Their Invincibility* (1:10)

No power shall be able to withstand the mighty sweep of the Chaldeans. They shall march with derision over all who dare to resist. **Heap dust** refers to the military tactic of raising mounds to the heights of defenders' walls. Thus the attacking warriors were on a level with the defenders and nullified the protection of the walls.

### 6. *Their Exaltation* (1:11)

The first clause is exceedingly difficult.[7] There are apparently three stages in the self-elevation of the Chaldees: (1) They were so elated by the fortresses they had taken that they changed direction and moved on to new conquests, perhaps to Judah. (2) "And they became guilty" (Lehrman) is a phrase omitted by the KJV. (3) The third step is making might their god. This is the consensus in distinction to the KJV, which says they impute

---

[6]E. Henderson, *The Book of the Twelve Minor Prophets* (New York: Sheldon and Co., 1864), *ad loc.*

[7]See Taylor, *op. cit.*, p. 983.

**his power unto his god.** In any case it possibly means that in deifying their own might they became guilty of denying God.

Eaton contends that this description (6-11) does not accurately describe the advance of the Babylonian armies. If this judgment be accepted, it need not disturb us. Habakkuk's vision is an apocalyptic-type description of a visitation of judgment. In fact, some have maintained these invaders to be apocalyptic figures without any particular historical counterparts. An acceptable position seems to be that, whereas this may not be detailed historical description, it is a reference to a definite people and their task as God's instrument.

We have here an implicit philosophy of history which accords with the insights of the great prophets like Isaiah. God is the Lord of history, who makes even the wrath of men to praise Him. He uses men who have other aims, and who attribute their power to other sources, to carry out His purposes in history. Thus His government is assured and at the same time the nations remain accountable for their actions. This faith, however, raises another and perhaps even more acute problem for Habakkuk, which he proceeds to present.

# Section III   Habakkuk Questions God's Answer

Habakkuk 1:12-17

Habakkuk's question now seems to be not, Why this kind of world? but, Why is God like He is? Here is a new kind of speculation in Israel. The prophet has a basic faith in the kind of God known to Israel, and it seems to him inconsistent that such a God could use an instrument so unrighteous as the Chaldeans. **We shall not die** (12) may read, "You shall not die" (Moffatt). However, RSV retains the KJV meaning. If this reading be retained, it becomes an expression of faith in spite of the prophet's doubts. The meaning also fits the last part of the verse, which relates why God has established the Chaldean nation —**for correction**, or the chastisement of His people.

Habakkuk has no question about the holiness of God. It is absolute, and moral in its nature: **Thou art of purer eyes than to behold evil, and canst not look on iniquity** (13). God's holiness cannot tolerate sin and evil in any form. But the problem is that the nation chosen for chastisement is **more righteous** than the one administering punishment. Fear grips the heart of the prophet as he now beholds the rapacious advance of the Chaldeans and realizes that soon his own people, even the righteous remnant, will be caught in its net.

Men become like hapless **fishes of the sea** (14), or earthworms, leaderless in the face of the relentless advance. The picture of fishing is carried through. The fisherman (Chaldea) takes them **with the angle** (15; hook), and draws multitudes of fish from the sea by his **net and drag** (seine). This continues until he is filled and then he piles the fish on the shore to die.[1]

Sacrificing **unto their net** (16) would seem to compare to v. 11 and indicates that they were worshipping their power and might. Burning **incense** to their seine, they live in luxury, gloating in self-adoration, making might their god.

In despair, Habakkuk closes his lament with these pathetic words:

*Shall he keep on emptying his net forever,*

*And never cease slaying the nations?* (17, Smith-Goodspeed)

---

[1]David A. Hubbard, "Habakkuk," *The Biblical Expositor*, ed. Carl F. H. Henry (Philadelphia: A. J. Holman Co., 1960), II, 348.

Section **IV** *The Prayer Watch*

Habakkuk 2:1-6a

This passage is perhaps the best known of any part of Habakkuk's prophecy. There are at least two oft-quoted verses which abound with meaning for both the day of Habakkuk and the present. It is no doubt the central passage of the book. Seemingly taken aback by his own outburst of rashness in impeaching God before the bar of human justice, the prophet feels sure that God's answer this time will be in the form of a rebuke. How surprised he must have been when the answer came, as if God was not at all disturbed by the railings of this poor mortal!

A. HABAKKUK'S SOLILOQUY, 2:1

Not now conversing with God, the prophet is musing within his own mind as to the outcome of the past events. He proposes to betake himself to his **tower.** This is no doubt a figurative term, possibly being his place of prayer. There he will station himself "as a watchman looks out from his watchtower into the distance"[1] (cf. II Sam. 18:24; II Kings 9:17). The watchtower refers figuratively to some part of the fortification on which a watchman might naturally place himself (cf. Nah. 2:1). Driver suggests the word "muniment." This may suggest that he has built his case (fortification) against God, now he wants to see how God will attack the problem. On the other hand, it may suggest that he has a rampart to guard, the heritage of truth from the past which now needs to be clarified by this new turn of events. **Will watch to see** means he will "look forth" to see.

**When I am reproved** is literally "the complaint of me," which is ambiguous. In the light of the context, Douglas, Driver, *et al.,* think this means the complaint *by* the prophet, rather than *against* the prophet. Just the reverse is understood by the RSV, KJV, and others. The poignant words of Taylor lend support to the KJV: "One cannot overlook the element of arrogance implicit in the demand that God answer to man for his behavior."[2]

This was a time of withdrawal, where in quietness of soul the prophet could see what was indiscernible in the bustle of life. In times of crisis, men need to come apart for a time to commune with God, to get their vision clarified and their perspectives straight.

[1]Davidson, *op. cit.,* p. 74.    [2]*Op. cit.,* p. 986.

275

## B. The Tarrying Vision, 2:2-3

The Lord answered without rebuking Habakkuk for his complaint. The answer came to him in the form of a **vision** (2), i.e., a prophecy or revelation. It was to be written on tablets, not **tables**—first, so that all might read; and second, because it was for the future. The tablets were of baked clay, having great enduring quality. It is suggested that the customary use of such tablets was for public notices (cf. Isa. 8:1).[3]

**Make it plain** is a reference to Deut. 27:8. It probably refers to "distinct writing" so that **he may run that readeth it.** Lehrman translates this phrase, "that a man may read it swiftly." However, Adam Clarke objects to this view on the basis that God never intends that His words shall be understood by the careless. He argues that the Bible is not to be read like a signboard, but with study, meditation, and prayer. Consequently he interprets the words as meaning that whoever attentively peruses it may speed to save his life from the attack of the Chaldeans. By others it is understood to mean that whoever reads it might be able to run and publish it to all within his reach. It is called by some a Hebrew idiom, but at any rate it has become an English idiom, "to read on the run."

**The vision is yet for an appointed time** (3). The vision is for the future and is directed toward **the end.** The vision itself is personified, the second phrase being literally translated, "It pants toward the end." The verb in the clause **it shall . . . not lie** is the same used to refer to streams which dry up in the summer.[4] This prophecy is eagerly moving forward to its accomplishment, and will not "dry up" until it has been fulfilled.

The prophet adds encouragement to patience so that the reader may not faint in his expectation, even in the face of delay. Compare the proclamation to the saints in tribulation, to whom the angel cried literally, "There shall be no more delay" (Rev. 10:6).

According to Driver, the word **tarry** means literally "be behind," thus implying that the fulfillment will arrive on time, and will not be late. "It will come, if not in Habakkuk's time, yet in God's Time."[5]

---

[3]Davidson, *op. cit.*, p. 75.        [4]Lehrman, *op. cit.*, p. 219.

[5]J. E. McFadyen, "Habakkuk," *Abingdon Bible Commentary* (New York: Abingdon-Cokesbury Press, 1929), p. 806.

Once again we glimpse an insight into the prophetic philosophy of history which is linear, with a terminal point. The ancient Greeks thought of history as circular, it being "the moving image of eternity" (Plato). Many moderns see history as meaningless because going nowhere. Unlike these, the prophet believes history to be under divine control, and moving toward a culmination when "God's righteous judgment will be revealed." While apocalyptic thought, on which this verges, arises especially in periods of persecution, the Hebrew-Christian tradition is through and through apocalyptic in its essence.[6]

C. The Divine Response, 2:4

This verse really is the climax of the book, for in it we have the culmination of the prophet's search. Unfortunately the text is quite corrupt.

**His soul which is lifted up is not upright in him.** There seem to be alternate readings, both of which the KJV has adopted and which literally would read: "Behold it is puffed up; not right is his soul in him." The Ain Feshka commentary supports "puffed up" rather than "not made straight."[7] By changing one letter in the Hebrew word for the second reading, the RSV comes out with the very good, "He whose soul is not upright in him shall fail." This has strength because it thus takes the form of an antithetic parallelism with two subjects in contrast: the "wicked" (so Aramaic paraphrase) and **the just.**

The Septuagint has a somewhat different implication and the New Testament quotation of this verse in Heb. 10:38 follows this rendering: "If any man draw back, my soul shall have no pleasure in him." It is this also which Smith-Goodspeed follows in its translation, "Verily, the wicked man—I take no pleasure in him."

However the verse be phrased, the meaning is clear. Men like the Chaldeans who are puffed up with the sense of their own value, yet who are not right in God's sight, will soon perish. "They are like the chaff which the wind driveth away" (Ps. 1:4). This is God's answer to Habakkuk's first problem. Cook makes an excellent summary: "In one short saying, the two general aspects of the prophet's inquiry are dealt with; the pride and injustice of the invader are dealt with, and the just man is assured of life, i.e.,

---

[6]Cf. H. H. Rowley, *The Relevance of Apocalyptic.*
[7]Taylor, *op. cit.,* p. 988.

preservation from evil and salvation on the condition that he hold steadfastly to the principle of faith."[8]

**The just shall live by his faith.** The word rendered **faith** is the Hebrew *emunah,* from a verb meaning originally "to be firm," and is used in the Old Testament in the physical sense of steadfastness.[9] Thus the better rendering is "faithfulness." Faith is a word for which, in the New Testament active sense, the Hebrew has no equivalent—though the term "believe" is derived from the same root as *emunah.*[10]

*Emunah* is the word used to describe the uplifted hands of Moses, which were steady (Exod. 17:12). It is also used of men in charge of money who "dealt faithfully" (II Kings 12:15). It is closely akin, if not identical, to the English idiomatic statement, "Hold steady," implying that if one does not "bolt," the circumstances that surround him will alter. Lehrman's suggested meaning of the intention of this exhortation is good: "The righteous Israelite, who remains unswervingly loyal to the moral precepts, will endure, although he has to suffer for his principles; whereas the wicked, who enjoy a temporary ascendency through their violation of right, are in the end overthrown and humbled."[11]

So, as Farrar says, this oracle "contains all that is necessary for the justification of God and the consolation of man."[12]

The Septuagint translated *emunah* by *pistis* (faith). It was this translation which the New Testament writers made use of and thus incorporated the vision of Habakkuk into the very heart of the Christian preaching (*kerygma*). Paul quotes this clause twice (Rom. 1:17; Gal. 3:11) in support of his doctrine of justification by faith. By it he "intends that single act of faith by which the sinner secures forgiveness and justification." It is also quoted along with the last clause of v. 3 in Heb. 10:37-38 to illustrate the benefits of faith.

In 1:12 and 2:1-4 we see "Living by Faith." The text, **The just shall live by his faith.** (1) Faith in God's holiness, His justice, His might, 1:12; (2) Faith demonstrated and rewarded in watchful prayer, clearer vision, and obedience, 2:1-3 (G. B. Williamson).

---

[8]Farrar, *op. cit.,* p. 165.         [9]Smith, *op. cit.,* p. 140.
[10]IB, VI, 989.                  [11]*Op. cit.,* p. 219.
[12]*Op. cit.,* p. 168.

D. THE FATE OF THE GREEDY, 2: 5-6a

This passage has a double difficulty: to which paragraph
should it be joined? and how shall it be translated? It gives to
some the impression of being a climactic description of the character of the Chaldeans. Others wish to associate it with the woes
which follow, making it to be their introduction.

**Wine** seems to be the subject. The ASV reads: "Yea, moreover, wine is treacherous, a haughty man, that keepeth not at
home; who enlargeth his desire as Sheol [hell]." The man given
to wine is seldom at home, and is subject to inflamed desires
and passions.

Eaton declares that the ASV translation has little meaning
but he has defended this type of "personification," saying that the
cultic prophet often resorted to riddle when uttering a condemnation which he could not speak plainly because of danger to his
safety. This then would be an oblique oracle, directed as a
"dark parable" toward the enemy. It is the adoption of a proverb
about the deceitful nature of wine which becomes a *de facto*
description of the greedy conquerors.

Eaton, as many others, combines 6a with 5 and gives his own
translation: "Shall not these all raise a parable against him,
oblique speech riddles against him, saying . . . ?" Most modern
translators describe this as a taunt-song—"a song with hidden
and provocative allusions."[13] Thus it provides a transition into
the following section.

[13]Taylor, *op. cit.*, p. 990.

Section **V** *The Five Woes*

Habakkuk 2:6b-20

Davidson considers the preceding section of the book preliminary while in this section is the real subject of the prophecy. The writer, however, considers this section to be subsidiary to the central concern, which is the passage just preceding.

Most scholars consider the "woes" of this section to be addressed to the Chaldeans, and perhaps a primary intention in this direction may be granted. However, the principles of evil described are subject to God's judgment and wrath wherever they appear. These "woes" may therefore be considered as parallel with the "woes" of Isa. 5:8-25 and related to the wickedness of Habakkuk's own people.

## A. THE MERCILESS CAPITALIST, 2:6b-8

The Chaldean is compared to one who multiplies his own wealth at the expense of another, unmindful of and not caring for the despair of his victims. He is motivated by insatiable lust for gain.

**Thick clay** (6) means pledges. Chaldea is a merciless usurer who requires the nations to give him heavy pledges. The word **increaseth** seems to allude to the custom of exacting usury, a custom hated by the Jews. "The Chaldean is represented as a creditor who exacts heavy interest; the victimized nations are thus debtors, but also 'biters,' who, when their day comes, will punish him remorselessly for his exactings."[1] Perhaps it may be paraphrased in English slang, "You have put the bite on them; they will soon put the bite on you." The tables will soon be turned and those who are victimized will see themselves vindicated in the overthrow of their oppressors.

**Vex thee** (7) is a stronger word than the English indicates. It has the significance of "shaking violently," like the wind shakes the tree so that its fruit falls to the ground.[2] This will be done to cause them to disgorge their plunder, to "shake them loose" from their ill-gotten gain.

[1]Driver, *op. cit.*, p. 79.    [2]Lehrman, *op. cit.*, p. 220.

280

**Booties** (spoils) is plural and thus intensive, revealing the extent of the plunder to be torn from the oppressor. The faith behind this cry is that there is a *lex talionis* in history, a principle of retribution that the wrong will be punished; "he who has spoiled will be spoiled," measure for measure (cf. Isa. 33:1).

### B. THE WEALTHY VILLAIN, 2:9-11

In this "taunt-song," the cry is against the Chaldean's rapacity and self-aggrandizement. It describes the nation which is establishing itself by plunder and making efforts only at selfish self-security. This is indeed **an evil covetousness to his house** (9). In this effort the enemy has "set high his nest, to save him from the grasp of calamity."[3]

The first song affirmed Habakkuk's faith in a law of retribution. This one pictures the nation attempting to evade this law. But though having secured himself like the eagle in its **nest** (9) among the crags, and having silenced every witness against him, he has **sinned against** his own **soul** (10). The **stone . . . beam** and **timber** (11) of his very house cry out in protest. "His would indeed be a haunted house."[4]

### C. THE DECEITFUL RULER, 2:12-14

The same condemnation voiced in 12 is made of Jerusalem in Mic. 3:10 and of Jehoiakim in Jer. 22:13, 17: **Woe to him that buildeth a town with blood!**

Verse 13 has two possible meanings. One is that the oppressed people will not forever see their labors go up in smoke. More probable is the idea that the labors of the Chaldeans are destined for the **fire** (13), which will destroy the cities they have built. Their work will end in **vanity**. This same word is used by *Koheleth* ("the Preacher") to describe life without God (Eccles. 1:2). It means "emptiness" or, literally, "striving after wind." Thus the cities and kingdoms built on blood are self-defeating, such establishments being acts of historical suicide.

In contrast to the perishing kingdoms of unrighteousness are the conquests of Jehovah, whose kingdom will overthrow the kingdoms of this world and be established over the whole earth. **For the earth shall be filled with the knowledge of the glory of**

---

[3]Smith, *op. cit.*, p. 146.    [4]McFadyen, *op. cit.*, p. 807.

**the Lord, as the waters cover the sea** (14). The members of this Kingdom do not toil only to have their works burned up in the fire. They have their treasures where moth and rust do not corrupt nor thieves break through and steal (Matt. 6:19).

## D. THE DRUNKEN EXPLOITER, 2:15-17

The reference in 15 is to the intoxicating effects of strong drink which cause one to become insensible, thus exposing himself to the gaze and exploitation of any who would take advantage. The prophet is possibly thinking of Noah (Gen. 9:21) or Lot (Gen. 19:30-35).

The actual reading is obscure in meaning. In order to use the word **bottle** (15) as in the KJV, the vowel points must be altered. As it stands in the Hebrew text, the word is "wrath," very similar to **bottle**. The text itself says that wrath was mixed with the drink. Consequently Douglas translates, "Woe unto him that giveth his neighbor drink, that addest thy venom thereto, and makest him drunken also, that thou mayest look on their nakedness." The meaning perhaps is that the Babylonians make their proposed victims drink (metaphorically) drugged wine to increase their stupefaction and helplessness.[5]

But once again the principle of retribution operates. These who have given the cup will themselves be forced to drink the **cup of the Lord's right hand** (16). In so drinking, they become intoxicated. In fact they are already **filled with shame** (sated), and the ensuing helplessness will issue in disaster to themselves. The wicked man will suffer the same thing he has perpetrated on others.

**Shameful spewing** is one word in the Hebrew, an intensive form of the word "shame." It seems to be a play on words comparing the first phrase—**filled with shame for** (instead of) **glory** —with this second intensive use, **Shameful spewing shall be on thy glory.** Lehrman translates **shameful** as "filthiness" and quotes Kimchi as interpreting it to be a compound word composed of "disgrace" and "vomiting," indicative of the vomiting that follows a drunkard's orgy. Thus the KJV translation is excellent.

According to Isa. 14:8 the Babylonians stripped the Lebanon forest, which explains the meaning of v. 17. It is interesting that

---

[5]Lehrman, *op. cit.*, p. 222.

Habakkuk conceives of this rape of nature as an injustice which is worthy of divine retribution. One may conclude that here is a view which encompasses the whole of life as being under divine rule. Wholesale violation of nature should not be carried on lightly even for religious purposes (the building of temples, as the enemy had done).

### E. The Stupid Idolater, 2:18-20

The denunciation in these verses is unique in that the **woe** is restrained until later in the oracle (v. 19) rather than appearing at the beginning, as in the case of the preceding ones. Perhaps it is intended to be more intense because it is of a strictly religious nature, dealing with the worship of idols. The stupidity of idolatry is caricatured in poignant language. The term translated **idols** (18) is a contemptuous word meaning "nonentities." The Smith-Goodspeed translation has clearly captured the striking picture:

> *Of what use is an idol when its designer has designed it*
> *Or a molten image, and a teacher of lies?*
> *For he who designed his own image trusts in it*
> *So that he makes dumb nonentities!*

**Arise, it shall teach!** (19) Habakkuk is astounded that men call upon inert matter to communicate. He has noted, however, that the dumb idol teaches lies, because the idol says only what is put into its mouth. A nature perverted to the point of worshipping idols will place within its mouth approbation for those things in which a perverted nature would delight. Here, however, Habakkuk shows the absurdity of expecting a real revelation from these human creations. The affirmative statement should perhaps be cast in the form of a question, as, "Can this give revelation?" (RSV)

One is reminded of Elijah's taunts at the prophets of Baal who in agony pled with their dumb deity to answer (I Kings 18:26-29), or of Jeremiah's parody on idolatry in Jer. 10:3-16.

Verse 20 is one of the most thrilling passages in the Old Testament. In vivid contrast to the dumb idols, who sit in silence in their morbid temples surrounded by vile worship, **The Lord is in his holy temple: let all the earth keep silence before him.** This may have been a call to worship in the language of the

Temple service and provides a fitting transition to the liturgical hymn which follows in c. 3.

**Silence** is a Hebrew exclamation meaning, "Hush!" or, "Be still!" Thus the series of woes begins with a revelation that God is working. It is a call to the righteous to be faithful. This affirmation of faith is an appropriate capstone to v. 4, the golden text of Habakkuk: "The just shall live by his . . . [faithfulness]."

# Section VI *A Liturgical Hymn*

Habakkuk 3:1-19

## A. INTRODUCTION, 3:1

This section is designated as **a prayer,** but the prayer proper is limited to v. 2. The central petition is, **Revive thy work** (2), and the whole psalm then is an amplification of this petition. Therefore it may be called a psalm of supplication in which the prophet is praying for the realization of his vision of God's intervention.

**Upon Shigionoth** (1) means "in dithyrambic." The Septuagint renders the phrase as "on stringed instruments." Henderson translates it, "with triumphal music," quoting Delitzsch as pointing out this particular type of irregular music to be particularly suited for songs of victory. The phrase is also found in the title of Psalms 7 and might be rendered, "to the music of psalms of ecstasy." "It denotes a wandering, devious, crooked course, where thought, feeling, and time rapidly change with the new strophe."[1] Thus this is an instruction as to the mode of rendering the psalm musically.

The consensus of scholars is that the key to understanding the chapter is the Exodus and its resulting effect upon the thinking of Israel. This historical event moulds the prophet's expectation of and prayer for another great divine deliverance. It takes the form of a "revelation of God in nature for the deliverance of Israel."[2]

The musical signs indicate that this was a psalm used in the Temple liturgy. It has also found a large place in the preaching and poetry of the Christian Church. St. Augustine, in *The City of God* (18:32), gives an exposition of it, spiritualizing it to apply to the first and second comings of Christ.

It may also represent the vision from the prophet's watchtower (2:2), being what he *saw,* in the same way as 2:4-20 is what he *heard.*

---

[1]Ewald, quoted in Farrar, *op. cit.,* p. 171.
[2]Smith, *op. cit.,* p. 149.

285

B. The Prayer, 3:2

Habakkuk is speaking on behalf of the people. The background is **thy speech,** the report of the fame of Jehovah in His deliverance of Israel from Egypt (Num. 14:15; Deut. 2:25). It does not refer to an immediate ecstatic vision which he is receiving, but has clear, historical roots. The whole Old Testament story is understood to be a record of *heilsgeschichte* (saving history), preserving and interpreting the mighty acts of God. Consequently prophetic proclamations are usually declared in the light of its events, especially the Exodus. Habakkuk is in the mainstream of Old Testament thought in seeing the deliverance from Egypt as the pattern of a present, or future, deliverance.

Having heard, he **was afraid.** The people were not fearful of hurt from the earlier theophany (Exodus) but the thought of it created awe. The prophet's prayer is that God will renew His **work** of the Exodus. **Revive thy work** does not quite carry the significance of Habakkuk's point. Lehrman correctly paraphrases it: "May God reproduce His redemptive power in the years of crisis which are upon them."[3]

**In the midst of the years** is difficult to interpret and many simply pass it by. Davidson has it mean, "At this late time in our history, make thy work known," which is contextually sound. **Make known** is reflexive, meaning, "Make thyself known."

**In wrath remember mercy.** G. A. Smith contends that **wrath** should be translated "turmoil." Nowhere in the Old Testament, he says, does the term mean wrath; but either roar or noise of thunder (Job 37:2) and of horse's hoofs (Job 39:24), or the raging of the wicked (Job 3:17), or the commotion of fear (Job 3:25; Isa. 14:3).[4] If the traditional historical setting be maintained as just prior to the Chaldean invasion, this is a piercing observation. He is supported in this translation by C. L. Taylor, Jr.[5]

In 1-2 there is "A Prayer for Revival." (1) Revival is needed because sin is rampant, religion is decadent, and judgment is imminent, 1:4; 2:18-20; (2) The time of revival is now—**in the midst of the years;** (3) The way of revivals is through **prayer;** (4) The hope of revival is in God's **mercy** (G. B. Williamson).

---

[3]*Op. cit.,* p. 224.                   [4]*Op. cit.,* p. 150, n.
[5]*Op. cit.,* p. 997.

Thus ends the petition. Next begins the description of the new manifestation of God to men, the **work** of Jehovah **in the midst of the years.**

### C. The Work, 3:3-16

The pattern for this redemptive visitation is the earlier great work, and Habakkuk sees God coming as of old **from Teman** (3), in the northwest of Edom, and **Paran,** between Sinai and Edom (see map 1). The Song of Deborah (Judg. 5:4) also pictured God as coming from this region to aid His people. He comes like a great storm in the heavens. This is a characteristic way the Hebrews had of describing Jehovah when He visits His people. Jehovah is concealed in dark thunderclouds, from which lightning flashes, illuminating heaven and earth. "The earth quakes, the hills sink, and neighboring desert-tribes look on in dismay."[6]

We have here highly picturesque language which is difficult to translate but which even in the best of translation can have only figurative significance, i.e., it does not always admit of precise interpretation. The awesome sense of God's presence and the confident assurance of deliverance for His people are of prime importance. However, both nature-descriptions and geographical allusions reveal that the prophet had in mind the Exodus pattern for this latter-day deliverance.[7]

*The Berkeley Version* with its poetic form conveys the mood of the passage. The footnotes help the reader understand the prophet's historical allusions.

> *God comes from Teman,*[8] *the Holy One from Mount Paran.*[9]
> *Selah.*
> *His majesty covers the heavens, and the earth is full of His praise.*
> *His brightness is like the light;*[10] *rays flash from His hand, and there is the hiding of His power.*
> *Before Him the pestilence goes out, and burning fever follows at His feet.*

[6]Driver, *op. cit.,* p. 87.  [7]Smith, *op. cit.,* p. 150.
[8]A district northwest of Edom.
[9]Between the Sinaitic Peninsula and Kadesh-barnea.
[10]The full light of the sun.

*He stands and surveys the earth; He looks and startles the
    nations.*[11]
*The eternal mountains are scattered;*[12]
*the everlasting hills bow; His goings are as of old.*[13]
*I see the tents of Cushan in distress;*
*the curtains of the land of Midian*[14] *are trembling.*
*Is the Lord displeased with the rivers?*
*Is Thy anger against the rivers,*
*or Thy wrath against the sea,*
*that Thou dost ride upon thy horses,*
*upon Thy victory-chariots?*
*Thou dost strip the sheath from Thy bow and puttest arrows
    to the string.  Selah.*
*Thou cuttest through the earth with rivers;*
*The mountains see Thee and are in pangs;*
*the raging rivers sweep on.*[15]
*The deep utters its voice and lifts its hands on high.*[16]
*The sun and the moon stand still in their habitations;*[17]
*at the light of Thy arrows as they speed,*
*at the shining of Thy glittering spear.*
*Thou dost bestride the land in indignation;*
*Thou dost thresh the nations in Thy anger.*
*Thou dost march out for the deliverance of Thy people,*
*for the salvation of Thy anointed.*
*Thou dost demolish the top of the ungodly's house,*
*laying bare the foundation even to the nethermost stone.
    Selah.*
*Thou dost pierce with his own shafts*[18] *the head of his war-
    riors;*
*who come like a whirlwind to scatter me,*
*rejoicing as if to devour the innocent*[19] *in secret.*

[11]The Judge's look made them quail with terror.
[12]Cleft assunder before Him (Mic. 1:4).
[13]When He stood in the stream of history during the Exodus.
[14]The country on the east side of the Gulf of Aqabah.
[15]The rush of waters, pouring down the mountainside, dug out channels
in the earth and filled dry waddies with terror.
[16]Its waves mounted high.          [17]Josh. 10:12-13.
[18]Enemies will be thrown into a panic and will turn their weapons
against themselves (Zech. 14:13).
[19]Suffering and afflicted people of God.

*Thou dost tread the sea with Thy horses;*
*the mighty waters are piled up.*

Having recounted this awe-inspiring manifestation of divine power, Habakkuk says, **I trembled** (16). "His bosom throbs, his teeth chatter and he is ready to collapse."[20] How much more should it terrify those against whom God's power is directed! But more than instilling fear, the vision grants the prophet calmness and patience. He is going to wait quietly for **the day of trouble.** Although the text is obscure, the meaning is apparently that the **trouble** will come upon those who are invading Israel, i.e., the Chaldeans.

## D. THE AFFIRMATION OF FAITH, 3:17-19

Whether the description in 17 is of the results of invasion or a natural calamity is not clear. However, this in no wise alters the basic expression of confidence. In the face of adverse conditions, Habakkuk's faith in Jehovah will remain unchanged. These verses form a fitting climax, not only to the psalm, but to the entire book. They are a beautiful expression, in its widest ramifications, of 2:4, "The just shall live by his faith." Henderson's description is fitting: "The passage contains the most beautiful exhibition of the power of true religion to be found in the Bible. The language is that of a mind weaned from earthly enjoyments, and habituated to find the highest fruition of its desires in God."[21]

This is a "but-if-not" religion that does not depend on prosperity or well-being to keep its faith in God or its determination to be faithful to Him. Like the three Hebrew princes who recognized the contingency of deliverance (Dan. 3:17-18), Habakkuk intends to remain true despite the external developments.

The strength of such a view of religion is expressed in the words, **He will make my feet like hinds' feet** (19). The hind (gazelle) is noted for its fleetness and its surefootedness in rough terrain. It is said that greyhounds are liable to be killed by overexertion in pursuit of it. In the rocky crags of tribulation, and of uncertain footing beneath, faith gives unerring guidance and stability to tread the precarious path. These elevated places are

[20]Driver, quoted in Lehrman, *op. cit.,* p. 228.
[21]*Op. cit.,* p. 318.

not the normal paths, but are sought only in times of war or danger when the enemy is in hot pursuit. **Walk upon mine high places** may also mean a triumphal possession of the high place. Thus there is a veiled promise of victory through suffering and trial. The faith that endures is real.

The closing sentence is more or less a repetition of 3:1. It probably shows us that this psalm found use in the public worship. "Selah" in this chapter is a musical rest, and is found elsewhere only in the Psalms.

*The Book of*

# ZEPHANIAH

H. Ray Dunning

# Introduction

## A. The Prophet

Our knowledge of Zephaniah, which is scanty, is confined to the information given in the prophecy bearing his name. Three other men in the Old Testament had the same name, which means "Jehovah hides." There is, however, a unique feature in the brief biographical sketch in 1:1. The genealogy is traced back through four generations, to Hezekiah. Since such a family tree is quite rare, most students are agreed that this is King Hezekiah and that therefore Zephaniah was of royal lineage. There are also other evidences of this noble descent: the prophet was a citizen of Jerusalem (1:4); he shows little preoccupation with the poor; he does not hesitate to denounce the royal family or household, although he spares the king himself.[1]

One problem is the fact that the superscription of the book dates Zephaniah's preaching in Josiah's reign, who was himself a descendant of Hezekiah but only the fourth removed, while Zephaniah was the fifth removed. This is usually countered by observing that the custom of marrying very young could make this difference in generations.

Zephaniah's work was during Josiah's reign but the question still remains as to which part of this period. Josiah's rulership is divided into two eras: one before the discovery of the code of Deuteronomy in 621 B.C.; the other, following that time. The contents of the book point to the former part. Thus Zephaniah probably preached between 638 B.C. and 621 B.C.

This makes the prophet a contemporary of Jeremiah and a predecessor of Nahum and Habakkuk. He is placed after them in the canon because he "had the last word. While Nahum and Habakkuk were almost wholly absorbed with the epoch that is closing, he had a vision of the future."[2]

Zephaniah is not nearly as original as some of the other prophets. He seems to have been greatly influenced by Isaiah, who was in a comparable situation so far as position in the court

[1]C. L. Taylor, "Zephaniah" (Introduction), *The Interpreter's Bible*, VI (New York: Abingdon Press), 1009.

[2]G. A. Smith, "Zephaniah," *The Expositor's Bible* (New York: A. C. Armstrong & Son, 1896), p. 26.

and relationship to royalty were concerned. It may be that Zephaniah was a counsellor to Josiah. Yet when the book of the law was discovered, the king turned to Huldah, the prophetess, rather than to Zephaniah (II Kings 22:8-20). There is also some evidence of the influence of the eighth-century prophet Amos in the preaching of Zephaniah.

Zephaniah's message, like that of most of the prophets, is shaped by the situation in which he lived. Consequently we must give careful consideration to his times.

## B. THE POLITICAL SITUATION

In Judah, the long reign of Manasseh was marked by spiritual darkness. There was no lifting of the pall under the short reign of his son, Amon, who managed to keep the throne for only two years.

The Assyrian power was beginning to totter even during its greatest expansion under Ashurbanipal. The last appearances of Assyria in Palestine were in 655 and 647 B.C., and even then Ashurbanipal did not attempt to reconquer Egypt, which had earlier revolted. Upon the death of Ashurbanipal in 626 B.C., things began to develop rapidly; and in 612 B.C., Nineveh lay in ruins under the combined attack of the Medes and Babylonians. (Cf. Introduction to Nahum.)

During this period of weakened Assyrian domination, Egypt's power was rising and she was able to establish a stronghold in western Asia at the fortress of Carchemish until dislodged by the Babylonians in 605 B.C. The Babylonians at that time established themselves as the world power.

Another significant factor in forming Zephaniah's preaching was the rise to prominence of barbaric hordes in the north known as Scythians. These were fierce, bloodthirsty tribes, "black and pregnant with destructions." They came from the Caucasian region, pouring down across Asia into Palestine and to the doors of Egypt. This invasion is recorded by Herodotus, the Greek historian. They were not dependent upon infantry and chariots, but were cavalrymen and rushed headlong into conquest as had no others before them. According to Herodotus, the Egyptian Pharaoh succeeded in buying them off, so they stopped short of overrunning the kingdom of the Nile and returned to their homeland as swiftly as they had come.

They had probably followed the Assyrian warpaths in the plains and thus Judah in her hill country apparently escaped the brunt of their attack. But the danger threw the populace into dismay.

## C. The Religious Situation

Corresponding to the political dangers without were ethical declensions within the Hebrew nation. The prophet saw these to be correlated circumstances. Under Manasseh, the true religion of Jehovah had been suppressed and the king had advocated an adulterated religion which incorporated Assyrian customs and worship. According to II Kings 21:6, Manasseh practiced human sacrifice of his own children, erected shrines to "the hosts of heaven" (astral deities of the Assyrians) in the Lord's house, and revived soothsaying, divination and traffic with the dead.

When Zephaniah came on the scene, this influence was still predominant. King Josiah early began to serve the Lord, but it was not until 621 B.C. that his reforms took on large proportions. Therefore the prophet would have been crying out against the continuation of the spiritual blight from Manasseh's evil influence. Graham describes the utterances of Zephaniah as being those of "a member of the opposition party, a record of the emotions and judgments of a puritan, himself of royal birth, who had thrown in his lot with the opponents of the then dominant elements in his own house."[3]

## D. The Nature of the Book

The characteristic phrase and chief emphasis of the book is "the day of the Lord." This was not new, for it had been frequently used by the prophets. At the time of Amos the idea of the day of the Lord was in frequent use (Amos 5:18). It was a popular conception that God would appear in the near future and confer some great victory upon His people. Therefore they desired and cried out for the day of the Lord. Amos transformed this concept from a kind of automatic bestowal of blessing into a day of ethical import. What this day would be, he said, depended upon their moral condition. It would be a day when Jehovah would manifest himself against sin, whether in His own people or among foreign nations. "Amos thus transformed a popular idea; and the prophets used the expression in this transformed sense to denote the day on which Jehovah is conceived as manifesting Himself in His fullness, striking down wrong and illusion and

---

[3]"Zephaniah," *Abingdon Bible Commentary*, ed. F. C. Eiselen, *et al.* (New York: Abingdon-Cokesbury Press, 1929), p. 810.

human pride, and giving the final victory to righteousness and truth."[4]

Zephaniah probably draws directly from Isaiah for his inspiration (cf. Isa. 2:12 ff.) and conceives of the "day" under the imagery of war and invasion. This is due to the fact that its near approach was suggested to him by the irruption of the Scythian hordes into Asia.

Zephaniah makes his own modification in the concept of the day of the Lord. To the earlier prophets, it was a crisis in the world which was a definite point in history. But its events are "natural" even if tumultuous—and afterwards history continues to flow on. Zephaniah, however, sees it as a terminal event, with the manifestation of supernatural intervention. G. A. Smith's classic interpretation is apropos: "In short, with Zephaniah the Day of the Lord tends to become the Last Day. His book is the first tinging of prophecy with apocalypse: that is the moment which it supplies in the history of Israel's religion."[5]

## *Outline*

I.  Superscription, 1:1

II.  The Threat of World Judgment, 1:2—3:7
    A.  Description of the Judgment, 1:2-18
    B.  Judgment on the Nations, 2:1—3:7

III.  A Word to the Faithful, 3:8-13
    A.  A Purified Speech, 3:8-9a
    B.  A Purified Worship, 3:9b-10
    C.  A Secure Remnant, 3:11-13

IV.  Conclusion, 3:14-20
    A.  Hymn of Gladness, 3:14-15
    B.  Assurance of Faith, 3:16-18
    C.  Promise of Restoration, 3:19-20

[4]S. R. Driver, "The Minor Prophets," II, *The New Century Bible*, ed. Walter F. Adeney (New York: Oxford University Press, 1906), 115.
[5]*Op. cit.*, p. 49.

# Section I Superscription

The name Zephaniah means "Jehovah hides" (see Intro.; cf. I Chron. 6:36; Jer. 21:1; and Zech. 6:10, 14). It has been suggested from this that the prophet was born during the "killing time of Manasseh." This is the most detailed of any genealogy given for a prophet, and is best accounted for on the basis of its purpose to show Zephaniah to be of royal lineage.

Zephaniah's claim to authority, however, is in the fact that he spake **the word of the Lord.** While his natural descent may have gained him admission to the courts of royalty, the supernatural origin of his message gave it the urgency, certainty, and power which it manifested.

# Section II The Threat of World Judgment

Zephaniah 1:2—3:7

## A. DESCRIPTION OF THE JUDGMENT, 1:2-18

### 1. *Universal Scope* (1:2-3)

This divine visitation through human instrumentality is to be worldwide in scope, taking in not only man himself but all other living creatures: beasts, fowls, and fish (cf. Ezek. 38:19-20).

Here is the announcement of the major theme, universal catastrophe, which Zephaniah afterwards proceeds to apply in various ways and to different groups. The world has become exceedingly wicked, much as in the days of Noah, and God has determined to administer justice. Zephaniah knows no mercy. "There is no great hope in his book, hardly any tenderness and never a glimpse of beauty . . . no hotter book lies in all the O.T."[1]

**The stumblingblocks with the wicked** (3) is a difficult phrase that some have considered to be an editorial addition because it doesn't seem to fit and sounds redundant. However there is no real reason for denying it to Zephaniah. As Henderson says, "The enumeration of particulars is designed to augment the fearful and universal character of the punishment."[2] **Stumblingblocks** is used in another place for idols, and it is proper that the causes of moral offense should be removed along with the offenders.

### 2. *Application to Judah* (1:4-13)

*a. An idolatrous people* (1:4-6). In this passage the prophet turns his attention to his own people, since the day of vengeance will affect them also. This is inevitable because of the raging idolatry which Zephaniah sees on every hand and describes in detail. **The remnant of Baal** (4) has been used for an argument to support the position that Zephaniah prophesied after 621 B.C., when Baal worship had been crippled by the reforms of Josiah. However, this view would be in too great a contrast to the other denunciations to be feasible.

---

[1]G. A. Smith, "Zephaniah," *The Expositor's Bible,* ed. W. Robertson Nicoll (New York: A. C. Armstrong, 1896), p. 48.

[2]*The Book of the Twelve Minor Prophets* (New York: Sheldon and Co., 1864), *ad loc.*

The Septuagint renders the word "names" rather than **remnant** and many understand this to be the original.[3] Others think it means "even to the last remnant," thus stating that Baal worship would be completely destroyed. Baalism, a Canaanite and Phoenician religion, played a major role in the religious failure of the northern kingdom of Israel. Much of the Old Testament is unintelligible apart from a knowledge of the conflict between Baalism and the worship of the true God. Baalism was a fertility cult which fostered immoral practices in its worship and to which the Israelites seemed to have an unusual affinity.[4]

**This place** refers to Jerusalem, indicating incidentally that the prophet was in the city. Fundamentally, we are to see Jerusalem as the center of the nation, both politically and religiously. In a very real sense as the leaders go, so go the people. Therefore a decisive judgment upon idolatry must concentrate upon the capital city.

**Chemarims** is an Aramaic word for "priests," used in the Old Testament only for idolatrous priests. Perhaps it refers to the priests of foreign cults which were introduced into Israel. These, along with the degenerate regular priests of Jehovah, are to be cut off. The latter are more fully described in 3:4. It is suggested that they encourage idolatry either by their indifference or by the inconsistency of their conduct, or both.

**Them that worship the host of heaven upon the house tops** (5) refers to the worship of the Assyrian astral deities which were brought in during Manasseh's evil reign (cf. II Kings 21:3). A strong warning against such practices is issued in Deut. 4:19 and 17:3. This false worship involved offering incense and libations from the flat rooftops, normal places of activity in an oriental house and natural places to worship the heavenly bodies. Smith-Goodspeed renders this: "And those who prostrate themselves upon the roofs."

**The host of heaven** includes all the heavenly bodies—the sun, moon, and stars. Certain ones were special objects of worship. Job 31:26-28 describes how this worship may have been performed. In Ezekiel's vision in Babylon he saw this type of worship being carried on in the Temple by priests (Ezek. 8:15-18). It was a practice which seems to have been confined to

[3]G. A. Smith, *op. cit.*, p. 56.
[4]See article "Baalism" in IDB or ISBE.

Judah (not practiced in Israel) because it was the result of Assyrian influence and Judah was a vassal state of the Assyrian Empire.

They **that swear by the Lord** render an allegiance to Jehovah but they also **swear by Malcham,** the national god of the Ammonites. Here is a divided loyalty, against which all prophets of Jehovah inveighed. The correct pronunciation is "Milcom" according to the Septuagint and others. Some scholars think it refers to Molech, the Phoenician god whose inhuman worship (II Kings 23:10; Jer. 7:31) was prevalent in Zephaniah's day.

Several translators render **Malcham** "their king." Even though they rendered lip service to Jehovah, they honored Molech as king. To swear by a deity means to acknowledge him in a public manner, i.e., openly to pledge oneself to his service. This divided loyalty and service Jesus condemned in no uncertain terms: "Ye cannot serve God and mammon" (Matt. 6:24).

Two other classes of people are mentioned in 6 as being included in the judgment: the backsliders and the indifferent. **Them that are turned back** had evidently once followed the Lord but now have become apostates. **Those that have not sought the Lord** simply gave no heed to the things of Jehovah. **Enquired for him** very nearly means "to worship at the Temple" and thus has a parallel in Ps. 10:4, which may be paraphrased, "The wicked in the pride of his countenance does not go to church."[5]

Thus we have three types of persons who fall under God's judgment and who may be thought of as being in eternal jeopardy in "the day of the Lord": (1) the indifferent who go their own way without concern for spiritual things, (2) the backslider who has turned away from a former experience, and (3) the halfhearted who give lip service to God but who honor another god as king in their lives and do not give total allegiance to the Lord. Jehovah will be Lord of all or He will not be Lord at all.

b. *Court officials and royal house condemned* (1:7-9). **Hold thy peace** (7) is literally, "Hush." The same term is used in Hab. 2:20. In view of the approaching judgment, the prophet bids all to be reverent as they prepare to meet it. **The day of the Lord** is the technical term (see Intro.) for the approaching judg-

[5]C. L. Taylor, "Zephaniah," *The Interpreter's Bible* (New York: Abingdon Press, 1956), VI, 1015.

ment which is the major concern of Zephaniah. His central message may be summed up in the phrase, **The day of the Lord is at hand.** This is the day when God will manifest himself as Judge. It is not just any day of calamity, but a special time, the full and final manifestation of God.

This day is seen under the symbolism of a great **sacrifice,** and the **guests** have been prepared for their role. **Bid** means "consecrated." It is not absolutely clear who are the guests, but apparently it is the menacing host from the north who remain unnamed throughout. It is probably the Scythians whom Zephaniah had in mind. Perhaps the victims are not all named but at least the upper classes are included (8). A New Testament parallel is Rev. 19:17-21, where the vultures are invited to the supper of the great God to "eat the flesh of kings, and the flesh of captains, and the flesh of mighty men."

After the first phrase of verse 8, the first-person form of speech resumes and there is a continuation of the description of judgment with a listing of those who will be punished.

**The king's children** may or may not refer to Josiah's offspring. Most take it to refer to the royal house in general, since Josiah's sons were only about ten and twelve years old at the time (II Kings 23:31-36). The Septuagint reads "house" for **children.** They are commonly interchanged words.[6]

**Strange apparel** is better translated "foreign attire" (RSV). Here is another overtone from the reign of Manasseh when Assyrian customs, including dress, infiltrated the land. To the true Hebrew, this adoption of Assyrian fashions symbolized acceptance of the alien culture and religion. It was consequently and correctly condemned as a betrayal of faithfulness to Jehovah.

"The garments they wear reveal the nature of their ideal. They do not hesitate to surrender their distinctive national characteristics in their desire to make themselves and the nation one with the neighboring peoples."[7]

**Those that leap on** (leap over) **the threshold** (9) is a phrase that has been variously interpreted. The key is said by some to

[6]A. B. Davidson, *Nahum, Habakkuk, and Zephaniah,* "The Cambridge Bible for Schools and Colleges," gen. ed. A. F. Kirkpatrick (Cambridge: University Press, 1896), p. 114.

[7]S. M. Lehrman, "Zephaniah," *The Twelve Prophets,* ed. A. Cohen. (London: The Soncino Press, 1948), Stonehouse is quoted, p. 236.

be I Sam. 5:5, where the practice of the Philistine priests was to avoid treading on the threshold of the temple because the idol, Dagon, had fallen on it. This would make it a superstitious practice which would also be a capitulation to Philistine idolatry.

Most scholars, however, lean to an interpretation based more on the text itself, which seems to indicate a violent action. If it is tied to the next phrase, it would imply the forcible invasion of the privacy of the homes to rob and plunder.

c. *Merchants and traders to be cut off* (1:10-13). Verse 10 further extends the scope of judgment upon Jerusalem by showing **that there shall be the noise of a cry** from all quarters of the city, not just the royal palace. **The fish gate** was on the north side of Jerusalem. The significance of this reference seems to be that this is the direction from which the attack will come. The fish gate is mentioned in Neh. 3:3 and is probably so called because the men of Tyre traded in dried fish at the market by the north wall.[8]

**An howling from the second** indicates another place. **Second** is translated "Mishneh" by G. A. Smith, who notes that it means the second or new town. So Smith-Goodspeed renders it "the New Town," while the RSV reads "Second Quarter." The phrase may refer to a second division of the city, which had been recently added. In II Chron. 33:14, Manasseh is said to have built an outer wall extending as far as the fish gate; "New Town" may have been the name of the ground encompassed by Manasseh's wall. To the north was the only direction the city could expand, but it would be vulnerable to attack.

**The hills** does not refer to all the hills about Jerusalem but to those on which the northern part of the city was built. **Howling** means a "loud crash," the noise of which resounds from the hills.

**Maktesh** (11) is probably the hollow between the western and eastern hills. It is literally "the mortar" but is translated "hollow place" in Judg. 15:19. It is supposed to have been the resort of traders and liable to invasion by a foe from the north. It has also been identified with the "Phoenician quarter" of Jerusalem (Driver). The literal term, "the Mortar," means "a pounding place." Thus there could be a connection between the name and the fate of the inhabitants. It is a place where they shall be pounded by the foe.

---

Taken together, these four locations are inclusive of the city's business life. This is further indicated by the final phrase of 11, "all who weigh out silver" (RSV).

**The merchant people** is "the people of Canaan" in the Hebrew, and Smith-Goodspeed renders it this way. However, **merchant people** is a correct paraphrase because the Canaanites (Phoenicians) were the chief traders in Palestine and so the term came to be used to denote a merchant.[9]

Verse 12 is a summary which pictures the Lord searching out the city of Jerusalem so as to render true justice upon those who are responsible for the spiritual indifference of the times. It is not certain whether or not Zephaniah intended to mean that the invaders would be the instrument of the Lord to search out the hidden transgressors. However it is done, the people involved are the indifferent who withdraw from public concerns. In the pictures of Zephaniah as a saint, he is represented as carrying a lantern.[10]

**Settled on their lees** (12) is a striking metaphor. **Settled** is an incorrect rendering. "Thickened" or "congealed" (cf. Exod. 15:8) is a better translation. The picture is taken from wine producing. During the process, wine was supposed to be poured from vessel to vessel (see Jer. 48:11-12) and left on its lees (dregs) only long enough to fix its color and body. Unless it was drawn or poured off, it grew thick and oversweet. Hence "to thicken upon one's lees" became a proverb for sloth, indifference, and the muddy mind.[11]

Judah was spiritually benumbed by security. Those who ought to have been leaders were relaxed into a selfish, idle existence, doing nothing about the situation in the land. It was an outlook that is so contemporary as to be startling. Either for good or evil, they thought, God will not act. Theirs was an absentee Deity, or one who was asleep—a practical atheism. It sounds very much like Ernst Renan, who said: "It has, in fact, never been established by observation that a superior being troubles himself, for a moral or immoral purpose, with the things of nature or the affairs of mankind."[12] A contemporary theologian has made a very similar faithless statement, "We cannot

[9]Driver, *op. cit.*, p. 117.          [10]Davidson, *op. cit.*, p. 116.
[11]G. A. Smith, *op. cit.*, p. 52.
[12]Quoted in Davidson, *op. cit.*, p. 117.

meet our time if we remain bound to a God who no longer appears in time and space. It is precisely by freely willing the death of God that we can be open to our time."[13]

In v. 12 we have the "criminal apathy of the well-to-do classes sunk in ease and religious indifference," which gives rise to G. A. Smith's classic comment: "The great causes of God and humanity are not defeated by the hot assaults of the devil, but by the slow, crushing, glacier-like mass of thousands and thousands of indifferent nobodies. God's causes are never destroyed by being blown up, but by being sat upon."[14]

There follows another denunciation of these apathetic people. The expression, **They shall also build houses, but not inhabit them** (13), implies desolation. Those things which, in their ease, they contemplated enjoying would be snatched from them and they would not enjoy the fruit of their labors.

### 3. *A Wider Application* (1:14-18)

**The day of the Lord** was introduced in v. 7. In 14-18 this figure is developed and the terrors of the approaching **great day** (14) are pictured. The striking detail is probably drawn from the irruption of the Scythian hordes from the north into Asia. This vision seems to take on more universal proportions than the preceding one, which was directed specifically to Jerusalem. **The day** here is not so much a measure of time as expressive of a supreme crisis.

**The day** is seen to be near at hand and hastening rapidly. There are to be disturbances in the natural world as well as in the political order. "What the prophet expects here is a day when a corrupt international order will dissolve in the confused self-destructive conflict of its various elements and be swept away by calamitous manifestations of natural forces."[15]

Taylor has shown how a simple rearrangement of letters in a line of the Massoretic text changes a section in 14 to a quite different and clearer reading without doing violence to the original.[16] **The voice of the day of the Lord: the mighty man shall cry there bitterly** becomes, "Swifter than a runner, the day of the Lord, and speedier than a warrior" (cf. Moffatt).

[13]Thomas J. J. Altizer, "Creative Negation in Theology," *Christian Century*, July 7, 1965, p. 866.

[14]*Op. cit.*, p. 54.

[15]Graham, *op. cit.*, p. 812.          [16]*Op. cit.*, p. 1019.

Zephaniah's description of **the day of the Lord** (15-16) is closely akin to Joel 2:2 and Amos 5:20. But Zephaniah's account is fuller, and places chief emphasis upon the fact that this is to be a day of wrath. The original is a poem which cannot be adequately reproduced in translation. Even in the English version, however, one catches the tumultuous spirit and atmosphere of terror which it is designed to produce. Moffatt renders it:

> *A day of wrath, that day, of woe and anguish,*
> *A day of stress and distress, darkness and gloom,*
> *A day of cloud and thundercloud,*
> *A day of trumpet blast and battle cry,*
> *Against towers fortified and ramparts high.*

The lives of men shall be worthless: **Their blood shall be poured out as dust, and their flesh as dung** (17). Their material possessions will give them no protection: **Neither their silver nor their gold shall be able to deliver them** (18). The closing phrase of 18 reads literally, "For an end, surely a terrible [or sudden] destruction will he make." A universal devastation will mark this final day when God will "make an end of all the inhabitants of the earth" (RSV).

### B. Judgment on the Nations, 2:1—3:7

#### 1. *The Summons* (2:1-3)

This appeal is directed to Judah, Zephaniah's own people. The opening words, **Gather yourselves together** (1), are difficult to interpret. They may be taken to mean much the same as the colloquialism, "Pull yourselves together," and so Eaton translates them. However the main word is formed from the term "stubble" and is used in the sense of assembling together. Using yet another possible root, Ewald would have it read "turn pale," which fits in with the context.[17]

Judah is described as a **nation not desired.** This may be connected with an Aramaic root which means "colorless," thus "pale." The nation does not "turn pale," hence it is not ashamed.[18] The RSV translates it, "O shameless nation." This is a call to Judah to be aware of the tragedy that awaits, and to

---

[17]Quoted in Davidson, *op. cit.*, p. 120.
[18]Taylor, *op. cit.*, p. 1021.

take advantage of the respite to repent before the storm. **Before the decree bring forth** (2) refers to God's decree of judgment. Before it produces its fruit of destruction the people are exhorted to **seek ye the Lord** (3).

The Septuagint clarifies the obscure clause **before the day pass as the chaff** (2) as "before you become like drifting chaff." The Hebrew phrase for the last half of 2 would literally suggest, according to Davidson, "before the day fixed by God breaks forth from the dark womb of the future." There is a cumulative, rhetorical address in these declarations leading up to the expressed appeal in v. 3. This call is directed to the **meek of the earth.** There is some hope that they may escape the day of vengeance. Perhaps this is the remnant that played such a major role in Isaiah's thinking. Even here, however, there is no absolute assurance of deliverance, only **it may be.** These humble ones who obey the commandments are to continue seeking the Lord in the face of the approaching day of trouble. Smith notes the "absence of all mention of the Divine mercy as the cause of deliverance. Zephaniah has no gospel of that kind. The conditions of escape are sternly ethical—meekness, the doing of justice and righteousness."[19]

In 1:14—2:3 we see Zephaniah's picture of "The Great Day of the Lord." It has two sides: (1) The heavy hand of God's justice: will bring terror, 14; wrath, 15; and destruction, 16; because of flagrant sin, 17; and trusting in wealth, 18; (2) The high hope of God's mercy: in His long-suffering, 2; giving opportunity to seek Him in meekness, obedience, and righteousness, 3 (W. T. Purkiser).

### 2. Oracles Against Foreign Nations (2:4-15)

There are four heathen nations chosen as examples of the coming judgments. Two of them are small and near at hand. The Philistines, mentioned first, are actually in Palestine. The latter two are large and far away. Assyria, mentioned last, was the great threat to God's people in Zephaniah's time. She had destroyed the Northern Kingdom and had now lured the Southern Kingdom to the brink of ruin. These four nations are also Israel's enemies to the west, east, south, and north (see map 1).

*a. The Philistines* (2:4-7). The Philistines were like the Israelites in being located between the great military powers of

[19]*Op. cit.,* p. 59.

Mesopotamia and the Kingdom of the Nile. They were therefore constantly threatened by opposing armies in their journeys of conquest. The four cities mentioned (see map 2) were the chief remaining strongholds of the Philistines. **They shall drive out Ashdod** (4) "suggests that Zephaniah's expectation here was of a sudden, irresistible military onslaught."[20] Undoubtedly Zephaniah still has in mind the invading Scythians. **Noon day** is the time when inhabitants of hot countries are accustomed to lounging and would thus be unprepared.

The Philistines are **the inhabitants of the sea coast** (5), having lived along the Mediterranean since about 1200 B.C., when they invaded the area. They had migrated from the Mediterranean islands including Crete, with which the term **Cherethites** is connected.

Eaton suggests that **Canaan** may be more than a designation of the district. It is, perhaps, a description of the greedy commercialism associated with the Canaanites. He offers this possible rendering: "A Canaan (a land of grasping merchants) is the land of the Philistines."[21] The land shall be depopulated and stripped of its splendor. Her once great cities shall become **cottages for shepherds, and folds for flocks** (6).

In 7, Zephaniah promises that this country adjoining Judah shall be possessed by **the remnant.** There are two specific things that God will do for them. First He will **visit them.** This word means literally "to turn one's attention to" and therefore the RSV renders it "will be mindful of them." The same term is used in 1:7 and there translated "punish." The significance is that when God turns His attention to a people the results are dependent upon the spiritual condition of those people. It is very much like the approach of the returning father, whose coming is reacted to variously by his children according as they have kept his commandments. When God was mindful of Jerusalem (1:7) in its wickedness, punishment was the result. When He is mindful of the righteous **remnant,** the result is deliverance. Therefore the second thing that God promises Judah is to **turn away their captivity.** This does not necessarily refer to the Exile, although it may legitimately be a prediction of the return. Many commentators interpret it to be a promise of a return of an original state of paradise, the restoration of a former happy

---

[20]Graham, *op. cit.,* p. 813.      [21]Eaton, *op. cit.,* p. 139.

condition. Thus Smith-Goodspeed renders the phrase, "restore their fortunes."

b. *Moab and Ammon* (2:8-11). Condemnation is pronounced upon **Moab** and **Ammon** because they reproached and reviled Israel **and magnified themselves against** her (8). This enmity is referred to in Amos 1:13-15; 2:1-3. These people lived directly to the east of Canaan (see map 2). They were never particularly friendly with Israel, and when the eastern tribes were weakened they seized the land of Reuben and Gad. **Magnified themselves against their border** means literally, "They enlarged [their mouths in arrogance] concerning their border." That is, they boasted that they would annex Israel's land.[22]

As a punishment, their country would be desolated like **Sodom** and **Gomorrah** (9), Bible examples of utter destruction. Their land would be possessed of **nettles**, a plant characteristic of poor, salt soil and uncultivated places. It would be turned into **saltpits**. "Salt for Jerusalem is still procured chiefly from this district, being partly obtained from pits dug into the sand or slime of the shore, into which the waters of the Dead Sea are admitted, and then allowed to evaporate."[23]

Zephaniah makes it clear that Moab and Ammon are in trouble because they have despised **the people of the Lord of hosts** (10). The clause, **He will famish** (make lean) **all the gods of the earth** (11), means that they will be rendered powerless by the Lord and unable to defend their worshippers.

c. *The Ethiopians* (2:12). This brief declaration is difficult to place. Douglas suggests that it is as if he said, "Also ye Ethiopians! No, I cannot address *you;* ye are dead and gone: *they* are those slain by my sword."[24] Some think that this verse refers to Egypt and is called Ethiopia (*Kush*) because of its long subjection to Ethiopic dynasties.[25] It was the king of Ethiopia ruling over Egypt who had been the object of hope and trust against Assyria by many in Jerusalem at the time of Hezekiah.[26]

d. *Assyria* (2:13-15). This description of the destruction of Nineveh is rivalled only by the fiery eloquence of Nahum, to which it is closely related. This is the climactic oracle, and

---

[22]Lehrman, *op. cit.,* p. 243.           [23]Driver, *op. cit.,* p. 126.
[24]*The Intermediate Prophets,* p. 147.
[25]G. A. Smith, *op. cit.,* p. 64.        [26]Douglas, *op. cit.,* p. 147.

probably the chief one, since Assyria was the colossus of the ancient world of Zephaniah's time and she was now beginning to totter (see Introduction). The fulfillment of this oracle, then, would be the close of an epoch.

Nineveh lay 500 miles northeast of Judah (see map 1). That she is pictured as coming from the north is due to the fact that the army would cross the Euphrates at the great ford of Carchemish, 300 miles west of Nineveh, and so would approach Palestine from the north.[27]

The **cormorant** (14) is a wild creature thought by some to be the pelican, which is mentioned in Ps. 102:6. It is also translated "vulture" (RSV) and "jackdaw" (Smith-Goodspeed) and is mentioned in the list of unclean birds in Lev. 11:18 and Deut. 14:17. The **bittern** is translated "hedgehog" (RSV) or "porcupine." The porcupine is a shy, solitary animal, which might well choose its home among desolate ruins.

We have here a picture of desolation and death. The great city which once revelled in splendor is now the haunt of wild beasts. Her dirge recounts the sins that brought her to the brink of doom.

> *This is the exultant city*
> *that dwelt secure,*
> *that said to herself,*
> *"I am and there is none else."*
> *What a desolation she has become,*
> *a lair for wild beasts!*
> *Everyone who passes by her*
> *hisses and shakes his fist* (15, RSV).

Compare the denunciation of Nineveh in Nahum.

### 3. *Further Word to Jerusalem* (3:1-7)

Having given attention to the foreign nations, the prophet now turns home again with his oracles and speaks to his own city. Jerusalem is a city that is **filthy** (rebellious) and defiled because she is filled with oppression. The word translated **polluted** (1) means blood-stained and is so translated in Isa. 59:3. It is largely the leading classes that are morally rotten (3). Jerusalem cannot be spared from the judgment of God.

[27]Driver, *op. cit.*, p. 128.

Verses 1-2 describe the fundamental nature of sin as rebellion against God. This is seen especially in the words, **She trusted not in the Lord** (2). Sin is thus self-idolatry; one who does not wholly trust the Lord has made a basic denial of the faith.

> *She listens to no voice,*
> *she accepts no correction.*
> *She does not trust in the Lord,*
> *she does not draw near to her God* (2, RSV).

*Living Prophecies* interprets v. 3, "Her leaders are like roaring lions hunting for their victims—out for everything that they can get. Her judges are like ravenous wolves at evening time, who by dawn have left no trace of their prey."

Even the spiritual leaders have failed in their function. The **prophets are light and treacherous persons** (4). As Henderson says, "Her prophets are vainglorious, hypocritical men."[28] **Light** here seems to mean boastful, reckless in assertion and action. "Instead of being humble declarers of the will of God, they sought to give utterance to their own ideas."[29] They are **treacherous** (not to be trusted) because they have given out their own imaginations as revelations from God.

The **priests have polluted the sanctuary**. The word **sanctuary** is an incorrect translation. The RSV correctly renders the clause, "Her priests profane what is sacred." Their function was to be "guardians of holiness ensuring conditions for the meeting of God and man in worship."[30] But instead they had become worldly, making no distinction between the holy and profane, and distorting the meaning of the law (Torah) (cf. Hab. 1:4).

How can God in justice overlook these corruptions? The fact that **the just Lord is in the midst** (5) of the people makes their conduct even more reprehensible. **He will not do iniquity** seems to be directed especially at the priests whose misinterpretations of the law denied this aspect of the nature of God.

**Every morning** the light of day testifies to God's faithfulness in the laws of nature; and He is just as faithful in the administration of the moral laws of His universe. But nothing seems to move **the unjust**—the calloused Israelites. The clear evidence of God's moral government does not stir them to action. Not even

[28]*Op. cit., ad loc.*      [29]Driver, *op. cit.*, p. 132.
[30]Eaton, *Obadiah, Nahum, Habakkuk and Zephaniah* (London: SCM Press, 1961), p. 147.

the visitation of judgment upon other nations (6-7) has shaken their carelessness and indifference. God says, **Surely thou wilt fear me** (7), but the results have been just the opposite. **They rose early, and corrupted all their doings.** The RSV says, "All the more they were eager to make all their deeds corrupt."

In 3:1-7 we see "God's Concern for the Careless." (1) A message to people who have once known God, 1; (2) The nature of sin, 2; (3) Backsliding is no respecter of persons, 3-4; (4) God is faithful with His warnings, 5-6; (5) The seeking God always hopes for repentance, 7ab; (6) Man can persist in sin in spite of all that divine love can do, 7c (A. F. Harper).

Section **III** *A Word to the Faithful*

Zephaniah 3:8-13

This is a call for patience until God rises up in execution of judgment upon **the nations** (8). It is clearly in anticipation of the promise contained in 9-13. For **rise up to the prey**, the Septuagint translates, "rise up for a witness." If this is correct, it would mean as a witness against **the nations**. They shall be assembled for the day of **indignation**, a picture often repeated in the prophets (Isa. 66:16; Jer. 25:31, 33; Ezekiel 38—39; Joel 3:11-16). It is a proclamation of universal punishment.

The prophet then turns to a brighter word, and sees the conversion of the nations. This is still the day of the Lord but in its positive aspects. In its total picture the day is first one of judgment, which is then followed by blessings, specifically defined in several cases as an outpouring of the Spirit.

### A. A PURIFIED SPEECH, 3:8-9a

The divine activity in bringing this to pass is a bit obscure in the KJV but is clarified in the RSV, which says: "Yea, at that time I will change the speech of the peoples to a pure speech." Literally, the Hebrew says "lip" (see margin). The natural meaning is caught by "speech" or **language** (9), since the lip is the organ of speech. Also the Hebrew is "purified" rather than **pure**. Once more we are reminded that the divine work is brought to pass through divine agency. God's people are to be "made pure."

The speech is a symbol of the inner condition. Isaiah in the Temple cried, "I am a man of unclean lips" (Isa. 6:5), to which God's response was, "Thine iniquity is taken away, and thy sin purged" (6:7). We have here a promise of a purified heart which issues in a purified language. So the day of the Lord is given its characteristic New Testament focus—the coming of the sanctifying Spirit.

### B. A PURIFIED WORSHIP, 3:9b-10

The result of the purified language was a sanctified worship. They shall **serve him with one consent** (9)—literally, "with one shoulder." The Septuagint renders it "under one yoke." This is

312

understandable in terms of the contemporary colloquialism, "Stand shoulder to shoulder." It is very close to the prayer of Jesus that His disciples should be one as a result of their sanctification (John 17:21).

These purified worshippers shall come from the uttermost parts of the earth. **Ethiopia** (10) is variously understood, but perhaps the most correct view is to consider it as a type of distant nations, the limits of the known world to the south.

Even more uncertain is the remainder of the verse, **My suppliants, even the daughter of my dispersed, shall bring mine offering.** One interpretation is that the converted nations shall bring back God's dispersed people, the Jews, as an offering to Him. Thus the heathen are giving practical proof of their conversion by surrendering the Israelites whom they hold.[1] This is supported by Isa. 66:20.

## C. A Secure Remnant, 3:11-13

The safety of the remnant will be secured by the removal of the proud and haughty ones from their midst. In contrast to 5, where "the unjust knoweth no shame" (see comment there), this purified remnant will have no need of shame. Why? Because sin, the source of true shame, has been removed. The people are to be like their Lord, who does no wrong (cf. 5). Unlike the haughty (2) who did not trust in God, the humble **shall trust in the name of the Lord** (12). "They are set in a transfigured world which lies beyond the devastation of the old order, and they themselves are made so pure and perfect before God that without exaggeration they could be termed new creatures."[2]

It has been suggested that Isa. 53:9 was in Zephaniah's mind when he describes the people as not having **a deceitful tongue** (13). There the Suffering Servant is described: "Neither was any deceit [guile] found in his mouth." This passage is clearly Messianic and, like Isaiah, Zephaniah wishes to compare the people with the Messiah.

[1]Lehrman, *op. cit.*, p. 249.            [2]Eaton, *op. cit.*, p. 155.

Section **IV** *Conclusion*

Zephaniah 3:14-20

## A. HYMN OF GLADNESS, 3:14-15

These verses reflect the joy of the redeemed in the presence of the Lord, who promises to be in their midst. Here is final deliverance, the golden age which is the climax of the day of the Lord. The verbs are in the prophetic perfect; the events, though yet in the future, are described as having taken place already.

There are three reasons for rejoicing:

1. The **judgments** (15) are removed. These are the **judgments** that have fallen upon Israel through all her history. Zephaniah, with Isaiah, sees that in this day "her warfare is accomplished . . . her iniquity is pardoned" (Isa. 40:2).

2. The enemy is **cast out.** Note that this promise and prediction is in the singular. The chief enemy of Israel was sin in conduct and sin in the heart. It is altogether possible that this final consummation is seen by Zephaniah to be also a final victory over the trouble of Israel, "a wandering heart." The word translated **taken away** (15) is the same as is rendered "prepared" in Isa. 40:3 and means "to clear away the debris," or free the ground from obstacles. Thus the removal of sin prepares the way for a fully victorious existence.

3. **The Lord, is in the midst.** He is present to protect, and therefore Israel need have no more fear. Conversely, she is now prepared for His presence in her midst by virtue of the removal of her sin.

## B. ASSURANCE OF FAITH, 3:16-18

**In that day it shall be said . . . Fear thou not** (16). God's presence gives peace of heart. Hence the exhortation, **Let not thine hands be slack,** meaning to "droop" or "drop." The reason for encouragement is that **the Lord thy God in the midst of thee is** "a victorious warrior" (17, Smith-Goodspeed).

Furthermore, those who are exiled in sorrow will be gathered to **the solemn assembly** (18). The word so translated means "a

314

stated place or time," and applies to the sacred seasons of the Jewish year.[1] Douglas suggests that "tryst" is the only English word comparable to the Hebrew. Those yet in exile are separated from the great feasts but they shall be brought again. The following translation of the verse reflects this meaning: "I will gather them that are removed from the solemn assembly; they shall be with thee, that thou bear not reproach because of them."

### C. Promise of Restoration, 3:19-20

"With a general picture of the Messianic days, but with no special mention of the Messianic King, the prophet ends."[2] The promise is, "I will bring you home" (20, RSV), with a repetition of 2:7, **when I turn back your captivity** (20). It shall be done in **your day.**

Zephaniah's concluding psalm exalts the Lord as "Mighty to Save," 17. God's power to save is the basis for His people's: (1) Joy, 14; (2) Protection, 15; (3) Confidence and zeal, 16; (4) Restoration, 18, 20; and (5) Achievement, 19 (W. T. Purkiser).

Moffatt has cast the promise in moving poetic form:

> *I will deal with all your oppressors,*
>    *and gather your outcasts, rescue the lame,*
> *lifting them out of their shame*
> *to world-wide praise and fame,*
>    *when I gather you home,*
>    *when I do good to you;*
> *for I will grant you praise and fame*
> *among all nations of the world,*
> *when I turn your fortunes*
>    *under your own eyes—*
> *'tis the Eternal's promise.*

---

[1]Driver, *op. cit.*, p. 139.          [2]Farrar, *op. cit.*, p. 157.

*The Book of*

# HAGGAI

H. Ray Dunning

# Introduction

Israel had seen a long period of humiliation and spiritual anxiety through the seventy years of the Exile prior to Haggai's ministry. One must know something of these trying years and the events at their close which issued in the return of the Jews to Canaan in order to understand the problems faced by this postexilic prophet.[1]

## A. The Historical Setting

Through a decree of Cyrus, the Persian conqueror of the Babylonian Empire, the Babylonian Captivity came to an end. At least the Jews were no longer forbidden to return to their homeland. Cyrus made a positive declaration giving them permission to return to reestablish their nation and to restore their worship. Many of the Jews were so rooted in Babylon that they were not interested in returning. But there was a group of some fifty thousand who returned with high hopes under the leadership of Zerubbabel. "The select company that followed Zerubbabel must have consisted of the most earnest, godly and enterprising members of the captive nation."[2]

However, due to the opposition which they faced in their homeland, chiefly from the neighboring Samaritans, they were unable to carry out their plans of rebuilding the Temple and restoring the city.

Upon the ascent to the Persian throne of Darius Hystaspes the decree which had stopped the work was reviewed and reversed. Therefore "the prophets Haggai and Zechariah strongly urged their countrymen to resume the work. . . . The work of rebuilding the temple was accordingly resumed."[3] This new impetus came after a period of about seventeen years during which the work had been at a standstill. It is against the background of this situation that Haggai's ministry is to be seen and understood.

---

[1]For a brief account of the whole period, cf. W. T. Purkiser, et al., *Exploring the Old Testament* (Kansas City: Beacon Hill Press, 1957), pp. 361-69.

[2]Blaikie & Matthews, *A Manual of Bible History* (New York: The Ronald Press, 1940), p. 282.

[3]*Ibid.*, p. 283.

## B. The Prophet

Of Haggai's personal life, little is known. The name means "The Festal" or if abbreviated from Haggiah (I Chron. 6:30), "feasts of Jehovah."[4] Unlike Zephaniah, no genealogy is attached to his name and he is mentioned outside his own book only in Ezra 5:1 and 6:14.

Haggai's chief work, along with Zechariah, was in providing the challenge to resume the restoration of the Temple. "One might almost say: 'No Haggai—no temple.' "[5] It is generally agreed that he was an old man when he prophesied. This is inferred from the indication in 2:3 that he still remembered Solomon's Temple, which had been destroyed nearly seventy years before.

Talmudic tradition lists Haggai with Zechariah and Malachi as the founders of "the Great Synogague," an assembly of Jewish scholars and rabbis originating in Ezra's time. Several psalms in the Septuagint are attributed to him. He stands with these other two as the last of the prophets. The Talmud declares that with their death the Holy Spirit departed from Israel.[6]

## C. The Book

This prophecy is composed of four messages which Haggai preached. The "sermons" are carefully dated and all were delivered within a brief period of four months. Each one was a further step in the process of encouraging Zerubbabel and the faithful to finish the Temple, and each came at a period when the work lagged. The four messages form the natural outline of the book.

[4]F. W. Farrar, *The Minor Prophets* (London: James Nisbet and Co., n.d.), p. 187.

[5]Eli Cashdan, "Haggai," *The Twelve Prophets,* ed. A. Cohen (London: The Soncino Press, 1948), p. 253.

[6]*Ibid.,* p. 254.

# *Outline*

Section **I** *The Call to Action*

Haggai 1:1-15

A. SUPERSCRIPTION, 1:1

This verse gives the basic data for the chronological and historical setting of the prophecy. It was **in the second year of Darius.** This would be 520 B.C., and Darius was king of Persia (see Introduction). The word of the Lord came to the prophet on **the first day of the month** which compares to our month of September—the **sixth month** in the Jewish calendar, known as Elul.[1]

**The first day of the month,** being the appearance of the new moon, was a religious holiday, and a day of religious pilgrimage (cf. II Kings 4:23; Amos 8:5). Consequently there would be a large audience to hear the prophet's message. They would also be more sensitive to their failure to build the Temple.

The message was specifically addressed to **Zerubbabel the son of Shealtiel . . . and to Joshua the son of Josedech, the high priest.** Thus the prophet spoke to the key men in the community, in the presence of the assembled worshippers. He issued to them a ringing call to action. Zerubbabel is said in I Chron. 3:19 to have been the son of Pedaiah. This may be explained as the result of a levirate marriage in which Zerubbabel, while actually the son of Pedaiah, was legally the son of Shealtiel (cf. BBC, II, 524). Zerubbabel was a Jew, of the house of David, being a direct descendant of the great king since his grandfather was the son of Jehoiachin (Jeconiah; I Chron. 16:3-17). This lineage gave rise to hope in certain hearts that he would be the king who would sit on David's throne, thus fulfilling a Messianic expectation. These hopes were, of course, groundless, as Zerubbabel was not the king. His position was that of governor, appointed by the Persian king as the civil head of the community.

**Joshua,** the first high priest after the restoration, returned with the first contingent of exiles and thus was the religious head of the community. His name appears often in the Book of Haggai. His father, **Josedech** or Jehozadah, was the high priest who was

[1]Cashdan, *op. cit.,* p. 255.

322

taken captive to Babylon (I Chron. 6:15). His grandfather, Seraiah, was the high priest who was put to death by Nebuchadnezzar when he destroyed Jerusalem in 586 B.C. (II Kings 25:18-21).

### B. The Cause of Delay, 1:2

The people were waiting to build the Temple at a convenient time, which they said had not yet arrived. The altar had been erected, and a simple ritual observed. This they considered sufficient for the time. It also seems that the people had been kept from completing the Temple by a meticulous interpretation of Jeremiah's mention of seventy years (Jer. 25:11), which they thought was not yet complete.[2]

Another suggested reason for their failure was that the Lord had not blessed them with good harvests, which indicated that He was still angry with them—and so **the time** was **not come.** Providence, on this view, had not created favorable conditions for building.

A further reason for the lack of interest in renewing efforts to build may have been fear of the Samaritans. These people had opposed the work before, on the pretext that the Jews had refused to allow them to share in the construction. This resentment showed itself in their successful efforts to prevent the Jews from securing timber for the building. This hindrance stopped when the Temple work ceased, and apparently there had been no objection to the Jews building their own houses (see 1:4). But to resume the Temple work would undoubtedly cause the Samaritans to renew their opposition.[3]

### C. Attack upon the Delay, 1:3-6

While neglecting the Temple for the reasons discussed above, the returned exiles had found both time and convenience to build their own houses. It was time for **the word of the Lord** (3) to be spoken. Furthermore, the people had built their houses well and extravagantly. **Ceiled** (4) means "panelled." They had finished the walls of their homes with costly woodwork. This was a practice which was considered luxurious even for a king (Jer. 22:14). Yet they were unable to restore the house of the

---

[2]Cashdan, *op. cit.*, p. 256.

[3]G. A. Smith, "Haggai," *The Expositor's Bible*, ed. W. Robertson Nicoll, (New York: A. C. Armstrong, 1896), p. 235.

Lord. It is even suggested that they used for their homes the cedarwood which had been procured for the Temple. In contrast, the house of worship lay in ruins. As Marcus Dods says: "Their own comforts were their condemnation. If they had found means, leisure, and security to furnish such houses for themselves, it could scarcely be the times which prevented them from building God's house."[4]

Now the Lord asks the people to **consider your ways** (5). This is a characteristic phrase, occurring four times in the book. Literally it says, "Set your heart upon your ways," but is well translated, "Consider how you have fared" (RSV). What are the results of this tragic neglect? There is a fivefold consequence: "You have sown much, but you have brought in little; you eat, but you do not have enough; you drink, but you do not have your fill; you clothe yourselves, but no one is warm; and he who earns wages earns wages for a purse with holes" (6, Berk.). There is no prosperity in the community; all their undertakings have failed. By failing to honor the Lord and spending their energy and possessions on themselves, they are operating on the law of diminishing returns. Positively, Haggai is saying, "It pays to serve God." The final figure of speech is expressive. One who waits until his economic circumstances improve before honoring God with his substance is playing a losing game.

All this Haggai attributes to the displeasure of Jehovah for their failure to build the Temple.

### D. CHALLENGE TO ACT, 1:7-11

In 7 we have again the ringing declaration, **Thus saith the Lord of hosts.** And again comes the challenge, **Consider your ways.** "Move yourselves out of this indolence and indifference and immediately go to the hills to gather timber for the task," is the import of 8a. The stones of Solomon's Temple would still remain strewn over the Temple site, but the woodwork would have been burned. If they would move into action, God's favor toward them and the Temple would be forthcoming. This is His glorious promise. The phrase **and I will be glorified** (8) is incomplete, omitting a letter from the Hebrew text which stands for the figure five. The Jews saw in this a mystery and from it argued that, in spite of the glory of this second Temple, five things

[4]*The Post-Exilian Prophets* (Edinburgh: T. and T. Clark, 1881), *ad loc.*

would be missing from it. There is not full agreement what these are but the usual list includes: (1) the ark and the mercy seat, (2) the Shekinah, or glory cloud in the holiest, (3) the fire that descended from heaven, (4) the Urim and the Thummim, and (5) the Spirit of prophecy.

In 9 the prophet repeats God's message regarding the spiritual cause of the famine. It is God's activity in response to their failure which has brought them scarcity. Haggai recognizes their high hopes—**Ye looked for much** (9). This expectation had been based on glowing promises found chiefly in Isaiah 40—66. He further pointed out that these promises had not been fulfilled, and the people were consequently disillusioned and discouraged. But he goes on to show that it is their own fault—**Mine house . . . is waste, and ye run every man unto his own house.** "That is why I am holding back the rains from heaven and giving you such scant crops. In fact, I have called for a drought upon the land, yes, and in the highlands, too; a drought to wither the grain and the grapes and olives and all your other crops; a drought to starve both you and all your cattle, and ruin everything you have worked so hard to get" (10-11, *Living Prophecies*).

### E. Response to the Challenge, 1:12-15

The two leaders, **Zerubbabel** and **Joshua** (see comment on 1:1), along with **the remnant of the people, obeyed the voice of the Lord** (12). Most commentators understand this to mean the remainder of the people besides the leaders, that is, the small portion of people who returned from captivity in contrast to the former population. **Remnant** came to be a technical term for that part of the nation which returned from the Babylonian Captivity.

The people "stood in awe of the Lord" (12, Berk.) and immediately set to work rebuilding the Temple. As soon as the work began, the prophet issued a promise from God, **I am with you** (13). The odd construction **the Lord's messenger in the Lord's message** means, "The messenger of the Lord, spoke to the people with the Lord's message" (Berk.). It is God's work and therefore God will do more than stand by as an interested onlooker; He will become an active Participant in the task. This assurance had historical rootage, for the words would remind the people of God's presence with their forefathers (Gen. 28:15; Exod. 3:12; Josh. 1:5). "This short but all-sufficient promise, varied sometimes by the corresponding expression of faith, 'God with us,' or by the record of its fulfillment, 'Jehovah was with him,' shines out like a bright star in times of darkness and need to individual saints, and to the church at large in the Old Testament."[5]

The indifference was broken and the discouragement was turned to courage as **the people . . . came and did work in the house of the Lord of hosts, their God (14).** Three weeks after Haggai's prophecy, the foundation stone was laid (cf. v. 1 and v. 15). They had probably spent the intervening time in clearing away the rubbish that had accumulated on the Temple site.

[5]T. T. Perowne, *Haggai, Zechariah, and Malachi,* "The Cambridge Bible for Schools and Colleges," gen. ed. J. J. S. Perowne (Cambridge: University Press, 1893), p. 31.

# Section II  The Call to Courage

The second message preached by the prophet came after the lapse of about a month. Apparently the work had lagged. The occasion of this address was, like the first, a public assembly—this date being the last day of the Feast of Tabernacles (Lev. 23: 33-36, 39-43). The reason for the slowdown in labor was that the Temple had been sufficiently formed for the people to compare it with Solomon's Temple and it presented a disheartening comparison. They saw that it was a poor substitute for the magnificent structure that had previously stood on Mount Zion. It was to counteract such despondency that the prophet spoke. "Haggai's new word is a simple one of encouragement. The people's conscience had been stirred by his first, they needed now some hope."[1]

## A. DELAY IN THE WORK, 2:1-5

The discouragement of the people and its source are reflected in the words of 3. Obviously, only a small proportion of the people present had actually seen the glory of Solomon's Temple. Most scholars believe that the words indicate that Haggai himself was among this group. He would thus have been an old man at this time, since the Temple had been destroyed seventy years before.

Pusey gives a striking description of the magnificence of Solomon's Temple which will point up the contrast to this simple house of worship:

> Besides the richness of the sculptures in the former Temple, everything which admitted of it was overlaid with gold; Solomon overlaid the whole altar by the oracle, the two cherubims, the floor of the house, the doors of the Holy of Holies and the ornaments of it, the cherubims thereon, and the palm trees he covered with gold fitted upon the carved wood; the altar of gold and the table of gold, whereupon the shewbread was, the ten candlesticks of pure gold, with the flowers and the lamps and the tongs of gold, the bowls, the snuffers and the basons and the spoons and the censers of pure

[1]G. A. Smith, op. cit., p. 241.

gold, and hinges of pure gold for all the doors of the Temple. The porch that was in the front of the house, twenty cubits broad and 120 cubits high, was overlaid within with pure gold; the house glistened with precious stones . . . Six hundred talents of gold were employed in overlaying the Holy of Holies. The upper chambers were also of gold, the weight of the nails was fifty shekels of gold.[2]

Clearly the poor community of returned exiles would be ill prepared to duplicate such an extravagant structure. Yet Haggai addresses himself to **Zerubbabel, Joshua,** and the **people** (4), calling upon them to **be strong.** These words would be filled with special meaning as the people remembered the story of the first chapter of Joshua. Here God had talked to the earlier Joshua, who had just been chosen as the successor of Moses and the leader of Israel. There too, in the face of a great task, God had given this same exhortation to strength and courage—**Be strong.**

Although some would criticize Haggai for calling upon the people to undertake the assignment in their own strength, this is a misreading of the prophet. There are two sides to his message: (*a*) the people are to **be strong . . . and work;** but as they do, (*b*) God promises, **I am with you.** The strongest assurance to Israel of Jehovah's presence and power to help was that He is the same God who delivered them **out of Egypt** (5). Haggai, like most of the prophets, reminds the people that God had entered into a covenant with them, a relationship which He will not break.

"It is remarkable that the presence of the Spirit should be used as equivalent to a fulfillment of the covenant on God's part; the idea which pervades the N.T."[3]

In 2:1-5 we see "How to Face Discouraging Circumstances." (1) Don't try to fool yourself—face the facts, 3; (2) Be courageous, 4; (3) Recall God's promises and help in previous hard places, 5*a*; (4) Listen for God's promise and encouragement—**I am with you, saith the Lord of hosts . . . my spirit remaineth among you: fear ye not,** 4-5 (A. F. Harper).

### B. THE PROPHECY ITSELF, 2:6-9

In this passage we see the actual prophecy which gave the people grounds for encouragement. The RSV translates 6: "Once again, in a little while, I will shake the heavens and the

[2]Quoted in Perowne, *op. cit.*, p. 34.
[3]Dods, *op. cit.*, p. 53.

earth and the sea and the dry land." Here, as so often in prophecy, the future is foreshortened. This is a vision of "incredible audacity which reveals the prophet's unconquerable faith."[4]

**Yet once** (again) . . . **I will shake** . . . **the earth** has been referred by some to the great shaking at Mount Sinai when God initiated the covenant. In like manner He will once again manifest His glory and cause all nations to tremble at His presence.

The cataclysms which Haggai foresees are thought by most to be reflections of the revolts then going on in the Persian world during the early reign of Darius. These upheavals Haggai sees as a prelude to the Messianic age. The prophetic picture indicated that the Messianic age would be preceded by "messianic woes."[5]

In this case, the Messianic age and its glory are associated with the Temple. Although these impoverished exiles do not have access to wealth sufficient to match the Temple of Solomon, yet God is the Possessor of all **silver** and **gold** (8).

Commentators are agreed that the singular **desire of all nations** (7) in the KJV is a mistaken translation since the verb is plural and demands the plural subject. J. McIlmoyle expresses the conservative position with great clarity: "Much as the hearts, especially of those who have found Him who is all their desire, would wish to follow ancient Jewish expositors and find a personal reference here to the Messiah, and great as would be the truth that would be thus expressed, the difficulty in so rendering the words seems insuperable."[6]

The Septuagint renders it "the choice things," or it may be translated, "the desirable things of all nations." The reference is to the costly treasures which will be brought to beautify the Temple (cf. Isa. 60:5—"The wealth [marg.] of the Gentiles [nations] shall come unto thee").

The prophet continues his bold prophecy with two further predictions: **The glory of this latter house** (the new Temple) **shall be greater than of the former** (Solomon's Temple), and God will give it **peace** (9).

Perhaps what is to make it greater are the splendid offerings of gold and silver brought to it by the nations. But this seems

[4]J. E. McFadyen, "Haggai," *Abingdon Bible Commentary,* ed. F. C. Eiselen, *et al.* (New York: Abingdon-Cokesbury Press, 1929), p. 817.

[5]Millar Burrows, *An Outline of Biblical Theology* (Philadelphia: The Westminster Press, 1946), pp. 195 ff.

[6]"Haggai," *New Bible Commentary,* ed. F. Davidson, *et al.* (Grand Rapids: Wm. B. Eerdmans Publishing Co., 1953), p. 747.

rather inadequate in face of the fact that the prophet recognizes the real glory of the Temple to be the presence of God. Also the literal meaning of this verse does not imply two houses, but one, the latter being in continuity with the first. This was literally true since certain standing walls of the old became part of the new. The literal translation puts it, "The latter glory of this house shall be greater than the former."

"The glory here promised is first and most obviously material glory," says Perowne, "the desirable things, the precious gifts of all nations." But he is undoubtedly nearer the truth when he adds, "but it includes the spiritual glory, without which in the sight of God material splendor is worthless and unacceptable."[7]

The second promise gave assurance that God's people should have security in the midst of the earth-shaking convulsions among the nations.

But were these prophecies fulfilled? Marcus Dods noted that they were literally fulfilled inasmuch as the means of building did not fail. But this did not constitute the greatest fulfillment. The tribute of the nations involved the recognition that this was the "visible center of God's kingdom and place of his manifestation."[8]

---

[7]*Op. cit.*, p. 39.          [8]*Op. cit.*, p. 54.

# Section III *The Call to Patience*

In this section, Haggai addresses some questions to the priests. His message came three months after the work had begun and two months after the previous prophecy. It was a further means of encouraging the people to work by showing them the need of patience. The message may be titled "The Power of the Unclean" (G. A. Smith) and is based on a judgment which the priests gave in response to Haggai's questions. He asks the priests to "decide this question" (11, RSV). The Hebrew says, "Ask for a Torah." In this case it was an oral decision ("direction") for which the Book of Deuteronomy makes provision in case there are no written instructions (Deut. 17:8-13). These decisions were given as an interpretation based on the traditional material and came to mean "a body of technical direction."[1]

Haggai asked two questions: Would a garment bearing **holy flesh** make holy what it touches? **And the priests answered and said, No** (12). The second question was, Will that which is made **unclean** by touching **a dead body** defile what it touches? The priests answered, **It shall be unclean** (13).

The point of the questions is that it is much easier to become defiled than to become clean—unholiness is more contagious than holiness. The sum of the argument is that what was ceremonially holy could not hallow what it touched. On the contrary, what was ceremonially unclean infected not only the person in contact with it, but whatever he touched as well (Num. 19:11-22).

In 14, Haggai makes his application. **This people** refers to the Jews. **That which they offer there** specifically points to the altar which had been erected. The people thought that their ritual enacted at the restored altar would remove their past negligence. But Haggai is trying to show them that this is not the case. Rather their former activities had polluted them until even their offerings were unclean.

It is easy to acquire defilement, but it is not easily cleansed. This is the lesson from the answer of the priests. Men are not to think that a mere change of direction will free them from the

[1]Driver, *op. cit.*, p. 163.

consequences of their former failures. Sin may be forgiven but its consequences sometimes remain to hinder. Thus the exhortation to patience was needed. The people would have to labor against difficulties which their sin had created. "If contact with a holy thing has only a slight effect, but contact with an unclean thing has a much greater effect, then their attempts to build the Temple must have less good influence upon their condition than the bad influence of all their past devotion to themselves and their secular labors."[2]

Having thus introduced the principles of God's government and applied them to the people, Haggai proceeds to illustrate the point. He calls attention to the seventeen years which had passed since the return from Babylon, with the succession of poor harvest seasons. God had smitten their crops **with blasting and with mildew** (17), two diseases which Moses had predicted as chastisements for disobedience (Deut. 28:22). **Hail** also had been destructive of the vines.

From the time that the people had begun to rebuild—**the day that the foundation of the Lord's temple was laid** (18)—there were yet no natural signs that the situation would change. This is probably to be understood as a result of the clinging remains of uncleanness, as the priests' answers indicated. Now, however, God intends to change their circumstances. *Living Prophecies* gives a clear interpretation of 18-19. "But now note this: From today, this 24th day of the month [the 24th day of Kislev; this corresponds to early in our December] as the foundation of the Lord's temple is finished, and from this day onward, I will bless you. Notice, I am giving you this promise now before you have even begun to rebuild the temple structure, and before you have harvested your grain, and before the grapes and figs and pomegranates and olives have produced their next crops: *from this day I will bless you.*"

---

[2]Smith, *op. cit.*, p. 249.

Section **IV** *The Call to Faith*

Haggai 2:20-23

The final message of Haggai is addressed to **Zerubbabel (21)** alone. It was given on the same day as the preceding sermon. In it, the prophet conceives of Zerubbabel as the predecessor and type of the true King of the Jews. To him and in him to the nation which he represented, a gracious promise of safety and distinction is given.[1]

Haggai sees the **throne of kingdoms** (22; powers of the world) being overthrown, and repeats the prophecy of 2:6, **I will shake the heavens and the earth** (21). In this upheaval, Zerubbabel's position will remain secure and God will make firm His trusted representative.

Zerubbabel is to be God's **signet** (23). This was a ring with the owner's name engraved on it and was guarded by him with jealous care. It was used to impress a seal and therefore became the symbol of authority. It was sometimes given by an Eastern monarch to an important minister as a mark of confidence and authority (cf. Gen. 41:42). Thus Zerubbabel's leadership is to bear the stamp of divine authority.

"The Messianic aspirations which attached formerly to the Davidic king are transferred by Haggai to Zerubbabel who becomes, in virtue of the position thus assigned to him, a type of Christ."[2]

Many must have had high hopes that Zerubbabel was actually the Messianic king, for to him the prophet speaks in the name of the Lord, **I have chosen thee.** But as G. A. Smith observes, this signet-ring of Jehovah (Zerubbabel) was not acknowledged by the world. He does not seem even to have challenged its briefest attention. Thus what we really have here is a reassertion of the Jewish Messianic hope of a divine Deliverer from the house of David who would sit on David's throne. This great hope came to its culmination in the Son of David—Jesus Christ. His kingdom shall arise above the fallen kingdoms of this world and His throne shall be established forever. Amen.

[1]Perowne, *op. cit.*, p. 45.
[2]Driver, *op. cit.*, p. 169.

*The Book of*

# ZECHARIAH

William M. Greathouse

# Introduction

## A. The Prophet

The name Zechariah was not uncommon in Israel. It means "Jehovah remembers" or "Jehovah has remembered" (i.e., by answering the parents' prayers for a baby son). Zechariah, the prophet, is described as "the son of Berechiah" and the grandson "of Iddo the prophet" (1:1). Ezra, on the other hand, refers to him as "the son of Iddo" (Ezra 5:1; 6:14). This discrepancy is more apparent than real. It may be easily removed by assuming that Berechiah died before Iddo and that Zechariah succeeded his grandfather in the headship of David's priestly course.[1] There are several instances in the Old Testament where men are called the sons of their grandfathers (Gen. 29:5; cf. Gen. 24:47; I Kings 19:16; cf. II Kings 9:14, 20). "As in these cases," George Adam Smith observes, "the grandfather was the reputed founder of the house, so in that of Zechariah Iddo was the head of his family when it came out of Babylon and was anew planted in Jerusalem."[2] Ezra's reference to Zechariah as the *son* of Iddo is therefore to be taken in the more general sense of descendant.

In any event the prophet Zechariah was a member of the priestly family of Iddo which returned to Jerusalem from Babylon under Cyrus (Neh. 12:4). The Book of Nehemiah adds the further note that in the high priesthood of Joiakim, the son of Joshua, the head of the house of Iddo was named Zechariah (Neh. 12:10, 16). If this is our prophet, as it is reasonable to suppose, he was a young man in 520 B.C. and had come to Jerusalem as a child in a caravan from Babylon. The Book of Ezra informs us that Zechariah shared with Haggai in the work of encouraging Zerubbabel and Joshua to rebuild the Temple (Ezra 5:1-2; 6:14).

Zechariah's prophetic career began "in the eighth month of the second year of Darius" (1:1), that is, in November, 520 B.C. The first phase of his ministry continued until the ninth month of the fourth year of the king's reign, or until December, 518 B.C. (7:1). We know nothing of the remaining years of the prophet's

---

[1] G. N. M. Collins, "Zechariah," *The New Bible Commentary* (Grand Rapids, Mich.: Wm. B. Eerdmans Publishing Co., 1953), p. 748.

[2] "The Book of the Twelve Prophets," *The Expositor's Bible,* ed. W. Robertson Nicoll (New York: George H. Doran Co., n.d.), II, 264-65.

life or ministry except for our Lord's statement that he was slain "between the temple and the altar" by rebellious Jews (Matt. 23:35).

## B. THE BOOK

The unity of the book has been seriously questioned by scholars. The two main divisions—chapters 1—8, which, for purposes of this discussion, may be designated as Zechariah I; and chapters 9—14, as Zechariah II—are so dissimilar in historical standpoint and style that it has become common to assign these divisions to different authors.

Zechariah I consists of prophecies dated according to the years of King Darius I Hystaspis, from his second to his fourth year (520-518 B.C.). In this division Darius is reigning and the Exile is over (1:12; 7:5). Many Jews, however, are still in Babylon (2:6); others are scattered over the world (8:7). The community in Jerusalem is small and feeble, composed mostly of young and middle-aged men who came to it from Babylon; there are few children and old people there (8:4-5). Joshua and Zerubbabel are the ecclesiastical and political heads of the community (3:1-10; 4:6-10; 6:11-15). The foundations of the Temple are laid but its completion is still future (4:6-10). But as the book unfolds, the Temple is so far built by December, 518 B.C., that the priests are said to belong to it (7:3), and there is no further need of continuing the fasts of the Exile (7:5-7; 8:18-19). The future is bright with Messianic hopes (8:20-23). Most of all, the hard struggles with nature seem to be past and the people have time to lift their eyes to behold nations coming from afar to worship in Jerusalem (8:20-23). These features leave no doubt that the first eight chapters of the book come from the prophet himself and from the period to which he assigns them, November, 520, to December, 518 B.C.

When we pass into chapter 9 we find ourselves in an altogether different historical situation, and the atmosphere is in sharp contrast to that of chapters 1—8. Israel is facing a new set of historical forces, and the words addressed to her breathe a different spirit. There is no reference to the building of the Temple or a single reflection of the events under the shadow of which Zechariah I was written. We encounter the names of heathen powers not mentioned in the first division: Damascus, Hadrach, Hamath, Assyria, Egypt, and Greece. The peace, and the love of peace, so prominent in Zechariah I, have disappeared. War, if not actual, is imminent. For these and other reasons, chiefly stylistic, modern biblical criticism has assigned Zechariah II to another hand.

In 1683, Joseph Mede advanced what has come to be known as the preexilic theory concerning the authorship of Zechariah II. Struck by the facts above and moved by a desire to vindicate the correctness of Matthew's ascription of Zech. 11:12-13 to the prophet Jeremiah (see Matt. 27:9-10), Mede ascribed a preexilic date to Zechariah II. He believed also that many things in the first division apply better to the time of Jeremiah than to that of Zechariah.[3] Mede's view eventually gained wide acceptance, and down to the late nineteenth century Zechariah II was regarded by many interpreters as a collection of preexilic prophecies attached by accident to the postexilic prophecy of Zechariah.

Although Grotius (1644) and H. Corrodi (1792) opposed the preexilic theory of Mede and argued for a post-Zecharian dating of Zechariah II,[4] it was Bernard Stade who is credited with turning the course in criticism to what is now known as the post-Alexandrian theory. In 1881, Stade published an article in which he demonstrated, by a study of literary relationships and historical allusions, that these chapters could not be earlier than Ezekiel.[5] His own view was that Zechariah II was written during the wars of the Diadochi (the successors of Alexander the Great who fought for control of his empire after his death), from 323 B.C. to about 278 B.C.[6]

At the present time biblical scholarship is divided between those who hold to the unity of the entire book, dating Zechariah II after 480 B.C. in view of the reference in 9:13 to the threat of Greece,[7] and those who would place the second division in the Grecian or post-Alexandrian period (after 330 B.C.). Those who

---

[3]Matthew 27, however, does not quote exclusively from Zechariah II. The fulfillment to which Matthew refers pertains to the purchase of a potter's field, and this points to Jer. 32:6-9 (cf. Jer. 18:2; 19:2, 11). In the light of these passages in Jeremiah we may understand Zechariah's casting of the money to the potter as a renewal of the older symbol in Jeremiah. Since Matthew combines both Jeremiah and Zechariah, only Jeremiah as the older prophet, is mentioned. See Gleason L. Archer, Jr., *A Survey of Old Testament Introduction* (Chicago: Moody Press, 1964), p. 411.

[4]Edward J. Young, *An Introduction to the Old Testament* (Grand Rapids: Wm. B. Eerdmans Publishing Company, 1953), p. 270.

[5]Robert C. Dentan, "Zechariah," *The Interpreter's Bible* (New York and Nashville: Abingdon Press, 1956), p. 1090.

[6]Young, *op. cit.*, p. 271; Dentan, *ibid.*

[7]Archer, *op. cit.*, p. 410.

hold the former view see Zechariah II as coming from the hand of the prophet in his old age. Advocates of the post-Alexandrian view, although they have not been able to agree upon any alternate theory of composition (dating Zechariah II variously from 333 B.C. to 140 B.C.), must of necessity reject the Zecharian authorship of the second division of the book.

## C. THE UNITY OF ZECHARIAH

Conservative scholarship has raised serious objections to the post-Alexandrian and post-Zecharian view of Zechariah on the following grounds:

1. The strongest argument adduced in favor of the post-Alexandrian theory is the reference to the sons of Greece in 9:13. Greece is thought to be a threat against Zion and is regarded as the dominant world power of the day. The prophecy, however, is one of a defeat, not a victory, for the sons of Greece. Moreover, 9:12-13 is not a description of an actual battle but is *predictive* of a future confrontation of Zion and Greece in which Zion would be triumphant. In Zechariah's own time the victories of the Greeks over Xerxes at Salamis, Platea, and Mycale (480-479 B.C.) would be sufficient to bring them to the attention of his contemporaries. Unless one rejects the possibility of predictive prophecy on dogmatic grounds, there is no reason why Zechariah could not have penned these words in the 470's.[8]

2. Literary arguments are also advanced. The style of Zechariah II is said to differ from that of Zechariah I. The phrase "thus saith the Lord," so frequent in chapters 1—8, occurs but once in the second division. On the other hand, the expression "in that day" is used eighteen times in Zechariah II as against only three occurrences in Zechariah I. Furthermore, the style of the later section is regarded as more poetic. Conservative scholars, however, point out that there are even more significant traits of style common to both sections. Admittedly, an author's style changes with the passing of years and in dealing with a different historical situation. In the days when the prophet was summoning his fellow Jews to rebuild the Temple, the prophetic "thus saith the Lord" was necessary to enforce the divine authority of that summons. On the other hand, the eschatological phrase "in that day" is more appropriate in prophecies that look to the more distant future of Israel, the theme of Zechariah II.

[8]Archer, *op. cit.*, p. 413; Young, *op. cit.*, p. 272.

Defenders of the unity of the authorship of Zechariah point out the persistence of the following stylistic traits:

*a.* "Saith the Lord" occurs fourteen times in Zechariah I and six times in Zechariah II.

*b.* The Hebrew phrase "the eyes of the Lord" is found twice in Zechariah I (4:10; 8:6) and once in Zechariah II (9:8; twice if 12:4, "mine eyes," be allowed).

*c.* The divine title "the Lord of hosts" is found three times in both divisions.

*d.* The verb translated "to sit" or "to dwell" in the special sense of "be inhabited" is found twice in each division and very seldom anywhere else in the Old Testament.

*e.* There is a peculiar five-member type of Hebrew parallelism which is scarcely found outside Zechariah but which occurs once in Zechariah I (6:13) and three times in Zechariah II (9:5, 7; 12:4).[9]

As far as language is concerned, all scholars agree that the Hebrew in both parts is pure and remarkably free of Aramaisms. Pusey remarks, "In both there is a certain fullness of language, produced by dwelling on the same thought or word: in both, the whole and its parts are, for emphasis, mentioned together. In both parts, as a consequence of this fullness, there occurs the division of the verse into five sections, contrary to the usual rule of Hebrew parallelism."[10]

3. Finally, it should be observed that those who reject the Zecharian authorship of chapters 9—14 are in hopeless disagreement among themselves in regard to an alternate theory. References in cc. 9—14 have led to various datings of its several component parts, ranging all the way from about 330 to 140 B.C., depending on what correlations are made with episodes and characters connected with Hellenistic history.

The admitted dissimilarities between Zechariah I and Zechariah II can be accounted for without surrendering belief in the unity of authorship. Collins has put the case well:

> . . . in i—viii the prophet is principally concerned with contemporary events, particularly the rebuilding of the temple; while in ix—xiv he deals with such future events as the coming of the Messiah and the glory of His reign. Naturally, therefore, the former division is

[9]Archer, *op. cit.,* p. 414-15.
[10]Quoted by Young, *op. cit.,* p. 273.

historical in style, whereas the latter is apocalyptic. It is probable also that the first part of the prophecy belonged to Zechariah's early life, and the second to his old age. The internal evidence of the book is favourable, as W. H. Lowe so clearly shows, to the post-exilic origin of both divisions, as well as to the unity of authorship.[11]

# *Outline*

[11]*Op. cit.*, p. 748.

# Section I *Oracles During the Building of the Temple*

**Zechariah 1:1—8:23**

The first eight chapters of Zechariah are prophecies dated according to the reign of Darius, the king, from his second year to his fourth.[1] Although these chapters contain some exhortations to rebuild the Temple, most of the prophecies presuppose the progress of this work and seek to encourage it by giving historical retrospect and inspiring hopes of the Messianic effects of the Temple's completion. In these chapters Zechariah demonstrates his true prophetic calling, for he begins his oracles by calling the people to repentance.

## A. A CALL TO REPENTANCE, 1:1-6

Late in the year 520 b.c. the Lord led Zechariah to summon His people to return to Him, with the assurance that if they would do so He would return to them. They are not to be like their fathers, who rebelled against the warnings of the preexilic prophets and thereby brought God's judgment upon themselves. Their fathers and the prophets are no more. But the effective power of God's word remains, as the people whom he warns well know, for it has overtaken them.

**The eighth month,** in which **the word of the Lord** (1) came to the prophet, corresponds with our October-November. Before the Exile it was called Bul (I Kings 6:38), but after the return of the Jews it came to be known as Marchesvan. This name probably derived from a word which meant "wet" or "rainy" and suggests the constant dripping rain which characterized the month. The day of the month is not given.

Zechariah began his prophetic career exactly two months after Haggai (Hag. 1:1). His summons to repentance was appropriate even after the promises made by Haggai, because the promises were conditioned on repentance.[2]

[1]See Introduction, "The Book."

[2]Marcus Dods, *The Post-Exilian Prophets* (Edinburgh: T. and T. Clark, 1881), p. 67.

**In the second year of Darius** indicates the Captivity practice of using the dates of the foreign kings to whom the Israelites were subject. They had formerly dated their history by the years of the reigns of their own kings. Concerning the identity of **Zechariah, the son of Berechiah, the son of Iddo the prophet,** see Introduction, "The Prophet." The title **prophet** is descriptive of Zechariah, but Cashdan points out that "according to the Massoretic accentuation it belongs to Iddo. . . . The Rabbis remove all doubt by the following comment: 'Whenever a prophet's name is given as well as his father's, it is to indicate that he was a prophet the son of a prophet.' "[3]

God's word to Zechariah is strong: **The Lord hath been sore displeased with your fathers** (2), literally, "has been displeased with displeasure." Dods says the word meant originally "breaking out in long-controlled indignation."[4] **Your fathers** is a reference to the generation before the Captivity. The displeasure of God had fallen heavily upon their ancestors. "Now, for the first time in this new era of their history, God is sending them, as He did to their fathers of old, His servants the prophets, himself and Haggai, with a call to repentance and a promise of reconciliation."[5]

**Turn ye unto me . . . and I will turn unto you, saith the Lord of hosts** (3). This is better translated, "Return unto me . . . and I will return unto you." The verb *return* indicates a change of conduct. God promises a change of attitude toward His people if they will mend their ways. "There had been a revival, and the people have returned to the land of God's choice. Yet evidently they had not fully returned in a spiritual way to the Lord Jehovah."[6] The threefold repetition of **saith the Lord of hosts** gives prominence to the authority of the message.

The prophet warns his hearers that they must not be like their **fathers,** who turned a deaf ear to **the former prophets** of the

[3]Eli Cashdan, "Zechariah," *The Twelve Prophets,* ed. A. Cohen (London: The Soncino Press, 1948), p. 271.

[4]*Loc. cit.*

[5]T. T. Perowne, *Haggai, Zechariah and Malachi,* "The Cambridge Bible for Schools and Colleges," gen. ed. J. J. S. Perowne (Cambridge: University Press, 1893), "Zechariah," p. 5.

[6]G. Coleman Luck, *Zechariah* (Chicago: Moody Press, n.d.), p. 15. For Zechariah's strong ethical emphasis, cf. v. 4; 7:1-10; 8:16-17, 19.

preexilic period (7:7, 12) and refused to amend their **ways** (4). Should they be like them in their sin, they should be like them in their punishment also. By this oracle God was countering the thought which naturally occurred to those who had been restored to their own country. They were not to assume that they were a new people without the ominous threats hanging over them such as their fathers had incurred. Their fathers' fate was actually a strong prophetic word to them. "Your fathers and the prophets are alike gone, but the testimony your fathers bore to the truth of the prophets' warning remains. You have not the same warnings ringing in your ears that your fathers had, you have not men like Jeremiah to move you to godliness, the prophets do not live forever; but you have what your fathers had not, you have the awful truthfulness of God's words of warning written in your fathers' fate."[7]

**But my words and my statutes . . . did they not take hold of your fathers?** (6) An apparent contradiction of v. 4 is avoided by adopting *The Berkeley Version:* "But My words and My decrees . . . did they not overtake your fathers?" A rebellious people was forced to confess, **Like as the Lord thought to do unto us . . . so hath he dealt with us.**

## B. THE VISIONS OF ZECHARIAH, 1:7—6:8

The visions of Zechariah are a characteristic feature of his prophecy. Some are quite brief, while others contain a wealth of imagery. By their means the prophet expresses the same lofty message found elsewhere in his book. Among these visions occurs the most spiritual of all his utterances: "Not by might, nor by power, but by my spirit, saith the Lord of hosts" (4:6). They express the need of divine pardon, emphasize the reality of sin, and declare the power of God to banish it from His people. They contain the promise of Jerusalem as the City of Peace, her only rampart the Lord himself. They predict the overthrow of the heathen empires as the act of God; and from all the visions there are absent both the turmoil and the glory of war.[8]

The visions are not dreams but "a series of conscious and artistic allegories—the deliberate translation into a carefully con-

[7]Dods, *op. cit.,* p. 68.

[8]George Adam Smith, *The Book of the Twelve Prophets* (New York: Harper and Brothers, 1940), II, 273.

structed symbolism of the Divine truths with which the prophet was entrusted by his God."[9]

For all the visions there is one date, **upon the four and twentieth day of the eleventh month, which is the month Sebat, in the second year of Darius**—i.e., January or February, 519 B.C. There is also one divine impulse, **the word of the Lord unto Zechariah, the son of Berechiah, the son of Iddo the prophet** (7).

### 1. *The Four Horsemen* (1:8-17)

The seventy years Jeremiah had set for the duration of the Babylonian Captivity (Jer. 25:12) were swiftly drawing to a close. It was now four months since Haggai had assured the people that in "a little while" God would shake the kingdoms and out of this shaking bring new glory to the Temple and the nation (Hag. 2:7). The people of Jerusalem were growing impatient with the delay. The world was *not* shaken; no political movement which promised to restore the glory to Jerusalem was apparent. A very natural disappointment had begun to set in and the people were beginning to question whether the promise of God was meant to have any practical fulfillment. In this state of affairs the word of the Lord came to Zechariah.

In the vision Zechariah sees a troop of horsemen in one of the myrtle-covered glens near Jerusalem. Their leader is in front. The prophet is told that these are God's scouts who have been patrolling the earth and who have brought back the report that the world is at peace. The purport of the vision is to indicate that the time is ripe for the Lord to fulfill His promise of mercy to Jerusalem and prosperity to the cities of Judah. The vision is followed by a proclamation of restoration and prosperity.

The prophet sees **a man** seated **upon a red horse** (8). His horse was standing **in the bottom** or valley-bottom **among the myrtle trees.** The scene of the vision was probably a well-known valley in the environs of Jerusalem. Possibly it was a spot to which Zechariah frequently retreated for prayer and reflection. At first the prophet thought he was witnessing a rendezvous of Persian cavalry scouts, the leader up front and the rest behind him, having just arrived on **red . . . speckled, and white** horses to give their reports. Some significance probably attaches to the colors of the horses, though what this significance is, is not clear. The view that the colors have a reference to different missions on

[9]*Ibid.*

which the scouts had been sent is not supported by the context; all bring back the same report (the case of Rev. 6:2, 4-5, and 8 is obviously different). Most probably the colors stand in some relation to the quarters of the earth where the horsemen have been patrolling.[10] The problem is complicated by the fact that the word translated **speckled** is not found elsewhere in the Bible and no agreement has been reached as to what color is meant by the Hebrew word.

Zechariah is soon made aware, however, that these are not men but angels; and with a quick, dissolving change of function and figure which characterizes all angelic appearances, they explain to him their mission.[11] **O my lord, what are these?** the astonished prophet questions (9). These words are addressed to the interpreting angel at his side, called throughout these visions **the angel that talked with me** (9; cf. 13-14, 19; 2:3; 4:1, 4-5; 5:10; 6:4). **The man** on the front horse answers. The horsemen are scouts of God come in from their survey of the whole **earth.** They speak for themselves and report to **the angel of the Lord** that the whole **earth sitteth still, and is at rest** (11). The implication is that all the nations are enjoying security while Jerusalem and Judah alone are in a state of misery and oppression. At this point **the angel of the Lord** turns intercessor: **O Lord of hosts, how long wilt thou not have mercy on Jerusalem and on the cities of Judah, against which thou hast had indignation these threescore and ten years?** (12) The seventy years predicted by Jeremiah are drawing to a close (Jer. 25:11-12; cf. Hag. 1:2). It is time for God to act.

The Lord himself now intervenes and answers the interpreting angel with comforting assurances. Under what form He appeared we are not told (cf. 7:1-9; 8:1-3; 9:1). He is introduced abruptly, just as the interpreting angel in v. 9 and "the angel of the Lord" in v. 11. Zechariah apparently did not hear the Lord's answer, so the interpreting **angel** gave him the divine oracle: **I am jealous for Jerusalem and for Zion with a great jealousy** (14). "I have been and still am jealous," is the literal Hebrew. Jehovah's jealousy for His people (cf. 8:2) prompts Him now at last to interpose on their behalf (cf. Isa. 42:13; 59:17; Ezek. 36:5-6; 38:19). His jealousy is His zeal for His people. Moffatt

---

[10]S. R. Driver, *The Minor Prophets,* "The New Century Bible," ed. Walter F. Adeney (New York: Oxford University Press, 1906), II, 185.

[11]Cf. Collins, *op. cit.,* p. 749.

translates: "I am stirred, deeply stirred, on behalf of Jerusalem." The Lord declares that He is **very sore displeased with the heathen that are at ease** (15), for they have done more mischief to Jerusalem than they were commissioned to do. God had raised up the heathen to punish His people (Isa. 10:5-6; Hab. 1:5-6), but they had gone beyond the divine intention: "for while I was angry but a little they furthered the disaster" (15, RSV). They carried matters entirely too far, outrunning the divine purpose which had used them for judgment. Accordingly God's wrath against Judah has become compassion. The Temple and the city shall be rebuilt, and the people shall again enjoy prosperity: **Thus saith the Lord of hosts** (16-17).

The scope of this first vision is clear. It conveys a distinct promise of three future events: (1) **My house shall be built** (16). The rebuilding of the Temple, in which the Lord might again, as of old, take up His abode (cf. 2:10), would be final proof that His anger was at an end. The Temple was completed four years later, in the sixth year of Darius (Ezra 4:15). (2) **A line shall be stretched forth upon Jerusalem** (16)—i.e., the measuring line. This is a figure of speech for "The city shall be rebuilt." Some seventy years later Nehemiah accomplished this task (Neh. 6:15). (3) **My cities through prosperity shall yet be spread abroad** (17). The fulfillment of this came later under the Hasmonean princes. Beyond this the prophecy does not expressly go. The concluding words, **The Lord shall yet comfort Zion, and shall yet choose Jerusalem,** point, however, toward the Messianic kingdom.[12]

In this first vision we encounter **the angel of the Lord** (vv. 11-12). Throughout the Old Testament He appears, speaking and acting everywhere as Jehovah himself. In Exod. 3:2, for example, we read that "the angel of the Lord appeared" to Moses. With reference to the same person the account says a few sentences later, "When the Lord saw" (Exod. 3:4). Whether the Angel of the Lord has a distinct existence or is a mode of the Lord's self-manifestation is difficult to determine. He appears to be the Word of God personified. Acting as God's mouthpiece, He is so merged with Jehovah that He speaks of himself by the divine I. Robertson Smith declares "that he represents God to man so directly and fully that when he speaks or acts God Himself is felt

---

[12]Perowne, *op. cit.*, p. 72.

348

to speak or act."[13] On the other hand, in the above passage (v. 12) He represents man to God. Here He is the Interceding Angel, presenting the cause of men to the Father. "What we see in these theophanies," G. A. F. Knight writes, "is a groping effort to describe in pictorial terms an experience of God who could not be fully known till He revealed Himself in Christ. But when He did do so, the NT revelation was found to be astonishingly akin to that dimly discovered in and through the OT." The reality that is being expressed in this passage, Knight continues, "is that God is indeed a communion with Himself, an organism, the Trinity."[14]

F. B. Meyer accordingly is right in his insistence that the Angel of the Lord here in Zechariah is "none other than the Angel of the Covenant, our blessed Lord Himself."[15] His comment on vv. 12-14 is fully justified: "It was as though the Father had heard and answered the pleadings of the Son, and returned Him an answer, which is passed on to Zechariah's angel-guide." Then he asks:

> Are you, my reader, desolate through the pressure of long-continued sorrow? God's chastenings have been greatly exaggerated by those who have helped forward the affliction. Yet, be of good cheer! There is One that ever liveth to intercede. Jesus has graven you upon the palms of His hands. Your sad lot is ever before Him. He will yet talk with you with good words and comfortable ones. "Turn"—they are His own words—"O backsliding children; for I am married unto you, saith the Lord." "I will heal their backsliding, I will love them freely; for mine anger is turned away." "He is able to save them to the uttermost that come unto God by him, seeing he ever liveth to make intercession for them."[16]

In 7-17 we see "God's Message to the Discouraged." (1) Even those who have failed God have a divine Intercessor, 12; (2) God is deeply concerned for His people, 13-14; (3) Man is accountable for his sin, but God recognizes the power of circumstances that **helped forward the affliction,** 15; (4) God is ready to strengthen and restore—**I am returned to Jerusalem with mercies, 16b** (A. F. Harper).

---

[13]Quoted by Smith, *op. cit.,* p. 311.

[14]"A Biblical Approach to the Doctrine of the Trinity," *Scottish Journal of Theology,* Occasional Paper No. 1, gen. eds. T. F. Torrance and J. K. S. Reid (Edinburgh: Oliver and Boyd, Ltd., 1953), pp. 27-28.

[15]*The Prophet of Hope* (London: Morgan and Scott, n.d.), p. 16.

[16]*Ibid.,* pp. 17, 19.

## 2. *The Four Horns and the Four Smiths* (1:18-21)

This vision follows closely upon the first and complements it in a striking way. The prophet sees four horns towering up, with threatening mien. He is told that these are the gentile powers which have scattered Judah. Thereupon **four carpenters** (20), or smiths, appear. These, he learns, are to terrify and strike down the horns of the nations. The vision symbolizes the destruction of the heathen nations which have oppressed Judah and Jerusalem and now threaten the fulfillment of the promises given in the previous vision (vv. 16-17).

**Then lifted I up mine eyes, and saw, and behold four horns** (18). In the language of a pastoral people like the Jews, horns represented the cruel threat of a ravener of the flock. "The wild fury of man against the people of God is aptly described by the irruption of a herd of tusked boars, by the charge of a rhinoceros, or the rush of a wild ox on a harmless, defenceless flock, which has no power of resistance, but only of flight."[17]

Some interpreters identify the four horns with the kingdoms of Daniel's vision: Babylon, Medo-Persia, Greece, and Rome (Dan. 2:31-45).[18] Yet only two of these powers had arisen by 519 B.C., the time of this vision, whereas v. 19 says: **These are the horns which have** (already) **scattered Judah, Israel, and Jerusalem.** Orelli comments: "In distinction from Daniel, Zechariah is fond of simultaneous survey, not the presenting of a succession."[19] The four horns point to the four quarters of the heavens (cf. 2:6). Marcus Dods's view is generally accepted: *"Four* horns were seen as representing the totality of Israel's enemies—her enemies from all quarters."[20] Wherever the people looked— north, south, east, or west—there were foes sworn to resist their efforts to rebuild the Temple and renew their national life.

To destroy the four horns **four carpenters** (20) appear. The original word used here means "workers in wood, stone, or metal." It is generally translated "smiths" in the modern versions. Driver suggests *"iron*-smiths, the horns being, no doubt, pictured as made of iron (Mic. iv. 13)."[21] **These are come to fray them,** the Lord answers Zechariah (21). **To fray** is an archaic

---

[17]*Ibid.,* p. 21.

[18]Cashdan, *op. cit.,* p. 276; Meyer, *op. cit.,* p. 21; Luck, *op. cit.,* p. 25.

[19]Quoted by Smith, *op. cit.,* p. 287.

[20]*Op. cit.,* p. 71.                    [21]*Op. cit.,* p. 189.

expression for "to terrify," and it is so translated by the RSV. In using the word, Zechariah is thinking, as in the case of **scattered** (19), not of the **horns** (which could not be terrified), but of the peoples the horns represent. The enemies of Judah are to be thrown into panic by the divinely appointed smiths. Here the figure is resumed. They shall **cast out the horns of the Gen tiles, which lifted up their horn over the land of Judah to scatter it** (21).

It is not clear just who the smiths are. The purport of the vision, however, is unmistakable: the Lord will deliver Judah so that His promise in vv. 16-17 may be fulfilled.

For the modern reader the four horns represent the evil forces that are arrayed against the Church or against us in our efforts to live for Christ and serve Him. But there is something more: "The Lord showed me four smiths" (RSV). We have no problem in locating our enemies, but we need a Divine Hand to reveal our promised deliverance. "And Elisha prayed, and said: Lord, I pray thee, open his eyes, that he may see. And the Lord opened the eyes of the young man; and he saw: and, behold, the mountain was full of horses and chariots of fire round about Elisha" (II Kings 6:17). Here is God's word to us in the second vision: "If God be for us, who can be again us?" (Rom. 8:31-39)

### 3. *The Man with the Measuring Line* (2:1-13)

Like the second vision, the third follows from the first and becomes another, and still more significant, supplement to it. The first promises the rebuilding of Jerusalem, and now the prophet beholds a young man (cf. 4) going forth with a measuring line to define the limits of the city. In light of what follows, there can be no doubt that the prophet meant to symbolize by the young man's act the intention to make Jerusalem again the fortress she had previously been. The man had restricted ideas as to what the city should be, for he seemed intent on defining it on its old lines. The interpreting angel who was conversing with Zechariah was dispatched by another angel to run and give the man a message. In the future Zion shall be an unwalled city, not only because of the multitude of her population, but also because God himself shall be her ramparts.

To this vision is added a lyric epilogue in which the prophet summons the people who are yet in Babylon to return to their own land. He calls upon Zion to exult because the Lord is about to take up His abode once more in Zion, and many nations shall join themselves to Him as He returns to Jerusalem.

*a. Jerusalem of the future* (2:1-5). **I lifted up mine eyes again, and looked** (1), is a repetition of the formula with which the second vision opened (1:18). This third vision, **And behold a man with a measuring line in his hand,** is based on the promise in the first: "A line shall be stretched forth upon Jerusalem" (1:16). The city was about to be restored. Zechariah put a question to the man: **Whither goest thou?** (2) Whereupon the man responded: **To measure Jerusalem, to see what is the breadth thereof, and what is the length thereof.** From what follows it is evident that this young man represents the narrow thinking of the returned exiles whose view of the future was limited to a restoration of the city of Jerusalem to its former condition as a mountain fortress. The past was to be the measure of the future. This, however, is never God's method of operation. We are not surprised, therefore, when another angel comes forward to interrupt the one who is talking with Zechariah and send him running to **speak to this young man.** He is directed to tell him two things.

First, the angelic messenger informs him that **Jerusalem shall be inhabited as towns without walls for the multitude of men and cattle therein** (4). The young man must know that his purpose in marking out the boundaries and walls of Jerusalem is useless. The city is destined to exceed the dimensions of the past and become so great that no walls will be capable of containing it. "Thus far," the young man keeps saying to himself. "The city will never grow beyond this boundary line. Grow as it may, it will never exceed those limits." But God says: "It will overflow into suburbs, adjoining villages, and even annex the neighbouring towns, so as to present the appearance not of a walled city but of a densely populated district."[22] The prediction that she **shall be inhabited as towns without walls** is more than a promise of magnitude and populousness; it is a divine assurance of security against her enemies.

This is certainly a word from God to us. We are all given to forecasting the future and placing limits on the growth of the City of God. But this, God has never designed. It is not for us to impose boundaries, or insist on our narrow conceptions. "For

[22]Dods, *op. cit.*, p. 73.

my thoughts are not your thoughts, neither are your ways my ways, saith the Lord. For as the heavens are higher than the earth, so are my ways higher than your ways, and my thoughts than your thoughts" (Isa. 55:8-9).

> *For the love of God is broader*
> *Than the measure of man's mind;*
> *And the heart of the Eternal*
> *Is most wonderfully kind.*
> —F. W. FABER

It is essential to observe further that the prophetic vision involved a Jerusalem beyond the historical Zion which was to be rebuilt. This prophecy envisions "the Jerusalem which is above . . . which is the mother of us all" (Gal. 4:26). To insist on a wooden literalism in interpreting this vision is to make the very mistake it is intended to correct. Zechariah here sees the City of God glimpsed by John on Patmos. In this city there is a "multitude, which no man could number, of all nations, and kindreds, and people, and tongues" (Rev. 7:9).

In the second place, the angel is instructed to give the young man with the measuring line a gracious and comforting word concerning the presence of God. **For I, saith the Lord, will be unto her a wall of fire round about, and will be the glory in the midst of her** (5). This image was probably borrowed from the campfires with which hunters surround themselves to frighten off wild beasts. Just as no marauder could break through a cordon of flame, "so the unseen but almighty presence of God would be a bulwark on which the powers of earth and hell would break to their undoing."[23] To rest on this promise is to exclaim with the Psalmist: "But thou, O Lord, art a shield for me; my glory, and the lifter up of mine head" (Ps. 3:3). F. B. Meyer observes: "Some put circumstances between them and God; it is far wiser to put God between oneself and the circumstances."[24]

The true protection of the Church is God's presence in her midst. The Shekinah of God is our only safeguard against the foes which would destroy His work. The Holy Spirit is the only

[23]F. B. Meyer, *op. cit.*, p. 29.
[24]*Ibid.*, p. 30.

Conserver of true doctrine, the sole Protector of spirituality, and Guardian of the moral law. The safety of Zion today, as in the days of Zechariah, is **the glory in the midst.**

*b. Zechariah's appeals* (2:6-13). Appended to the third vision is a lyrical epilogue. This consists of two appeals: (1) to the exiles yet in Babylon, vv. 6-9; (2) to the inhabitants of Zion, vv. 10-13.

There were still vast numbers of Jews in Babylon, and to these an earnest invitation is addressed: **Ho, ho, come forth, and flee from the land of the north, saith the Lord** (6). *"The north country,* although its capital and centre was Babylon, was the whole Babylonian empire, called 'the north' because its invasions always came upon Israel from the north."[25] God's word continued: **For I have spread you abroad as the four winds of heaven.** The Book of Esther is witness to the fact that sixty years later Jews were dispersed over the 127 provinces of the Persian Empire, from India to Ethiopia (Esther 1:1; 3:8, 12-14; 8:5, 9). The Lord called to the Jews of the dispersion: **Deliver thyself, O Zion** (i.e., Escape to Zion), thou **that dwellest with the daughter of Babylon** (7).

The Lord promised protection to those who return. "For thus says the Lord of hosts: Afterwards glory! He sent me to the Gentiles who plundered you, for he who touches you touches the pupil of His eye. See, I am shaking my hand at them; they shall be plunder for their servants, and you shall know that the Lord of hosts sent me" (8-9, Berk.). Thomas comments: "The pupil of the eye is sensitive and vulnerable, and therefore highly prized by its owner. Who touches Judah, so highly prized by Yahweh, touches him at a sensitive point."[26] God promises to be as quick to protect Judah as a man to raise his arm when injury is threatening his eye. On the other hand, the Jews are warned of certain danger they incur by lingering. The Lord is already shaking His hand over Babylon as a signal to the nations she has oppressed to gather to her overthrow and to share her spoils.

A second appeal is made: **Sing and rejoice, O daughter of Zion: for, lo, I come, and I will dwell in the midst of thee, saith the Lord** (10).

[25]Pusey; quoted by Perowne, *op. cit.,* p. 77.
[26]"Zechariah," *The Interpreter's Bible,* ed. George A. Buttrick, et al. (New York: Abingdon Press, 1956), VI, 1066.

When the tabernacle of God is with men, and he dwells with them, wiping away all tears, there is no mourning or crying or pain; but the mouth is filled with laughter, and the tongue with singing. Sometimes the Christian gets a vision of this. He realizes that since God has come into the midst of his work, it is no longer his, but God's; he is only the agent. . . . God comforts and teaches the people; God restores the ruins; God builds the walls of Jerusalem; God does good in his good pleasure to Zion; God attracts the people, who join themselves not to a congregation, a church, or a minister, but to the Lord, and become his. He is not only a wall of fire round about, but the glory in the midst.[27]

There is yet another reason for exultation. **And many nations shall be joined to the Lord in that day, and shall be my people** (11). The apostles of Christ understood such prophecies as these to be predictions of the gathering of the gentiles into the Israel of faith, the Christian Church (Rom. 9:22-26; I Pet. 2:9-10; cf. Eph. 2:11-22).

The prophecy, however, moves out into an even wider promise: **And the Lord shall inherit Judah his portion in the holy land, and shall choose Jerusalem again** (12). While insisting on a spiritual application of this vision we must not lose sight of certain literal aspects of the prophecy. The prophet was envisioning historical events connected with the actual city of Jerusalem. And from an absolute perspective these prophecies are the promise of God that in some way beyond our imagining "all Israel shall be saved" (Rom. 11:26; cf. 11:25-32). God has an ultimate plan for His people Israel, and when this purpose shall be fulfilled these visions will be translated into a reality we can now only guess. No wonder Zechariah closes with a passage which approaches in mood the doxology of Paul in Rom. 11:33-36—**Be silent, O all flesh, before the Lord: for he is raised up out of his holy habitation** (13).

> *Glorious things of thee are spoken,*
> *Zion, city of our God;*
> *He whose word cannot be broken*
> *Formed thee for His own abode.*
> *On the Rock of Ages founded,*
> *What can shake thy sure repose?*
> *With salvation's walls surrounded,*
> *Thou mayst smile at all thy foes.*
> —JOHN NEWTON, 1725-1807

[27]Meyer, *op. cit.,* p. 32.

### 4. *Joshua and Satan* (3:1-10)

At this point the visions begin to deal with the moral condition of the people of Judah and their standing before God. The former visions have predicted that God is about to disturb the "rest" of the nations and at long last to act in Jerusalem's behalf (1:8-17). The enemies of Judah are to be "cast out" (1:18-21), and Zion shall become once again the habitation of the Lord (2:1-13). But in order that these prophecies be fulfilled there must be a moral and spiritual transformation of the people. "Israel is rescued, but not sanctified. The nation's troubles are over: their uncleanness has still to be removed."[28]

*a. The vision* (3:1-5). In the preceding vision God had promised: "I will dwell in the midst of thee." The people realized that both they and their priests had sinned. They felt the justice of Ezekiel's charge, "Her priests have violated my law, and have profaned mine holy things" (22:26), and they were troubled that God might not be disposed to receive their services. The vision takes as its starting point this feeling of guilt and unworthiness felt keenly by the Jews.

Zechariah sees **Joshua the high priest standing** as a representative of Israel **before the angel of the Lord.** The guilty fears of the people find a mouthpiece in Satan, who appears to accuse Joshua. Before a charge can be preferred, however, God himself intervenes and rebukes the accuser. Should He, who has rescued His people as a brand plucked from the burning, cast them back into the fire? Not that they are without guilt. Joshua's very garb betrays their sin and pollution. But by an act of sheer grace this obstacle shall be removed. He commands the angel attendants to reclothe Joshua. This typifies the forgiveness and cleansing of Joshua and Israel.

Moreover at Zechariah's suggestion **a fair mitre** is placed on the high priest's head. The angel of the Lord stands by in approval. He does not leave until he has disclosed to Joshua the full dignity of the priesthood to which he has been restored. If he remains loyal to the Lord, he shall have right of access into the presence of God in behalf of Israel. But more, he and his colleagues foreshadow and prepare the way for "Him who, himself the chief cornerstone, shall rear the true Temple on which the

---

[28]Smith, *op. cit.*, II, 293.

eyes of Jehovah are fixed, who by one act shall remove iniquity forever, and restore prosperity and festal joy to man."[29]

**Joshua the high priest** (1) is called elsewhere Jeshua (Ezra 2:2; 3:2; *et al.*). His grandfather, Seraiah, was taken captive after the destruction of the Temple and slain by Nebuchadnezzar at Riblah (II Kings 25:18-21). His father—Josedech, Jehozadak, or Jozadak—was captured at the same time and taken captive to Babylon (I Chron. 6:15), where Joshua was probably born. During the time the Temple lay in ruins the office of high priest ceased. Now, after an interval of fifty-two years, Josedech having meanwhile died, the office is restored in the person of his son.

Zechariah sees **Joshua . . . standing before the angel of the Lord** as before his judge. It is a judicial scene. The high priest stands indicted for the sins of Israel. "The sins that stain him are the people's sins; and the case to be tried is, whether he, as the people's representative and priest, is to be accepted or rejected."[30] **Standing at his right hand,** the place occupied by the plaintiff in a Jewish court of law (cf. Ps. 109:6), is **Satan,** the accuser (cf. Job 1:6-12; 2:1-6; Rev. 12:10). Satan, once the great archangel of God, fell through pride, to become the adversary of man and God. He is prepared to argue that God cannot receive Joshua and his people, for He is a holy God. "This is precisely what the thoughtful and conscience-stricken minds among the Jews conceived to be going on in the presence-chamber of Jehovah."[31]

Before Satan can make his charge, however, the divine Advocate speaks: **The Lord rebuke thee, O Satan** (2). Luck comments: "These words are incomprehensible unless there is more than one Person in the Godhead."[32] This is another clear foreshadowing of the priestly intercession of our "advocate with the Father, Jesus Christ the righteous" (I John 2:1). Satan is rebuked by **the Lord that hath chosen Jerusalem.** It is because God delights in Jerusalem and has not cast her off that He silences Satan. "Who shall lay any thing to the charge of God's elect?" (Rom. 8:33) This is the truth conveyed by the question, **Is not this a brand plucked out of the fire?** (Cf. Amos. 4:11.) Would the same hand which plucked from the fire the brand, charred and half-consumed already, cast it back into the flames? And

[29]Perowne, *op. cit.,* p. 79.          [30]Dods, *op. cit.,* p. 76.
[31]*Ibid.*                              [32]Luck, *op. cit.,* p. 37.

should He who has delivered His people from the fiery furnace of Babylonian Captivity now listen to the charges of Satan and yield them again to utter destruction?

Not that the people are guiltless. The very raiment of their high priest testifies against them. Instead of the pure linen in which he should have been arrayed, he is clothed in **filthy garments** (3), symbolic of the sinfulness and pollution of Israel (cf. Isa. 4:4; 64:6). But the God who is holy is also merciful and gracious. In an act which prefigures the propitiatory offering of Christ, the angel of the Lord orders the removal of Joshua's foul raiment: **Take away the filthy garments from him** (4). He then turns directly to the high priest and explains this action: **Behold, I have caused thine iniquity to pass from thee, and I will clothe thee with change of raiment** (cf. Lev. 16:4). "The word here literally refers to *festal* (or *rich*) *apparel.* Thus not only is sin to be removed, but a gift of righteousness is to be given, represented by this fine clothing."[33]

Zechariah now makes a suggestion to the angel: **Let them set a fair mitre upon his head** (5). The mitre is described in Exod. 28:36-38. A gold plate across the front bore the inscription, "Holiness to the Lord." The priest wore it that the services of the people "may be accepted before the Lord." **So they set a fair mitre upon his head, and clothed him with garments.** Joshua was now fully authorized to offer sacrifices in behalf of his people. **The angel of the Lord** looked on with satisfaction and approval.

b. *Admonition of the angel* (3:6-10). God's messenger then **protested unto** (enjoined) **Joshua: Thus saith the Lord of hosts; If thou wilt walk in my ways, and if thou wilt keep my charge, then thou shalt also judge my house, and shalt also keep my courts** (6-7). In effect the angel defined the high priest's duties. He must observe God's commandments—i.e., keep the moral law (Deut. 8:6; 10:12; Ps. 128:1). He must also be zealous in the maintenance of the Temple service and in the ruling of God's house (Lev. 8:35; Ezek. 44:15-16). To this solemn enjoinder God added a promise: **And I will give thee places to walk among those that stand by** (7). This is better rendered, "I will give you the right of access among those who are standing here" (RSV). Joshua could now be sure his prayers would reach heaven. "Like

[33]*Ibid.,* p. 39.

the angels who stand in attendance upon God, the High Priest is promised the privilege of direct communion with God. He will have the right to approach God at any time as the intercessor of His people."[34]

The angel next made a Messianic promise to Joshua and the assistant priests who sat before him to receive his instructions (8). He declares that **they are men** to be **wondered at** (8), or that "men are a sign" (ASV). *The Berkeley Version* translates it "significant men." The Jewish scholar, Cashdan, notes: "The restored priesthood is an omen of the advent of the Messiah."[35] This is clearly the meaning of the promise; it continues: **For, behold, I will bring forth my servant the BRANCH** (8). Perowne paraphrases the promise: "To Joshua and his fellows I foretell the coming of 'my servant, Branch,' because they, the priesthood, in all their office and ministry, as well as in what has just happened to them in the vision in the person of their chief, are types of Him."[36]

**My servant** is a frequent name of Messiah in Isaiah (42:1; 49:6; 52:13; 53:11) and is perhaps the most characteristic Messianic motif in the New Testament (Acts 8:30-35; I Pet. 2:21-25; in Acts 3:13, 26; 4:27, 30 the Greek word translated "Son" or "child" in the KJV is properly translated "servant" in all the revised and modern versions. **The BRANCH,** without the article, is literally "shoot" or "sprout." Cashdan declares: "Modern as well as ancient interpreters agree in explaining *the Shoot* as the expected Messiah. *Shoot* means that which sprouts or shoots from the ground. . . . 'The old tree of the Jewish State was dead, but the prophet foreshadows a new life through the springing up of a new shoot of David's house' (Barnes)."[37]

In the next verse the figure changes to that of **the stone that I have laid before Joshua** (9). The primary and immediate reference is to the Temple, in the rebuilding of which Joshua was at that time involved. **The stone** is difficult to identify. It is thought by some to have been the foundation stone of the Temple, which had already been employed as a symbol of Messiah (cf. Isa. 28:16). Others prefer the topstone or coping stone of the Temple (cf. 4:7, 9), which would complete the building. Thomas sees in it the stone or precious gem which was to be worn by Joshua on

---

[34]Cashdan, *op. cit.,* p. 281.                    [35]*Ibid.,* p. 282.
[36]*Op. cit.,* p. 82.                                        [37]*Op. cit.,* p. 282.

the breast or forehead (cf. Exod. 28:11-12, 36-38).[38] After considering various interpretations George Adam Smith concludes, "We must rather suppose that the stone is symbolic of the finished Temple."[39] T. T. Perowne's view seems to have merit:

> The ultimate reference is to Him, who as "the Branch" should hereafter "build the temple of the Lord" (vi. 12), of which He is not only the Foundation-stone (Isaiah xxviii. 16; I Peter ii. 4, 5), but also the chief Corner-stone (Ps. cxviii. 22; Matt. xxi. 42; Ephes. ii. 20). The two fulfillments of the prophecy are intimately connected. The first is, in the purpose of God, the necessary preparation for the second.[40]

**Upon one stone shall be seven eyes** (9). These are "the eyes of the Lord, which run to and fro through the whole earth" (4:10), and symbolize the full expression of His providence and care. God never takes His eyes off this stone, in either type or antitype, until His purpose relating to it is fulfilled.

An additional promise is added: **Behold, I will engrave the graving thereof, saith the Lord of hosts.** Perowne paraphrases: "My eyes, I have said, are fixed upon the stone. My hand shall engrave upon it whatever is needed to beautify it and fit it for the place of honour it is to hold."[41] But that is not all; he adds, **And I will remove the iniquity of that land in one day.** The immediate reference is probably to the expiation of the nation's sin in **one day,** the annual Day of Atonement (cf. Lev. 16:21, 30, 34), which would be reinstituted upon the completion of the Temple. But the goal of the prophecy looks beyond this type to the day that Christ died. On that great Day of Atonement, He "once for all in the end of the age . . . put away sin by the sacrifice of himself" (Heb. 9:26, lit.).

One final touch is given this prophecy: **In that day, saith the Lord of hosts, shall ye call every man his neighbour under the vine and under the fig tree** (10). In the Messianic age which is coming men will again, as in the glorious days of Solomon (I Kings 4:25), entertain their friends in peace and security under the vine and under the fig tree (cf. Mic. 4:4).[42] This final victory of the Messianic kingdom is yet future.

---

[38]IB, VI, 1071.                    [39]*Op. cit.,* p. 297.
[40]*Op. cit.,* p. 83.                [41]*Ibid.*
[42]Thomas, IB, VI, 1071.

### 5. *The Golden Lampstand and the Two Olive Trees* (4:1-14)

As the fourth vision unfolded the dignity and significance of the high priest, the fifth promised the joint glory of Joshua and Zerubbabel, the civil head of the Jewish community. To this was added an oracle for Zerubbabel himself.

The prophet sees a seven-branched, golden lampstand with an inexhaustible supply of oil. Above the stand is a bowl, and to the right and left of it are two olive trees. These trees feed the bowl through two spouts, and the bowl supplies the olive oil to the lampstand through seven golden pipes. The lampstand is a symbol of the restored Jewish community in which God is himself present. The two olive trees which supply the lamps with oil represent Zerubbabel and Joshua as the channels of divine grace.

Many interpreters think that vv. 6b-10a, beginning with **This is the word of the Lord** and ending with **in the hand of Zerubbabel,** are out of place as they now stand. In our present text they seem to be inserted in the middle of the vision, for they interrupt the connection between verses 6a and 10b. This message of encouragement to Zerubbabel fits well after 4:1-6a, 10b-14, and the comment upon it will be given at that point.

*a. The vision and its meaning* (4:1-6a, 10c-14). After the last vision Zechariah seems to have fallen into a reverie, meditating on what had been shown him. **And the angel of the Lord that talked with me came again, and waked me, as a man that is wakened out of his sleep** (1). The prophet was aroused by the interpreting angel in order that he might apprehend the significance of a fresh vision. Giving attention, he saw **a candlestick all of gold** (2), a seven-branched lampstand like the one in the Tabernacle (cf. Exod. 37:17-24). This lamp, however, was replenished with oil by no human hands. A bowl above the lampstand supplied the oil to it through **seven pipes**. There were **two olive trees by it, one upon the right side of the bowl, and the other upon the left side** (3). The supply of oil was not from any vessel but from two living trees; it was thus perennial and unfailing.

Mystified by the vision, the prophet asked the interpreting angel, **What are these, my Lord?** (4) The angel was surprised that Zechariah did not know, but he did not hesitate to supply the answer: **They are the eyes of the Lord, which run to and fro through the whole earth** (10b). While the lampstand represented the community of Israel, in a yet deeper sense it was a symbol of the divine presence in the midst of the community. "The Temple so near completion will not of itself reveal God: let not the Jews put their trust in it, but in the life behind it."[43] The seven lights are symbolic of the eyes of Jehovah.

But **what are these two olive trees upon the right side of the candlestick and upon the left side thereof?** Zechariah asks (11). In 12 he put the question a second time, enlarging on it. "What are the two branches of the olive trees, which are beside the two golden pipes from which the oil is poured out?" (RSV) Again the angel was puzzled at the prophet's ignorance: **Knowest thou not what these be?** Zechariah answered: **No, my lord** (13). He then told the prophet plainly: **These are the two anointed ones that stand by the Lord of the whole earth** (14). Although he does not name them, these can only be Joshua and Zerubbabel, the religious and the civil leader, respectively, of the Jewish community. The two olive trees which provide an unfailing supply of oil to the lamps are the two anointed heads of Israel. "Theirs [is] the equal and co-ordinate duty of sustaining the Temple, figured by the whole candelabrum, and ensuring the brightness of the sevenfold revelation. . . . The Temple, that is to say, is nothing without the monarchy and the priesthood behind it; and these stand in the immediate presence of God."[44] Joshua and Zerubbabel are simply the channels of divine grace; the Fountain is God himself.

b. *The word to Zerubbabel* (4:6b-10b). **This is the word of the Lord unto Zerubbabel, saying, Not by might, nor by power, but by my spirit, saith the Lord of hosts** (6b). Here is one of the great texts of the Bible. It is more than a word to Zerubbabel; it is a message to everyone who engages in the work of God. Spiritual success is possible only when we are Spirit-filled and Spirit-cleansed. Marcus Dods has given a beautiful commentary on this verse:

> You have taken your own measure, you feel your weakness to cope with your circumstances, you are painfully conscious of your inability to shine and scatter the surrounding darkness; but you are to understand that it is God's Spirit who is the source of every brilliant and enlightening action that reflects glory upon God. You have not to create a holy spirit in yourself. Holiness sufficient for the need of all creatures exists in God. And there is in God life enough to uphold all creatures in life, so there is in Him holiness

[43]Smith, *op. cit.*, p. 298.                    [44]Smith, *ibid.*

sufficient for every good thing that needs to be done. You can never find yourself face to face with any duty for which there is not grace enough. In yourself there may be far too little, but in God is a living fountain."[45]

**Who art thou, O great mountain? before Zerubbabel thou shalt become a plain: and he shall bring forth the headstone thereof with shoutings, crying, Grace, grace unto it (7).** All the obstacles which had arisen before Zerubbabel, and which by his fears had been magnified into a **great mountain,** would be overcome in the power of the Spirit resting upon him. **The headstone** of the Temple would at last be brought out of the hewer's shed with shouts of triumph and with the earnest supplication that God would add His grace to the finished work and long keep that stone in its place. **Moreover the word of the Lord came unto me, saying, The hands of Zerubbabel have laid the foundation of this house; his hands shall also finish it (8-9).** The final clause of 9 means, "By the fulfilment of these promises Zerubbabel and the whole nation will realize that it was the Divine word speaking through the prophet."[46]

**For who hath despised the day of small things? (10)** All who scoffed at the small beginnings of the Temple and expressed doubts as to its completion will now **rejoice** when they **shall see the plummet in the hand of Zerubbabel** as he sets the capstone in its place. God never begins a work He does not intend to complete. When we are fully committed to Him and filled with His Spirit, we may say with Paul: "Being confident of this very thing, that he which hath begun a good work in . . . [us] will perform it until the day of Jesus Christ" (Phil. 1:6).

### 6. *The Flying Roll* (5:1-4)

The two visions of this chapter are given to encourage God's people to expect that their land would be purged of evildoers and wickedness. The vision of the flying roll pictures the judgment of God upon individual sinners; the vision of the woman in a barrel symbolizes God's determination to banish the very principle of sin from Israel.

The first of these is a vision of the removal of the curse brought upon the land by its criminals, especially thieves and perjurers—the two forms which crime takes in a rude community

---

⁴⁵*Op. cit.,* pp. 80-81.                    ⁴⁶Cashdan, *op. cit.,* p. 285.

like that of the returned exiles in Judah.[47] The prophet sees a giant scroll, inscribed with curses against sins of all kinds, flying through the air. It enters the house of every thief and perjurer in the land, and destroys it like a plague.

Zechariah was fully alert when this vision began. He turned his head, lifted his eyes, and saw **a flying roll** (1). He uses the common word for skin or parchment upon which writing was done. The scroll was unfurled like a giant sheet and was **flying** in swift pursuit of its object, like a bird of prey. It apparently came from heaven (4), which indicated that it was a judgment proceeding from the throne of God.

The dimensions of the scroll—**twenty cubits** in **length** and **ten cubits** in **breadth** (thirty by fifteen feet; 2)—are "an indication of the number of curses inscribed on it."[48] Some interpreters, however, point out that the measurements correspond to the size of the holy place in the Tabernacle, and they see this as more than a coincidence. C. H. H. Wright observes: "Men are not to be judged as to sin by their own measure, or weighed in their own false balances—*the measure of the sanctuary* is that by which man's actions are to be weighed (I Sam. 2:3)."[49]

The interpreting angel explained the roll to Zechariah: **This is the curse that goeth forth over the face of the whole earth** (3). **Earth** is not quite correct; the word should be translated "land," since this is a judgment upon Israel. Only those who have the law shall be judged by the law; those without law shall be judged by the law of nature (Rom. 2:12-15). The angel continued: Every thief and every perjurer **shall be cut off** (3), literally "cleared" or "emptied out." The Hebrew word, however, is frequently given a figurative meaning, "to clear from guilt, hold guiltless, leave unpunished." Smith-Goodspeed accordingly translates the passage: "How long now have all thieves remained unpunished? And how long have those foresworn remained unpunished?" Crime has been hitherto practiced with impunity; this will no longer be the case.[50]

The two sins specified are inscribed **on this side** and **on that side** (3) of the scroll (i.e., on opposite sides). Stealing and

[47]Smith, *op. cit.*, p. 301.
[48]Driver, *op. cit.*, p. 205; cf. Dods, *op. cit.*, p. 83.
[49]Quoted by Luck, *op. cit.*, pp. 52-53; cf. Cashdan, *op. cit.*, p. 287.
[50]Driver, *op. cit.*, p. 206.

perjury correspond to the eighth and the third commandments. These are the middle commandments of the second and first tables of the Decalogue respectively, and thus probably represent the entire law. The two sides of the scroll then would represent the two tables of the law, the first having to do with man's relationship to God, the second with his relationship to his neighbor.[51] We are reminded of the words of James in the New Testament: "For whosoever shall keep the whole law, and yet offend in one point, he is guilty of all" (Jas. 2:10).

The Lord then speaks: **I will bring it forth . . . and it shall enter into the house of the thief, and into the house of him that sweareth falsely by my name, and it shall remain in the midst of his house, and shall consume it with the timber thereof and the stones thereof** (4). Smend gives this possible explanation: "It appears that in ancient times curses were written on pieces of paper and sent down the wind into the houses" of those to whom they were directed.[52] The divine threat is that the scroll will **remain in the midst of** the **house** until it has effected its deadly judgment upon the entire household. It is a solemn warning.

> How terribly those words have been fulfilled in the case of people and families we have known! It has seemed as though there were a plague in the house. The fortune which had been accumulated with such toil has crumbled; the children turned out sources of heartrending grief; the reputation of the father has become irretrievably tarnished. "There is a plague spread in the house; it is a fretting leprosy, it is unclean." No man can stand against that curse. It confronts him everywhere. It touches his most substantial effects, and they pulverize, as furniture eaten through by white ants.[53]

Such is the terrible truth of this vision. God has two ways of dealing with sin. The first is that of grace and mercy. "Let the wicked forsake his way, and the unrighteous man his thoughts: and let him return unto the Lord, and he will have mercy upon him; and to our God, for he will abundantly pardon" (Isa. 55:7). But if sinners persist in their wickedness and refuse to receive God's grace, then His method of dealing with sin is that of judgment. "Sin must be purged away, iniquity must be stamped out

---

[51]Luck, *op. cit.*, p. 53; Driver, *ibid.*    [52]Cited by Smith, *op. cit.*, p. 300.
[53]Meyer, *op. cit.*, pp. 51-52.

in the city of God; and when the sinner is so wedded to his sin that he is no longer separable from it, he becomes the object of God's curse, and must be cleansed away from the earth."[54]

### 7. *The Woman in the Barrel* (5:5-11)

This vision is even more searching than the preceding, "for it is not so much the sinner as the very principle of sin that has to be eradicated."[55]

The prophet saw an ephah, a small barrel with a circular, lead lid. The lid was lifted and Zechariah gimpsed the form of a woman inside. The woman, so the interpreting angel explained, was the personification of wickedness. She apparently attempted to escape, but was thrust back into the barrel. The lid was quickly secured and the ephah was carried by two female figures, with wings like those of a stork, to Babylon, where a shrine might be erected for the worship of the ephah.

During the interval between this vision and the previous one while Zechariah was lost in contemplation, the interpreting angel falls into the background. He now reappears and invites the prophet to consider what is coming into view: **an ephah** emerging from the surrounding darkness (5-6). **The ephah** was the largest vessel of measurement used by the Jews. It had a capacity of more than seven gallons and was shaped somewhat like a barrel.

**What is it?** Zechariah asks the angel (6). The reply is difficult: **This is their resemblance through all the earth** (6). Apparently it means, "This is the resemblance [of the wicked] in all the earth." By a slight change in the Hebrew, **resemblance** becomes "iniquity." So the RSV translates the sentence, "This is the iniquity in all the land." "Land" is also better than "earth," since this vision encompasses only the Holy Land. The **talent of lead** (7) is better translated "disc of lead" (Moffatt) or "leaden cover" (Berk.). The Heb., *kakkar*, means "circle" as well as "talent." This lid is **lifted up** and the prophet sees **a woman** sitting **in the . . . ephah. This is wickedness**, the angel explains (8). The word should be capitalized (as it is in modern versions), since the woman is the personification of sin. In the Hebrew **wickedness** is feminine. indicative of the seductive power of

[54]Baron; quoted by Luck, *op. cit.*, pp. 51-52. Cf. John 12:31; 16:7-11.

[55]J. E. McFadyen, "Zechariah," *Abingdon Bible Commentary*, ed. David D. Downey (New York: Abingdon Press, 1929), p. 823.

temptation. Sin is personified here for the further purpose of distinguishing the *principle* of sin from the *acts* in which it expresses itself; it is therefore eradicable.[56]

Apparently the woman attempted to escape, for the angel thrust her (not **it**, as KJV) back into the **ephah** and closed the heavy lead top securely upon its **mouth** (8). Thereupon **two women** come forth from the surrounding darkness with **wind** in their powerful, stork-like **wings**; they **lifted up the ephah between the earth and the heaven** and swiftly bore it away (9). **Whither do these bear the ephah?** Zechariah queries (10), and the answer was given by the angel: **To build it an house in the land of Shinar** (11), or Babylon (Gen. 11:2; Isa. 11:11). Babylon has the general significance of the counterpart of the Holy Land. It is the epitome of wickedness and an appropriate place for the dumping of Judah's concentrated sin. But more than this, a temple is to be built there for the ephah, which shall be **set there upon her own base** as an image (11). "Sin thus not only finds its natural home in Babylon, but worship is to be paid to it!"[57]

We must not let the curious imagery of this vision blind us to its deep spiritual teaching. Zechariah is not satisfied with the mere ritual atonement for sin (3:1-10), or even with its divine punishment (5:1-4). George Adam Smith observes: "The living power of sin must be banished from Israel; and this cannot be done by any efforts of men themselves, but by God's action only, which is thorough and effectual." He then shows the meaning of this vision for the Christian gospel: "Let us lay to heart [the] eternally valid doctrine, that sin is not a formal curse, not only expressed in certain social crimes, nor exhausted by the punishment of these, but, as a power of attraction and temptation to all men, *it must be banished from the heart, and can be banished only by God.*"[58]

Here in Oriental imagery is the grand New Testament promise of the destruction of sin by the sanctifying activity of the Holy Spirit. This vision reminds us that the suppression of sin is necessary but only as a prelude to its banishment from the heart

---

[56]Dods, *op. cit.*, p. 84. Dods writes, "This symbol presents wickedness as full-grown, seductive, plotting, prolific, but also as separable from the life and customs of the people with which it had seemed inextricably involved."

[57]Thomas, IB, VI, 1077.        [58]*Op. cit.*, pp. 304-5.

by the power of God! What is promise in the Old Testament becomes experience in the New Testament. "The law of the Spirit of life in Christ Jesus hath made me free from the law of sin and death," Paul joyfully witnesses. "For what the law could not do, in that it was weak through the flesh, God sending his own Son in the likeness of sinful flesh, and for sin, condemned sin in the flesh: that the righteousness of the law might be fulfilled in us, who walk not after the flesh, but after the Spirit" (Rom. 8:2-4).

### 8. *The Four Chariots* (6:1-8)

In this eighth and last vision the prophet sees four chariots drawn by horses of various colors coming forth from between two mountains of brass. They are commissioned by God to execute judgment upon different quarters of the earth. The chariots which go to the north country—to Babylon—have the special task of executing divine wrath upon Jerusalem's enemy *par excellence*.

As the series of visions opened with a depiction of the universal providence of God, so they close with another of the same nature. The first vision had postponed God's overthrow of the nations until His own time. With the religious and moral needs of Israel having been met in the intervening visions, and every obstacle to God's action of deliverance having been removed, this final vision promises divine judgment upon the nations of earth, Babylon in particular.

The prophet beholds **four chariots** coming forth from **between two mountains . . . of brass** (1). These are war chariots, the most formidable of ancient military machines (I Kings 10:28-29). They were also used on great state occasions and came to be symbolic of authority and resistless might (cf. Ps. 68:17; Isa. 66:15; Hab. 3:8; Hag. 2:22). The two **mountains of brass** are possibly Mount Zion and the Mount of Olives viewed as the source of divine judgments upon the world. Brass is symbolic of might.

The chariots were drawn by horses of various colors: **the first** by **red horses, the second** by **black horses** (2), **the third** by **white horses, and the fourth** by **grisled and bay horses** (3; "dappled gray horses," RSV; **and** does not appear in the Heb.). As in the first vision, the colors are debatable and of uncertain significance. The word rendered **white** also means "strong," and in v. 7 where the KJV reads **the bay** the Hebrew has the same meaning ("the steeds," RSV). It is unlikely that the colors are intended to be symbolic.

The interpreting angel informs the prophet that **these are the four spirits** (or winds) **of the heavens, which go forth from standing before the Lord of all the earth** (5). The RSV translates, "These are going to the four winds of heaven" (cf. 2:6). The preposition *to,* however, is not in the Hebrew text. **The four spirits** are the servants of Him "who maketh his angels spirits; his ministers a flaming fire" (Ps. 104:4; Heb. 1:7). They are dispatched to different quarters of the world. "The prophet," George Adam Smith rightly observes, "has not been admitted to the Presence, and does not know exactly what they have been commissioned to do; that is to say, Zechariah is ignorant of the actual political processes by which the nations are to be overthrown and Israel glorified before them."[59] The deliverance is to be by divine action.

The destination of the four chariots has not been uniformly understood. It is clear that **the black horses** are dispatched to **the north country** (6), i.e., Babylon. The KJV follows the Hebrew closely in translating the next clause, **and the white go forth after them.** This seems to mean that two chariots are sent to execute judgment on Babylon. In order to make four, the KJV divides **the grisled** (6) from **the bay** (7), the former being dispatched **toward the south country** (6), or Egypt, the latter to the length and breadth of **the earth** (7). No reference is made to dispatching the red horses. However, there is no Hebrew conjunction **and** in 3b and hence there is no justification for dividing the grisled and bay into two separate teams. Some scholars "suspect there is a clerical error, and that we should read 'red' in place of 'bay' "[60] in v. 7.

Other interpreters[61] support the RSV translation of 6b, "The white ones go toward the west country." A slight modification of the Hebrew text makes this translation possible. Wellhausen suggests another variant reading of v. 6, which would cause the white horses to be sent "to the land of the east";[62] he thinks that "the west" has probably fallen out after "they go forth" in v. 7.

[59]*Ibid.,* pp. 305-6.            [60]Dods, *op. cit.,* p. 87.
[61]Smith, *op. cit.,* p. 306; Thomas, IB, VI, 1078; Cashdan, *op. cit.,* p. 291.
[62]Cf. Driver, *op. cit.,* p. 210.

According to this construction the chariots are sent north, east, south, and west. George Adam Smith takes note of Wellhausen's theory, but argues for the view suggested by the RSV translation. No chariot is sent eastward, for there was no power oppressing or threatening Jerusalem from that direction; but in the north there was Babylon, to the south Egypt, still a possible master of the world, and to the west new forces of Europe that in less than a generation were to prove themselves a threat to the countries of the Near East. We should probably follow the RSV in rendering the first part of v. 7, "When the steeds came out, they were impatient to get off and patrol the earth." This may mean the horses of the fourth chariot, or the red horses. Or it may be a general statement concerning all four teams and chariots.

The center of the world's power in that day was in **the north country** (8), so called because Babylon's invasions always came from the north (cf. 2:6). The horses were dispatched in that direction with the explicit charge to quiet ("set at rest," RSV) God's **spirit** (8). "Spirit" here means "anger" (cf. Prov. 16:32). God's "anger" or "wrath" is His strong displeasure at sin (cf. Rom. 1:18-32). His "anger" will be "set at rest" when His judgment is executed on Babylon. This is admittedly a human way of speaking of God, but what other way is there to speak? What God is in himself, finite man can never fathom, so we attribute to Him human ways of feeling and acting. In the unfolding of divine revelation, however, it is made absolutely certain that God's wrath is not a petulant emotion. It is rather the recoil of God's holy love, the antipathy of the divine nature at man's sin.

Since God is holy, His wrath at sin is inevitable. *In* Christ, said Luther, "God is love"; *outside* Christ, "Our God is a consuming fire." Both Scripture and experience confirm the justice of this claim. Nor is this a denial of God's love; the opposite of love is not anger but hate. Elsewhere Martin Luther spoke of God's wrath as "the underside of His love." To soften the paradox between love and judgment in the nature of God is to destroy the biblical revelation of Deity. So the chariots of the Lord go forth to execute God's judgment upon Babylon for the injury she has done His people.

The close connection between this last vision and the first given to Zechariah (1:7-17) should once again be noted. At the beginning of this unforgettable night the prophet saw angel riders, led by the angel of Jehovah, coming to give their reports to the Lord after riding "to and fro through the earth." Their report that the wicked nations were at rest while God's people suffered in distress greatly displeased Jehovah. "Now, in the present vision, shown to Zechariah just before the break of dawn, the angels are seen going forth, not to reconnoiter as before, but to execute God's judgment upon the nations."[63] This vision discloses God's control over all destructive forces used by Him in the punishment of peoples deserving His wrath. It is therefore similar to the detailed picture of God's judgments recounted in Revelation 6—18. Zechariah's visions may quite fittingly be called "the Old Testament Apocalypse."

### C. THE CROWNING OF THE KING, 6:9-15

The heathen nations overthrown, Zion is now free to have her own king again. Zechariah is therefore ordered—the visions of the night now past—to visit a deputation of Jews lately come from the captivity in **Babylon, Heldai** (called **Helem** in v. 14), **Tobijah,** and **Jedaiah,** at **the house of Josiah the son of Zephaniah** (10), and to select from the gifts they had brought for the Temple enough **silver and gold** to make circlets for a crown to be used in a coronation ceremony for **the high priest** (11). None of the men named is otherwise identified in the Old Testament.

A problem in interpretation here arises. The Hebrew text of this passage has the Lord instructing Zechariah to crown **Joshua the son of Josedech, the high priest** (11), rather than Zerubbabel. This would in effect make the high priest the king of Israel. This is an interesting possibility, especially in the light of the New Testament picture of Christ as our great Priest-King. There are, however, some textual problems we cannot ignore. The student is advised to read the passage thoughtfully in several versions. The evidence from close study points toward an early corruption of the text upon which our translations are based.

First, Zechariah is ordered to make **crowns** (11) but in v. 14 the Hebrew verb is in the singular, while in the Septuagint Version both subject and verb are in the singular. This is not an insurmountable problem, for v. 11 may mean "circlets for a crown." Was Zechariah instructed to make one or two crowns?

---

[63]Luck, *op. cit.*, pp. 60-61.

Some have suggested that the names of both Joshua and Zerub-babel were originally in v. 11, but if this is so why is the singular **unto him** found in v. 12 and the singular usage in v. 14?

Secondly, v. 13 should be translated, "There shall be a priest *by* his throne," rather than, **He shall be a priest upon his throne.** Otherwise, what is the meaning of the next clause, **and the counsel of peace shall be between them both?** Obviously there is a promise of concord between the king who shall be crowned and the priest beside his throne—i.e., between Zerubbabel and Joshua.

We can hardly escape the conclusion that an early copiest made an error and substituted the name of Joshua for that of Zerubbabel in v. 11. If we replace **Joshua** with the name of Zerubbabel, all difficulty of interpretation vanishes and we are given a significant prophetic word. This seems to be the best solution to the problem.[64]

God's word to Zechariah is a Messianic prophecy. Zerubbabel is **The BRANCH** (12), or better, "the Shoot," to whom reference has already been made (3:8). From Zerubbabel shall spring Him who shall be "King of kings and Lord of lords," who shall build the true temple of the Lord, "himself being the chief corner stone; in whom [believers in His name] . . . are builded together for an habitation of God through the Spirit" (Eph. 2:20-22; cf. I Pet. 2:4-5).

Admittedly, this prophecy has a double reference. It is primarily a promise that the Temple then being erected should be completed by the hands of Zerubbabel and an assurance to Zechariah that in the rehabilitated Jerusalem both Zerubbabel, the prince, and Joshua, the high priest, should work together in concord and peace. Yet it is a word which points beyond the then present to the days of the Messiah, in whose kingdom and temple the roles of both King and Priest should be glorious fulfilled in Him who should make them one in His own majestic person and ministry. In those days we now live; "and it doth not yet appear what we shall be: but we know that, when he shall appear, we shall be like him; for we shall see him as he is" (I John 3:2).

[64]Such a reconstruction of the text in no way invalidates the inspiration of Zechariah's prophecy. The New Testament command to "rightly divide the word of truth" puts upon us the responsibility to make every effort to establish what that word actually is. Such a reconstruction also har-monizes 6:12b-13a with 4:9. "The hands of Zerubbabel have laid the foundation of this house; his hands shall also finish it."

The crown which Zechariah is instructed to place **in the temple of the Lord** (14) is to be **a memorial** and a token of the fulfillment of this prophecy. **Build in the temple** (15) means "help to build the temple" (RSV). "The arrival of the deputation with gifts foreshadows the arrival of further reinforcements of Jews from afar—and perhaps Gentiles too (cf. viii. 22 and Hag. ii. 7)—and the work of the temple will progress rapidly."[65] **Ye shall know that the Lord of hosts hath sent me unto you** means that the completion of the Temple will testify to the divine authority of the prophet's word. Note, however, the conditional nature of the promise: **And this shall come to pass, if ye will diligently obey the voice of the Lord your God.**

## D. An Inquiry and Reply Regarding Fast Days, 7:1—8:23

After a lapse of about two years Zechariah was again called upon to prophesy. The occasion was the arrival in Jerusalem of a deputation, probably from Bethel, which had been sent to inquire whether they should continue to observe the national fast that had been instituted at the time of the Captivity (7:1-3). God's answer by the prophet falls into four sections, each introduced by the same formula (7:4, 8; 8:1, 18). The return in the last section to the question out of which the answers arose (8:19) shows that the prophecy is really one whole.

First, the people are reminded that their fasting, like their feasting, had not been by divine commandment and was therefore devoid of spiritual meaning, in accordance with the teaching of the preexilic prophets (7:4-7).

In the second section Zechariah recalls what the commandments of the Lord had been when the land was inhabited and enjoying prosperity. They were not ceremonial, they were ethical; they required justice, mercy, and compassion on the poor. To the neglect of these ethical obligations the prophet traces the calamities of the Captivity and Exile (7:8-14).

The mood changes in the third section. The prophet gives a word of promise concerning the bright days of holiness and prosperity which are in store for Zion, in contrast with her earlier condition of distress. On the strength of these promises Zechariah urges the people to holy obedience (8:1-17).

[65]Cashdan, *op. cit.*, p. 294.

Finally comes a prediction that the fasting of the people shall give way to joyous feasting, to which great multitudes shall throng from all over the land. Even heathen nations will join in the celebration, counting it a privilege to be associated with a Jew (8:18-23).

### 1. *The Inquiry* (7:1-3)

**In the fourth year of king Darius** (1; i.e., in 518 B.C.) would have been about two years after Zechariah saw his visions (1:7) and about the same length of time before the completion of the Temple (cf. Ezra 6:15). **Chisleu** was the Babylonian name of the month corresponding to our November-December. **The word of the Lord came unto Zechariah,** the occasion being the arrival of a deputation in Jerusalem. They had come, first, "to seek favor from the Lord" (2, Berk.), and, second, to inquire whether to continue to observe the fast in **the fifth month** (3), as they had done during the time of the Exile. Their coming to the Temple would imply that at least some of its services were probably resumed.[66]

The phrase **unto the house of God** (2) is better rendered "of Bethel." The sentence thus would properly read, "Now they of Bethel had sent." The burden of the deputation's mission was to consult with the Temple **priests** and **prophets** (3), the latter being Haggai and Zechariah, regarding the continuation of the fast of the fifth month, which commemorated the burning of Jerusalem and the Temple (II Kings 25:8-9). **Should I weep?** the spokesman asked. "The *I* represents the whole community of the exile. 'Weeping' stands here for all the practices which made up the day of fasting and humiliation: shedding tears of contrition, fasting, rending the garments, putting on sackcloth and scattering earth on the head."[67] The question was natural. Now that the Temple was in the course of construction and national life was being restored in the Holy Land, it seemed inconsistent to continue the fasts which commemorated the destruction of the city and sanctuary.

### 2. *Zechariah's Reply* (7:4—8:23)

The deputation inquired only regarding the fast of the fifth month; "but with a breadth of view which reveals the prophet

---

[66]Cf. 7:3: "the priests of the house of the Lord" (RSV).

[67]Cashdan, *op. cit.,* p. 295.

rather than the priest, Zechariah replies in the following chapter upon the fasts by which Israel for seventy years had bewailed her ruin and exile."[68] His answer, intended to reach the ears of **all the people** (5), is of special significance when we remember his profound love for the Temple. It shows Zechariah to be a true prophet infinitely more concerned with righteousness than with ritual.

*a. The emptiness of fasting* (7:4-7). With a boldness and vocabulary reminiscent of the prophet Amos, Zechariah asks the people whether in their fasts they fasted at all to God. He refers to two fasts, that of **the fifth month** and that of **the seventh month** (5), which commemorated the assassination of the Jewish governor Gedaliah, appointed over the people left in the land by Nebuchadnezzar (cf. II Kings 25:25; Jer. 41:1-10). The Lord had not commanded these fasts, and in their fasting the people had fasted to themselves, just as in eating and drinking they had feasted to themselves (5-6). They should rather heed the words of **the former prophets, when Jerusalem was inhabited and in prosperity** (7). Fasts or feasts are of no concern to God unless they have a positive effect upon daily life. The preexilic prophets had spoken the word to which the people should have listened. They had preached that God is indifferent to ritual, that what He demands is a moral life which manifests itself in brotherly love and social justice. To that old teaching the people must pay heed and return. It was uttered in the time of their national prosperity. By neglecting it, that prosperity was lost. Only by returning to it can prosperity be gained. **The south and the plain,** i.e., "the Negeb [the desert at the south of the land, still so named] and the Shephelah [the foothills southwest of Jerusalem, now part of the Gaza section]" (Berk.). When fully populated, these otherwise wilderness portions of Palestine would be inhabited.

*b. A lesson from the past* (7:8-14). Zechariah proceeds to give a summary of the teachings of the preexilic prophets (9-10). He follows this epitome of the prophetic message with a graphic account of Israel's disobedience and consequent punishment (11:14).

The demand of God, voiced by the prophets of old, was for **true judgment** (9) or social justice (the message of Amos; cf. Amos 5:24), **mercy** or covenant love and loyalty (the message

[68]Smith, *op. cit.*, p. 321.

of Hosea; cf. Hos. 6:6), and pity toward the poor and defenseless (10; the message of Micah, cf. Mic. 3:1-3). **Imagine evil** would be to "plot evil" (Moffatt). In Isaiah and Jeremiah all these emphases blended and came to full flower.

Zechariah's description of the people's rebellion against the prophetic message is picturesque and striking. First **they refused to hearken** (11); they took an entirely negative attitude. Next **they pulled away the shoulder,** showing childish and spiteful disrespect to the messengers of God. Then **they stopped their ears, that they should not hear,** making futile every effort of God to instruct them. Finally **they made their hearts as an adamant** (flint or diamond) **stone, lest they should hear the law** (12). God could make absolutely no impression on their hard hearts. Since the Lord had sent this message "by his Spirit through the former prophets" (12, RSV), Israel's rejection of it was in effect a resisting of the Holy Spirit (cf. Acts 7:51).

Because of their deliberate apostasy **a great wrath from the Lord of hosts** came upon Israel. Their selfish cries were ignored by the Almighty and **with a whirlwind He scattered them . . . among all the nations whom they knew not** (14). Moreover, a great desolation came to **the pleasant land** of Judah.

In 8-14 there is a powerful lesson on "The Wickedness and Tragedy of Apostasy." (1) Disobedience, 11-12c; (2) Destruction, 12d-13; (3) Desolation, 14 (cf. Matt. 23:34-38).

c. *Precious promises for Zion* (8:1-17). **Again the word of the Lord of hosts came to me** (1): Zechariah continues his answer to the delegation (cf. comments on 7:1-3). The mood, however, now changes to one of hope for the future. But as the promises unfold we get a vivid glimpse of the forlorn conditions of the people and the land. Few old people and few children were seen in Jerusalem (4-5). Many of their fellow Jews were still in exile (7), and they themselves were slack and disheartened (9, 13). Unemployment was widespread, neighboring peoples were hostile, and the city was torn with dissension (10). A drought had ruined their crops (12; cf. Hag. 1:11), and their name was a byword among the heathen (13). The situation was so desperate that only a miracle could remedy it (6).

Seven shining promises, however, are given by the Lord. "At each word and sentence, in which good things, for their greatness almost incredible, are promised, the prophet promises, Thus saith the Lord of hosts, as if he would say, Think not that what I would pledge you are my own, and refuse me not credence as man. What I unfold are the promises of God" (Jerome).[69]

(1) God is **jealous** (zealous) in His determination to restore **Zion** (2). He expresses on the one hand His love for Zion and on the other His indignation against her foes.

(2) The Lord is about to return to Zion after seventy years, **and Jerusalem shall be called a city of truth; and the mountain of the Lord of hosts the holy mountain** (3).

(3) Jerusalem shall become a scene of serene old age and joyful childhood (4-5). Old folk will sit watching happy boys and girls play in the streets. A partial fulfillment of this promise has been recorded from the days of Simon the Maccabee: "And the land had rest all the days of Simon . . . the ancient men sat in the streets, communing together of good things, and the young men put on glorious and warlike apparel. . . . He made peace in the land, and Israel rejoiced with great joy; for every man sat under his vine and his fig-tree, and there was none to fray them" (I Maccabees 14: 4, 9, 11 f.).[70]

(4) **Nothing is too hard for the Lord** (6). Will it take a miracle to transform Zion? "Very well," says Zechariah, "God is equal to the miracle, it is no miracle for Him."[71] *Living Prophecies* renders the verse, "This seems unbelievable to you—a remnant, small, discouraged as you are—but it is no great thing for Me."

(5) God shall regather His people in the Holy Land (7-8). He shall bring them **from the east** and **from the west** (7) and **they shall dwell in the midst of Jerusalem** (8); He shall be **their God** and they His people **in truth and in righteousness.**

(6) Anxious times shall pass with the restoration of the Temple (9-13). **Let your hands be strong** (9), the Lord exhorts the people of Zion. "Take courage and persevere in the rebuilding of the Temple," Rashi paraphrases, "and fear not the people of the land who 'weakened the hands of the people of Judah and harried them while they were building' (Ezra 4: 4)."[72] Times

[69]Quoted by Perowne, *op. cit.,* p. 102.

[70]Quoted by Cashdan, *op. cit.,* p. 298.

[71]McFadyen, *op. cit.,* p. 824.

[72]Quoted by Cashdan, *op. cit.,* p. 298.

have been desperate (10), **but now** (11) a new state of things has come about. **For the seed shall be prosperous; the vine shall give her fruit, and the ground shall give her increase, and the heavens shall give their dew** (12). The **curse** that rested upon the land shall be removed, for with the building of the Temple a new era has dawned (13).

(7) God shall **do well unto Jerusalem** if she will practice justice and mercy (14-17). As God punished the nation for its sin when they provoked Him to wrath, He will now show mercy and favor upon the land (14-15). In view of His beneficent purposes God enjoins once again the moral demands He had made through the old prophets (cf. 7:9-10). **Speak ye every man the truth to his neighbour; execute the judgment of truth and peace in your gates: and let none of you imagine** (plot) **evil in your hearts against his neighbour; and love no false oath: for all these are things that I hate, saith the Lord** (16-17). These are the words of an authentic prophet of righteousness, and they are timeless in their demands upon the conscience of man. "Think not that I am come to destroy the law, or the prophets," said Jesus; "I am not come to destroy, but to fulfil" (Matt. 5:17). The Christian ethic is based solidly upon the prophetic ethic of the Old Testament.

*d. Fasts turned to feasts of rejoicing* (8:18-23). Zechariah now comes to the climax of his answer to the delegation (see comments on 7:2-3). Let the people drop their fasts—the two already mentioned and two other fasts of the Exile—and turn them into cheerful feasts. So attractive would the happy days of Jerusalem be that returning Jews would be joined by men of many nations, and together they would make their way to Zion, where they would join in worshiping Jehovah God. **Lord of hosts** (18, *passim*) is a common title for God among the prophets. It stands for the power and sovereignty of the Lord.

The fast of neither **the fourth month** nor **the tenth** (19) is mentioned in 7:3 or 5. In **the fourth month** (the month of Tammuz) the Babylonians had made a breach in the walls of Jerusalem and begun to enter the city (II Kings 25:3-4; Jer. 39:2). This fast is still observed by Jews today on the seventeenth day of this month.[73] In **the tenth** (the month of Tebeth) the Babylonians had begun the siege of Jerusalem (II Kings 25:1). The

[73]*Ibid.*, p. 301.

four Exile fasts, says Zechariah, henceforth **shall be to the house of Judah joy and gladness, and cheerful feasts.** Then he adds the conditions for all these promises: **Therefore love the truth and peace.** In substance the prophet is saying: Drop your fasts and practice the moral virtues the neglect of which made your fasts necessary.

Finally Zechariah adds the crowning promise: **The inhabitants of one city shall go to another, saying, Let us go speedily to pray before the Lord, and to seek the Lord of hosts . . . Yea, many people and strong nations shall come to seek the Lord of hosts in Jerusalem, and . . . In those days . . . ten men . . . shall take hold of the skirt of him that is a Jew, saying, We will go with you: for we have heard that God is with you** (21-23). **Take hold of the skirt of,** or "coat of," is an expression meaning to seek identification with and protection from.

Have these prophecies been fulfilled? In part, yes. The inhabitants of the earth *have* gone up to Jerusalem to worship God. The Jews are the recognized religious teachers of mankind. Their Sacred Writings have become the very Word of God to multitudes of races, tongues, and nations. To them we owe the New Testament, as well as the Old. Their lawgivers, prophets, psalmists, apostles, and saints have given us our conception of God and the life He requires and imparts. Long before the Christian era, the synagogues of the Jews were lights shining in a world of pagan darkness. These assemblies later became the bridges over which the knowledge of God and Christ passed to the Gentiles. From the Jewish nation came the Saviour of mankind and the earliest apostles of the Christian faith. In Jerusalem, Jesus of Nazareth presented himself as the promised Messiah. In Jerusalem this same Jesus offered himself as the one perfect Sacrifice for the sins of mankind. In Jerusalem, He arose from the dead, ascended to the Father, and inaugurated the kingdom of God on earth. In Jerusalem the Holy Spirit descended, on a Jewish festival day, and began His mighty work of convicting the world of sin, righteousness, and judgment. Surely "Jerusalem which is above . . . is the mother of us all" (Gal. 4:26).

There is also a time, yet future, but possibly not far away, when "all Israel shall be saved" (Rom. 11:26) and these prophecies shall have a still more literal fulfillment. Some see in the modern Zionist movement and the restoration of the State of Israel signs that the ultimate fulfillment of Zechariah's prophecy may be at our very doors.

And we must never forget that it was the Captivity which purified Israel from idolatry and set her faith free to become a universal religion.

> They entered [the Captivity] imbued with polytheism and left it the strictest monotheists the world has ever seen. Their sorrows gave birth to some of their noblest Scriptures, and made their hold on the sacred Canon more tenacious than ever. Cast out by man, they fled to the bosom of God. Divorced from the outward rites of the Temple, they were driven to cling to spiritual realities, of which the Levitical institutions were only transient types. Israel owes all the influence she has wielded in the world to the anguish which culminated in the conflagration of the Temple; and, if she were wise, she would evermore keep those ancient anniversaries of despair as birthdays of her power.[74]

[74]Meyer, *op. cit.*, p. 70.

Section **II** *Oracles After the Building*

*of the Temple*

Zechariah 9:1—14:21

As we open the second section of Zechariah's prophecy we are made immediately aware that we have passed into a new era and a new prophetic situation. Abruptly and without warning the precious promises of a glorious future for Zion end and we find ourselves reading tidings of sorrow and disaster for nations and cities which appear in Zechariah's account for the first time. There is also a significant change in phraseology. No longer is it "the word of the Lord" but **the burden of the word of the Lord** prefixed to two groups of prophecies composed of three chapters each (9:1; 12:1).

Zechariah is now well advanced in years, and these burdens rest heavily upon his spirit. As they unfold, however, the glories of the Messiah and of His universal reign come into view. While the visions of the first section were concerned primarily with contemporary events, particularly the rebuilding of the Temple, the second division is primarily *futuristic*. It points the way toward the coming of Christ and describes affairs in Israel and in the world when the kingdom of Christ shall be consummated and "Holiness unto the Lord" shall be the watchword of the whole earth.

## A. The Burden of Hadrach, 9:1—11:17

This is the first of two "burdens" which constitute the material of the second division of Zechariah. The Hebrew word means "oracle" as well as **burden** (1). It is probably from a root meaning to "lift up"—i.e., the voice, especially when the announcement is of a "burdensome" or threatening character.[1]

### 1. Preparation for the Messiah (9:1-8)

The early troubles of the returned remnant in the reconstruction of the city and Temple are now at an end, but Jerusa-

[1]Collins, *op. cit.*, p. 755.

381

lem finds herself hemmed in and pressed by Syria and Tyre on the north and by Ashkelon, Gaza, and Ekron on the south (see map 2). It is therefore for the encouragement of the Jews that Zechariah foretells an approaching invasion before which these strong and hostile neighbors shall be swept away. *Living Prophecies* renders the verse, "This is the message concerning God's curse on the lands of Hadrach and Damascus; for the Lord is closely watching all mankind, as well as Israel." The oracle declares that the cities of Syria were under the judgment of God— **Hadrach, and Damascus** (1) and **Hamath** (2) being singled out specially. **Hamath** was one hundred miles north of **Damascus;** the city of **Hadrach** was probably in the same neighborhood, although its exact site is not known. The second part of v. 1 is obscure, but it probably means that the eyes of man (better, perhaps, "Aram" or Syria, RSV), as well **as of all the tribes of Israel, shall be toward the Lord** in awesome contemplation of His just judgments.

Next to fall would be **Tyrus** (Tyre) and **Zidon** (Sidon), the chief cities of Phoenicia, despite the fact that they were in a worldly sense very wise (2). The prophet declares that although **Tyrus did build herself a strong hold, and heaped up silver as the dust, and fine gold as the mire of the streets . . . the Lord will cast her out, and . . . smite her power in the sea; and she shall be devoured with fire** (3-4). Tyre was situated on an island about a half mile from the mainland and completely surrounded by massive walls. But although she considered herself impregnable, the calamities foretold by Zechariah actually came upon her. Alexander the Great built an artificial mole from the mainland to the island and after a seven-month siege completely destroyed the proud city and murdered thousands of its inhabitants.

Philistia lay south of Tyre, and the fall of Tyre would naturally cause alarm to the less fortified cities in Alexander's path. **Ashkelon shall see it, and fear; Gaza also . . . and be very sorrowful;** likewise **Ekron; for her expectation** (that Tyre would be able to assist her) **shall be ashamed** (5). Gaza's **king** was to perish, and **Ashkelon** was to be depopulated. A "mongrel people" (instead of **bastard**) were to inhabit **Ashdod,** and **the pride of the Philistines** was to be utterly crushed (6). The prophet predicts that, after abandoning the heathen practice of eating blood, the remnant of Philistia **shall be for our God** (7). This means that they were to be converted to the faith of Israel. **And**

**he shall be as a governor in Judah** means "that the Philistine
. . . shall take his place, ruler and people, as one of the divisions
of the Jewish nation."[2] **Ekron as a Jebusite** means that this
Philistine city would become like Jebus (Jerusalem). Josephus
declares that such an incorporation of Philistines into the Jews
actually occurred. Verse 8 is a promise of protection for Judah
while her neighbors were being devastated by the invader: **I will
encamp about mine house because of the army, because of him
that passeth by, and . . . returneth.**

The prophet thus foresees the conquering career of Alexander the Great (336-323 B.C.). It is no accident that this passage
precedes the prediction of the Messianic King. In the eyes of
Zechariah the great warrior was preparing the way for Christ.
"In this anticipation the prophet read the future more truly than
he at that time could have realized," J. E. McFadyen rightly
observes; "for, through the spread of the Greek language which
followed in the wake of his conquests, Alexander was all unconsciously preparing the way for the LXX [Septuagint] and
the New Testament in which the story of our Lord was told to all
the world: so that in a sense little dreamed of either by Alexander
or Zechariah, Alexander was one of those who prepared the way
for the coming of the Lord."[3] Such an interpretation of Zechariah's prediction seems to be in harmony with Peter's view of Old
Testament prophecy (see I Pet. 1:10-11).

### 2. *Presentation of the Messiah* (9:9-12)

The way having been prepared for His advent, the Messianic
King now appears (9). Interpreters, liberal and conservative
Christians as well as Jewish, see this as an indubitable Messianic
prediction. Dentan comments: "The prophet sees the army of
Alexander as only a tool in the hand of God. Riding invisibly
with it is the God of Israel and the long expected Prince of Peace,
who is about to enter Jerusalem and reestablish . . . the spiritual
glories of the ancient kingdom of David."[4] Collins claims, "The
reference to Christ is direct and immediate."[5] The Jewish interpreter Eli Cashdan quotes Rashi to the same effect: "This can
only refer to King Messiah of whom it is said, *And his dominion
shall be from sea to sea*, since we do not find any ruler with such

[2]Perowne, *op. cit.*, p. 111.          [3]*Op. cit.*, pp. 826-27.
[4]*Op. cit.*, pp. 1095-96.          [5]*Op. cit.*, p. 756.

wide dominion during the days of the Second Temple."[6] And T. T. Perowne justly observes: "No event in Jewish history answers even typically to this prediction."[7] When Jesus of Nazareth entered Jerusalem on the first "Palm Sunday," He was consciously fulfilling this great prophecy and presenting himself to the city as the long-awaited Messianic King.

The entrance of the King, says Zechariah, is to be the occasion for great rejoicing in Jerusalem. See Luke 19:37-40 for the fulfillment of this prediction.

The Messiah's character is described by the prophet: **He is just, and having salvation** (9). The RSV translates: "Triumphant and victorious is he." **Having salvation** is a passive participle in Hebrew and should be literally rendered "being saved" (in the sense of being divinely vindicated).[8] By raising Jesus from the dead, God ratified our Lord's Messianic claims and vindicated Him before the eyes of His crucifiers. Peter declared at Pentecost: "God hath made this same Jesus, whom ye have crucified, both Lord and Christ" (Acts 2:36). This is also the sense of Paul's assertion that Jesus was "designated Son of God in power according to the Spirit of holiness *by his resurrection from the dead*" (Rom. 1:4, RSV). By entering Jerusalem mounted on a donkey, Jesus not only proclaimed himself the Zecharian Messiah; He also committed himself to His enemies and to God— in the confidence that in His impending death the Father would vindicate Him by raising Him from the dead (cf. Mark 10:32-34). Therefore His entry *was* "triumphant and victorious," as the prophet had foretold.

**He is . . . lowly, and riding upon an ass** (9), for He is the promised Prince of Peace. The Messiah is to be no worldly conqueror riding upon a war horse, says Zechariah, but a humble King riding upon a lowly beast of burden, the animal used for peaceful purposes. "To this day in the East asses are used, as they are represented in the Song of Deborah, by great officials, but only when these are upon civil, and not upon military, duty."[9]

---

[6]*Op. cit.,* p. 305                    [7]*Op. cit.,* p. 113.

[8]Cashdan comments on this phrase: "The Hebrew *tsaddik,* usually translated 'just, righteous,' probably means here: shown to be in the right, vindicated in face of opposition, hence *triumphant.* The Hebrew *jasha* ('having salvation,' KJV) is a passive participle and strictly should be rendered 'the recipient of salvation'" (*op. cit.,* p. 306).

[9]Smith, *op. cit.,* p. 467.

Moreover, His reign shall resemble His character: **I will cut off the chariot from Ephraim, and the horse from Jerusalem, and the battle bow shall be cut off: and he shall speak peace unto the heathen: and his dominion shall be from sea even to sea, and from the river even to the ends of the earth** (10). The Prince of Peace shall banish all military equipment when His kingdom is fully established (cf. Isa. 2:4). **Ephraim** (Israel) as well as **Jerusalem** shall enjoy the promised blessing of peace in the Messianic age. The seas mentioned by Zechariah were undoubtedly the Mediterranean and the Dead Sea, while **the river** was the Euphrates. The language means that the Messianic kingdom shall extend to the earth's utmost bounds. Compare Isaiah's prophecy of Christ: "For every tramping soldier's boot in the middle of the battle turmoil and every coat rolled in blood shall be burned—fuel for the fire. For to us a Child is born, to us a Son is given; the government shall be upon His shoulder; and His name shall be called Wonderful, Counselor, Mighty God, Everlasting Father, Prince of Peace. There shall be no end to the increase of [His] government or to the peace upon the throne of David and upon His kingdom, in that it is firmly established and supported in justice and righteousness from now on and forever. The zeal of the Lord of hosts shall do this" (Isa. 9:5-7, Berk.)

Speaking still to the **daughter of Zion,** Zechariah likens her in her captive state to **prisoners in a pit wherein is no water** (11). Such captives faced inevitable and horrible death. Such would be the fate of Israel but for **the blood of thy covenant** (cf. Exod. 24:5-7). Because of this covenant they are termed **prisoners of hope** and exhorted to **turn . . . to the strong hold** (12).

3. *Program of the Messiah* (9:13—10:12)

a. *The promised victory of Zion over Greece* (9:13-17). "The next oracle seems singularly out of keeping with the spirit of the last, which declared the arrival of the Messianic peace," George Adam Smith admits. But he quotes Stade's observation that frequently in chapters 9 through 14 "a result is first stated and then the oracle goes on to describe the process by which it is achieved."[10] We should bear this in mind as we study these chapters.

Most commentators agree that there should be a full stop at v. 12, for in 13 a new topic is introduced, as Smith points out

[10]*Op. cit.,* pp. 467-68.

above. In vv. 13-17 God gives a promise of victory and freedom to Judah. The victory, we should note, is to be God's. He simply uses His people as His weapons: **Judah** as a bow, **Ephraim** as arrows, and **Zion** as a **sword** (13). The thrust of Zion is to be against **Greece**. In Zechariah's day the Greeks had already come to the attention of the Near East. Jews returning from the Captivity would have heard of the burning of Sardis (in 499 B.C.) and the battle of Marathon (in 490 B.C.) More recently the victories of the Greeks over Xerxes at Salamis, Platea, and Mycale (in 480-479 B.C.) would have come to the attention of Nehemiah and his contemporaries. The word **Greece** (Heb. *Javan*) should be understood in its widest meaning as applicable to all Hellenists in the Mediterranean area.

"The Jewish commentators regarded this verse as a prediction of the wars waged successfully by the Maccabean heroes against the Greek rulers of Syria. Rashi gives the following paraphrase: 'In the end, the Greeks will take the kingdom from the hand of the kings of Persia; they will ill-treat you, but I will bend Judah for Me as a war-bow, and they shall make war against Antiochus in the days of the Hasmoneans.' "[11]

Verses 14 and 15 underscore the truth that it is God who shall accomplish the victory for His people. Verse 14 probably means He will use the powers of nature to accomplish His purposes. In v. 15 the prophet describes the completeness of the victory: "He will defend His people and they will subdue their enemies, treading them beneath their feet. They will taste victory and shout with triumph. They will slaughter their foes, leaving horrible carnage everywhere" (*Living Prophecies*). Verse 16 brings out the preciousness of God's people: they are His **flock** and the **stones** (jewels) **of a crown.** In v. 17 Zechariah catches a glimpse of the restored land of Judah: "Yea, how good and how fair it shall be!" (RSV)

*b. Encouraging prospects* (10:1-5). The promise of temporal prosperity with which the preceding chapter ends is continued and expanded in 10:1-2. The people are to look to God for **the latter rain** (1), which fell in the spring and ripened the maturing grain and vineyards. **Bright clouds** is better translated "storm clouds," for these accompany **the latter rain.**

The injunction, **Ask . . . of the Lord rain,** is endorsed by a reminder of the vanity of looking to **idols** (2). In the past **they**

---

[11]Cashdan, *op. cit.*, p. 307.

**went their way** (in the sense of straying) and **were troubled** (afflicted), **because there was no shepherd** to tend them; their rulers had proven false. God's **anger was kindled against the shepherds, and . . . the goats** (3; cf. Ezek. 34:17). In their dire straits God himself became the Shepherd and made them "splendid steeds for his campaign" (3, Moffatt). "In this passage," Collins observes, "the prophetic perfect, the equivalent of the future, is used. In the fixity of the divine purpose, the promised transformation was as good as effected."[12] Verse 4 amplifies the promise that out of Judah should come conquerors. Smith-Goodspeed makes the imagery clear:

> *From them shall come the cornerstone,*
> *from them the tent-pin,*
> *From them the bow for war, and from*
> *them all the officers.*

**And they shall fight, because the Lord is with them** (5). Such great warriors and leaders did arise from Judah during the Maccabean period, but the ultimate reference may be to "the Lion of the tribe of Juda," by whose almighty power the kingdom of God shall, in the end, triumph over all its opposition. "For he must reign, till he hath put all enemies under his feet" (I Cor. 15:25).

### c. The restoration of the nation (10:6-12)

> *I will make the house of Judah strong,*
> *and rescue the house of Joseph,*
> *bring them home in my compassion,*
> *till they be as though I had never expelled them* (6, Moffatt).

With the **hiss** (8, cf. Isa. 5:26) or whistle, as a beekeeper summons his bees (cf. Isa. 7:18) or a shepherd his flock, God promises to bring back **into the land of Gilead and Lebanon** (10) His people who are "scattered" (RSV) **in far countries** (9), especially in **Egypt** and **Assyria** (10). One problem of Zechariah's day was too few inhabitants in Judah. God promised a massive return of His people until **place shall not be found for them.** Nothing will deter Him, but as of old His people "shall pass through the sea of Egypt" (11, RSV; cf. Isa. 11:15-16). And

---

[12]*Op. cit.,* p. 757.

their strength shall come from Jehovah himself. **And I will strengthen them in the Lord; and they shall walk up and down in his name, saith the Lord** (12).

4. *The Two Shepherds* (11:1-17)

*a. The destruction of Jerusalem* (11:1-3). In this chapter we have a companion picture to that drawn in c. 10. There the picture is bright with the coming of the Messiah, the victories He would achieve, and the blessings He would bestow. This picture is dark with His rejection and the tragic consequences which would ensue. The chapter opens with a vivid description of these consequences:

> *Open your doors, O Lebanon,*
> *to let fire burn up your cedars!*
> *Wail, O pine-tree,*
> *the cedar is down*
> *[[the glorious trees despoiled]].*
> *Wail, O oaks of Bashan,*
> *the thick-set forest is felled!*
> *Hark to the shepherds deploring*
> *their glorious pastures ruined!*
> *Hark to the young lions roaring,*
> *for the jungle of Jordan is blasted!* (1-3, Moffatt.)

"The desolating scourge, approaching as it ever did from the north, overthrows the pride of Lebanon and Bashan, and then, sweeping southward down the Jordan valley, falls upon the shepherds of Israel."[13] The cedars of Lebanon, the oaks of Bashan, and the other similar phrases signify the rulers and leaders of the doomed nations. Both Assyria and Egypt are compared in Scripture to the stately **cedar** (cf. Isa. 10:33-34; Ezek. 31:3-15).

As we shall see from what follows, it is the destruction of Jerusalem by the Roman armies which the prophet foretells.[14]

*b. The rejection of the Good Shepherd* (11:4-14). The causes of the above judgment are dealt with in this section, called by S. R. Driver "the most enigmatic in the Old Testament." The basic idea, however, seems clear enough. The catastrophe which befell Jerusalem flowed from the age-long, persistent misconduct

[13]Perowne, *op. cit.,* p. 122.      [14]Collins, *op. cit.,* p. 758.

of the people and their shepherds (or rulers). It climaxed in their rejection of the Good Shepherd, sent by God to feed His flock.

Zechariah himself was called upon to enact the role of the Good Shepherd in an allegory which recalls the pictures in Jeremiah and Ezekiel of the overthrow of false shepherds and the appointment of a true shepherd (cf. Jer. 23:1-8; Ezek. 34; 37: 24-28). "Thus says the Lord my God: Shepherd the flock destined for slaughter, whose owners will slay them and say they are not guilty; while those who sell them say, 'Blessed be the Lord, I have become rich. Their shepherds do not spare them'" (4-5, Berk.). Their rulers, both civil and religious, were so devoid of patriotism and spirituality they had no sense of responsibility toward the people entrusted to their care. Because they had no pity on the people, therefore God said, **I will no more pity the inhabitants of the land . . . but, lo, I will deliver the men every one into his neighbour's hand, and into the hand of his king: and they shall smite the land** (6).

The prophet did as he was told and took upon himself the task of shepherd of Israel. "So I became the shepherd of the flock doomed to be slain . . . And I took two staffs; one I named Grace [symbolizing the divine favor promised God's people], the other I named Union [symbolizing the unity that should exist between Judah and Israel]. And I tended the sheep" (7, RSV). **In one month** he cut off **three shepherds** (8). This is an obscure point but Calvin understood it to signify that God "took the greatest care of His flock, for He loved it, and omitted nothing necessary to defend it." Some think the sentence is a scribal gloss.

Despite all the care bestowed upon the flock, the shepherd's services were unappreciated. "So I said, 'I will not be your shepherd; what is dying, let it die, let the lost be lost, and let the survivors devour one another" (9, Moffatt). The prophet then took his "staff Grace, and . . . broke it" (RSV), thereby annulling the covenant of grace with Israel. This signified that the nation was to become prey to her enemies. Those who watched this dramatic act **knew that it was the word of the Lord** (11).

Zechariah then requested his wages for services rendered, if they felt disposed to pay him. He left it to the people to decide what their services were worth. **So they weighed for my price thirty pieces of silver** (12), the price of an injured slave (cf. Exod. 21:32).

Up to this point the prophet has spoken as the representative of the Lord. Now the Lord himself speaks, **Cast them to the potter**[15] **in the house of the Lord** (13). Zechariah ironically calls this **a goodly price.** The amount shows how meanly they thought of him and his services. The fact that the silver was cast **in the house of the Lord** means that it was God himself to whom they paid the wretched sum.

> It is impossible to read of the insulting response accorded by the people to the good shepherd without feeling how prophetic the whole passage is. Israel had not had an abundance of good shepherds in the course of her history (cf. Ezek. 34); but when the greatest shepherd of all came, ready to lay down his life for the sheep (cf. John 10:15), he was despised and rejected, sold for a price of a slave (Mt. 26:15) and nailed to a cross. "The guilty sacrifice the innocent, but in this execute their own doom. This is a summary of the history of Israel" (G. A. Smith).[16]

In Matt. 27:10 this symbolical incident of the shepherd is shown specifically to have been fulfilled in the betrayal of Jesus. He was sold for "thirty pieces of silver," and this amount was later cast down in the Temple by the remorseful Judas and then used to purchase a "potter's field." In Matt. 27:9 this prophecy is assigned to Jeremiah. One possible explanation for this is that a scribe mistook "Zechariah" for "Jeremiah" in copying the text. The probability is that Matthew was quoting from a group of Old Testament passages dealing with this theme and listed under "Jeremiah."[17]

After this incident the prophet broke the "second staff Union," thus signifying the "annulling [of] the brotherhood between Judah and Israel" (14, RSV).

*c. The worthless shepherd* (11:15-17). Having enacted the role of the Good Shepherd, the prophet is now called upon to impersonate a foolish ("worthless," Moffatt) shepherd (15). **For, lo, I will raise up a shepherd in the land, which shall not visit those that be cut off, neither shall seek the young one, nor heal that that is broken, nor feed that that standeth still: but he shall eat the flesh of the fat, and tear their claws in pieces** (16). "By

---

[15]The RSV translates this "treasury," reading *otsar* instead of *yotser.* However the footnote reads: "Syr: Heb *the potter.*"

[16]Quoted from McFadyen, *op. cit.,* p. 829.

[17]See Introduction, "The Book."

the unfaithful shepherd in this passage is to be understood the Roman oppressor, who destroyed the Jewish state and mercilessly harassed the Jews subsequent to their rejection of Christ."[18] This "worthless shepherd" must bear responsibility for his own actions and be punished accordingly:

> *May the sword strike his arm*
> *and his right eye!*
> *May his arm be withered,*
> *and his right eye blinded!* (17, Moffatt.)

## B. THE BURDEN OF ISRAEL, 12:1—14:21

As in the former burden (9:1), this section opens with the general title, **The burden of the word of the Lord** (1); and like it, this title belongs to the entire group of prophecies which follow, extending to the end of the book. Here, however, the **burden** is not "upon" or "against" (Heb., *bh*) Israel, but **for** or "concerning" (Heb., *al*) Israel. Her enemies are to be severely punished by the Lord because of their ruthless mistreatment of His people.[19]

The predictions of this final section of Zechariah are tied together by the phrase **in that day**, which occurs sixteen times in these three chapters.[20] This certainly means that the ultimate fulfillment of this oracle to Israel will occur in "the day of the Lord" (14:1). That is the eschatological day which shall be ushered in at the second coming of Christ, when "his feet shall stand . . . upon the mount of Olives" (14:4), from which He ascended after His resurrection (Acts 1:11-12).

### 1. *Final Victories of Israel* (12:1—13:6)

*a. The deliverance of Jerusalem* (12:1-9). An unusual solemnity attaches to the opening words of this oracle. To remove all doubt as to His ability to deliver His people, God prefaces the prediction of this glorious event by an appeal to His creative and sustaining power. He speaks as the Creator, who **stretcheth forth the heavens, and layeth the foundation of the earth, and formeth**

[18]Collins, *op. cit.*, p. 759.
[19]*Ibid.*
[20]12:3, 4, 6, 8, 9, 11; 13:1, 2, 4; 14:4, 6, 8, 9, 13, 20, 21.

the spirit of man within him (1). He would make sure that we stagger "not at the promise of God through unbelief" but be "fully persuaded that, what he" hath "promised" he is "able also to perform."

"The vision itself," F. B. Meyer reminds us, "refers to a time yet future, though perhaps not far away, when the Jewish people shall have returned to their own land, but still in unbelief."[21] The nations of earth will be in league against Jerusalem, but their confederacy is doomed to be overwhelmed with infinite disaster. **Behold, I will make Jerusalem a cup of trembling unto all the people round about, when they shall be in the siege both against Judah and against Jerusalem** (2). Jerusalem is a great bowl or cup about which the nations gather, eager to drink its inviting contents, but it becomes "a cup that causes reeling" (Berk.); it causes them to stagger and fall (cf. Isa. 51:22). In v. 3 the figure changes: **In that day will I make Jerusalem a burdensome stone for all people: all that burden themselves with it shall be cut in pieces.** The moving of heavy stones in antiquity was often the occasion for tragic accidents and loss of life. George Adam Smith thinks the reference is to the effort of workmen to dislodge giant boulders from the earth. Their hands would be lacerated by the stones as they attempted to tear them from their bed or to carry them.[22] Jerome thought the figure was taken from a weight-lifting contest such as he had seen in Palestine. The lift proves too much for the contestants, who drop the stone from their grasp, cutting and wounding themselves.

**I will open mine eyes upon the house of Judah** (4) is a metaphor denoting a favorable attitude. Her enemies would be put to confusion; **every horse** would be struck "with panic, and its rider with madness" (RSV). **Every horse of the people** would be all the horses of Israel's enemies. Seeing the confusion of the attackers, **the governors of Judah shall say in their heart, The inhabitants of Jerusalem shall be my strength in the Lord of hosts their God** (5).

The princes of Judah will share in Jerusalem's triumph. In this connection two arresting similes are employed. "In that day I will make the clans of Judah like a little fire that sets the forest aflame—like a burning match among the sheaves" (6,

---

[21]*Op. cit.*, p. 100.                    [22]*Op. cit.*, p. 479.

*Living Prophecies).* The result of this conflagration among Jerusalem's enemies will be the survival of the city **in her own place (6).**

In this deliverance **the tents of Judah first** are saved, so that **the inhabitants of Jerusalem do not magnify themselves against Judah (7).** In a footnote, *The Berkeley Version* notes that it was not from Jerusalem but from Bethlehem of Judea that the Messiah was to come. The glory shall belong neither to Judah nor to Jerusalem but to the Lord. By His help **he that is feeble . . . shall be as David; and the house of David shall be as God, as the angel of the Lord before them (8).** Wardlaw writes regarding this promise: "The general meaning is that the Lord God will strengthen the weakest and give additional elevation, honour, and influence to the highest, and add divinely to the might of the mightiest, so that no opposing power shall ever stand before them, any more than when that divine angel of the covenant was commissioned to be their conductor and guardian of Whom Jehovah said, MY NAME IS IN HIM."[23]

*b. Repentance of Israel* (12:10-14). Following their deliverance from their enemies, God **shall pour upon the house of David, and upon the inhabitants of Jerusalem, the spirit of grace and of supplications (10).** The word **grace** here means the gifts and influences of the Spirit.[24] The word continues: **And they shall look upon me whom they have pierced, and they shall mourn for him (10).** T. T. Perowne rightly observes: "The Speaker is Almighty God. The Jews had pierced Him metaphorically by their rebellion and ingratitude throughout their history. They pierced Him literally and as the crowning act of their contumacy, in the Person of His Son upon the Cross, John xix. 39."[25] The fulfillment of this prophecy in the mourning of those who pierced Him is still future, awaiting the return of the long-rejected Messiah. This prophecy is supported by the prophecy of John on Patmos: "Behold, he cometh with clouds; and every eye shall see him, and they also which pierced him: and all kindreds of the earth shall wail because of him. Even so. Amen" (Rev. 1:7).

[23]Quoted from Collins, *op. cit.,* p. 760.

[24]See John 1:16; I Cor. 15:10; and for the expression "the Spirit of grace" see Heb. 10:29.

[25]*Op. cit.,* p. 133.

The mourning for Christ will be as the wailing of one for the death of **his only son . . . as one that is in bitterness for his first-born (10)**, and as the mourning of **Hadad-rimmon (11)**, i.e., the mourning of the nation over the death of King Josiah. **Hadad-rimmon** is believed to have been a city **in the valley of Megiddon,** where Josiah was slain. Although only **Jerusalem** is mentioned as being involved in the mourning, it is clear from the verses that follow that the city stands for all Israel.

Several interpreters see the families specifically mentioned in vv. 12 and 13 as representative of the leading classes of the people: **the family of the house of David**—the royal family; **the family of the house of Nathan**—the prophetic line **(12)**; **the family of the house of Levi**—the priesthood; **the family of Shimei**—the scribes and teachers of Israel **(13)**. The mourning will not only be universal; it will be lonely: **every family apart, and their wives apart (14)**. We sin alone; we repent alone. "The mention of their wives as mourning **apart** is in reference to the practice of males and females sitting and worshipping separately."[26]

Mourning for Christ began at the time of the Crucifixion (Luke 23:48). The number of mourners increased greatly at Pentecost (Acts 2:36-41). Since by their sins all men were involved in the piercing of Christ, the mourning of every penitent is a partial fulfillment of this word of prophecy. But the final fulfillment will occur when Christ appears the second time. Then "a nation shall be born in a day," for in connection with the Messiah's return in glory "all Israel shall be saved" (Rom. 11:26; cf. comments on 14:16-19).

c. *The conversion and sanctification of Israel* (13:1-6). **In that day there shall be a fountain opened to the house of David and to the inhabitants of Jerusalem for sin and for uncleanness (1)**. The **day** is the same as that in 12:11. The piercing of the rejected Messiah was in reality the opening of the **fountain,** but the provisions of Calvary will not effect the *national* salvation of Israel until Christ returns on clouds of heaven (Rev. 1:7).[27]

[26]Collins, *op. cit.,* p. 760.

[27]Although Israel of the flesh as a whole has rejected Christ (Rom. 10:1-3, 18-21), "at this present time also there is a remnant according to the election of grace" (Rom. 11:5). During "the times of the Gentiles" Israel is said to be "cast away" (Rom. 11:7-22). But when "the fulness of the Gentiles be come in . . . all Israel shall be saved" (Rom. 11:23-32). Zechariah 12—14 as a whole throws light on this last prediction by St. Paul.

Henderson declares that v. 1 "exhibits the two grand doctrines of the gospel—justification and sanctification."[28] Christ's death opened **a fountain** (1) **for sin** and (2) **for uncleanness.** Justification is by the Blood of atonement (Rom. 3:21-26); sanctification is by "the Spirit of grace" (II Thess. 2:13; I Pet. 1:2). Justification means the putting away of our sin, the rectification of a wrong relationship with God, so that by faith we are restored to the favor of a holy and just God. Sanctification in the broadest sense means the entire moral renewal of our fallen natures, beginning with "the washing of regeneration, and renewing of the Holy Ghost" (Titus 3:5) and being made complete by the baptism with the Holy Spirit and fire (Matt. 3:11; Acts 1:4-5; 15:8-9).

On the Day of Pentecost, Peter pointed to the cleansing fountain: "Repent, and be baptized every one of you in the name of Jesus Christ for the remission of sins, and ye shall receive the gift of the Holy Ghost" (Acts 2:38).

With marvelous eloquence John Bunyan brought out the force of these words, "every one of you":

> "But I struck Him on his head with the rod: is there any hope for me?" *Every one of you,* saith the apostle. "But I spat in his face: is there forgiveness for me?" Yes, is the reply, for *every one of you.* "But I drove the spikes into his hands and feet, which transfixed him on the cross: is there cleansing for me?" Yes, cries Peter, for *every one of you.* "But I pierced his side, though he had never done me wrong; it was a ruthless, cruel act, and I am sorry for it now: may that sin be washed away?" *Every one of you,* is the constant answer.

As it was at the beginning of this age, so it will be at its close—with this difference, that whereas then some few thousand souls stepped into the fountain, "in that day" the vast majority of Israel shall wash there and be clean. Then the words of the Apostle Peter, spoken in the very dawn of this era, will be fulfilled. When Israel repents and is converted, "the times of refreshing shall come from the presence of the Lord; and he shall send Jesus Christ, which before was preached unto you: whom the heaven must receive until the times of restitution of all things, which God hath spoken by the mouth of all his holy prophets since the world began" (Acts 3:19-21).

[28]Quoted by Collins, *op. cit.,* p. 760.

Since the beginning of the Christian age the true fountain opened for sin and for uncleanness has availed for millions of penitent seekers in the Church of Jesus Christ. But Perowne sees more: "Beyond that in another age, in which in all its particulars, and with a completeness, it may be, and exactness of detail which it had never before attained to, the whole prediction shall be fulfilled."[29]

**In that day, saith the Lord of hosts . . . I will cut off the names of the idols out of the land** (2)—their very memory will be banished. **False prophets and the unclean spirit** by which they are moved shall be expelled. So great will be the zeal for pure religion that parents of any false prophet who may remain shall destroy him for speaking **lies in the name of the Lord** (3). Such discredit will be cast on the false prophet **in that day** that he will be ashamed of the things of which he was formerly proud. He will no longer wear **a rough garment to deceive** (4) the people into thinking him a prophet; **but he shall say, I am no prophet, I am an husbandman; for man taught me to keep cattle from my youth** (5). And if any shall still regard him with suspicion, because of **wounds in his hands** (6), he will say, **I was wounded in the house of my friends**. These **wounds** refer to "incisions which false prophets made on themselves" (I Kings 18:28).

This last verse has generally been associated with the marks of the nails in the hands of Christ. This, however, is not the natural meaning of the statement, and it is nowhere so applied in the New Testament. The passage is more accurately rendered, "What are these wounds between your hands?" (Berk.) A footnote explains: "Hebrew, 'between your hands,' means 'in the chest' or 'in the back,' the same as 'between your arms.' " A footnote in *Living Prophecies* comments: "That this is not a passage referring to Christ, is clear from the context. This is a false prophet who is lying about the reason for his scars."

2. *Final Victories of the Shepherd-King* (13:7—14:21).

a. *The smiting of the Shepherd* (13:7-9). The opening of this section is so abrupt that most modern critics place these verses at the end of chapter 11, after the account of the worthless shepherd. They are a continuation of the Good Shepherd motif (cf. 11:1-17), but they fit well here as a sequence to the preceding

[29]*Op. cit.,* p. 136.

prophecies of the deliverance, repentance, conversion, and sanctification of Israel. "Moreover, it was not because He claimed to be a prophet, nor because they were impatient with any such claim . . . but because 'He made Himself the Son of God' (John xix. 7), that the Jews took their part in the smiting of the Shepherd."[30]

The apparently abrupt transition may be explained by the fact that this section is parallel with, rather than consecutive upon, the preceding passage. Having pictured the future conversion and transformation of Israel, the prophet now turns back to a point even earlier than that with which the previous section began. He opens once more with a new view of the vista from the smiting of the Shepherd to the goal of true sanctification which was reached before.[31]

**Awake, O sword, against my shepherd . . . saith the Lord of hosts: smite the shepherd** (7). This is a distinct prophecy of Christ, who is Jehovah's Shepherd entrusted with the care of His flock. "In His Person, He is uniquely suited to His task, being a man and yet Jehovah's fellow (7). The word *gebher,* rendered man, is emphatic, indicating that the shepherd is a man *par excellence;* while the word *Kamith, fellow,* contains the idea of fellowship on equal terms. The smiting of any mere Jewish ruler . . . could not therefore be regarded as the ultimate and true fulfillment of this prophecy."[32] While it is said that He was crucified by the hands of wicked men, it is also stated that He was "delivered by the determinate counsel and foreknowledge of God" (Acts 2:23).

The immediate effect of the smiting of the Shepherd is given: **the sheep shall be scattered.** Christ leaves no doubt as to the meaning of these words. "Then saith Jesus unto them, All ye shall be offended because of me this night: for it is written, I will smite the shepherd, and the sheep of the flock shall be scattered abroad" (Matt. 26:31). The flock, however, was not to be left in this scattered condition, for the prophecy continues: **I will turn mine hand upon the little ones.** A literal rendering of this passage is, "I will turn back my hand over the humble ones," in

---

[30]Perowne, *op. cit.,* p. **138.**

[31]Cf. the parallel series of seals, trumpets, and vials in the Book of Revelation.

[32]Rollins, *op. cit.,* p. 761.

the gracious sense of Isa. 1:25. "The hand and power of God in the *risen* Shepherd returned from death is turned upon them and gathers them together" (Stier). Scattered by His crucifixion, the dispersed disciples were gathered again by His resurrection (Matt. 26:32).

Verses 8 and 9 are the basis for the New Testament doctrine of "the remnant of grace" (Rom. 11:5). It is not necessary to interpret **two parts** (8) and a **third part** (9) literally. The truth of this prophecy is that while there was a widespread destruction of the Jews after Christ's crucifixion (in the siege of Jerusalem by Titus in A.D. 70 and in subsequent attacks upon the Jews), a remnant of Israel did believe on Jesus as the Christ and became the nucleus of the Christian Church which evangelized the Graeco-Roman world. **I will say, It is my people: and they shall say, The Lord is my God** (9).

b. *The day of the Lord* (14:1-15). **Behold, the day of the Lord cometh** (1). It is impossible to regard this mysterious and sublime prophecy as fulfilled already. There is nothing either in the capture of Jerusalem under the Maccabees or in its subsequent destruction by the Roman armies which adequately fulfills the conditions of Zechariah's words. When have **all nations** been gathered together **against Jerusalem to battle** (2)? When has **the mount of Olives** been cleft **in the midst** (4)? What day has ever broken in the east as described in vv. 6 and 7?

> Of course it is possible to put metaphorical and spiritualizing interpretations on all these touches. But to do so is to jeopardize the whole force and value of prophetic Scripture. If the predictions of the Advent of our Lord in the days of his humiliation were so literally fulfilled, why should we suppose that the predictions of the Second Advent in great glory must be treated in metaphor?[33]

This chapter returns to the prophetic picture of the siege of Jerusalem depicted in c. 12. The nation is still in unbelief. The prophecy opens with a fresh account of the great siege but goes on to reveal the wonderful deliverance God will bring about for Jerusalem. The picture is as vivid as if the prophet were describing an actual historic event he had witnessed.

In 1919 David Baron wrote of this prediction:

> First of all we have to suppose a restoration of the Jews in a condition of unbelief—not a complete restoration of the whole na-

[33]Meyer, *op. cit.,* p. 109.

tion, which will not take place till after their conversion, but of a representative and influential remnant. It seems from Scripture that in relation to Israel and the land there will be a restoration, before the second advent of our Lord, of very much the same state of things as existed at the time of His first advent when the threads of God's dealing with them nationally were finally dropped, not to be taken up again "until the times of the Gentiles shall be fulfilled."[34]

The creation of the State of Israel in 1948 augurs an approaching fulfillment of Zechariah's prophecy. "Now learn a parable of the fig tree," said Jesus; "When his branch is yet tender, and putteth forth leaves, ye know that summer is nigh: so likewise ye, when ye shall see all these things, know that it is near, even at the doors" (Matt. 24:32-33).

**The day of the Lord** was an eschatological phrase which had long been used by prophets (cf. Amos 5:18-20; Isa. 2:12). This prediction is of the "great and notable day of the Lord" when Christ shall return to execute the end-time judgment of history. According to the biblical view, history is moving toward an end. **The day of the Lord** has had many *inner-historical* fulfillments in times of crisis, when God has judged history and brought about a partial victory of His kingdom. The most significant of these fulfillments was the death and resurrection of Jesus, when the kingdom of Christ was inaugurated.[35] There is yet to be a *suprahistorical* fulfillment of history, when Christ returns to consummate the Kingdom. The inner-historical fulfillment was anticipatory of this future suprahistoric fulfillment. When **the day of the Lord** here envisioned by Zechariah is *complete,* there shall "be time no longer" (Rev. 10:6). "Then cometh the end," when God shall be "all in all" (cf. I Cor. 15:24-28).

This **day of the Lord** will begin with the nations of the earth gathering against Jerusalem, **and the city shall be taken** (2). The siege will be successful in its beginnings. Scenes of horror and brutality are described, such as accompany the fall of a city into the hands of an angry enemy. **Half of the city shall go forth into captivity,** the prophet declares, but **the residue of the people shall not be cut off** (2). Jerusalem is to be preserved for the great event which is next announced: **Then shall the Lord go forth, and fight against those nations** (3). The

[34]Quoted by Luck, *op. cit.,* p. 117.
[35]John 12:31-33; 16:11; Mark 9:1; Acts 1:3.

Apostle John says of the same event, "Behold, he cometh with clouds; and every eye shall see him, and they also which pierced him: and all kindreds of the earth shall wail because of him" (Rev. 1:7).

Zechariah is foretelling a literal appearance of the rejected Saviour. Where His feet often stood when He was here in the days of His flesh they shall be placed once again. **And his feet shall stand in that day upon the mount of Olives, which is before Jerusalem on the east . . . and the Lord my God shall come, and all the saints with thee** (4-5; cf. Matt. 25:31; Col. 3:4; I Thess. 4:14; Jude 14). This can only mean that there will be a glorious fulfillment of the words of the two men who stood by the apostles on Olivet: "Ye men of Galilee, why stand ye gazing up into heaven? this same Jesus, which is taken up from you into heaven, shall so come in like manner as ye have seen him go into heaven" (Acts 1:11). F. B. Meyer observes with spiritual insight:

> It was when his brethren were in the greatest straits that Joseph made himself known unto them, and when the Jews are in their dire extremity, they will cry aloud for help and deliverance from Him whom they rejected. That memorable scene in the ancient land of the pyramids will be reproduced in all its pathos, when the long-rejected Brother shall say to His own brethren after the flesh, "I am Jesus, your Brother whom ye sold unto Pilate; and now be not grieved, nor angry with yourselves, that ye delivered Me up to be crucified: for God did send Me before you to preserve a remnant in the earth, and to save you alive by a great deliverance" (see Gen. xlv. 1-15).[36]

When the chosen people shall have recognized their great Deliverer, He will begin to deliver them. "It may be that they will recognize Him in the act of their deliverance. The cleaving mountain shall make a way of escape, as of old the cleaving sea."[37] These are the travail pains of the end. **And it shall come to pass in that day, that the light shall not be clear, nor dark: but it shall be one day which shall be known to the Lord, not day, nor night** (6-7). This will be a special day understood only by the Lord. With the natural light abated, this particular day will be neither day nor night as we understand them. No doubt the literal and the figurative are blended in the next prediction: **But it shall come to pass, that at evening time it shall be light** (7).

[36]*Op. cit.*, p. 111.                    [37]*Ibid.*

And it shall be in that day, that living waters shall go out of Jerusalem; half of them toward the Dead Sea, and half of them toward the Mediterranean Sea (8). Living waters shall flow out of **Jerusalem** "for the healing of the nations."[38] These waters will flow unabated **in summer and in winter**, unaffected by the seasons.

And the Lord shall be king over all the earth (9). John on Patmos also glimpsed this day and wrote, "The kingdoms of this world are become the kingdoms of our Lord, and of his Christ; and he shall reign for ever and ever" (Rev. 11:15). Since God is sovereign Lord of creation and history, this victory is certain. The day of the Lord *shall* come. **In that day**, the prophet continues, **shall there be one Lord, and his name one.** This will be the ultimate fulfillment of the Old Testament *Shema* (Deut. 6: 4-5). The unity of God's nature must mean the final acknowledgment of His sovereign name. The New Testament makes it clear that this sovereignty God shall exercise in "the name of Jesus" (Phil. 2:9-11).

While this passage predicts the literal return of Christ, there are many figurative touches upon the account, and it is impossible in each case to separate the literal from the metaphorical. It speaks of the cleaving of the mount of Olives (4-5), the irruption of God's own day (6-7), the issue of living waters (8), the depression of the surrounding country **as a plain from Geba to Rimmon south of Jerusalem** (10, the extremities of the land of Judah) with the exaltation of the city (**lifted up**), and the removal of the curse of sin (11). These are stars in the heaven of God's prophecy.

Coming to v. 12, however, we seem to touch more literal ground again. Since the advent of nuclear fission we understand something of the horror of men's **flesh** consuming away **while they stand upon their feet** (12). The confusion which God shall send to the armies of the enemies of Jerusalem is reminiscent of many an Old Testament account of battle (13). Moreover, the descriptions in vv. 14 and 15 seem easy enough to grasp. This is the language of Jewish apocalypse, and it describes a scene which John depicts in rich and glowing eloquence in the Christian Apocalypse (cf. Rev. 19:11-18).

c. *The millennial reign of Christ* (14:16-21). The quickened eye of the prophet now catches sight of the coming victory

---

[38]Cf. Ezek. 47:2-12; Joel 3:18; Rev. 22:1-2.

of the kingdom of God on earth. **And it shall come to pass, that every one that is left of all the nations which came against Jerusalem shall even go up from year to year to worship the King, the Lord of hosts, and to keep the feast of tabernacles (16).** The fair vision which filled the horizon for the great Hebrew prophets was always that of Jerusalem exalted as the religious metropolis of the world. Spiritually, the whole trend of the world's religious thought has been toward the city where Christianity was born and cradled (cf. comments on 8:21-23). But such a prophecy as this cannot be entirely spiritualized. Honest exegesis demands that we understand this prediction to be that the literal city of Jerusalem will become the religious capital of the world during the millennial reign of Christ.[39]

It is imperative that we exercise care, however, lest we fail to recognize those metaphorical elements which are certainly a part of this prophecy. It is not required that we understand v. 16 to be a prediction of the restoration of the literal feasts of the Old Covenant[40] but rather an assurance "that the gladness, the restfulness, the festal array, which pervaded the city at that time of the year, in the olden days, shall characterise the religious life of the world, the focus of which will be 'the beloved city.' "[41]

**And it shall be, that whoso will not come up of all the families of earth unto Jerusalem to worship the King, the Lord of hosts, even upon them shall be no rain (17).** This and the next two verses remind us that, even in the great day when the glory of the Lord shall cover the earth as the waters cover the sea, some will be impenitent. Egypt (18-19) here, as so often in the Old Testament, symbolizes defiant rebellion against the true God. "The true conception of the Millennium does not imply that every single soul will be regenerate; but that the preponderating influences of the world shall be in favour of things that are just, pure, lovely and of good report."[42]

**In that day shall there be upon the bells of the horses, HOLINESS UNTO THE LORD; and the pots in the Lord's house shall be like the bowls before the altar. Yea, every pot in Jerusalem and in Judah shall be holiness unto the Lord of hosts**

[39]The word millennium comes from a Greek word meaning *one thousand;* the only specific biblical reference to a thousand years is in Rev. 20:1-7.

[40]Nor v. 21 to be a prediction of the restoration of animal sacrifice.

[41]Meyer, *op. cit.,* p. 116.     [42]*Ibid.,* p. 117.

(20-21). When the victory of Christ shall be accomplished, the sacred words which were inscribed on the mitre of the high priest, "HOLINESS UNTO THE LORD," will be inscribed on the bells of the horses and the common vessels of household use. This symbolizes the abolition of the distinction between the sacred and the secular. In the Old Testament law, special days, places, and articles were set apart to God as holy. It was not possible for God to teach men what holiness meant except by this process of prohibition and separation. But when the lesson was fully learned, the Levitical code was abolished. The horses which were formerly taboo for the people of God will be as sacred **in that day** as the vessels of the temple of Jehovah. Christ sanctifies the whole of life, and when He is fully regnant in the affairs of this world, all shall be consecrated to Him.

> *"Holiness unto the Lord" is our watch-*
> *word and song,*
> *"Holiness unto the Lord" as we're*
> *marching along.*
> *Sing it, shout it, loud and long.*
> *"Holiness unto the Lord," now and*
> *forever!*
> —Mrs. C. H. Morris

*The Book of*

# MALACHI

William M. Greathouse

# *Introduction*

## A. The Prophet

—Of the life of the prophet Malachi we know absolutely nothing historically. All we know of him we infer from his utterances. We cannot be sure whether "Malachi," which means "my messenger,"[1] is the prophet's personal name or simply his title. Josephus, who mentions Haggai and Zechariah, makes no reference to Malachi. The Targum[2] paraphrases 1:1 "as by the hand of my messenger, whose name is called Ezra the scribe."[3] The Septuagint[4] also translates "my messenger" but entitles the book "Malachias" or Malachi. Archer observes, "Every other prophetic book in the Old Testament bears the name of its author. It would be strange if this one were left anonymous."[5] Since the question is open, we shall refer to the prophet as Malachi.

Although we cannot be certain as to the prophet's name, we have no difficulty in forming a clear-cut conception of Malachi's personality. The little book which comes from his hand witnesses to a forceful and vigorous preacher who pled for sincerity in worship and holiness of life. He had an intense love for Israel and the services of the Temple. It is true that he laid more stress upon worship than upon inward spirituality. However, "for him ritual was not an end in itself, but an expression of the people's faith in the Lord."[6]

## B. The Situation

The Jews had returned from the Captivity with high hopes. Interpreting the fair promises of Ezekiel and Zechariah as of immediate fulfillment, many of the devout believed the Messianic age was at hand. The nation, it was expected, was about to recover the lost glory of the kingdom of David. The land would become miraculously fruitful and the cities populous. The ideal

[1]Cf. 3:1, where the Hebrew word is rendered "my messenger."

[2]An Aramaic paraphrase of a portion of the OT.

[3]Cited by Gleason L. Archer, Jr., *A Survey of Old Testament Introduction* (Chicago: Moody Press, 1964), p. 416.

[4]Greek version of the OT.

[5]*Loc. cit.*

[6]J. T. H. Adamson, "Malachi," *The New Bible Commentary* (Grand Rapids: Wm. B. Eerdmans Publishing Co., 1956), p. 764.

King would be soon raised up, and all the nations would come to Jerusalem to serve the Lord.

As the years passed, however, disillusionment set in. The anticipated prosperity and blessing did not materialize. Life was hard. Crops were poor, parasites ruined the plants, and the fruit was disappointing. As these conditions persisted year after year and the bright dreams of earlier times were not realized, a spirit of dull depression settled down upon the community. The priests became careless in the performance of their duties and neglected the religious instruction of their charges. The people began to complain that God no longer loved them or cared for them. A spirit of cynicism spread to the entire population, and even those who remained true to the faith began to ask the question, "Why?" Many withheld their tithes and offerings. Social injustice became common. Intermarriage with the heathen of the land was freely practiced. Divorce became the order of the day as the people forgot their covenant with God. Everyone was disposed to question the authority and ways of God.

Such is the background against which the prophecies of Malachi must be studied. It was a situation which called for a fearless prophet. Malachi was God's man for the crisis. His book might be subtitled "A Message for an Age of Discouragement."[7] It therefore speaks to our day and to every period of spiritual depression.

## C. DATE

The conditions described above point to the period immediately preceding the work of Ezra and Nehemiah. The abuses are precisely those described in the Book of Ezra[8] and those which occupied the attention of Nehemiah.[9] Ezra returned from Babylon in 458-457 B.C. Nehemiah became governor for the first time in 444 B.C. and then had a second administration beginning in 433. It was during his second term that Nehemiah dealt with the problem of mixed marriages, but it would be too precarious to locate Malachi between the two administrations of Nehemiah. Since the prophet makes no reference to Nehemiah, his prophecies must antedate by a few years the beginning of his first period as governor. A date between 460 and 450 B.C. is generally accepted.

[7]Robert C. Dentan, "Malachi," *The Interpreter's Bible* (New York and Nashville: Abingdon Press, 1956), p. 764.
[8]Ezra 5:3; 9:1-2; 10:17.
[9]Neh. 13:1-29.

## D. THE BOOK

The Book of Malachi bears evidence of having been "hammered out in the actual discipline of public debate."[10] It differs greatly from the other prophetic writings. Malachi does not present his sermons or addresses in formal fashion as do the other prophets but launches into an argument with his hearers. The dialogue of question and answer reflects the actual situation in which the prophet found himself and the frequent verbal conflicts he was involved in with his contemporaries. In these questions and answers we can hear Malachi publicly defending the honor and justice of God against the attacks of skeptical opponents. The master debater takes up each objection and answers it before going on to another. "Throughout the entire dialogue he is describing the divine love, revealing the faithlessness and ingratitude of the people, calling for genuine repentance, answering the skeptics, challenging the current godlessness, and making glorious promises for those who are faithful."[11] It was no longer possible for a prophet of God to gain a hearing simply by saying, "Thus saith the Lord." It was an age of rationalism and even the Jews were beginning to require a logical and reasoned argument. They demanded that assertions be justified and objections met.[12]

Employing the device of dialogue, Malachi condemned the sins of the people and summoned them to repentance. Their ultimate salvation, however, was not to be found in their repentance but in God's action. The great day of the Lord would dawn in which He would purify the godly and destroy the wicked. That day would be heralded by the coming of Elijah.[13]

With Malachi, Old Testament prophecy ceased until the coming of John the Baptist. Yet in the closing verses of this book we have a shining prophecy of God's new age. "Malachi is like a late evening which closes a long day, but he is at the same time the morning twilight, which bears in its womb a glorious day."[14]

[10]Dentan, op. cit., p. 1119.

[11]Kyle M. Yates, *Preaching from the Prophets* (New York: Harper and Brothers, 1942), p. 217.

[12]Dentan, op. cit., p. 1119.

[13]Adamson, loc. cit.

[14]Negelsbach; cited by W. H. Lowe, "Minor Prophets," v. 3, *Layman's Handy Commentary on the Bible*, ed. Charles John Ellicott (Grand Rapids: Zondervan, 1961), p. 105.

# *Outline*

# *Section* I *Superscription*

Malachi 1:1

Malachi's message is described as **The burden of the word of the Lord to Israel** (1). The term **burden** is derived from a Hebrew word meaning "to lift up" (i.e., the voice). By a natural extension this came to refer to the words the voice uttered, the speaker's message or the prophet's oracle. The latter may appropriately be called his **burden,** since it is literally "that which is lifted up."[1] Jerome comments: "The word of the Lord is heavy, because it is called a burden, yet it hath something of consolation, because it is not 'against' but *to Israel."*[2]

For the significance of **by Malachi** see Introduction, "The Prophet."

[1]Dentan, *op. cit.*, p. 1122.

[2]Quoted by E. B. Pusey, "The Minor Prophets," II (Grand Rapids: Baker Book House, 1950), 465.

# Section II  *God's Love for Israel*

Malachi 1:2-5

The oracle begins almost abruptly with a tender and plaintive word of the Lord to Israel: **I have loved you** (2). This is the real burden of Malachi's prophecy; everything else is to be viewed in the light of this fundamental claim.[1] But the people are skeptical: **Wherein hast thou loved us?** They see no evidence of God's love. Poverty-stricken and suffering, they are a disheartened and disillusioned people. Their thought is clouded by doubt. Everything the prophet says is challenged: **Yet ye say.**[2] Malachi has to argue his points with a people who are at least critical and in part hostile. He here asserts a view of God's love that goes back to Deut. 7:8 (cf. Hos. 11:1), which declares that God chose **Jacob** because He **loved** him.

The proof of God's love for Jacob is seen in His overthrow of **Esau** (3). Esau and Jacob are here the nations of **Edom** (4) and **Israel** (5). God's love for Israel is proven by His punishment of Edom. Edom had not only failed to come to the help of Jerusalem when the city was besieged by the Babylonians in 586 B.C., but had actually rejoiced in its fall (Lam. 4:21-22; Ps. 137:7). As a result, during the postexilic period Edom became a living symbol of cruelty and faithlessness, ripe for destruction (Ezek. 25:12; Obad., 21). Therefore the expulsion of the Edomites from their old territory of Mount Seir by the Nabatean Arabs was seen as an act of divine vengeance for their unbrotherly and inhuman conduct (3). We do not know the date of this event, but it was apparently recent enough at the time of the writing to be fresh in the minds of the Jews.

The Edomites regarded the calamity which had befallen them as merely a temporary setback and looked forward to reestablishing themselves in their original territory. But Malachi declares that their ruin is permanent: **They shall build, but I**

---

[1]G. Campbell Morgan, *An Exposition of the Whole Bible* (Westwood, N.J.: Fleming H. Revell Co., 1959), p. 414.

[2]J. E. McFadyen, "Malachi," *Abingdon Bible Commentary* (New York: Abingdon Press, 1929), p. 833.

will throw down; and they shall call them, **The border of wicked-ness, and, The people against whom the Lord hath indignation for ever** (4). This will provide incontrovertible evidence to future generations, Malachi is saying, of the wickedness of Edom and the judgment of God. Edom was called **The border of wick-edness** ("The Criminal Land," Moffatt). On the other hand, it will provide Israel with indisputable proof of God's sovereign care. Furthermore, this will prove that the Lord is no petty national deity; it will enable Israel to say, "Great is the Lord, beyond the border of Israel!" (5, RSV) "Malachi's prophecy proved correct," Dentan points out, "and Edom never returned to her former lands. The Edomites (Idumaeans) remained set-tled in southern Palestine. . . . By a curious irony of history it was from these same Idumeans that the family of the Herods came."[3]

[3]*Op. cit.*, p. 1124.

## Section **III** *Sins of the Priesthood*

Malachi 1:6—2:9

From the love of God for Israel, Malachi passes on to the nation's affront to the divine majesty. His indictment is specifically against the clergy. The priests were ordained to give spiritual instruction and guidance (2:6-7). Had they lived up to their high calling and given the laity a godly example and proper teaching, the nation would not have fallen into spiritual apathy and skepticism. Because the priests failed and set such a vicious example of hypocrisy and empty professionalism, they made God contemptible in the eyes of the people and became contemptible themselves (2:8-9).

This lengthy section falls into two divisions. First God indicts a slovenly priesthood (1:6-14) and then pronounces a curse upon them (2:1-9).

### A. God's Indictment, 1:6-14

#### 1. *The Character of God* (1:6a-6e)

The prophet opens with a statement of a general principle upon which there was widespread agreement. In so doing he employs two characteristic images of God's relation to Israel: His fatherhood and His lordship. **A son honoureth his father, and a servant his master: if then I be a father, where is mine honour? and if I be a master, where is my fear? saith the Lord of hosts unto you, O priests, that despise my name** (6).

"We are so accustomed to associate with the Divine Fatherhood only ideas of love and pity that the use of the relation to illustrate not love but Majesty, and the setting of it in parallel to the Divine Kingship, may seem to us strange."[1] But to the Israelites this was very natural. In the Semitic world honor was due before love. "Honour thy father and thy mother," the fifth commandment reads. And when God presents himself to Israel as their Father, it is to enhance His authority over them and to increase their reverence rather than to assure them of His love

[1]George Adam Smith, "The Book of the Twelve Prophets," *The Expositor's Bible* (New York: George H. Doran Company, n.d.), II, 353.

414

and pity. The accent is upon His creating the nation to be His obedient son (Exod. 4:22-23). The central idea is that God is Father of the *nation:* its Creator (2:10; Isa. 64:8; Jer. 31:9), its Redeemer (Deut. 32:6; Isa. 63:16), its Guide and Guardian (Jer. 3:4; Hos. 11:1-4).

Certainly the idea of divine love is present in these concepts, but in the forefront is the thought of divine majesty. Even in the Book of Psalms, where we find the most intimate fellowship of the believer with God, there is only one passage in which His love is compared to that of a human father (Ps. 103:13). This tendency toward what we might regard as an austere view of God's fatherhood may have been necessary to preserve Israel's religion from the sensual ideas of divine fatherhood prevalent among their Canaanite neighbors. But whatever the reason, the severity of the Old Testament idea of God's fatherhood enables Malachi to employ the image as a proof of the majesty and holiness of God.[2]

The prophet next employs a second image: God is **master** and Israel **a servant.** Paul made this one of the dominant figures by which he described the Christian's relation to Christ (I Cor. 7:22; Gal. 5:13; Col. 3:24). The thought is of divine ownership and God's right to claim absolute obedience.

The majesty and holiness of God had been wronged by the priests of Israel. "If then I am a father, where is My honor? And if I am a master, where is My reverence?" (Berk.) To think of God as Father is to honor Him as our Creator, Redeemer, and Sustainer. To regard Him as Master is to reverence and obey Him as Lord. "By the fear of the Lord men depart from evil" (Prov. 16:6).

### 2. *Despising God's Name* (1:6f-10)

In making this indictment Malachi charges the priests with despising the name of God. Their querulous voices raise the question, **Wherein have we despised thy name?** (6) The prophet replies, **Ye offer polluted bread upon mine altar** (7). The **bread** (*lechem*) here is not shewbread (this was not offered upon the altar), but the flesh of sacrificial victims (cf. Lev. 3:11, 16; 21:6; 22:25). This offering was **polluted** by not being offered in accord with the stipulations of the ceremonial law, as explained in v. 8. By disregarding God's plain commandment to bring only un-

[2]*Ibid.,* pp. 352-54.

blemished animals they were saying, **The table of the Lord is contemptible.** The expression **Ye say** here has the sense of "say to oneself" or "say by one's actions." By **the table of the Lord** is meant the altar of sacrifice.

Verse 8 specifies the charges. **Blind, sick,** and **lame** animals were being devoted to God. This was a clear violation of the law, which read: "And if there be any blemish therein, as if it be lame, or blind, or have any ill blemish, thou shalt not sacrifice it unto the Lord thy God" (Deut. 15:21). In its purest form sacrifice meant offering to God something as valuable as possible as a symbol of one's willing self-consecration. By offering sickly and lame animals the priests were making a mockery of the institution of sacrifice.

The priests, however, were apparently saying, "No harm!" Since a sacrifice is only a symbol, they were probably rationalizing that one kind of offering was as good as another. But God asks·

> And when you bring the blind to sacrifice, is there
> no harm?
> And when you bring the lame and the sick, is there
> no harm? (8, Smith-Goodspeed)

No harm? "Present that to your governor," Malachi suggests; "will he be pleased with you or show you favor?" (8, RSV) The reference here to the **governor** proves that Malachi was writing during the Persian period, when Judah was ruled by appointees of the Persian monarch. The Hebrew word is the same as used of the governorships of Zerubbabel (Hag. 1:1) and Nehemiah (Neh. 5:14).

W. J. Deane has paraphrased the ninth verse: "Come now and ask the favour of God with your polluted sacrifices; intercede, as is your duty, for the people. Will he accept you? Will he be gracious to the people for your sakes?"[3] **This hath been by your means** is an awkward sentence. *The Berkeley Version* has given a plausible rendering of 9b: "With such a gift from your hand, will He show favor to any of you?" Better that sacrifice should cease than that offerings should be made in such a spirit!

[3]"Malachi," *The Pulpit Commentary.* XIV (Grand Rapids: Wm. B. Eerdmans Publishing Co., 1950), 3.

Moffatt clarifies the first part of 10 thus: "Will no one close the temple-doors, to keep you from kindling useless fires upon my altar?"

### 3. God Honored Among the Gentiles (1:11-12)

A remarkable and disputed statement follows in v. 11: **For from the rising of the sun even unto the going down of the same my name shall be great among the Gentiles; and in every place incense shall be offered unto my name, and a pure offering: for my name shall be great among the heathen, saith the Lord of hosts.** From the days of the Church Fathers this verse has been understood as a prophecy of the Messianic age and the universal worship of the Christian Church.[4] Deane writes: "The course of the thought is this: God does not need the worship of the Jews and their impious priests; he needs not their maimed sacrifices; his majesty shall be recognized throughout the wide world, and pure worship shall be offered to him from every nation under heaven."[5] This interpretation requires that the reference to the Jewish ritual be understood metaphorically: "The pure oblation is a symbol of the Christian sacrifice of praise and thanksgiving; and the prophet, rising superior to Jewish prejudices, announces that this prayer and sacrifice shall no longer be confined to one specifically favoured country, but be universal, worldwide."[6] Many have gone even further and seen in the verse a prophecy of the Christian Eucharist, the "pure offering" commemorating Christ's sacrifice, which is offered wherever the name of Christ is adored.

The above interpretation rests upon the verbs **shall be** which occur twice in the verse, both times in italics in both the KJV and ASV. This indicates that the verb is lacking in the original. The Hebrew construction, while admitting a future, is most naturally understood as present. Pusey comments, "It is a vivid present, such as is often used to describe the future. But the things spoken of shew it to be future."[7] The Septuagint translates it, "My name *has been* and *is* glorified." The RSV translates "is" instead of "shall be." If there were no theological problem, the verse would be most easily interpreted as applying to the contemporary scene in Malachi's world. W. H. Lowe has posed the problem for the Christian interpreter:

[4]Pusey, *op. cit.*, gives a full summary of this view, pp. 471-74.
[5]*Op. cit.*, pp. 3-4.      [6]*Ibid.*            [7]*Op. cit.*, p. 471.

If we take the words as referring to the present, we are met by the unsurmountable difficulty that in no sense, at the time of Malachi, could the Lord's name be great over all the earth, or pure sacrifices be offered to Him in every place. Nor can we . . . suppose that heathen rites are here referred to as being offered ignorantly to the one true God. . . . We are compelled therefore to take the words as a prophetic announcement of the future rejection of Israel and calling of the Gentiles.[8]

The conservative *New Bible Commentary*, however, adopts the view that Malachi is describing the contemporary situation. "In the prophet's day the very Gentiles were offering worship which was more sincere than that in Jerusalem."[9] If this is a possible interpretation, Malachi is making a generous statement somewhat similar to St. Paul's on Mars' Hill: "Whom therefore ye ignorantly worship, him declare I unto you" (Acts 17:23). On this view all forms of heathen worship are ignorant gropings after the one true and living God and are therefore a witness to the great name of the Lord. All men worship because God is and every religion bears witness to God *in this sense.*

The very sincerity of some heathen worship, Malachi seems to be saying, is a stinging rebuke to the disgraceful hypocrisy of the Jewish priests. If the heathen are magnifying God's name, the priests of Jerusalem are profaning it by their contempt of the Lord's **table** (12). "The prophet's purpose is of course not to praise the heathen but to shame the Jews. The heathen by their carefulness and munificence are honoring God, while the Jews by their indifference are dishonoring him."[10]

### 4. A Curse on Insincere Religion (1:13-14)

Despising the altar, and performing their duties without heart or faith, the priests found their duties an intolerable burden. **What a weariness is it!** (13) They moan, and "have sniffed" (Berk.) at the altar. Many interpreters think this should read "sniff *at me.*" This is on the supposition that the scribes corrected the verse to read **at it** in order to avoid the appearance of irreverence. For **torn** *The Berkeley Version* follows the Septuagint in translating "taken by violence," i.e., stolen animals. This verse has the priests chiefly in mind, who as corrupt officials allow this practice to go on. The next verse condemns those who bring such offerings.

[8]*Op. cit.*, p. 110.                    [9]Adamson, *op. cit.*, p. 766.
[10]Dentan, *op. cit.*, p. 1129.

The laity was corrupted by the priesthood. In this case it was "like priest, like people" (contra, Hos. 4:9). Following the example of their priests the worshippers were stingy and deceitful. **But cursed be the deceiver, which hath in his flock a male, and voweth, and sacrificeth unto the Lord a corrupt thing** (14). In a time of sickness or distress a man prayed to God and vowed a perfect male from his flock. But when he recuperated and the time came to perform his vow, his stinginess took over and he decided to offer an injured or sickly animal (cf. Lev. 3:1, 6). God's curse is upon such irreverence and halfheartedness. It is more devout to ignore God altogether than thus to trifle with Him, for He is **a great King, and** (His) **name is dreadful among the heathen.**

### B. God's Judgment, 2:1-9

In the name of the Lord the prophet now proceeds to pronounce judgment upon the priesthood: **And now, O ye priests, this commandment is for you** (1). "As God said of old, upon obedience, *I will command my blessing upon you,* so now He would command . . . a curse."[11] **If ye will not hear, and if ye will not lay it to heart** (my rebukes), **to give glory unto my name . . . I will even send a curse upon you** (2). Yet, like all prophetic messages of doom, this word is conditional: "If you continue in your hypocrisy and heartless indifference, I will send my curse upon you." Clearly, God desires their repentance so that the curse will be stayed.[12] **I will curse your blessings,** God says. These **blessings** are not their priestly benedictions which they pronounced upon the people, but the benefits they enjoyed as ministers of the Temple (cf. Num. 18:8-19). These benefits God will withdraw. The latter part of the verse may mean that the curse had already gone forth and had begun to settle upon them from the moment they began to despise God's name.

The nature of this curse is indicated in v. 3: **I will corrupt** ("rebuke," ASV and RSV) **your seed,** or "your offspring" (Berk.). **And spread dung upon your faces, even the dung of your solemn feasts,** or "of your offerings" (RSV). Here "dung" does not mean the excrement of the animals but the contents of

---

[11]Pusey, *op. cit.,* p. 476.

[12]Cf. the prophecy of Jonah against Nineveh, Jonah 3:1-4.

the bowels of the slain victims. The last clause, **and one shall take you away with it,** may mean the priests will be removed from the city along with the dung of the sacrifice (cf. Lev. 4:12). Thus the priests shall be utterly degraded. As God said to Eli, "Them that honour me I will honour, and they that despise me shall be lightly esteemed" (I Sam. 2:30).

The performance of God's curse upon the priests was to be a proof of His justice and therefore a warning to those who would presume (4). Pusey notes: "God willed to punish those who at that time rebelled against Him, that He might spare those who should come after them."[13] This is because He is a covenant God (cf. Deut. 7:9-11).

God's **covenant . . . with Levi** (4) is not explicitly mentioned in the Old Testament. However, the idea of covenant here is not necessarily technical, and Deut. 33:8-11 clearly stands behind this claim of Malachi. God's covenant was intended to be a blessing to Levi and his descendants, as v. 5 indicates: "My covenant with him was a covenant of life and peace, and I gave them to him, that he might stand in awe; and he stood in awe of Me and regarded My name with reverence" (Berk.). Throughout this section **Levi** must be understood as a personification of the priestly order rather than as the Hebrew patriarch. This usage is characteristic of the Old Testament. Malachi's point is that the priesthood originally fulfilled its ministry with sincerity and faithfulness.

In vv. 6-7 the nature of true priestly service is portrayed in beautiful language. Remembering that Levi personifies the ideal priesthood, we read: **The law of truth was in his mouth, and iniquity was not found in his lips: he walked with me in peace and equity, and did turn many away from iniquity** (6). The priest in Israel was more than an expert in the ritual sacrifice; his duty was to give instruction in **the law** (*torah*) **of truth.** He was to be a man of **peace and equity** (uprightness), whose instruction would convert many from sin. "For the lips of a priest should keep knowledge, and men should seek the law from his mouth" (7, Berk.). What a lofty ideal! G. A. Smith exclaims, "In all the range of prophecy there is not any saying more in harmony with the prophetic ideal. . . . Every priest of God is a priest of truth."[14] This is because the priest **is the messenger of**

[13]*Op. cit.,* p. 477.           [14]*Op. cit.,* p. 361.

**the Lord of hosts.** The word **messenger** here is the word applied to the prophet himself (1:1) and to the figure who should usher in the day of the Lord (3:1). It is also the word often translated "angel" in the Old Testament.

How pathetically the priests of Malachi's time fell below the divine standard! Instead of walking humbly with the Lord, they **departed out of the way** (8). Rather than converting the sinful from their wickedness, by their own mischief they **caused many to stumble at the law.** Like the religious teachers of Jesus' day, they were blind leaders of the blind (Matt. 15:14). Moreover, they thereby **corrupted the covenant of Levi.** Since a covenant must be observed by both parties, the covenant which should have brought blessing upon them (v. 5) had been annulled and they were **made . . . contemptible and base before all the people** (9) who should have sought instruction from their lips. The final clause means that the priests had **been partial** to the wealthy upper class in their application of **the law.**

Section **IV** *Divorce and Foreign Marriages*

Malachi 2:10-16

This passage has been called "the most difficult section in the Book of Malachi."[1] The general meaning, however, seems clear enough. Although they were all children of one Heavenly Father, the Jews were dealing treacherously with one another and profaning the covenant of their fathers by divorcing their Jewish wives and contracting unholy marriages with heathen women. For this abomination God threatens to destroy both the offenders and their offspring. He declares that He hates divorce and warns the people to take heed to their spiritual lives.

## A. MARRIAGE WITH HEATHEN WOMEN, 2:10-12

Abruptly Malachi opens his charge. He does so by laying down, in the form of a question, a general principle which he proceeds to apply: **Have we not all one father? hath not one God created us?** (10) Although Calvin and others have suggested that the **one father** here mentioned is Abraham, the parallelism of the verse proves that He is the **one God** who **created** Israel. "He created them not only as He did all mankind," Pusey declares, "but by the spiritual relationship with Himself, into which He brought them."[2] So Isaiah says, "But now thus saith the Lord that created thee, O Jacob, and he that formed thee, O Israel, Fear not: for I have redeemed thee, I have called thee by thy name; thou art mine. . . . every one that is called by my name: for I have created him for my glory, I have formed him; yea, I have made him. This people have I formed for myself; they shall shew forth my praise" (Isa. 43:1, 7, 21). Malachi is making the point that God's creating them as His people gave them a new existence, a new relation to one another. Thus an offense of one against another was a violation of their relation to God, who, as their common Father, had given them this unity. This verse is often quoted as a sublime admonition to mankind

[1]J. M. Powis Smith, *Malachi*, "The International Critical Commentary" (New York: Charles Scribner's Sons, 1912), p. 47.

[2]*Op. cit.*, p. 481.

regarding the fatherhood of God and the brotherhood of man, but the context limits the full meaning of the concept to the fatherhood of those who are bound together by a common bond of redemption as the people of God. This is also true of the fatherhood of God in the New Testament.

Malachi's charge that the offenders were **profaning the covenant of** their **fathers** (10) proves that this verse is internally related to vv. 11-12, which by some interpreters[3] are regarded as an interpolation. It was intermarriage with heathen, condemned in vv. 11-12, which was "a menace to the distinctive faith which was the basis of God's covenant with Israel."[4] The law warned, "Neither shalt thou make marriages with them . . . For they will turn away thy son from following me, that they may serve other gods" (Deut. 7:3-4). Therefore Malachi continues: **Judah hath dealt treacherously, and an abomination is committed in Israel and in Jerusalem; for Judah hath profaned the holiness of the Lord which he loved, and hath married the daughter of a strange god** (11). The tragedy was compounded by the fact that the priests were the leaders in this offense (Ezra 9:1-2). The prophet calls this an **abomination.** The term is prevailingly used of things or acts which are abhorrent to the Lord—e.g., idolatry, uncleanness, irregularities of ritual, and violations of the moral law.[5] He also regards this as a profanation of **the holiness of the Lord.** The RSV translates this "the sanctuary of the Lord." The Hebrew permits this rendering and it is supported by the prohibition against heathen entering the sacred precincts of the Temple. Most commentators, however, favor the KJV translation. Israel itself was "holiness unto the Lord" (Jer. 2:3). "The general sense is that the Jews have despised the position of privilege assigned to them—the position of being 'holy' or 'separate' (Lev. xx. 24) to Jehovah—and have joined themselves to foreign women and (through them) to foreign gods" (cp. I Kings xi. 4)."[6]

**The Lord will cut off the man that doeth this, the master and the scholar** (12). The latter phrase has been a puzzle to

[3]Raymond Calkins, *The Modern Message of the Minor Prophets* (New York: Harper and Brothers, 1947), p. 131; G. A. Smith, *op. cit.*, pp. 363, 365.

[4]Eli Cashdan, "Malachi," *The Twelve Prophets,* ed. A. Cohen (London: The Soncino Press, 1948), p. 354.

[5]Powis Smith, *op. cit.*, p. 48.

[6]W. Emery Barnes, *Malachi*, "Cambridge Bible for Schools and Colleges," ed. F. S. Marsh (Cambridge: The University Press, 1934), p. 122.

exegetes; it means literally "the awakened and the awakener."
The Peshitta[7] and the Targum paraphrase: "his son and his son's
son." Marcus Dods agrees with those who take the phrase to
mean "every one who is alive."[8] The general sense is clear: The
Lord will destroy the males of the household of the man who
profanes the holiness of the Lord by marrying a foreign woman.
His household will have no one to perform the duty of sacrifice
(12b).

## B. DIVORCE OF JEWISH WIVES, 2:13-16

**And this ye have done again** (13) means literally, "And this,
a second thing, you do." Rashi elaborates the prophet's rebuke:
"The first crime for which I censure you, that you take to wife
not one of your own people but a foreign woman, is bad enough;
but that you already have a Jewish wife and bring into the house
a foreign woman as chief wife is unpardonable."[9] The following
verses, however, strongly imply that the Jews at this time were
practicing monogamy. Their crime consisted in divorcing their
Jewish wives in order to marry younger and more attractive
heathen women. Their **covering the altar of the Lord with tears,
with weeping, and with crying out** probably refers to all the
practices which go to make up a day of fasting and humiliation.
Such practices unaccompanied by an amendment of life were
repugnant to the Lord. "Yahweh refuses to recognize their gifts
because of their sins and so they redouble their efforts to pro-
pitiate him, but do not forsake their sins."[10] True mourning involves a forsaking of all wicked ways. Only this kind of weeping
is acceptable to the Lord.

**Yet ye say, Wherefore?** (14) That is, "Why does He not
accept our offerings?" The prophet answers this objection plainly: **Because the Lord hath been a witness between thee and
the wife of thy youth, against whom thou hast dealt treacherously: yet is she thy companion, and the wife of thy covenant.**
The special mention of **the wife of thy youth** shows that elderly
Jewish wives were being put aside so that husbands might

[7]The Syriac Version.
[8]*The Post-Exilian Prophets* (Edinburgh: T. & T. Clark, n.d.), p. 143.
[9]Quoted by Cashdan, *op. cit.*, p. 346.
[10]Powis Smith, *op. cit.*, p. 51.

marry young and attractive girls from their neighboring nations.[11] The phrase **wife of thy covenant** and the reference to God's being a **witness** to the covenant, point to a high view of marriage as a sacred compact made in the presence of Jehovah God. Douglas Rawlinson Jones observes: "Malachi plainly regarded a marriage witnessed by Yahweh, no doubt in a formal troth before the priest, as a covenant not to be broken. Man and wife are 'those whom the Lord hath joined together.' "[12] Whether or not Old Testament marriages were formalized in a troth before the priest, there are other references which point up the truth that marriage is a covenant relationship to which the Lord witnesses (cf. Gen. 31:50; Prov. 2:16-17). Malachi speaks beautifully here of **the wife of thy youth** as **thy companion** (cf. Gen. 2:18-24).

Verse 15 is one of the most difficult in the Bible. An examination of the standard commentaries reveals that there is practically no agreement as to its meaning. It is the opinion of this writer that the RSV probably gives the correct sense: "Has not the one God made and sustained for us the spirit of life? And what does he desire? Godly offspring. So take heed to yourselves, and let none be faithless to the wife of his youth." Some such rendering fits into the argument of the prophet. The purpose of Hebrew marriage was to insure "godly offspring." By divorcing their Jewish wives and marrying strangers the sinners of Judah were destroying the divine purpose of marriage, i.e., to rear children who hold fast the faith of Israel.

This situation led the prophet to announce a truth found nowhere else in the Old Testament. The RSV renders it: "I hate divorce, says the Lord the God of Israel" (16). This is a departure from the Hebrew text, which reads, "He hates." "Divorce although permitted and regulated by the Torah (Deut. xxiv. 1 ff.) is hateful to God," says Cashdan. He then quotes the Talmud: "Hateful is he that putteth away his first wife; even the altar sheddeth tears because of this."[13] The reference to covering **violence with his garment** is based in the ancient custom of claiming a woman as wife by casting one's garment over her

[11]Dentan, *op. cit.*, p. 1135.

[12]*Malachi,* "Torch Bible Commentaries," eds. John Marsh and Alan Richardson (London: SCM Press, Ltd., 1962), p. 196.

[13]*Op. cit.*, p. 348.

(cf. Deut. 22:30; Ruth 3:9; Ezek. 16:8). J. M. Powis Smith gives another possible translation of this verse which preserves the central idea: " 'For one who hates and divorces,' says the Lord God of Israel, 'covers his clothing with violence.' . . . So take heed of your spiritual life, and do not be faithless."[14] Such a man does injustice to her who is as near to him as his garment.

[14]*The Bible: An American Translation, loc. cit.*

# Section V Where Is the God of Judgment?

Malachi 2:17—3:5

In this section Malachi turns from the sinners of his people to those who weary the Lord with their complaint that sin is successful. They worded it, "Everyone who does evil is good in the sight of the Lord, and He delights in them"; and again, "Where is the God of justice?" (Berk.) They have lost faith in God. Therefore He will send His messenger to prepare for the coming day of judgment. Then there will be a purification of the priestly order and a full exposure and condemnation of sinners of every kind. For the Lord is unalterably opposed to sin, and the sinners of Judah must perish. It is uncertain whether this section closes with v. 5 or 6; the latter goes equally well with it or the following section. We shall follow *The Berkeley Version* and Moffatt in closing it with v. 5.

## A. THE COMPLAINT OF THE PEOPLE, 2:17

**Ye have wearied the Lord with your words,** the prophet charges (17). This is no novel idea. In Isaiah the Lord complains, "Your new moons and your appointed feasts my soul hateth: they are a trouble unto me; I am weary to bear them" (1:14). And again, "Thou hast wearied me with thine iniquities" (Isa. 43:24). In like manner St. Paul says, "Grieve not the holy Spirit of God" (Eph. 4:30). **Yet ye say, Wherein have we wearied him?** The prophet answers, **When ye say, Every one that doeth evil is good in the sight of the Lord, and he delighteth in them; or, Where is the God of judgment?** (17) Jerome comments appropriately:

> The people, when returned from Babylon, seeing all the nations around, and the Babylonians themselves, serving idols but abounding in wealth, strong in body, possessing all which is accounted good in this world, and themselves, who had the knowledge of God, overwhelmed with want, hunger, servitude, is scandalized and says, "There is no providence in human things; all things are borne along by blind chance, and not governed by the judgment of God; nay rather, things evil please Him, things good displease Him; or if God does discriminate all things, where is His equitable and just judgment?"[1]

[1]Quoted by Pusey, *op. cit.* p. 485

427

## B. The Answer of the Word, 3:1-5

The last question, "Where is the God of judgment?" provides the lead for a divine pronouncement, **Behold, I will send my messenger, and he shall prepare the way before me: and the Lord, whom ye seek, shall suddenly come to his temple, even the messenger of the covenant, whom you delight in: behold, he shall come, saith the Lord of hosts** (1). "Evil as the present may seem, God is coming soon to correct its inequities."[2]

Two events are here predicted: (1) the coming of the Lord's messenger to **prepare the way** for God; (2) the coming of the Lord himself, called particularly the **messenger** (angel) **of the covenant.**

### 1. *The Coming of the Forerunner* (3:1a)

The thought here is that of Isa. 40:3-5; 52:7; 57:14. The first of these prophecies is quoted along with our passage in the second Gospel, as being fulfilled by John the Baptist (Mark 1:2-3).

Douglas Rawlinson Jones has given the Christian interpretation of this prophecy: "The point here is that, though the contemporary priests are men-pleasers, the Lord will send a true messenger to prepare for his coming in judgment. Very soon this figure was understood to be a prophet, a veritable Elijah (4:5). Once the visitation of the Temple was seen to have been made by Jesus, then in all respects John the Baptist could be recognized as the one who fulfilled the promise of the herald."[3]

### 2. *The Coming of the Lord* (3:1b-5)

**The Lord, whom ye seek, shall suddenly come to his temple.** This teaches us that judgment begins at the house of the Lord (Ezek. 9:6; I Pet. 4:17). **The Lord** is not the sacred name Yahweh, nor is it *Adonai,* the form which is usually substituted for it in reading.[4] The word here is the rare *ha-Adon* (the literal equivalent of "the Lord"), which is occasionally prefixed to Yahweh as in Exod. 23:17; Isa. 1:24. On the Day of Pentecost, Simon Peter declared, "God hath made that same Jesus, whom ye have crucified, both Lord and Christ" (Acts 2:36). The earliest Christian confession was the words, "Jesus is Lord"

[2]Dentan, *op. cit.,* p. 1137.
[3]*Op. cit.,* p. 199.
[4]The name "Jehovah" is a hybrid word, never used by the Jews, composed of the consonants of *Yahweh* (YHWH) and the vowels of *Adonai.*

(cf. I Cor. 12:3; Phil. 2:11). The Christian conviction is that Jesus is God, not God the Father but *God the Son:* "God was in Christ" (II Cor. 5:19). Jesus Christ was no mere man among men, no angel masquerading as a man, no secondary divinity created in eternity, but God the Almighty, the only God who is, come down to us as Jesus of Nazareth. "No man hath seen God at any time; the only begotten Son, which is in the bosom of the Father, he hath declared him" (John 1:18). This we believe Malachi is foretelling.

**Even the messenger of the covenant.** J. M. Powis Smith notes: "This 'messenger' can hardly be identical with the forerunner, viz. 'my messenger,' at the opening [of the] verse; for his coming is here made simultaneous with that of 'the Lord,' who can hardly be other than Yahweh himself, and the coming of 'my messenger' is explicitly announced as preceding that of Yahweh."[5] T. T. Perowne has given a defintive treatment of this title of our Lord.

> The idea of *the messenger*, which pervades this prophecy, culminates (as do the Old Testament ideas of the prophet, the priest and the king) in the Messiah, who is in the highest sense the Messenger of God to man. The Angel, or Messenger, whose presence in the Church was recognized from the beginning (Acts vii. 38; Exod. xxiii. 20, 21; Isaiah lxiii. 9, *et al.*), follows up these "preludings of the Incarnation" by being "made flesh and dwelling among us." The covenant, which was before the Law (Gal. iii. 17) and yet by virtue of its later introduction "a new covenant" (Jer. xxxi. 31-34; Heb. viii. 7-13), He comes, in fulfilment of promise and prophecy (Isaiah xlii. 6, lv. 3), as its Messenger and Mediator (Heb. xii. 24), to inaugurate and ratify with His blood (Matt. xxvi. 28; Heb. xiii. 20); while He vindicates His claim to be "the God of judgment" whom they desired, by the work of discriminating justice which He performs (vv. 2-5).[6]

*a. The Lord shall purify* (3:2-4). There is a twofold object in the coming of the Lord: (1) To purify the priesthood and (2) to execute judgment upon sinners (3:5). In presenting this truth Malachi seems to blend the first and second comings of Christ. The First Coming, too, was a time of sifting and severance, according as those to whom He came did or did not receive

[5]*Op. cit.*, p. 63.

[6]*Malachi*, "The Cambridge Bible for Schools and Colleges," eds. J. J. S. Perowne and A. F. Kirkpatrick (Cambridge: The University Press, 1902), p. 29.

Him. "For judgment I am come into this world, that they which see not might see; and that they which see might be made blind" (John 9:39). Again we read in the Fourth Gospel: "He that believeth on him is not condemned: but he that believeth not is condemned already" (John 3:18). Every soul is in a state of grace or out of it, in God's favor or under His wrath, and "every one shall be salted with fire" (Mark 9:49), either the fire of the Holy Spirit baptism or the fire of Gehenna. Therefore we read here: **But who may abide the day of his coming? and who shall stand when he appeareth? for he is like a refiner's fire, and like fullers' soap (2).**

John the Baptist was most certainly echoing Malachi when he declared: "He shall baptize you with the Holy Ghost, and with fire: whose fan is in his hand, and he will throughly purge his floor, and gather his wheat into the garner; but he will burn up the chaff with unquenchable fire" (Matt. 3:11-12). "The power of fire, we know, is twofold," John Calvin comments; "for it burns and it purifies; it burns what is corrupt but it purifies gold and silver from their dross. The prophet no doubt meant to include both."[7] As "God is a consuming fire" (Heb. 12:29), who must burn out the dross, either He must by His grace consume the sin within us or must consume us with it, in hell.

He is also **like fullers' soap.** A fuller was a bleacher of cloth. "In the Anglo-Saxon Gospels John the Baptist is called 'The Fuller.'"[8] This idea is parallel to the idea of Refiner.

**And he shall sit as a refiner and purifier of silver: and he shall purify the sons of Levi, and purge them as gold and silver, that they may offer unto the Lord an offering in righteousness (3).** After the outpouring of the Holy Spirit at Pentecost we read in Acts that "a great company of the priests were obedient to the faith" (Acts 6:7). "But more largely," Pusey points out, "as Zion and Jerusalem are the titles for the Christian Church, and Israel who believed was the true Israel, so 'the sons of Levi' are the true Levites, the Apostles and their successors in the Christian priesthood."[9] The purpose of this purging is **that they may offer unto the Lord an offering in righteousness.** Peter declares of believers: "Ye also . . . are built up . . . an holy

---

[7]"Minor Prophets," *Calvin's Commentaries* (Grand Rapids: Wm. B. Eerdmans Publishing Co., 1950), V, 572.

[8]Adamson, *op. cit.*, p. 767.

[9]*Op. cit.*, p. 488.

priesthood, to offer up spiritual sacrifices acceptable to God by Jesus Christ" (I Pet. 2:5). The author of Hebrews says in the same vein: "For we have an altar. . . . By him therefore let us offer the sacrifice of praise to God continually" (13:10, 15). The most precious sacrifice we can offer the Lord is ourselves (Rom. 12:1).

Malachi continues, **Then shall the offering of Judah and Jerusalem be pleasant unto the Lord, as in the days of old, and as in former years** (4). These **days of old** are the days before the degeneracy of Israel (cf. Isa. 1:25-27; Jer. 7:21-26; Hos. 2:15; 11:1).

In 1-3 we find "Malachi's Vision of the Messiah." (1) The prophecy proclaimed, 1 (fulfilled in John the Baptist, Matt. 3:1-10; and in Jesus, the Messiah, Matt. 3:11-12; John 1:35-36); (2) Purity promised, 2; (3) Purging performed, 3 (G. B. Williamson).

b. *The Lord shall judge* (3:5). The RSV translates v. 5, "Then I will draw near to you for judgment; I will be a swift witness against the sorcerers, against the adulterers, against those who swear falsely, against those who oppress the hireling in his wages, the widow and the orphan, against those who thrust aside the sojourner, and do not fear me, says the Lord of hosts." This is the answer to the question, "Where is the God of judgment?" (2:17). After the Temple has been cleansed and the house of God prepared for the Master, God will come and set right the injustices which make men doubt His goodness. Sorcerers will fall under His judgment. This is the only "religious" sin condemned. The others are social sins—adultery, false swearing, injustice, and inhumanity. Like the greatest of the prophets, Malachi regards sins against the social order as those with which God is most particularly concerned. He lays chief emphasis upon the wickedness of those who exploit the weak and helpless, **those that oppress the hireling in his wages, the widow, and the fatherless, and that turn aside the stranger from his right** (5). Malachi was as deeply concerned about the morality of the people as he was about their worship.

Section **VI** *Tithing, the Way of Blessing*

Malachi 3:6-12

The prophet now takes up another obstacle in the way of the free outpouring of God's blessing upon Israel. The nation had been unwilling to pay the price of His favor. The "windows of heaven" are closed because the people have been withholding their "tithes and offerings." Let these be brought in to the full and "showers of blessing" will fall upon the land.

Before we charge Malachi with a legal spirit let us remember that Israel's refusal to tithe was "an outward sign of alienation from God."[1] Their neglect at this point was symptomatic of unbelief and disobedience, and their repentance could not therefore be shown in a more practical way than by the payment of tithes.

## A. The Charge, 3:6-9

Malachi opens the subject by making a contrast between the constancy of the Lord and the inconstancy and frailty of His people: **I am the Lord, I change not; therefore ye sons of Jacob are not consumed** (6). On the one hand, God is saying, "I am Yahweh—'I AM THAT I AM' (Exod. 3:14); you are still the 'sons of Jacob'—deceivers and cheats." On the other hand, He says, "Because I am the God of unchanging love, **therefore ye . . . are not consumed.**" Martin Luther once exclaimed, "If I were God, I would knock the world to pieces!" It is because God is God that we are not destroyed. Pusey paraphrases this verse beautifully: "God might justly have cast off them and us; but He changes not. He abides by the covenant which He made with their fathers; He consumed them not; but with His own unchangeable love awaited their repentance. Our hope is not in ourselves, but in God."[2]

In v. 7 God presses His charge: **Even from the days of your fathers ye are gone away from mine ordinances, and have not**

---

[1]Jones, *op. cit.*, p. 200.　　　　　　　　　[2]*Op. cit.*, p. 491.

**kept them.** God is faithful, but the people, like their fathers, are faithless. Their complaint is that God has failed them, but the Lord puts the blame where it belongs—on them. The connection between vv. 7 and 6 is given by Pusey: "I am not changed from good; ye are not changed from evil. I am unchangeable in holiness; ye are unchangeable in perversity."[3] By **mine ordinances** God meant every expression of His will found in the Torah (the first five books of the OT, but often extended to mean "the law" —God's revelation to Israel).

**Return unto me, and I will return unto you, saith the Lord.** The wayward must return to the road from which they wandered. "The thought is not that of merely turning in a particular direction, but of retracing one's steps."[4] This is the Old Testament idea of repentance and conversion (cf. Isa. 55:7). While repentance is basically a change of attitude and purpose (the thought of the New Testament word *metanoia*), yet such a change must necessarily manifest itself in action (cf. Matt. 3:8, "fruits meet for [worthy of] repentance"). But what action? As in previous instances (1:6; 2:17), the prophet's hearers demand that he be more specific: **Wherein shall we return?**

The prophet answers with a question which answered itself: **Will a man rob God?** (8) His tone is one of incredulity. Will a man in his weakness and creatureliness rob the Creator? **Yet ye have robbed me.** The Hebrew word translated **rob** is rare, found only here and in Prov. 22:33. The original text possibly read "cheat" instead, since there is only a slight difference between the two Hebrew words. **But ye say, Wherein have we robbed thee?** The prophet answers, **In tithes and offerings.** By the law (1) the tithe (tenth) of all produce, as well as of flocks and cattle, belonged to the Lord and must be offered to Him (Lev. 27:30, 32); and (2) this was assigned to the Levites for their services (Num 18:21, 24). Nehemiah had to deal more than once with the evil here rebuked (cf. Neh. 9:38; 10:32-39; 13:10-14).

**Ye are cursed with a curse: for ye have robbed me, even this whole nation** (9). The word translated **nation** (*goy*) usually means *heathen* nation. There is no way to render the word in English, but Barnes suggests, "O Gentiles all."[5] Both priests and

[3]*Ibid.*                                    [4]Dentan, *op. cit.*, p. 1139.
[5]*Op. cit.*, p. 129.

people fall under this charge. The curse is shown in the next verse to be crop failure and the sufferings which follow.

## B. The Challenge, 3:10*abcd*

The prophet now tells them how they can return to the Lord: **Bring ye all the tithes into the storehouse (10).** Evidently they had not ceased tithing altogether, but they were not paying in full. The people as a whole were possibly keeping back a part of the tenth, deeming that they needed it worse than the priests. More probably, large numbers of them had ceased tithing altogether, while the faithful pious were denying themselves in order that they might meet their religious obligations in full.[6] This laxity was probably encouraged and excused by their poverty. But Malachi sees it as a symbol of a deep-seated contempt for God and of their alienation from Him. So he commands them to bring their whole tithe **into the storehouse.** This was undoubtedly the great chamber which surrounded the Temple on three sides. Tobias about this time diverted it from its original purpose as a receptacle of the people's tithes and heave offerings and assigned it to the high priest, but Nehemiah restored it to its proper use (Neh. 10:38; 13:5-9, 12-13). T. T. Perowne has aptly written: "It is not unlikely that the 'chambers,' which abutted to the height of three stories on the walls of Solomon's Temple, were intended in like manner for storehouses (I Kings vi. 5, 6). In the great Reformation under Hezekiah such chambers were 'prepared,' either built or restored, in some part of the Temple area, to receive the enormous influx of tithes and offerings (2 Chron. xxxi. 11, 12)."[7]

God's design in requiring the people to bring their whole tithes into the storehouse was **that there may be meat in mine house.** Before Nehemiah's reformation "the Levites and the singers . . . were fled every one to his field" because "the portions of the Levites had not been given them." At Nehemiah's insistence, aided perhaps by Malachi's injunctions, "the tithe of the corn and the new wine and the oil" were brought into "the treasuries" (Neh. 13:10-12). "Even so hath the Lord ordained that they which preach the gospel [of Christ] should live of the gospel" (I Cor. 9:14). Although for private reasons St. Paul did not exercise this privilege, he considered it fully as justified as Old

[6]Powis Smith, *op. cit.*, pp. 70-71.          [7]*Op. cit.*, p. 52.

Testament practice (I Cor. 9:9-14). If the tithe was the percentage of giving for a Jew under the old covenant, will New Testament believers give less? (Cf. Heb. 7:8.) The Church of Jesus Christ has found no better way of providing for its needs than by reechoing Malachi's behest. A tithing church is a church sufficient to whatever challenge may arise. Moreover, a non-tithing Christian is hard put to defend his niggardliness. Can he escape the charge that his failure is likewise a sign of his contempt for God?

C. THE PROMISE, 3:10e-12

God attaches a glorious promise to His command to tithe: **And prove me now herewith, saith the Lord of hosts, if I will not open you the windows of heaven, and pour you out a blessing, that there shall not be room enough to receive it (10).** This is literally a promise of rain (cf. Gen. 7:11; 8:2; II Kings 7:2, 19). The phrase suggests that they had been experiencing drought and bad crops. However the sign of rain was often a symbol of blessing (see Zech. 10:1; 14:17). **That there shall not be room enough to receive it** is translated more aptly as "a more than sufficient blessing" (Berk.). **And I will rebuke the devourer** —"the locust *or* the drought *or* blasting *or* mildew *or* hail, whatever the devourer was at that time."[8] The promise continues: **and he shall not destroy the fruits of your ground; neither shall your vine cast her fruit before the time in the field, saith the Lord of hosts (11).**

"As in Haggai and Zechariah and indeed in the Old Testament generally (Hag. 2:19; Zech. 8:9-13), the idea of blessing is no rarefied, spiritual state, but a wholeness and health of total social life, the sign of which is fertility. In a land that is blessed, everyone and everything is fruitful to fulfil the function for which it is made."[9] The prophet foresees that **all nations shall call you blessed: for ye shall be a delightsome land, saith the Lord of hosts (12).** "When the surrounding nations see the prosperity which will follow liberality towards God, they will rightly judge that it is the Lord's action in blessing His people."[10]

We must of course apply a Christian footnote to vv. 10-12. Material prosperity and physical health do not invariably accom-

[8]Barnes, *op. cit.*, p. 130.      [9]Jones, *op. cit.*, p. 202.
[10]Adamson, *op. cit.*, p. 767.

pany faithfulness to God. But spiritual health and prosperity do. When adversity comes, the Christian whose tithes are all paid finds himself on praying ground. In the New Testament we find a higher formula than Malachi's. The elder John wrote to a believer named Gaius, "Beloved, I wish above all things that thou mayest prosper and be in health, even as thy soul prospereth" (III John 2). The highest reaches of faith are found in a passage like Rom. 8:28-39, where we are assured that God is working in every detail of the life of one who loves God and that nothing in the created universe can separate such a one from God's love in Christ.

An exposition of vv. 6-12 might follow this outline under the heading "Tithing, the Way of the Blessing": (1) The charge, 6-9; (2) The challenge, 10*abcd;* (3) The promise, 10*e*-12.

Another analysis could be "God's Call to Tithing." (1) A recognition of God's ownership, 8; (2) A criterion of total Christian stewardship, 9; (3) An expression of sincere worship, 10; (4) A confession of faith in God's promise, 10*b;* and His providence, 11-12 (G. B. Williamson).

# Section VII Final Triumph of the Righteous

Malachi 3:13—4:3

The prophet had previously given a penetrating analysis to those who failed to make a distinction between good and evil (2:17). He now returns to the same theme. Before, he said, "You have wearied the Lord with your words . . . By saying, 'Everyone who does evil is good in the sight of the Lord, and he delights in them'" (RSV). Now he repeats this more fully.

## A. SKEPTICISM, 3:13-15

**Your words have been stout against me, saith the Lord** (13). The attitude of the people seems to have been one of growing skepticism. Their criticism is now vocal. They say, **What have we spoken so much against thee?** This is not a question in good faith. It implies a denial of Malachi's charge and challenges him to further proof (cf. 1:2, 6; 2:14; 3:7-8). **Spoken so** means talking together. "When have we so spoken among ourselves?" is the sense. They seem to have been in the habit of conversing together and comparing the promises of God with their unhappy state. Yet they professed to be ignorant of criticizing God.

The prophet delivers his charge. **Ye have said, It is vain to serve God: and what profit is it that we have kept his ordinance, and that we have walked mournfully before the Lord of hosts?** (14) Remembering the proud and prosperous heathen of Babylon and noting the nations around them abounding in all things while they themselves were languishing in poverty and misery, they said, "What does it benefit us, that we worship the one true God, abominate idols, and pricked with a consciousness of sins, walk penitently before God?"

Who are these doubters and critics? Perowne calls their words "the open blasphemy of those who 'sat in the seat of the scorner.'"[1] But J. M. Powis Smith calls them "Yahweh-worshippers who have begun to lose faith and are in danger of apostasy from Yahweh."[2] Outwardly at least they served God and **kept**

---

[1] *Op. cit.*, p. 33          [2] *Op. cit.*, p. 76.

**his ordinance.** Their tendency, however, to regard mere outward observance as true religion smacks of the Pharisaism of New Testament times. The phrase **walked mournfully** has the same connotation. Although it does not exclude a genuine inner grief, the Hebrew phrase refers primarily to the outer garb these people wore as a sign of their humiliation and contrition. This calls to mind Jesus' warning in Matt. 6:16-18.

Verse 15 sums up their case against God. Jones has given a free translation of their beatitudes:

> *Blessed are the arrogant and godless;*
> *Blessed are the evil-doers, for they prosper;*
> *Blessed are those who put God to the test, for*
> *they escape all punishment.*[3]

"Stout" words indeed! This seems to be what is meant earlier by their question, "Where is the God of judgment?" (2:17) Bitterly they were compelled to congratulate wickedness in high places, with the Lord himself permitting it to go unpunished.

## B. MEN WHO BELIEVE GOD, 3:16-18

**Then they that feared the Lord spake often one to another** (16). Some interpreters, following the Septuagint, the Syriac, and the Targum, would read, "Thus (or such things) spake they that feared the Lord to each other."[4] But most interpreters see the persons in v. 16 as another group: Jones writes: "Over against the arrogant doubters are those who, despite the problems, *feared the Lord.* They are those who retain the spirit of humble reverence and awe. It is possible that the *then they . . . spake often one to another,* refers to the discussion roused among the faithful by the prophet's forthright analysis of the situation. If so, the prophet now supplies them with the divine assurance they need."[5] If this is the correct view, then, as the godless in Israel conversed together (vv. 13-14), so did the godly. Their conversations, however, differed greatly. What the pious remnant said to one another is not recorded, although it is hinted in the statement that they **thought upon his name.** They may have witnessed to each other about the goodness of the Lord they had experienced in spite of their sufferings. In any event, we

---

[3]*Op. cit.,* p. 203.                    [4]Cf. G. A. Smith, Powis Smith, Dentan.
[5]*Op. cit.,* p. 204.

are told that **the Lord hearkened, and heard it, and a book of remembrance was written before him for them that feared the Lord.** Those who fear the Lord may know that their names are recorded indelibly in the divine writing. "This is a permanence, which, associated with the Old Testament faith in the Living God, leads to the authentic biblical belief in the blessed life of the hereafter."[6]

**And they shall be mine, saith the Lord of hosts, in that day when I make up my jewels (17).** The word translated **jewels** (*segullah*) is used in Exod. 19:5, where it is better rendered "peculiar treasure." The *segullah* was that part of the property which a person claimed to himself as his own special treasure. "This is what Israel is to God in relation to the world; it is what those who fear him are in relation to Israel."[7] In the New Testament the Church is a people for God's own possession (I Pet. 2:9-10). **And I will spare them, as a man spareth his own son that serveth him.** The word **spare** is a remarkable one. It teaches us that those who are to God a *peculiar treasure* are so, not on their own merits, but by His great mercy. Pusey expresses this thought in an extended paraphrase: "I will spare them, although formerly sinners; I will spare them, repenting, and serving Me with a service of a pious confession, 'as a man spareth his son which serveth him.' For the Lord said of the son who refused to work in his Father's vineyard, and afterward repented and went, that 'he did the will of his Father.' "[8] This is Malachi's doctrine of salvation by grace.

**Then shall ye return, and discern between the righteous and the wicked, between him that serveth God and him that serveth him not (18).** On the day of judgment people will be able to distinguish the sheep from the goats, the wheat from the tares. God's final decision is the only ultimate solution to the problem raised in this section (cf. Dan. 12:2; Matt. 25:32-46).

C. THE DAY OF ANSWERS, 4:1-3

**For, behold, the day cometh, that shall burn as an oven; and all the proud, yea, and all that do wickedly, shall be stubble: and the day that cometh shall burn them up, saith the Lord of hosts, that it shall leave them neither root nor branch (1).**

[6]*Ibid.;* cf. Exod. 32:32; Neh. 13:14; Ps. 56:8; 69:28; Dan. 12:2; Rev. 20:12.
[7]*Ibid.*      [8]*Op. cit.,* p. 496.

The **oven** is a figure of fierce heat (cf. Hos. 7:4-7). The word is still used for an oven in which bread is baked in Palestine. A large hole is made in the earth, the sides are plastered, and a fierce fire is made at the bottom with twigs and thorns (**stubble**). After the embers are removed, bread is stuck to the plastered sides and quickly cooked.[9]

**The proud** are all those whom the murmurers called "happy" (3:15), and **all** who should thereafter be like them. Malachi insists on the universality of the judgment; "all the arrogant and all evildoers" (Bcrk.) **shall be stubble** (cf. Isa. 5:24; Obad. 18; Zeph. 1:18). To build a doctrine of the final annihilation of the wicked on this figure is to go beyond the limits of the metaphor as well as to contradict the specific teaching of Jesus (Matt. 25:46; Luke 16:23-28; cf. Rev. 20:10, 14-15). Pusey quotes an early authority who has caught Malachi's true point: "The proud and mighty, who in this life were strong as iron and brass, so that no one dared resist them, but they dared to fight with God, these, in the Day of Judgment, shall be most powerless, as stubble cannot resist the fire, in an everliving death."[10]

The further statement that this fire **shall leave them neither root nor branch** means that they shall have no hope of sprouting again to life, that life which is promised the righteous. "There is hope of a tree, if it be cut down, that it will sprout again, and that the tender branch thereof will not cease" (Job 14:7), but there is no hope for those who are condemned on the Day of Judgment.

**But unto you that fear my name,** God says, **shall the Sun of righteousness arise with healing in his wings** (2). Malachi's beautiful figure used here is unique in the Old Testament, although it is close to the thought of Isa. 60:1-5. The fathers and early commentators understood Christ to be the **Sun of righteousness.** They were right insofar as it is the period of His advent which the prophet foresees. Though **Sun** is feminine, both ASV and RSV render the phrase, "with healing in its wings." *The Berkeley Version* has "the sun of righteousness" with the footnote, "There is no fulfilment of this prophecy in any person or event as complete and satisfying as in the coming of Jesus Christ, who is for us 'the righteousness of God.'" Moffatt renders it,

[9]Barnes, *op. cit.,* p. 133.
[10]*Op. cit.,* p. 496.

"But for you, my worshippers, the saving Sun shall rise with healing in his rays." **And ye shall . . . grow up** ("gambol," ASV) **as calves of the stall.** The picture is of a happy, carefree existence. The glory of God in Christ disperses the darkness of sin and sorrow and makes glad the people of God. Pusey reminds us that the title "the Sun of righteousness" belongs to both of Christ's comings. "In the first, He diffused rays of righteousness, whereby He justified and daily justifies any sinners whatever, who will look to Him, i.e., believe in Him and obey Him, as the sun imparts light, joy and life to all who turn toward it."[11] Then he adds, "In the second, the righteousness which He gave, He will own and exhibit, cleared from all the misjudgment of the world, before men and angels."[12]

On v. 3, Jones makes the pertinent observation, "The Old Testament is the record of God's patient preparation of His people for the New. We must therefore expect to meet sentiments needing our Lord's correction."[13] For this correction read Matt. 5:38-48. As Christians, we must always read the Old Testament through the eyes of Christ, for the Old Testament is a progressive and preparatory revelation which finds its fulfillment in Him (see Heb. 1:1-2).

In 3:13—4:3, we may see reasons for the exhortation, "Keep Your Faith in God." (1) When faith fails, 3:13-15; (2) How faith grows stronger, 3:16-18; (3) God's last word, 4:1-3 (A. F. Harper).

---

[11]A quotation from Lap, cited by Pusey, *op. cit.*, p. 497.
[12]*Ibid.*              [13]*Op. cit.*, p. 205.

Section **VIII** *Conclusion*

Malachi 4:4-6

**Remember ye the law of Moses my servant, which I commanded unto him in Horeb for all Israel, with the statutes and judgments (4).** We are here reminded of the ending of Ecclesiastes: "Let us hear the conclusion of the whole matter: Fear God, and keep his commandments" (Eccles. 12:13).

The final note of the Old Testament is predictive: **Behold, I will send you Elijah the prophet before the coming of the great and dreadful day of the Lord (5).** In one sense this was a prophecy of John the Baptist, who should "go before him [the Lord] *in the spirit and power* of Elias" (Luke 1:17). It is significant that this passage from Luke actually quotes v. 6: **And he shall turn the heart of the fathers to the children.** This is a prophecy of John's preparatory work of converting Israel in order that they might receive Christ. In this sense Jesus could say of John, "This is Elias, which was for to come" (Matt. 11:14).

# Bibliography

## I. COMMENTARIES

ADAMSON, J. T. H. "Malachi." *The New Bible Commentary.* Edited by FRANCIS DAVIDSON, *et al.* Grand Rapids, Michigan: Wm. B. Eerdmans Publishing Co., 1956.

BARNES, W. EMERY. *Malachi.* "Cambridge Bible for Schools and Colleges." Edited by F. S. MARSH. Cambridge: The University Press, 1934.

CALVIN, JOHN. "Minor Prophets." *Calvin's Commentaries,* Vol. V. Grand Rapids, Michigan: Wm. B. Eerdmans Publishing Co., 1950 (reprint).

CASHDAN, ELI. "Zechariah." *The Twelve Prophets.* Edited by A. COHEN. London: The Soncino Press, 1948.

————. "Malachi." *The Twelve Prophets.* Edited by A. COHEN. London: The Soncino Press, 1948.

CHADWICK, S. "Micah." *The Expositor's Dictionary of Texts,* Vol. I. Edited by W. ROBERTSON NICOLL, JANE T. STODDARD, JAMES MOFFATT. New York: George H. Doran Co., n.d.

CLARKE, ADAM. *The Holy Bible with a Commentary and Critical Notes,* Vol. IV. New York: Abingdon-Cokesbury Press, n.d.

CLARKE, W. K. LOWTHER. *Concise Bible Commentary.* New York: Macmillan Co., 1954.

COLLINS, G. N. M. "Zechariah." *The New Bible Commentary.* Edited by FRANCIS DAVIDSON, *et al.* Grand Rapids, Michigan: Wm. B. Eerdmans Publishing Co., 1956.

DAVIDSON, A. B. *Nahum, Habakkuk and Zephaniah.* "The Cambridge Bible for Schools and Colleges." Edited by J. J. S. PEROWNE. Cambridge: University Press, 1896.

DEANE, W. J. "Hosea" (Exposition). *The Pulpit Commentary: Amos to Micah.* Edited by H. D. M. SPENCE and JOSEPH S. EXELL. New York: Funk and Wagnalls Co., n.d.

————. "Amos to Micah" (Exposition). *The Pulpit Commentary: Amos to Micah.* Edited by H. D. M. SPENCE and JOSEPH S. EXELL. New York: Funk and Wagnalls Co., n.d.

————. "Malachi." *The Pulpit Commentary,* Vol. XIV. Edited by H. D. M. SPENCE and JOSEPH S. EXELL. Grand Rapids, Michigan: Wm. B. Eerdmans Publishing Co., 1950 (reprint).

DENTAN, ROBERT C. "Malachi" (Exegesis). *The Interpreter's Bible.* Edited by GEORGE A. BUTTRICK, *et al.,* Vol. VI. New York: Abingdon Press, 1956.

DRIVER, S. R. *The Minor Prophets.* "The New Century Bible." Edited by WALTER F. ADENEY. 2 volumes. New York: Oxford University Press.

EATON, J. H. *Obadiah, Nahum, Habakkuk and Zephaniah.* London: SCM Press, 1961.

ELLIOTT, CHARLES. "Hosea." *A Commentary on the Holy Scriptures: Critical, Doctrinal and Homiletical.* Edited by J. P. LANGE, Vol. XIV. Grand Rapids, Mich.: Zondervan Publishing House, 1874 (reprint).

EXELL, JOSEPH S. (ed.). "Hosea." *The Biblical Illustrator: The Minor Prophets*, Vol. I. New York: Fleming H. Revell Co., n.d.

FAUSSET, A. R. *A Commentary on the Old and New Testaments*, Vol. IV. Grand Rapids, Mich.: Wm. B. Eerdmans Publishing Co., 1948 (reprint).

FOSBROKE, HUGHELL E. W. "Amos" (Exegesis). *The Interpreter's Bible*. Edited by GEORGE A. BUTTRICK, *et al.*, Vol. VI. New York: Abingdon Press, 1956.

FRASER, A., and STEPHENS-HODGE, L. E. H. "Micah." *The New Bible Commentary*. Edited by FRANCIS DAVIDSON, *et al.* Grand Rapids, Mich.: Wm. B. Eerdmans Publishing Co., 1953.

FREDERICK, P. W. H. "The Book of Amos." *Old Testament Commentary*. Edited by HERBERT C. ALLEMAN and ELMER E. FLACK. Philadelphia: The Muhlenberg Press, 1948.

GIVEN, J. J. "The Book of Hosea" (Exposition and Homiletics). *The Pulpit Commentary*. Edited by H. D. M. SPENCE and JOSEPH S. EXELL. New York: Funk and Wagnalls, n.d.

GRAHAM, WILLIAM C. "Nahum." *Abingdon Bible Commentary*. Edited by FREDERICK CARL EISELEN, *et al.* New York: Abingdon-Cokesbury Press, 1929.

———. "Zephaniah." *Abingdon Bible Commentary*. Edited by FREDERICK CARL EISELEN, *et al.* New York: Abingdon-Cokesbury Press, 1929.

HALDOR, ALFRED. *Studies in the Book of Nahum*. Uppsala: A. B. Lundequistreka Bokhandeln, 1946.

HAUPT, PAUL. *The Book of Nahum*. Baltimore: Johns Hopkins Press, 1907.

HENDERSON, EBENEZER. *The Book of the Twelve Minor Prophets*. New York: Sheldon and Co., 1864.

HENRY, MATTHEW. *Commentary on the Whole Bible*. 6 vols. New York: Fleming H. Revell Co., n.d.

HICKS, R. LANSING. "The Twelve Minor Prophets." *The Oxford Annotated Bible: RSV*. Edited by HERBERT G. MAY and BRUCE M. METZGER. New York: Oxford University Press, 1962.

HORINE, JOHN W. "The Book of Hosea." *Old Testament Commentary*. Edited by HERBERT C. ALLEMAN and ELMER E. FLACK. Philadelphia: The Muhlenberg Press, 1948.

HUBBARD, DAVID A. "Habakkuk." *The Biblical Expositor*. Edited by CARL F. H. HENRY, Vol. II. Philadelphia: A. J. Holman Co., 1960.

JAMIESON, ROBERT, FAUSSET, A. R., BROWN, DAVID. *A Commentary: Critical, Experimental and Practical*, Vol. I. Hartford: The S. S. Scranton Co., n.d.

JONES, DOUGLAS RAWLINSON. *Malachi*. "Torch Bible Commentaries." Edited by JOHN MARSH and ALAN RICHARDSON. London: SCM Press, Ltd., 1962.

KEIL, C. F., and DELITZSCH, FRANZ. "The Twelve Minor Prophets." *Biblical Commentary on the Old Testament*. Grand Rapids, Mich.: Wm. B. Eerdmans Publishing Co., 1954 (reprint).

KNIGHT, GEORGE A. F. *Hosea*. "Torch Bible Commentaries." Edited by JOHN MARSH and ALAN RICHARDSON. London: SCM Press, Ltd., 1960.

LANGFORD, NORMAN F. "Hosea" (Exegesis). *The Interpreter's Bible*. Edited by GEORGE A. BUTTRICK, *et al.*, Vol. VI. New York: Abingdon Press, 1956.

LEHRMAN, S. M. "Nahum. *The Twelve Prophets.* Edited by A. COHEN. London: The Soncino Press, 1948.

———. "Zephaniah." *The Twelve Prophets.* Edited by A. COHEN. London: The Soncino Press, 1948.

LOGSDEN, S. FRANKLIN. *Hosea.* Chicago: Moody Press, 1959.

LOWE, W. H. "Minor Prophets." *Layman's Handy Commentary on the Bible,* Vol. III. Edited by CHARLES JOHN ELLICOTT. Grand Rapids, Mich.: Zondervan Publishing House, 1961.

LUCK, G. COLEMAN. *Zechariah.* Chicago: Moody Press, n.d.

MAIER, WALTER A. *The Book of Nahum.* St. Louis: Concordia Publishing House, 1959.

McFADYEN, JOHN E. "Habakkuk." *Abingdon Bible Comentary.* Edited by FREDERICK CARL EISELEN, et al. New York: Abingdon-Cokesbury Press, 1929.

———. "Zechariah." *Abingdon Bible Commentary.* Edited by DAVID D. DOWNEY. New York: Abingdon Press, 1929.

———. "Malachi." *Abingdon Bible Commentary.* Edited by DAVID D. DOWNEY. New York: Abingdon Press, 1929.

MACLAREN, ALEXANDER. *Expositions of Scripture,* Vol. VI. Grand Rapids, Mich.: Wm. B. Eerdmans Publishing Co., 1944 (reprint).

MEYER, F. B. *The Prophet of Hope.* London: Morgan and Scott, n.d.

MORGAN, G. CAMPBELL. *Hosea.* London: Marshall, Morgan and Scott, Ltd., 1948.

———. "Jonah." *Biblical Illustrator.* Edited by J. S. EXELL. New York: Fleming H. Revell, n.d.

PEROWNE, T. T. *Haggai, Zechariah and Malachi.* "The Cambridge Bible for Schools and Colleges." J. J. S. PEROWNE, general editor. Cambridge: University Press, 1893.

PUSEY, E. B. *The Minor Prophets.* New York: Funk and Wagnalls, 1886.

REYNOLDS, H. R. "Hosea." *Commentary on the Whole Bible.* Edited by CHARLES JOHN ELLICOTT, Vol. V. London: Cassell and Co., 1897.

ROBINSON, D. W. B. "Jonah." *The New Bible Commentary.* Edited by FRANCIS DAVIDSON, et al. Grand Rapids, Mich.: Wm. B. Eerdmans Publishing Co., 1963.

SMITH, GEORGE ADAM. "The Book of the Twelve Prophets." *The Expositor's Bible.* Edited by W. ROBERTSON NICOLL. 2 vols. New York: George H. Doran Co., n.d.

———. "The Book of the Twelve Prophets." *The Expositor's Bible.* Edited by W. ROBERTSON NICOLL. 2 vols. New York: A. C. Armstrong and Son, 1896.

———. *The Book of the Twelve Prophets.* New York: Harper and Bros., 1928.

SMITH, J. M. POWIS. *Malachi.* "The International Critical Commentary." New York: Charles Scribner's Sons, 1912.

SNYDER, EDGAR E. "The Book of Joel." *Old Testament Commentary.* Edited by HERBERT C. ALLEMAN and ELMER E. FLACK. Philadelphia: The Muhlenberg Press, 1948.

TAYLOR, CHARLES L., JR. "Habakkuk" (Exegesis). *The Interpreter's Bible.* Edited by GEORGE A. BUTTRICK, et al., Vol. VI. New York: Abingdon Press, 1956.

———. "Zephaniah" (Introduction and Exegesis). *The Interpreter's Bible.* Edited by GEORGE A. BUTTRICK, *et al.,* Vol. VI. New York: Abingdon Press, 1956.

THOMAS, D. WINTON. "Zechariah" (Exegesis). *The Interpreter's Bible.* Edited by GEORGE A. BUTTRICK, *et al.,* Vol. VI. New York: Abingdon Press, 1956.

THOMPSON, JOHN A. "Joel" (Exegesis). *The Interpreter's Bible.* Edited by GEORGE A. BUTTRICK, *et al.,* Vol. VI. New York: Abingdon Press, 1956.

WOLFE, ROLLAND E. "Micah" (Exegesis). *The Interpreter's Bible.* Edited by GEORGE A. BUTTRICK, *et al.,* Vol. VI. New York: Abingdon Press, 1956.

WOLFENDALE, JAMES. "Minor Prophets." *The Preacher's Homiletical Commentary.* New York: Funk and Wagnalls, 1892.

## II. OTHER BOOKS

ANDERSON, BERNARD W. *Understanding the Old Testament.* Englewood, N.J.: Prentice-Hall, Inc., 1957.

ARCHER, GLEASON L., JR. *A Survey of Old Testament Introduction.* Chicago: Moody Press, 1964.

BAAB, OTTO J. *The Theology of the Old Testament.* New York: Abingdon-Cokesbury Press, 1949.

*Biblical Approach to the Doctrine of the Trinity, A.* Scottish Journal of Theology Occasional Paper No. 1. General editors, T. F. TORRANCE and J. K. S. REID. Edinburgh: Oliver and Boyd, Ltd., 1953.

BREWER, JULIUS A. *The Literature of the Old Testament.* New York: Columbia University Press, 1962.

BUBER, MARTIN. *The Prophetic Faith.* New York: The Macmillan Co., 1949.

CALKINS, RAYMOND. *The Modern Message of the Minor Prophets.* New York: Harper and Brothers, 1947.

CARTLEDGE, SAMUEL A. *A Conservative Introduction to the Old Testament.* Grand Rapids, Mich.: Zondervan Publishing House, 1943.

DAVIS, LEON J. *Bible Knowledge.* Edited by HENRY JACOBSEN. Wheaton, Ill.: Scripture Press, 1956.

DODS, MARCUS. *The Post-Exilian Prophets.* Edinburgh: T. and T. Clark, 1881.

DRIVER, S. R. *An Introduction to the Literature of the Old Testament.* New York: Charles Scribner's Sons, 1891.

EISELEN, FREDERICK CARL. *Prophecy and the Prophets.* New York: The Methodist Book Concern, 1909.

FARRAR, F. W. *The Minor Prophets.* New York: Fleming H. Revell Co., n.d.

GADD, C. J. *The Fall of Nineveh.* London: Department of Egyptian and Assyrian Antiquities, British Museum, 1923.

GAEBELEIN, A. C. *The Prophet Joel.* New York: Publication Office, *Our Hope,* 1909.

HENSHAW, T. *The Latter Prophets.* London: George Allen and Unwin, Ltd., n.d.

KNIGHT, GEORGE A. F. *A Christian Theology of the Old Testament.* Richmond, Va.: John Knox Press, 1959.

KNUDSON, ALBERT C. *The Beacon Lights of Prophecy.* New York: The Methodist Book Concern, 1914.

Morgan, G. Campbell. *The Analyzed Bible.* New York: Fleming H. Revell Co., 1908.

———. *An Exposition of the Whole Bible.* Westwood, N.J.: Fleming H. Revell Co., 1959.

Nygren, Anders *Agape and Eros.* Translated by Phillip S. Watson. Philadelphia: Westminster Press, 1953.

Oehler, Gustave F. *Theology of the Old Testament.* Translated by George E. Day. Grand Rapids, Mich.: Zondervan Publishing House, n.d.

Paterson, John. *The Goodly Fellowship of the Prophets.* New York: Charles Scribner's Sons, 1948.

Purkiser, W. T., et al. *Exploring the Old Testament.* Kansas City, Mo.: Beacon Hill Press, 1957.

———. "Jonah." *Aldersgate Biblical Series.* Edited by Donald Joy. Winona Lake, Ind.: Light and Life Press, 1963.

Robinson, George L. *The Twelve Minor Prophets.* New York: George H. Doran and Co., 1926.

Rosenberg, Stuart E. *More Loves than One: The Bible Confronts Psychiatry.* New York: Thomas Nelson and Sons, 1963.

Rowley, H. H. *The Relevance of Apocalyptic.* Second Edition. London: Lutterworth Press, 1947.

Sampey, John A. *The Heart of the Old Testament.* Nashville: Broadman Press, 1922.

Schultz, S. J. *The Old Testament Speaks.* New York: Harper and Brothers, 1960.

Sloan, W. W. *A Survey of the Old Testament.* New York: Abingdon Press, 1957.

Snaith, Norman H. *The Distinctive Ideas of the Old Testament.* Philadelphia: Westminster Press, 1946.

Vriezen, M. C. *An Outline of Old Testament Theology.* Boston: Charles T. Bradford Company, 1958.

Watts, John D. W. *Vision and Prophecy in Amos.* Grand Rapids, Mich.: Wm. B. Eerdmans Publishing Co., 1958.

Welch, Adam C. *Kings and Prophets of Israel.* London: Lutterworth Press, 1952.

Yates, Kyle M. *Preaching from the Prophets.* New York: Harper and Brothers, 1942.

Yoder, S. C. *He Gave Some Prophets.* Scottsdale, Pa.: Herald Press, 1964.


## III. ARTICLES

Davidson, A. B. "Hosea." *Dictionary of the Bible.* Edited by James Hastings, et al., Vol. II. New York: Charles Scribner and Sons, 1909.

Gillett, A. L. "Jonah." *New Standard Bible Dictionary.* Edited by M. W. Jacobus, E. C. Lane, A. C. Zenos, E. J. Cook. New York: Funk and Wagnalls, 1936.

Neil, William. "Joel." *The Interpreter's Dictionary of the Bible.* Edited by George A. Buttrick, et al. New York: Abingdon Press, 1962.

QUELL, GOTTFRIED, and STAUFFER, ETHELBERT. "Love." *Bible Key Words.* Edited by GERHARD KITTEL; translated and edited by J. R. COATES. New York: Harper and Brothers, 1951.

SMART, J. D. "Hosea." *The Interpreter's Dictionary of the Bible.* Edited by GEORGE A. BUTTRICK, *et al.* New York: Abingdon Press, 1962.

WILSON, J. A. "Jonah." *Princeton Theological Review,* XXV (1927), 636.

YOUNG, E. J. "Jonah." *Christianity Today,* III, No. 25 (September 28, 1959), 11-12.

*Map 1*

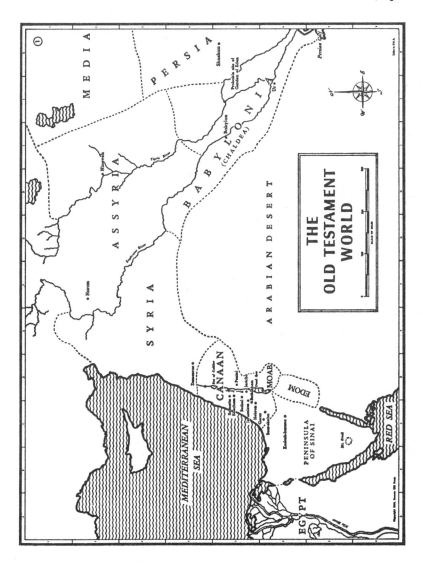

THE
OLD TESTAMENT
WORLD

**Map 2**

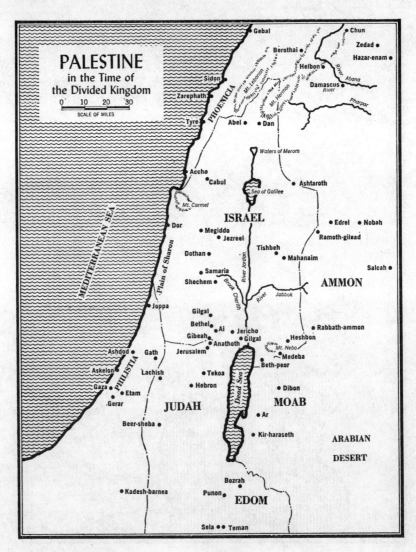

PALESTINE
in the Time of
the Divided Kingdom

0   10   20   30
SCALE OF MILES

MEDITERRANEAN SEA

PHOENICIA

Gebal
Berothai
Sidon
Zarephath
Tyre
Abel
Dan

Chun
Zedad
Hazar-enam
Helbon
Damascus
River Abana
Pharpar

Waters of Merom

Accho
Cabul
Mt. Carmel

Sea of Galilee

Ashtaroth

ISRAEL

Dor
Megiddo
Jezreel

Edrei   Nobah
Ramoth-gilead

Dothan
Tishbeh
Mahanaim

Salcah

Samaria
Shechem

AMMON

Brook Cherith
River Jordan
Jabbok River

Plain of Sharon

Joppa

Gilgal
Bethel
Gibeah   Ai
Jerusalem   Anathoth

Jericho
Gilgal

Rabbath-ammon

Heshbon
Mt. Nebo
Medeba
Beth-peor

Ashdod   Gath
Askelon
Lachish
Gaza   Etam
Gerar

Tekoa
Hebron

PHILISTIA

JUDAH

Dead Sea

Dibon

MOAB

Ar

Beer-sheba

Kir-haraseth

ARABIAN

DESERT

Kadesh-barnea

Bozrah
Punon

EDOM

Sela  Teman

450

# CHART OF THE KINGDOM PERIOD
# FROM 1010 to 586 B.C.

DAVID (1010-971)
SOLOMON (971-931)
DIVISION (931)

| ISRAEL (Northern Kingdom) | | JUDAH (Southern Kingdom) | |
|---|---|---|---|
| **Reigns** | **Co-regencies** | **Reigns** | **Co-regencies** |
| JEROBOAM............931-910 | | REHOBOAM .........931-913 | |
| NADAB ................910-909 | | ABIJAM ...............913-911 | |
| BAASHA ..............909-886 | | ASA ......................911-870 | |
| ELAH ....................886-885 | | | |
| ZIMRI.....................885 | | | |
| TIBNI ......................885-880 | 885-880 | | |
| OMRI .....................885-874 | 885-880 | | |
| AHAB ...................874-853 | | JEHOSHAPHAT ...870-848 | 873-870 |
| AHAZIAH ............853-852 | | | |
| JEHORAM ...........852-841 | | JEHORAM ...........848-841 | 853-848 |
| JEHU ...................841-814 | | AHAZIAH ...........841 | |
| JEHOAHAZ...........814-798 | | ATHALIAH ........841-835 | |
| | | JOASH ...............835-796 | |
| JEHOASH ............798-782 | | AMAZIAH ...........796-767 | |
| JEROBOAM II ......782-753 | 793-782 | AZARIAH ...........767-740 | 791-767 |
| ZACHARIAH .......753-752 | | (Uzziah) | |
| SHALLUM.............752 | | | |
| MENAHEM ..........752-742 | | | |
| PEKAHIAH ..........742-740 | | | |
| PEKAH ................740-732 | | JOTHAM .............740-732 | 750-740 |
| HOSHEA .......732-723, 722 | | AHAZ .................732-716 | |
| | | HEZEKIAH .........716-687 | 729-716 |
| | | MANASSEH..........687-642 | 696-687 |
| | | AMON .................642-640 | |
| | | JOSIAH ...............640-608 | |
| | | JEHOAHAZ ..........608 | |
| | | JEHOIAKIM .......608-597 | |
| | | JEHOIACHIN .......597 | |
| | | ZEDEKIAH ..........597-586 | |

**Chart B**

**Stevens-Wright reconstruction of Solomon's Temple**

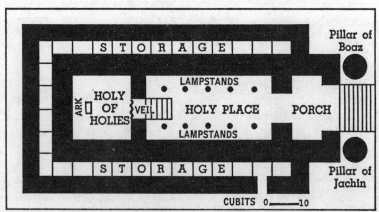

**Floor plan of the Temple (*adapted from Watzinger*)**

452

Chart C

# THE EXILE AND RETURN

## EXILIC PERIOD: CAPTIVITY (606-536 B.C.)

- **605-561** NEBUCHADNEZZAR in BABYLONIA
- **608-597** JEHOIAKIM, KING of JUDAH (II Kings 23:34-24:6)
  - VASSAL of EGYPT
  - VASSAL of BABYLONIA
- **606** FIRST CAPTIVITY—DANIEL (II Kings 24:1; Daniel 1:1-2; 6)
- **600** REBELLION against BABYLONIA
- **597** JEHOIACHIN, KING of JUDAH (II Kings 24:8-17)
  - JERUSALEM BESIEGED
  - SECOND CAPTIVITY—10,000 INCLUDING JEHOIACHIN and EZEKIEL
- **597-586** ZEDEKIAH, KING of JUDAH (II Kings 24:18-25:21)
- **592-570** EZEKIEL'S PROPHECIES
- **588** REVOLT against BABYLONIA
- **586** JERUSALEM DESTROYED
  - THIRD CAPTIVITY
- **585** OBADIAH'S PROPHECY
- **555** GEDALIAH SLAIN (Jeremiah 40-41)
  - JEREMIAH to EGYPT (Jeremiah 42-44)
- **550-535** DANIEL'S PROPHECIES (Daniel 5)
- **538** FALL of BABYLONIA

## POSTEXILIC PERIOD: RETURN (536-400 B.C.)

- **539-530** CYRUS of PERSIA (Isaiah 44:28; 45:1; II Chronicles 36:22; Ezra 1:1)
- **537** DECREE to RETURN (Ezra 1:1-4)
- **536** FIRST RETURN—ZERUBBABEL (Ezra 1:4-2:67)
  - REBUILDING BEGUN (Ezra 2:68-3:13)
  - HINDERED by SAMARITANS (Ezra 4:1-24)
- **522-486** DARIUS of PERSIA (Ezra 4:24; 6:1; Haggai 1:1; Zechariah 1:1)
- **520** HAGGAI and ZECHARIAH (Ezra 5; Haggai; Zechariah)
- **516** TEMPLE REBUILT and DEDICATED (Ezra 6)
- **485-465** AHASUERUS (Xerxes of Persia) (Book of Esther)
  - ESTHER and MORDECAI (Esther 1:1)
- **458** SECOND RETURN—EZRA (Ezra 7-8)
  - REFORMS at JERUSALEM (Ezra 9-10)
- **450-430** MALACHI'S PROPHECIES
- **444** THIRD RETURN—NEHEMIAH (Nehemiah 1:1-2:8)
  - REBUILDING of the WALL (Nehemiah 2:9-6:19)
  - INSTRUCTION in the LAW (Nehemiah 8-10)
- **432** NEHEMIAH BACK in JERUSALEM (Nehemiah 12)
  - REFORM MEASURES
  - PERIOD between the TESTAMENTS